Build a Large Language Model (From Scratch)

Build a Large Language Model (From Scratch)

SEBASTIAN RASCHKA

MANNING
SHELTER ISLAND

For online information and ordering of this and other Manning books, please visit www.manning.com. The publisher offers discounts on this book when ordered in quantity. For more information, please contact

Special Sales Department
Manning Publications Co.
20 Baldwin Road
PO Box 761
Shelter Island, NY 11964
Email: orders@manning.com

©2025 by Manning Publications Co. All rights reserved.

No part of this publication may be reproduced, stored in a retrieval system, or transmitted, in any form or by means electronic, mechanical, photocopying, or otherwise, without prior written permission of the publisher.

Many of the designations used by manufacturers and sellers to distinguish their products are claimed as trademarks. Where those designations appear in the book, and Manning Publications was aware of a trademark claim, the designations have been printed in initial caps or all caps.

♾ Recognizing the importance of preserving what has been written, it is Manning's policy to have the books we publish printed on acid-free paper, and we exert our best efforts to that end. Recognizing also our responsibility to conserve the resources of our planet, Manning books are printed on paper that is at least 15 percent recycled and processed without the use of elemental chlorine.

The authors and publisher have made every effort to ensure that the information in this book was correct at press time. The authors and publisher do not assume and hereby disclaim any liability to any party for any loss, damage, or disruption caused by errors or omissions, whether such errors or omissions result from negligence, accident, or any other cause, or from any usage of the information herein.

Manning Publications Co.
20 Baldwin Road
PO Box 761
Shelter Island, NY 11964

Development editor: Dustin Archibald
Technical editor: David Caswell
Review editor: Kishor Rit
Production editor: Aleksandar Dragosavljević
Copy editors: Kari Lucke and Alisa Larson
Proofreader: Mike Beady
Technical proofreader: Jerry Kuch
Typesetter: Dennis Dalinnik
Cover designer: Marija Tudor

ISBN: 9781633437166
Printed in the United States of America

brief contents

contents

preface

I've always been fascinated with language models. More than a decade ago, my journey into AI began with a statistical pattern classification class, which led to my first independent project: developing a model and web application to detect the mood of a song based on its lyrics.

Fast forward to 2022, with the release of ChatGPT, large language models (LLMs) have taken the world by storm and have revolutionized how many of us work. These models are incredibly versatile, aiding in tasks such as checking grammar, composing emails, summarizing lengthy documents, and much more. This is owed to their ability to parse and generate human-like text, which is important in various fields, from customer service to content creation, and even in more technical domains like coding and data analysis.

As their name implies, a hallmark of LLMs is that they are "large"—very large—encompassing millions to billions of parameters. (For comparison, using more traditional machine learning or statistical methods, the Iris flower dataset can be classified with more than 90% accuracy using a small model with only two parameters.) However, despite the large size of LLMs compared to more traditional methods, LLMs don't have to be a black box.

In this book, you will learn how to build an LLM one step at a time. By the end, you will have a solid understanding of how an LLM, like the ones used in ChatGPT, works on a fundamental level. I believe that developing confidence with each part of the fundamental concepts and underlying code is crucial for success. This not only helps in fixing bugs and improving performance but also enables experimentation with new ideas.

Several years ago, when I started working with LLMs, I had to learn how to implement them the hard way, sifting through many research papers and incomplete code repositories to develop a general understanding. With this book, I hope to make LLMs more accessible by developing and sharing a step-by-step implementation tutorial detailing all the major components and development phases of an LLM.

I strongly believe that the best way to understand LLMs is to code one from scratch—and you'll see that this can be fun too!

Happy reading and coding!

acknowledgments

Writing a book is a significant undertaking, and I would like to express my sincere gratitude to my wife, Liza, for her patience and support throughout this process. Her unconditional love and constant encouragement have been absolutely essential.

I am incredibly grateful to Daniel Kleine, whose invaluable feedback on the in-progress chapters and code went above and beyond. With his keen eye for detail and insightful suggestions, Daniel's contributions have undoubtedly made this book a smoother and more enjoyable reading experience.

I would also like to thank the wonderful staff at Manning Publications, including Michael Stephens, for the many productive discussions that helped shape the direction of this book, and Dustin Archibald, whose constructive feedback and guidance in adhering to the Manning guidelines have been crucial. I also appreciate your flexibility in accommodating the unique requirements of this unconventional from-scratch approach. A special thanks to Aleksandar Dragosavljević, Kari Lucke, and Mike Beady for their work on the professional layouts and to Susan Honeywell and her team for refining and polishing the graphics.

I want to express my heartfelt gratitude to Robin Campbell and her outstanding marketing team for their invaluable support throughout the writing process.

Finally, I extend my thanks to the reviewers: Anandaganesh Balakrishnan, Anto Aravinth, Ayush Bihani, Bassam Ismail, Benjamin Muskalla, Bruno Sonnino, Christian Prokopp, Daniel Kleine, David Curran, Dibyendu Roy Chowdhury, Gary Pass, Georg Sommer, Giovanni Alzetta, Guillermo Alcántara, Jonathan Reeves, Kunal Ghosh, Nicolas Modrzyk, Paul Silisteanu, Raul Ciotescu, Scott Ling, Sriram Macharla, Sumit

Pal, Vahid Mirjalili, Vaijanath Rao, and Walter Reade for their thorough feedback on the drafts. Your keen eyes and insightful comments have been essential in improving the quality of this book.

To everyone who has contributed to this journey, I am sincerely grateful. Your support, expertise, and dedication have been instrumental in bringing this book to fruition. Thank you!

about this book

Build a Large Language Model (From Scratch) was written to help you understand and create your own GPT-like large language models (LLMs) from the ground up. It begins by focusing on the fundamentals of working with text data and coding attention mechanisms and then guides you through implementing a complete GPT model from scratch. The book then covers the pretraining mechanism as well as fine-tuning for specific tasks such as text classification and following instructions. By the end of this book, you'll have a deep understanding of how LLMs work and the skills to build your own models. While the models you'll create are smaller in scale compared to the large foundational models, they use the same concepts and serve as powerful educational tools to grasp the core mechanisms and techniques used in building state-of-the-art LLMs.

Who should read this book

Build a Large Language Model (From Scratch) is for machine learning enthusiasts, engineers, researchers, students, and practitioners who want to gain a deep understanding of how LLMs work and learn to build their own models from scratch. Both beginners and experienced developers will be able to use their existing skills and knowledge to grasp the concepts and techniques used in creating LLMs.

What sets this book apart is its comprehensive coverage of the entire process of building LLMs, from working with datasets to implementing the model architecture, pretraining on unlabeled data, and fine-tuning for specific tasks. As of this writing, no other resource provides such a complete and hands-on approach to building LLMs from the ground up.

To understand the code examples in this book, you should have a solid grasp of Python programming. While some familiarity with machine learning, deep learning, and artificial intelligence can be beneficial, an extensive background in these areas is not required. LLMs are a unique subset of AI, so even if you're relatively new to the field, you'll be able to follow along.

If you have some experience with deep neural networks, you may find certain concepts more familiar, as LLMs are built upon these architectures. However, proficiency in PyTorch is not a prerequisite. Appendix A provides a concise introduction to PyTorch, equipping you with the necessary skills to comprehend the code examples throughout the book.

A high school–level understanding of mathematics, particularly working with vectors and matrices, can be helpful as we explore the inner workings of LLMs. However, advanced mathematical knowledge is not necessary to grasp the key concepts and ideas presented in this book.

The most important prerequisite is a strong foundation in Python programming. With this knowledge, you'll be well prepared to explore the fascinating world of LLMs and understand the concepts and code examples presented in this book.

How this book is organized: A roadmap

This book is designed to be read sequentially, as each chapter builds upon the concepts and techniques introduced in the previous ones. The book is divided into seven chapters that cover the essential aspects of LLMs and their implementation.

Chapter 1 provides a high-level introduction to the fundamental concepts behind LLMs. It explores the transformer architecture, which forms the basis for LLMs such as those used on the ChatGPT platform.

Chapter 2 lays out a plan for building an LLM from scratch. It covers the process of preparing text for LLM training, including splitting text into word and subword tokens, using byte pair encoding for advanced tokenization, sampling training examples with a sliding window approach, and converting tokens into vectors that feed into the LLM.

Chapter 3 focuses on the attention mechanisms used in LLMs. It introduces a basic self-attention framework and progresses to an enhanced self-attention mechanism. The chapter also covers the implementation of a causal attention module that enables LLMs to generate one token at a time, masking randomly selected attention weights with dropout to reduce overfitting and stacking multiple causal attention modules into a multihead attention module.

Chapter 4 focuses on coding a GPT-like LLM that can be trained to generate human-like text. It covers techniques such as normalizing layer activations to stabilize neural network training, adding shortcut connections in deep neural networks to train models more effectively, implementing transformer blocks to create GPT models of various sizes, and computing the number of parameters and storage requirements of GPT models.

Chapter 5 implements the pretraining process of LLMs. It covers computing the training and validation set losses to assess the quality of LLM-generated text, implementing a training function and pretraining the LLM, saving and loading model weights to continue training an LLM, and loading pretrained weights from OpenAI.

Chapter 6 introduces different LLM fine-tuning approaches. It covers preparing a dataset for text classification, modifying a pretrained LLM for fine-tuning, fine-tuning an LLM to identify spam messages, and evaluating the accuracy of a fine-tuned LLM classifier.

Chapter 7 explores the instruction fine-tuning process of LLMs. It covers preparing a dataset for supervised instruction fine-tuning, organizing instruction data in training batches, loading a pretrained LLM and fine-tuning it to follow human instructions, extracting LLM-generated instruction responses for evaluation, and evaluating an instruction-fine-tuned LLM.

About the code

To make it as easy as possible to follow along, all code examples in this book are conveniently available on the Manning website at https://www.manning.com/books/build-a-large-language-model-from-scratch, as well as in Jupyter notebook format on GitHub at https://github.com/rasbt/LLMs-from-scratch. And don't worry about getting stuck—solutions to all the code exercises can be found in appendix C.

This book contains many examples of source code both in numbered listings and in line with normal text. In both cases, source code is formatted in a `fixed-width font like this` to separate it from ordinary text.

In many cases, the original source code has been reformatted; we've added line breaks and reworked indentation to accommodate the available page space in the book. In rare cases, even this was not enough, and listings include line-continuation markers (➥). Additionally, comments in the source code have often been removed from the listings when the code is described in the text. Code annotations accompany many of the listings, highlighting important concepts.

One of the key goals of this book is accessibility, so the code examples have been carefully designed to run efficiently on a regular laptop, without the need for any special hardware. But if you do have access to a GPU, certain sections provide helpful tips on scaling up the datasets and models to take advantage of that extra power.

Throughout the book, we'll be using PyTorch as our go-to tensor and a deep learning library to implement LLMs from the ground up. If PyTorch is new to you, I recommend you start with appendix A, which provides an in-depth introduction, complete with setup recommendations.

liveBook discussion forum

Purchase of *Build a Large Language Model (From Scratch)* includes free access to liveBook, Manning's online reading platform. Using liveBook's exclusive discussion features, you can attach comments to the book globally or to specific sections or paragraphs. It's a snap to make notes for yourself, ask and answer technical questions, and receive help from the author and other users. To access the forum, go to https://livebook.manning.com/book/build-a-large-language-model-from-scratch/discussion. You can also learn more about Manning's forums and the rules of conduct at https://livebook.manning.com/discussion.

Manning's commitment to readers is to provide a venue where a meaningful dialogue between individual readers and between readers and the author can take place. It is not a commitment to any specific amount of participation on the part of the author, whose contribution to the forum remains voluntary (and unpaid). We suggest you try asking the author some challenging questions lest his interest stray! The forum and the archives of previous discussions will be accessible from the publisher's website as long as the book is in print.

Other online resources

Interested in the latest AI and LLM research trends?

- Check out my blog at https://magazine.sebastianraschka.com, where I regularly discusses the latest AI research with a focus on LLMs.

Need help getting up to speed with deep learning and PyTorch?

- I offer several free courses on my website at https://sebastianraschka.com/teaching. These resources can help you quickly get up to speed with the latest techniques.

Looking for bonus materials related to the book?

- Visit the book's GitHub repository at https://github.com/rasbt/LLMs-from-scratch to find additional resources and examples to supplement your learning.

about the author

Sebastian Raschka, PhD, has been working in machine learning and AI for more than a decade. In addition to being a researcher, Sebastian has a strong passion for education. He is known for his bestselling books on machine learning with Python and his contributions to open source.

Sebastian is a staff research engineer at Lightning AI, focusing on implementing and training LLMs. Before his industry experience, Sebastian was an assistant professor in the Department of Statistics at the University of Wisconsin-Madison, where he focused on deep learning research. You can learn more about Sebastian at https://sebastianraschka.com.

about the cover illustration

The figure on the cover of *Build a Large Language Model (From Scratch)*, titled "Le duchesse," or "The duchess," is taken from a book by Louis Curmer published in 1841. Each illustration is finely drawn and colored by hand.

In those days, it was easy to identify where people lived and what their trade or station in life was just by their dress. Manning celebrates the inventiveness and initiative of the computer business with book covers based on the rich diversity of regional culture centuries ago, brought back to life by pictures from collections such as this one.

1 Understanding large language models

This chapter covers

- High-level explanations of the fundamental concepts behind large language models (LLMs)
- Insights into the transformer architecture from which LLMs are derived
- A plan for building an LLM from scratch

Large language models (LLMs), such as those offered in OpenAI's ChatGPT, are deep neural network models that have been developed over the past few years. They ushered in a new era for natural language processing (NLP). Before the advent of LLMs, traditional methods excelled at categorization tasks such as email spam classification and straightforward pattern recognition that could be captured with handcrafted rules or simpler models. However, they typically underperformed in language tasks that demanded complex understanding and generation abilities, such as parsing detailed instructions, conducting contextual analysis, and creating coherent and contextually appropriate original text. For example, previous generations of language models could not write an email from a list of keywords—a task that is trivial for contemporary LLMs.

LLMs have remarkable capabilities to understand, generate, and interpret human language. However, it's important to clarify that when we say language models "understand," we mean that they can process and generate text in ways that appear coherent and contextually relevant, not that they possess human-like consciousness or comprehension.

Enabled by advancements in deep learning, which is a subset of machine learning and artificial intelligence (AI) focused on neural networks, LLMs are trained on vast quantities of text data. This large-scale training allows LLMs to capture deeper contextual information and subtleties of human language compared to previous approaches. As a result, LLMs have significantly improved performance in a wide range of NLP tasks, including text translation, sentiment analysis, question answering, and many more.

Another important distinction between contemporary LLMs and earlier NLP models is that earlier NLP models were typically designed for specific tasks, such as text categorization, language translation, etc. While those earlier NLP models excelled in their narrow applications, LLMs demonstrate a broader proficiency across a wide range of NLP tasks.

The success behind LLMs can be attributed to the transformer architecture that underpins many LLMs and the vast amounts of data on which LLMs are trained, allowing them to capture a wide variety of linguistic nuances, contexts, and patterns that would be challenging to encode manually.

This shift toward implementing models based on the transformer architecture and using large training datasets to train LLMs has fundamentally transformed NLP, providing more capable tools for understanding and interacting with human language.

The following discussion sets a foundation to accomplish the primary objective of this book: understanding LLMs by implementing a ChatGPT-like LLM based on the transformer architecture step by step in code.

1.1 What is an LLM?

An LLM is a neural network designed to understand, generate, and respond to human-like text. These models are deep neural networks trained on massive amounts of text data, sometimes encompassing large portions of the entire publicly available text on the internet.

The "large" in "large language model" refers to both the model's size in terms of parameters and the immense dataset on which it's trained. Models like this often have tens or even hundreds of billions of parameters, which are the adjustable weights in the network that are optimized during training to predict the next word in a sequence. Next-word prediction is sensible because it harnesses the inherent sequential nature of language to train models on understanding context, structure, and relationships within text. Yet, it is a very simple task, and so it is surprising to many researchers that it can produce such capable models. In later chapters, we will discuss and implement the next-word training procedure step by step.

LLMs utilize an architecture called the *transformer*, which allows them to pay selective attention to different parts of the input when making predictions, making them especially adept at handling the nuances and complexities of human language.

Since LLMs are capable of *generating* text, LLMs are also often referred to as a form of generative artificial intelligence, often abbreviated as *generative AI* or *GenAI*. As illustrated in figure 1.1, AI encompasses the broader field of creating machines that can perform tasks requiring human-like intelligence, including understanding language, recognizing patterns, and making decisions, and includes subfields like machine learning and deep learning.

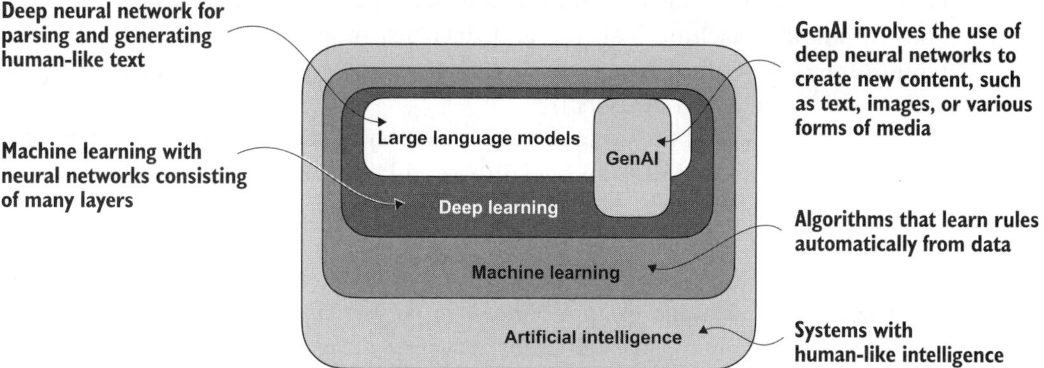

Figure 1.1 As this hierarchical depiction of the relationship between the different fields suggests, LLMs represent a specific application of deep learning techniques, using their ability to process and generate human-like text. Deep learning is a specialized branch of machine learning that focuses on using multilayer neural networks. Machine learning and deep learning are fields aimed at implementing algorithms that enable computers to learn from data and perform tasks that typically require human intelligence.

The algorithms used to implement AI are the focus of the field of machine learning. Specifically, machine learning involves the development of algorithms that can learn from and make predictions or decisions based on data without being explicitly programmed. To illustrate this, imagine a spam filter as a practical application of machine learning. Instead of manually writing rules to identify spam emails, a machine learning algorithm is fed examples of emails labeled as spam and legitimate emails. By minimizing the error in its predictions on a training dataset, the model then learns to recognize patterns and characteristics indicative of spam, enabling it to classify new emails as either spam or not spam.

As illustrated in figure 1.1, deep learning is a subset of machine learning that focuses on utilizing neural networks with three or more layers (also called deep neural networks) to model complex patterns and abstractions in data. In contrast to deep learning, traditional machine learning requires manual feature extraction. This means that human experts need to identify and select the most relevant features for the model.

While the field of AI is now dominated by machine learning and deep learning, it also includes other approaches—for example, using rule-based systems, genetic algorithms, expert systems, fuzzy logic, or symbolic reasoning.

Returning to the spam classification example, in traditional machine learning, human experts might manually extract features from email text such as the frequency of certain trigger words (for example, "prize," "win," "free"), the number of exclamation marks, use of all uppercase words, or the presence of suspicious links. This dataset, created based on these expert-defined features, would then be used to train the model. In contrast to traditional machine learning, deep learning does not require manual feature extraction. This means that human experts do not need to identify and select the most relevant features for a deep learning model. (However, both traditional machine learning and deep learning for spam classification still require the collection of labels, such as spam or non-spam, which need to be gathered either by an expert or users.)

Let's look at some of the problems LLMs can solve today, the challenges that LLMs address, and the general LLM architecture we will implement later.

1.2 Applications of LLMs

Owing to their advanced capabilities to parse and understand unstructured text data, LLMs have a broad range of applications across various domains. Today, LLMs are employed for machine translation, generation of novel texts (see figure 1.2), sentiment analysis, text summarization, and many other tasks. LLMs have recently been used for content creation, such as writing fiction, articles, and even computer code.

LLMs can also power sophisticated chatbots and virtual assistants, such as OpenAI's ChatGPT or Google's Gemini (formerly called Bard), which can answer user queries and augment traditional search engines such as Google Search or Microsoft Bing.

Moreover, LLMs may be used for effective knowledge retrieval from vast volumes of text in specialized areas such as medicine or law. This includes sifting through documents, summarizing lengthy passages, and answering technical questions.

In short, LLMs are invaluable for automating almost any task that involves parsing and generating text. Their applications are virtually endless, and as we continue to innovate and explore new ways to use these models, it's clear that LLMs have the potential to redefine our relationship with technology, making it more conversational, intuitive, and accessible.

We will focus on understanding how LLMs work from the ground up, coding an LLM that can generate texts. You will also learn about techniques that allow LLMs to carry out queries, ranging from answering questions to summarizing text, translating text into different languages, and more. In other words, you will learn how complex LLM assistants such as ChatGPT work by building one step by step.

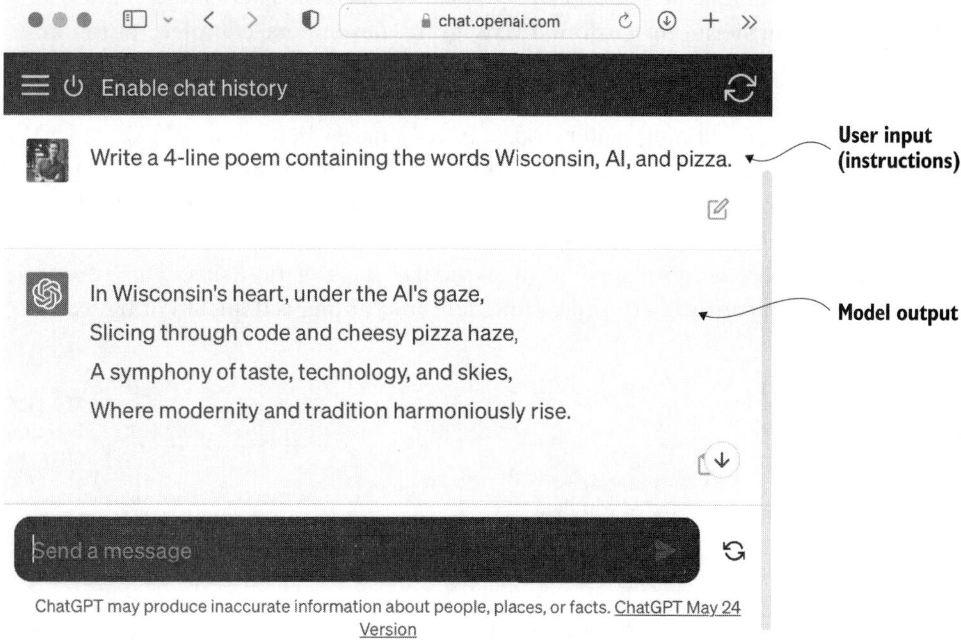

Figure 1.2 LLM interfaces enable natural language communication between users and AI systems. This screenshot shows ChatGPT writing a poem according to a user's specifications.

1.3 Stages of building and using LLMs

Why should we build our own LLMs? Coding an LLM from the ground up is an excellent exercise to understand its mechanics and limitations. Also, it equips us with the required knowledge for pretraining or fine-tuning existing open source LLM architectures to our own domain-specific datasets or tasks.

> **NOTE** Most LLMs today are implemented using the PyTorch deep learning library, which is what we will use. Readers can find a comprehensive introduction to PyTorch in appendix A.

Research has shown that when it comes to modeling performance, custom-built LLMs—those tailored for specific tasks or domains—can outperform general-purpose LLMs, such as those provided by ChatGPT, which are designed for a wide array of applications. Examples of these include BloombergGPT (specialized for finance) and LLMs tailored for medical question answering (see appendix B for more details).

Using custom-built LLMs offers several advantages, particularly regarding data privacy. For instance, companies may prefer not to share sensitive data with third-party LLM providers like OpenAI due to confidentiality concerns. Additionally, developing smaller custom LLMs enables deployment directly on customer devices, such as laptops and smartphones, which is something companies like Apple are currently exploring.

This local implementation can significantly decrease latency and reduce server-related costs. Furthermore, custom LLMs grant developers complete autonomy, allowing them to control updates and modifications to the model as needed.

The general process of creating an LLM includes pretraining and fine-tuning. The "pre" in "pretraining" refers to the initial phase where a model like an LLM is trained on a large, diverse dataset to develop a broad understanding of language. This pretrained model then serves as a foundational resource that can be further refined through fine-tuning, a process where the model is specifically trained on a narrower dataset that is more specific to particular tasks or domains. This two-stage training approach consisting of pretraining and fine-tuning is depicted in figure 1.3.

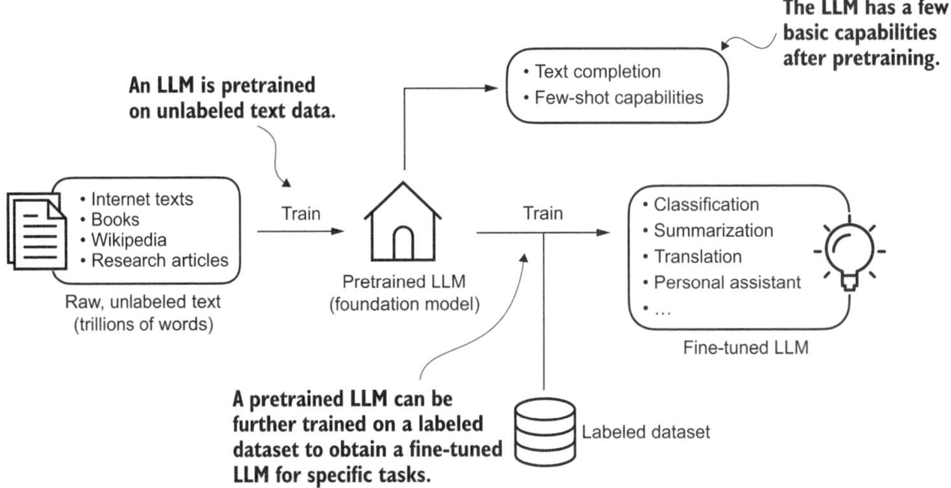

Figure 1.3 Pretraining an LLM involves next-word prediction on large text datasets. A pretrained LLM can then be fine-tuned using a smaller labeled dataset.

The first step in creating an LLM is to train it on a large corpus of text data, sometimes referred to as *raw* text. Here, "raw" refers to the fact that this data is just regular text without any labeling information. (Filtering may be applied, such as removing formatting characters or documents in unknown languages.)

NOTE Readers with a background in machine learning may note that labeling information is typically required for traditional machine learning models and deep neural networks trained via the conventional supervised learning paradigm. However, this is not the case for the pretraining stage of LLMs. In this phase, LLMs use self-supervised learning, where the model generates its own labels from the input data.

This first training stage of an LLM is also known as *pretraining*, creating an initial pretrained LLM, often called a *base* or *foundation model*. A typical example of such a model is the GPT-3 model (the precursor of the original model offered in ChatGPT). This model is capable of text completion—that is, finishing a half-written sentence provided by a user. It also has limited few-shot capabilities, which means it can learn to perform new tasks based on only a few examples instead of needing extensive training data.

After obtaining a pretrained LLM from training on large text datasets, where the LLM is trained to predict the next word in the text, we can further train the LLM on labeled data, also known as *fine-tuning*.

The two most popular categories of fine-tuning LLMs are *instruction fine-tuning* and *classification fine-tuning*. In instruction fine-tuning, the labeled dataset consists of instruction and answer pairs, such as a query to translate a text accompanied by the correctly translated text. In classification fine-tuning, the labeled dataset consists of texts and associated class labels—for example, emails associated with "spam" and "not spam" labels.

We will cover code implementations for pretraining and fine-tuning an LLM, and we will delve deeper into the specifics of both instruction and classification fine-tuning after pretraining a base LLM.

1.4 Introducing the transformer architecture

Most modern LLMs rely on the *transformer* architecture, which is a deep neural network architecture introduced in the 2017 paper "Attention Is All You Need" (https://arxiv.org/abs/1706.03762). To understand LLMs, we must understand the original transformer, which was developed for machine translation, translating English texts to German and French. A simplified version of the transformer architecture is depicted in figure 1.4.

The transformer architecture consists of two submodules: an encoder and a decoder. The encoder module processes the input text and encodes it into a series of numerical representations or vectors that capture the contextual information of the input. Then, the decoder module takes these encoded vectors and generates the output text. In a translation task, for example, the encoder would encode the text from the source language into vectors, and the decoder would decode these vectors to generate text in the target language. Both the encoder and decoder consist of many layers connected by a so-called self-attention mechanism. You may have many questions regarding how the inputs are preprocessed and encoded. These will be addressed in a step-by-step implementation in subsequent chapters.

A key component of transformers and LLMs is the self-attention mechanism (not shown), which allows the model to weigh the importance of different words or tokens in a sequence relative to each other. This mechanism enables the model to capture long-range dependencies and contextual relationships within the input data, enhancing its ability to generate coherent and contextually relevant output. However, due to

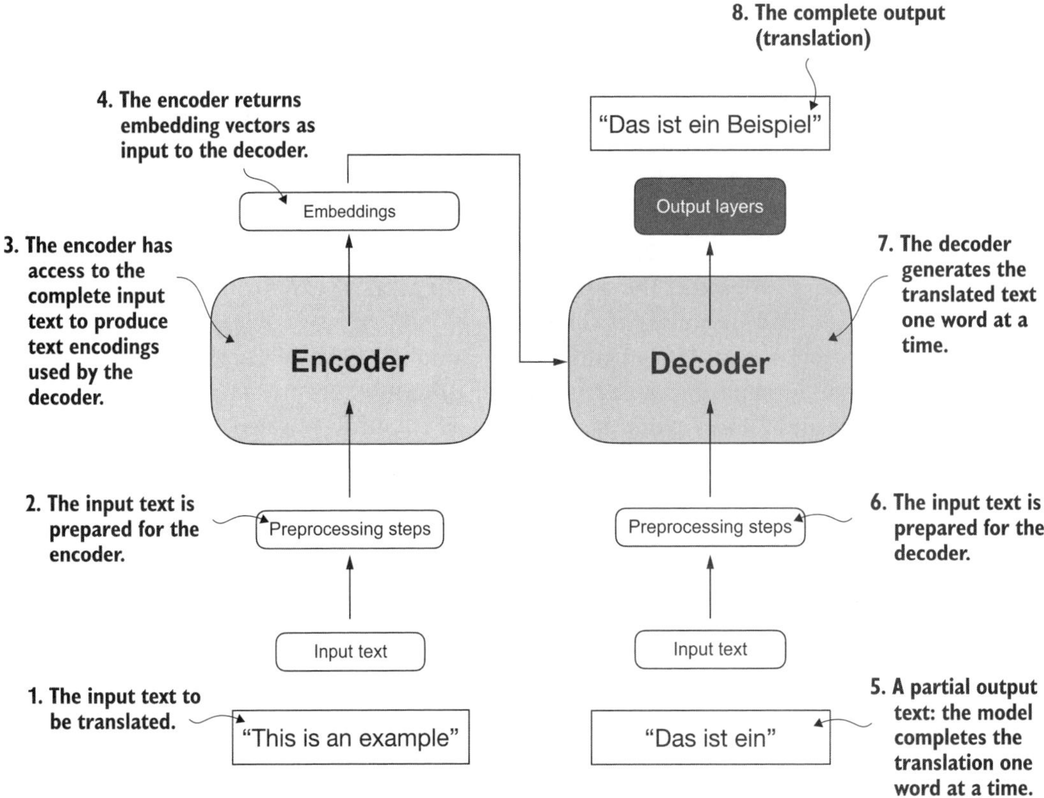
8. The complete output (translation)
"Das ist ein Beispiel"
4. The encoder returns embedding vectors as input to the decoder.
Embeddings
Output layers
3. The encoder has access to the complete input text to produce text encodings used by the decoder.
Encoder
Decoder
7. The decoder generates the translated text one word at a time.
2. The input text is prepared for the encoder.
Preprocessing steps
Preprocessing steps
6. The input text is prepared for the decoder.
Input text
Input text
1. The input text to be translated.
"This is an example"
"Das ist ein"
5. A partial output text: the model completes the translation one word at a time.

Figure 1.4 A simplified depiction of the original transformer architecture, which is a deep learning model for language translation. The transformer consists of two parts: (a) an encoder that processes the input text and produces an embedding representation (a numerical representation that captures many different factors in different dimensions) of the text that the (b) decoder can use to generate the translated text one word at a time. This figure shows the final stage of the translation process where the decoder has to generate only the final word ("Beispiel"), given the original input text ("This is an example") and a partially translated sentence ("Das ist ein"), to complete the translation.

its complexity, we will defer further explanation to chapter 3, where we will discuss and implement it step by step.

Later variants of the transformer architecture, such as BERT (short for *bidirectional encoder representations from transformers*) and the various GPT models (short for *generative pretrained transformers*), built on this concept to adapt this architecture for different tasks. If interested, refer to appendix B for further reading suggestions.

BERT, which is built upon the original transformer's encoder submodule, differs in its training approach from GPT. While GPT is designed for generative tasks, BERT and its variants specialize in masked word prediction, where the model predicts masked or hidden words in a given sentence, as shown in figure 1.5. This unique training strategy equips BERT with strengths in text classification tasks, including sentiment prediction and document categorization. As an application of its capabilities, as of this writing, X (formerly Twitter) uses BERT to detect toxic content.

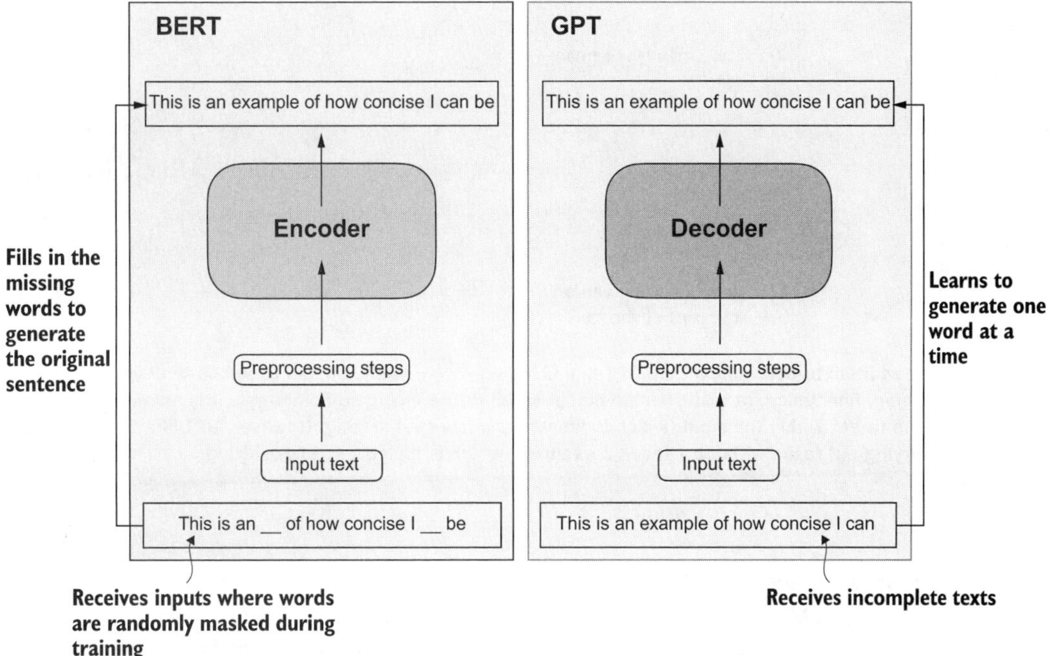

Figure 1.5 A visual representation of the transformer's encoder and decoder submodules. On the left, the encoder segment exemplifies BERT-like LLMs, which focus on masked word prediction and are primarily used for tasks like text classification. On the right, the decoder segment showcases GPT-like LLMs, designed for generative tasks and producing coherent text sequences.

GPT, on the other hand, focuses on the decoder portion of the original transformer architecture and is designed for tasks that require generating texts. This includes machine translation, text summarization, fiction writing, writing computer code, and more.

GPT models, primarily designed and trained to perform text completion tasks, also show remarkable versatility in their capabilities. These models are adept at executing both zero-shot and few-shot learning tasks. Zero-shot learning refers to the ability to generalize to completely unseen tasks without any prior specific examples. On the other hand, few-shot learning involves learning from a minimal number of examples the user provides as input, as shown in figure 1.6.

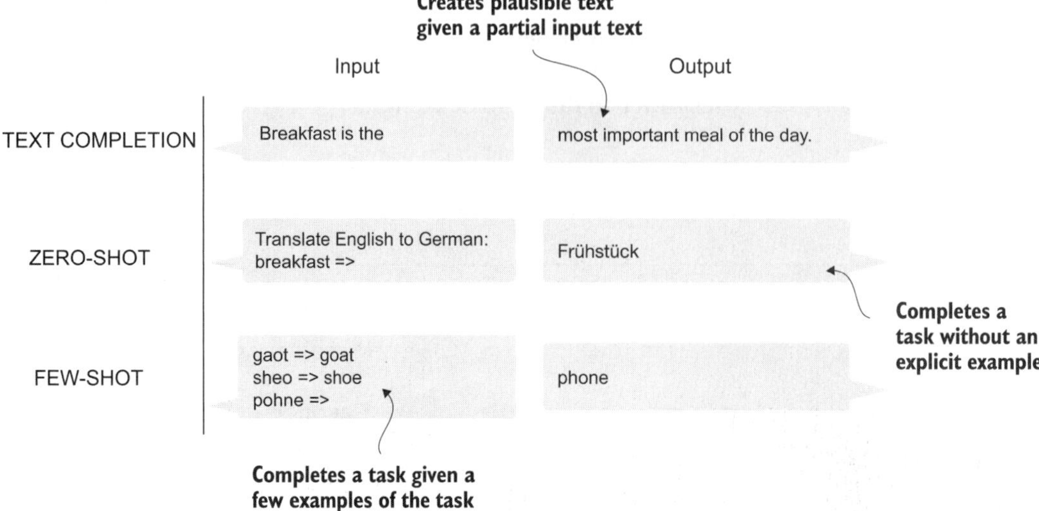

Figure 1.6 In addition to text completion, GPT-like LLMs can solve various tasks based on their inputs without needing retraining, fine-tuning, or task-specific model architecture changes. Sometimes it is helpful to provide examples of the target within the input, which is known as a few-shot setting. However, GPT-like LLMs are also capable of carrying out tasks without a specific example, which is called zero-shot setting.

Transformers vs. LLMs

Today's LLMs are based on the transformer architecture. Hence, transformers and LLMs are terms that are often used synonymously in the literature. However, note that not all transformers are LLMs since transformers can also be used for computer vision. Also, not all LLMs are transformers, as there are LLMs based on recurrent and convolutional architectures. The main motivation behind these alternative approaches is to improve the computational efficiency of LLMs. Whether these alternative LLM architectures can compete with the capabilities of transformer-based LLMs and whether they are going to be adopted in practice remains to be seen. For simplicity, I use the term "LLM" to refer to transformer-based LLMs similar to GPT. (Interested readers can find literature references describing these architectures in appendix B.)

1.5 Utilizing large datasets

The large training datasets for popular GPT- and BERT-like models represent diverse and comprehensive text corpora encompassing billions of words, which include a vast array of topics and natural and computer languages. To provide a concrete example, table 1.1 summarizes the dataset used for pretraining GPT-3, which served as the base model for the first version of ChatGPT.

Table 1.1 The pretraining dataset of the popular GPT-3 LLM

Dataset name	Dataset description	Number of tokens	Proportion in training data
CommonCrawl (filtered)	Web crawl data	410 billion	60%
WebText2	Web crawl data	19 billion	22%
Books1	Internet-based book corpus	12 billion	8%
Books2	Internet-based book corpus	55 billion	8%
Wikipedia	High-quality text	3 billion	3%

Table 1.1 reports the number of tokens, where a token is a unit of text that a model reads and the number of tokens in a dataset is roughly equivalent to the number of words and punctuation characters in the text. Chapter 2 addresses tokenization, the process of converting text into tokens.

The main takeaway is that the scale and diversity of this training dataset allow these models to perform well on diverse tasks, including language syntax, semantics, and context—even some requiring general knowledge.

GPT-3 dataset details

Table 1.1 displays the dataset used for GPT-3. The proportions column in the table sums up to 100% of the sampled data, adjusted for rounding errors. Although the subsets in the Number of Tokens column total 499 billion, the model was trained on only 300 billion tokens. The authors of the GPT-3 paper did not specify why the model was not trained on all 499 billion tokens.

For context, consider the size of the CommonCrawl dataset, which alone consists of 410 billion tokens and requires about 570 GB of storage. In comparison, later iterations of models like GPT-3, such as Meta's LLaMA, have expanded their training scope to include additional data sources like Arxiv research papers (92 GB) and StackExchange's code-related Q&As (78 GB).

The authors of the GPT-3 paper did not share the training dataset, but a comparable dataset that is publicly available is *Dolma: An Open Corpus of Three Trillion Tokens for LLM Pretraining Research* by Soldaini et al. 2024 (https://arxiv.org/abs/2402.00159). However, the collection may contain copyrighted works, and the exact usage terms may depend on the intended use case and country.

The pretrained nature of these models makes them incredibly versatile for further fine-tuning on downstream tasks, which is why they are also known as base or foundation models. Pretraining LLMs requires access to significant resources and is very expensive. For example, the GPT-3 pretraining cost is estimated to be $4.6 million in terms of cloud computing credits (https://mng.bz/VxEW).

The good news is that many pretrained LLMs, available as open source models, can be used as general-purpose tools to write, extract, and edit texts that were not part of the training data. Also, LLMs can be fine-tuned on specific tasks with relatively smaller datasets, reducing the computational resources needed and improving performance.

We will implement the code for pretraining and use it to pretrain an LLM for educational purposes. All computations are executable on consumer hardware. After implementing the pretraining code, we will learn how to reuse openly available model weights and load them into the architecture we will implement, allowing us to skip the expensive pretraining stage when we fine-tune our LLM.

1.6 A closer look at the GPT architecture

GPT was originally introduced in the paper "Improving Language Understanding by Generative Pre-Training" (https://mng.bz/x2qg) by Radford et al. from OpenAI. GPT-3 is a scaled-up version of this model that has more parameters and was trained on a larger dataset. In addition, the original model offered in ChatGPT was created by fine-tuning GPT-3 on a large instruction dataset using a method from OpenAI's InstructGPT paper (https://arxiv.org/abs/2203.02155). As figure 1.6 shows, these models are competent text completion models and can carry out other tasks such as spelling correction, classification, or language translation. This is actually very remarkable given that GPT models are pretrained on a relatively simple next-word prediction task, as depicted in figure 1.7.

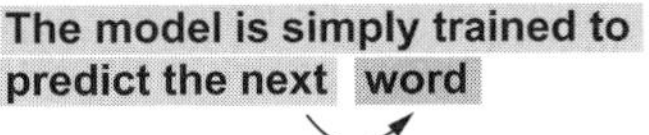
The model is simply trained to
predict the next word

Figure 1.7 In the next-word prediction pretraining task for GPT models, the system learns to predict the upcoming word in a sentence by looking at the words that have come before it. This approach helps the model understand how words and phrases typically fit together in language, forming a foundation that can be applied to various other tasks.

The next-word prediction task is a form of self-supervised learning, which is a form of self-labeling. This means that we don't need to collect labels for the training data explicitly but can use the structure of the data itself: we can use the next word in a sentence or document as the label that the model is supposed to predict. Since this next-word prediction task allows us to create labels "on the fly," it is possible to use massive unlabeled text datasets to train LLMs.

Compared to the original transformer architecture we covered in section 1.4, the general GPT architecture is relatively simple. Essentially, it's just the decoder part without the encoder (figure 1.8). Since decoder-style models like GPT generate text by predicting text one word at a time, they are considered a type of *autoregressive* model. Autoregressive models incorporate their previous outputs as inputs for future predictions. Consequently, in GPT, each new word is chosen based on the sequence that precedes it, which improves the coherence of the resulting text.

Architectures such as GPT-3 are also significantly larger than the original transformer model. For instance, the original transformer repeated the encoder and decoder blocks six times. GPT-3 has 96 transformer layers and 175 billion parameters in total.

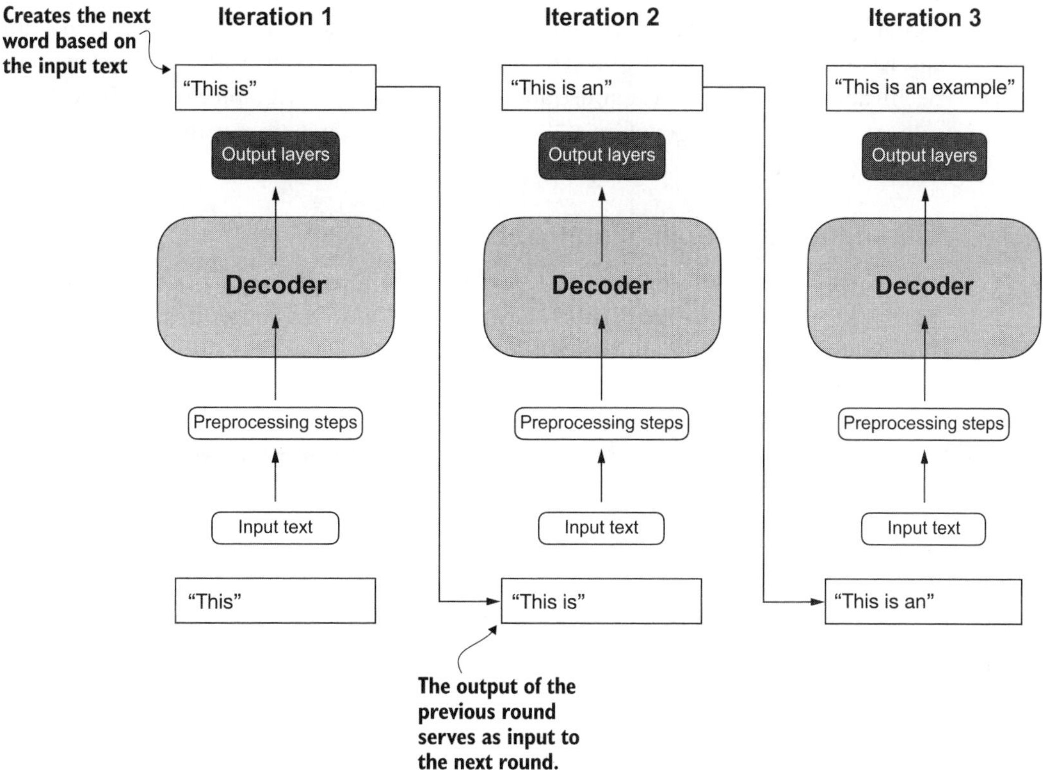

Figure 1.8 The GPT architecture employs only the decoder portion of the original transformer. It is designed for unidirectional, left-to-right processing, making it well suited for text generation and next-word prediction tasks to generate text in an iterative fashion, one word at a time.

GPT-3 was introduced in 2020, which, by the standards of deep learning and large language model development, is considered a long time ago. However, more recent architectures, such as Meta's Llama models, are still based on the same underlying concepts, introducing only minor modifications. Hence, understanding GPT remains as relevant as ever, so I focus on implementing the prominent architecture behind GPT while providing pointers to specific tweaks employed by alternative LLMs.

Although the original transformer model, consisting of encoder and decoder blocks, was explicitly designed for language translation, GPT models—despite their larger yet simpler decoder-only architecture aimed at next-word prediction—are also capable of performing translation tasks. This capability was initially unexpected to researchers, as it emerged from a model primarily trained on a next-word prediction task, which is a task that did not specifically target translation.

The ability to perform tasks that the model wasn't explicitly trained to perform is called an *emergent behavior*. This capability isn't explicitly taught during training but emerges as a natural consequence of the model's exposure to vast quantities of multilingual data in diverse contexts. The fact that GPT models can "learn" the translation patterns between languages and perform translation tasks even though they weren't specifically trained for it demonstrates the benefits and capabilities of these large-scale, generative language models. We can perform diverse tasks without using diverse models for each.

1.7 Building a large language model

Now that we've laid the groundwork for understanding LLMs, let's code one from scratch. We will take the fundamental idea behind GPT as a blueprint and tackle this in three stages, as outlined in figure 1.9.

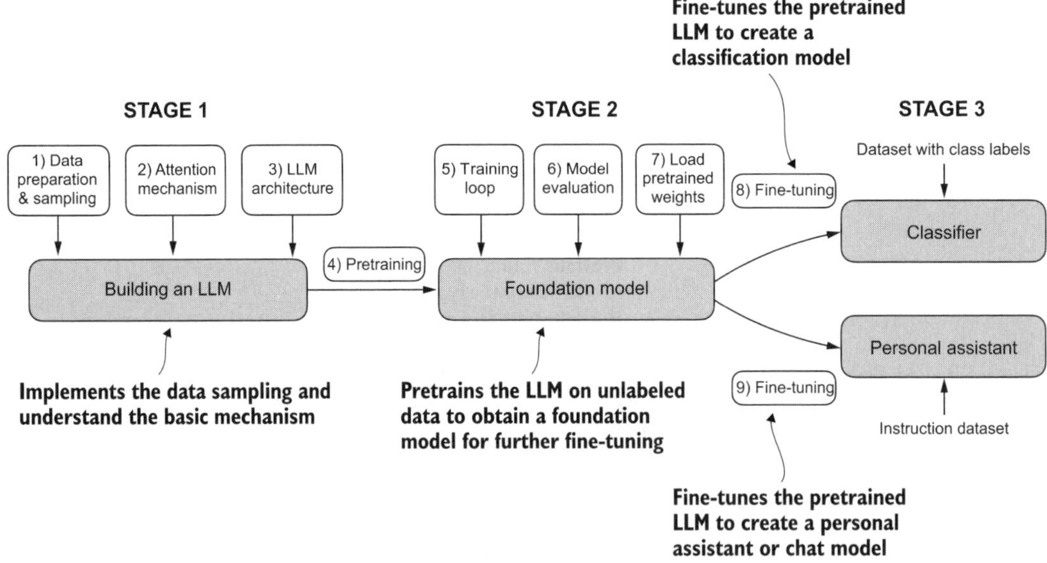

Figure 1.9 The three main stages of coding an LLM are implementing the LLM architecture and data preparation process (stage 1), pretraining an LLM to create a foundation model (stage 2), and fine-tuning the foundation model to become a personal assistant or text classifier (stage 3).

In stage 1, we will learn about the fundamental data preprocessing steps and code the attention mechanism at the heart of every LLM. Next, in stage 2, we will learn how to code and pretrain a GPT-like LLM capable of generating new texts. We will also go over the fundamentals of evaluating LLMs, which is essential for developing capable NLP systems.

Pretraining an LLM from scratch is a significant endeavor, demanding thousands to millions of dollars in computing costs for GPT-like models. Therefore, the focus of stage 2 is on implementing training for educational purposes using a small dataset. In addition, I also provide code examples for loading openly available model weights.

Finally, in stage 3, we will take a pretrained LLM and fine-tune it to follow instructions such as answering queries or classifying texts—the most common tasks in many real-world applications and research.

I hope you are looking forward to embarking on this exciting journey!

Summary

- LLMs have transformed the field of natural language processing, which previously mostly relied on explicit rule-based systems and simpler statistical methods. The advent of LLMs introduced new deep learning-driven approaches that led to advancements in understanding, generating, and translating human language.
- Modern LLMs are trained in two main steps:
  - First, they are pretrained on a large corpus of unlabeled text by using the prediction of the next word in a sentence as a label.
  - Then, they are fine-tuned on a smaller, labeled target dataset to follow instructions or perform classification tasks.
- LLMs are based on the transformer architecture. The key idea of the transformer architecture is an attention mechanism that gives the LLM selective access to the whole input sequence when generating the output one word at a time.
- The original transformer architecture consists of an encoder for parsing text and a decoder for generating text.
- LLMs for generating text and following instructions, such as GPT-3 and ChatGPT, only implement decoder modules, simplifying the architecture.
- Large datasets consisting of billions of words are essential for pretraining LLMs.
- While the general pretraining task for GPT-like models is to predict the next word in a sentence, these LLMs exhibit emergent properties, such as capabilities to classify, translate, or summarize texts.

- Once an LLM is pretrained, the resulting foundation model can be fine-tuned more efficiently for various downstream tasks.
- LLMs fine-tuned on custom datasets can outperform general LLMs on specific tasks.

2 Working with text data

This chapter covers

- Preparing text for large language model training
- Splitting text into word and subword tokens
- Byte pair encoding as a more advanced way of tokenizing text
- Sampling training examples with a sliding window approach
- Converting tokens into vectors that feed into a large language model

So far, we've covered the general structure of large language models (LLMs) and learned that they are pretrained on vast amounts of text. Specifically, our focus was on decoder-only LLMs based on the transformer architecture, which underlies the models used in ChatGPT and other popular GPT-like LLMs.

During the pretraining stage, LLMs process text one word at a time. Training LLMs with millions to billions of parameters using a next-word prediction task yields models with impressive capabilities. These models can then be further finetuned to follow general instructions or perform specific target tasks. But before we can implement and train LLMs, we need to prepare the training dataset, as illustrated in figure 2.1.

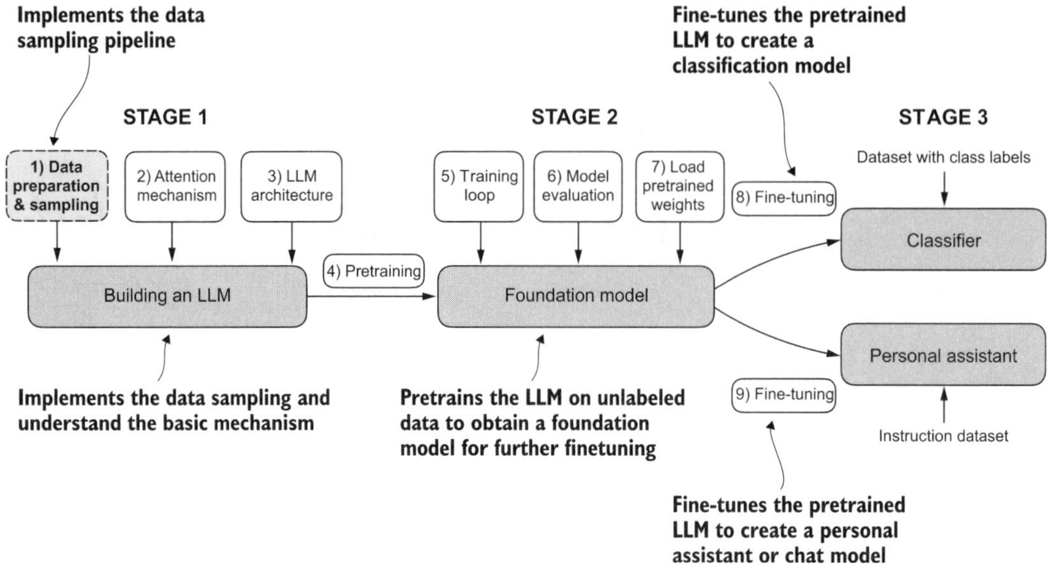

Figure 2.1 The three main stages of coding an LLM. This chapter focuses on step 1 of stage 1: implementing the data sample pipeline.

You'll learn how to prepare input text for training LLMs. This involves splitting text into individual word and subword tokens, which can then be encoded into vector representations for the LLM. You'll also learn about advanced tokenization schemes like byte pair encoding, which is utilized in popular LLMs like GPT. Lastly, we'll implement a sampling and data-loading strategy to produce the input-output pairs necessary for training LLMs.

2.1 Understanding word embeddings

Deep neural network models, including LLMs, cannot process raw text directly. Since text is categorical, it isn't compatible with the mathematical operations used to implement and train neural networks. Therefore, we need a way to represent words as continuous-valued vectors.

> **NOTE** Readers unfamiliar with vectors and tensors in a computational context can learn more in appendix A, section A.2.2.

The concept of converting data into a vector format is often referred to as *embedding*. Using a specific neural network layer or another pretrained neural network model, we can embed different data types—for example, video, audio, and text, as illustrated in figure 2.2. However, it's important to note that different data formats require distinct embedding models. For example, an embedding model designed for text would not be suitable for embedding audio or video data.

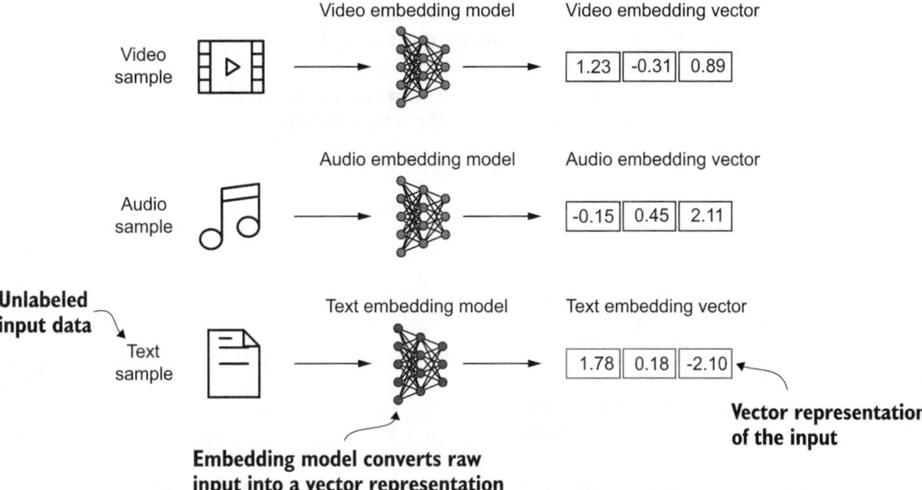

Figure 2.2 Deep learning models cannot process data formats like video, audio, and text in their raw form. Thus, we use an embedding model to transform this raw data into a dense vector representation that deep learning architectures can easily understand and process. Specifically, this figure illustrates the process of converting raw data into a three-dimensional numerical vector.

At its core, an embedding is a mapping from discrete objects, such as words, images, or even entire documents, to points in a continuous vector space—the primary purpose of embeddings is to convert nonnumeric data into a format that neural networks can process.

While word embeddings are the most common form of text embedding, there are also embeddings for sentences, paragraphs, or whole documents. Sentence or paragraph embeddings are popular choices for *retrieval-augmented generation*. Retrieval-augmented generation combines generation (like producing text) with retrieval (like searching an external knowledge base) to pull relevant information when generating text, which is a technique that is beyond the scope of this book. Since our goal is to train GPT-like LLMs, which learn to generate text one word at a time, we will focus on word embeddings.

Several algorithms and frameworks have been developed to generate word embeddings. One of the earlier and most popular examples is the *Word2Vec* approach. Word2Vec trained neural network architecture to generate word embeddings by predicting the context of a word given the target word or vice versa. The main idea behind Word2Vec is that words that appear in similar contexts tend to have similar meanings. Consequently, when projected into two-dimensional word embeddings for visualization purposes, similar terms are clustered together, as shown in figure 2.3.

Word embeddings can have varying dimensions, from one to thousands. A higher dimensionality might capture more nuanced relationships but at the cost of computational efficiency.

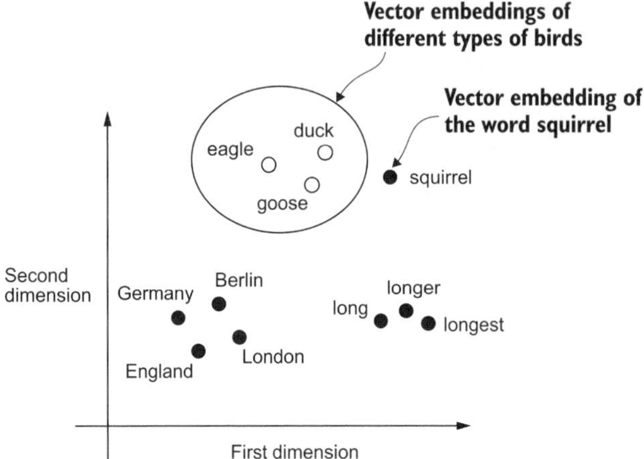

Figure 2.3 If word embeddings are two-dimensional, we can plot them in a two-dimensional scatterplot for visualization purposes as shown here. When using word embedding techniques, such as Word2Vec, words corresponding to similar concepts often appear close to each other in the embedding space. For instance, different types of birds appear closer to each other in the embedding space than in countries and cities.

While we can use pretrained models such as Word2Vec to generate embeddings for machine learning models, LLMs commonly produce their own embeddings that are part of the input layer and are updated during training. The advantage of optimizing the embeddings as part of the LLM training instead of using Word2Vec is that the embeddings are optimized to the specific task and data at hand. We will implement such embedding layers later in this chapter. (LLMs can also create contextualized output embeddings, as we discuss in chapter 3.)

Unfortunately, high-dimensional embeddings present a challenge for visualization because our sensory perception and common graphical representations are inherently limited to three dimensions or fewer, which is why figure 2.3 shows two-dimensional embeddings in a two-dimensional scatterplot. However, when working with LLMs, we typically use embeddings with a much higher dimensionality. For both GPT-2 and GPT-3, the embedding size (often referred to as the dimensionality of the model's hidden states) varies based on the specific model variant and size. It is a tradeoff between performance and efficiency. The smallest GPT-2 models (117M and 125M parameters) use an embedding size of 768 dimensions to provide concrete examples. The largest GPT-3 model (175B parameters) uses an embedding size of 12,288 dimensions.

Next, we will walk through the required steps for preparing the embeddings used by an LLM, which include splitting text into words, converting words into tokens, and turning tokens into embedding vectors.

2.2 Tokenizing text

Let's discuss how we split input text into individual tokens, a required preprocessing step for creating embeddings for an LLM. These tokens are either individual words or special characters, including punctuation characters, as shown in figure 2.4.

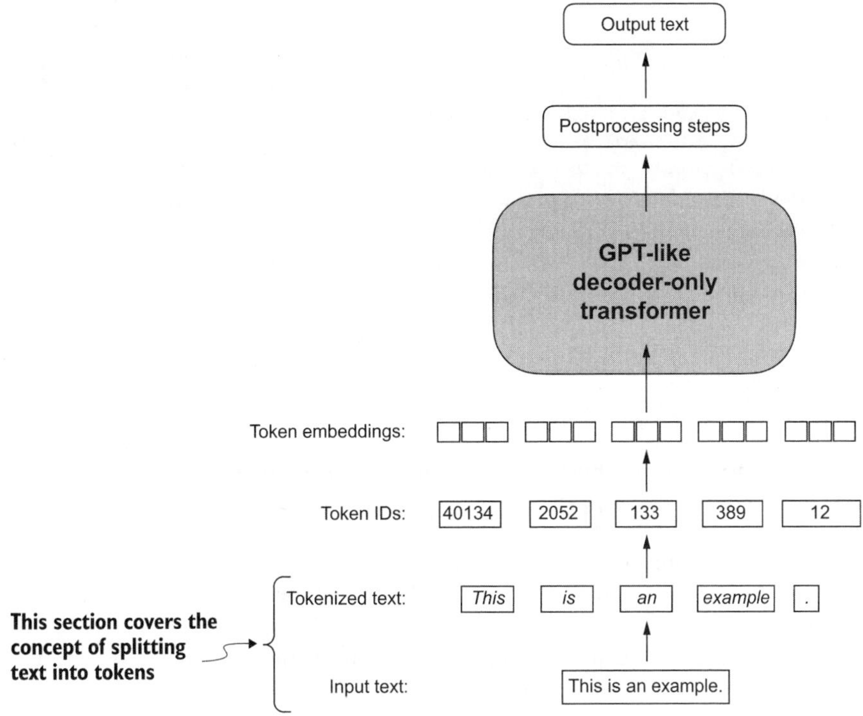

Figure 2.4 A view of the text processing steps in the context of an LLM. Here, we split an input text into individual tokens, which are either words or special characters, such as punctuation characters.

The text we will tokenize for LLM training is "The Verdict," a short story by Edith Wharton, which has been released into the public domain and is thus permitted to be used for LLM training tasks. The text is available on Wikisource at https://en.wikisource.org/wiki/The_Verdict, and you can copy and paste it into a text file, which I copied into a text file `"the-verdict.txt"`.

Alternatively, you can find this `"the-verdict.txt"` file in this book's GitHub repository at https://mng.bz/Adng. You can download the file with the following Python code:

```
import urllib.request
url = ("https://raw.githubusercontent.com/rasbt/"
       "LLMs-from-scratch/main/ch02/01_main-chapter-code/"
       "the-verdict.txt")
file_path = "the-verdict.txt"
urllib.request.urlretrieve(url, file_path)
```

Next, we can load the `the-verdict.txt` file using Python's standard file reading utilities.

Listing 2.1 Reading in a short story as text sample into Python

```
with open("the-verdict.txt", "r", encoding="utf-8") as f:
    raw_text = f.read()
print("Total number of character:", len(raw_text))
print(raw_text[:99])
```

The print command prints the total number of characters followed by the first 100 characters of this file for illustration purposes:

```
Total number of character: 20479
I HAD always thought Jack Gisburn rather a cheap genius--though a good fellow
     enough--so it was no
```

Our goal is to tokenize this 20,479-character short story into individual words and special characters that we can then turn into embeddings for LLM training.

> **NOTE** It's common to process millions of articles and hundreds of thousands of books—many gigabytes of text—when working with LLMs. However, for educational purposes, it's sufficient to work with smaller text samples like a single book to illustrate the main ideas behind the text processing steps and to make it possible to run it in a reasonable time on consumer hardware.

How can we best split this text to obtain a list of tokens? For this, we go on a small excursion and use Python's regular expression library `re` for illustration purposes. (You don't have to learn or memorize any regular expression syntax since we will later transition to a prebuilt tokenizer.)

Using some simple example text, we can use the `re.split` command with the following syntax to split a text on whitespace characters:

```
import re
text = "Hello, world. This, is a test."
result = re.split(r'(\s)', text)
print(result)
```

The result is a list of individual words, whitespaces, and punctuation characters:

```
['Hello,', ' ', 'world.', ' ', 'This,', ' ', 'is', ' ', 'a', ' ', 'test.']
```

This simple tokenization scheme mostly works for separating the example text into individual words; however, some words are still connected to punctuation characters that we want to have as separate list entries. We also refrain from making all text lowercase because capitalization helps LLMs distinguish between proper nouns and common nouns, understand sentence structure, and learn to generate text with proper capitalization.

Let's modify the regular expression splits on whitespaces (`\s`), commas, and periods (`[,.]`):

```
result = re.split(r'([,.]|\s)', text)
print(result)
```

We can see that the words and punctuation characters are now separate list entries just as we wanted:

```
['Hello', ',', '', ' ', 'world', '.', '', ' ', 'This', ',', '', ' ', 'is',
' ', 'a', ' ', 'test', '.', '']
```

A small remaining problem is that the list still includes whitespace characters. Optionally, we can remove these redundant characters safely as follows:

```
result = [item for item in result if item.strip()]
print(result)
```

The resulting whitespace-free output looks like as follows:

```
['Hello', ',', 'world', '.', 'This', ',', 'is', 'a', 'test', '.']
```

> **NOTE** When developing a simple tokenizer, whether we should encode whitespaces as separate characters or just remove them depends on our application and its requirements. Removing whitespaces reduces the memory and computing requirements. However, keeping whitespaces can be useful if we train models that are sensitive to the exact structure of the text (for example, Python code, which is sensitive to indentation and spacing). Here, we remove whitespaces for simplicity and brevity of the tokenized outputs. Later, we will switch to a tokenization scheme that includes whitespaces.

The tokenization scheme we devised here works well on the simple sample text. Let's modify it a bit further so that it can also handle other types of punctuation, such as question marks, quotation marks, and the double-dashes we have seen earlier in the first 100 characters of Edith Wharton's short story, along with additional special characters:

```
text = "Hello, world. Is this-- a test?"
result = re.split(r'([,.:;?_!"()\']|--|\s)', text)
result = [item.strip() for item in result if item.strip()]
print(result)
```

The resulting output is:

```
['Hello', ',', 'world', '.', 'Is', 'this', '--', 'a', 'test', '?']
```

As we can see based on the results summarized in figure 2.5, our tokenization scheme can now handle the various special characters in the text successfully.

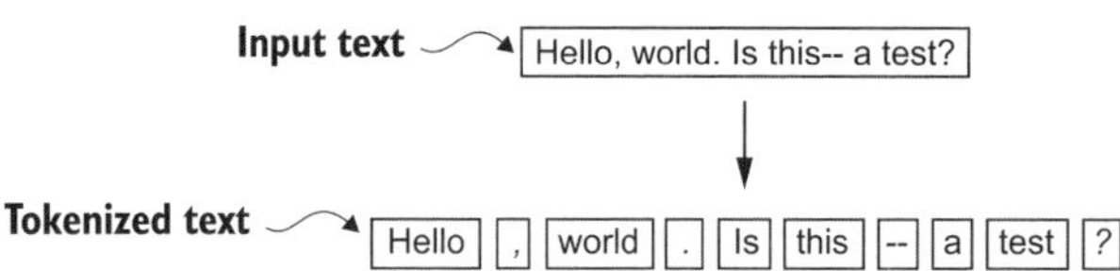

Figure 2.5 The tokenization scheme we implemented so far splits text into individual words and punctuation characters. In this specific example, the sample text gets split into 10 individual tokens.

Now that we have a basic tokenizer working, let's apply it to Edith Wharton's entire short story:

```
preprocessed = re.split(r'([,.:;?_!"()\']|--|\s)', raw_text)
preprocessed = [item.strip() for item in preprocessed if item.strip()]
print(len(preprocessed))
```

This print statement outputs `4690`, which is the number of tokens in this text (without whitespaces). Let's print the first 30 tokens for a quick visual check:

```
print(preprocessed[:30])
```

The resulting output shows that our tokenizer appears to be handling the text well since all words and special characters are neatly separated:

```
['I', 'HAD', 'always', 'thought', 'Jack', 'Gisburn', 'rather', 'a',
'cheap', 'genius', '--', 'though', 'a', 'good', 'fellow', 'enough',
'--', 'so', 'it', 'was', 'no', 'great', 'surprise', 'to', 'me', 'to',
'hear', 'that', ',', 'in']
```

2.3 Converting tokens into token IDs

Next, let's convert these tokens from a Python string to an integer representation to produce the token IDs. This conversion is an intermediate step before converting the token IDs into embedding vectors.

To map the previously generated tokens into token IDs, we have to build a vocabulary first. This vocabulary defines how we map each unique word and special character to a unique integer, as shown in figure 2.6.

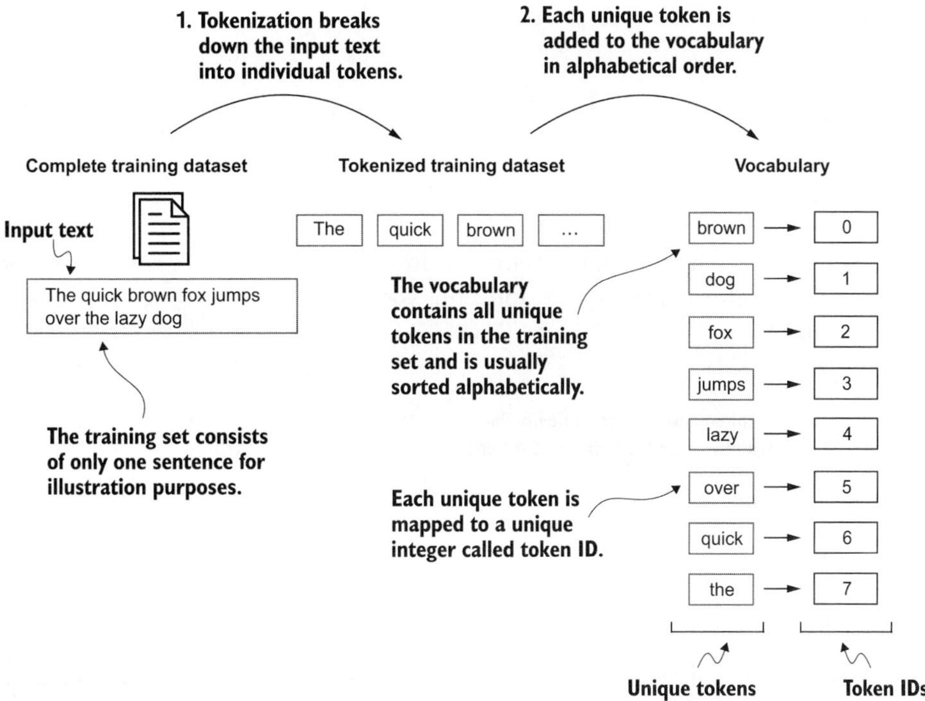

Figure 2.6 We build a vocabulary by tokenizing the entire text in a training dataset into individual tokens. These individual tokens are then sorted alphabetically, and duplicate tokens are removed. The unique tokens are then aggregated into a vocabulary that defines a mapping from each unique token to a unique integer value. The depicted vocabulary is purposefully small and contains no punctuation or special characters for simplicity.

Now that we have tokenized Edith Wharton's short story and assigned it to a Python variable called `preprocessed`, let's create a list of all unique tokens and sort them alphabetically to determine the vocabulary size:

```
all_words = sorted(set(preprocessed))
vocab_size = len(all_words)
print(vocab_size)
```

After determining that the vocabulary size is 1,130 via this code, we create the vocabulary and print its first 51 entries for illustration purposes.

Listing 2.2 Creating a vocabulary

```
vocab = {token:integer for integer,token in enumerate(all_words)}
for i, item in enumerate(vocab.items()):
    print(item)
    if i >= 50:
        break
```

The output is

```
('!', 0)
('"', 1)
("'", 2)
...
('Her', 49)
('Hermia', 50)
```

As we can see, the dictionary contains individual tokens associated with unique integer labels. Our next goal is to apply this vocabulary to convert new text into token IDs (figure 2.7).

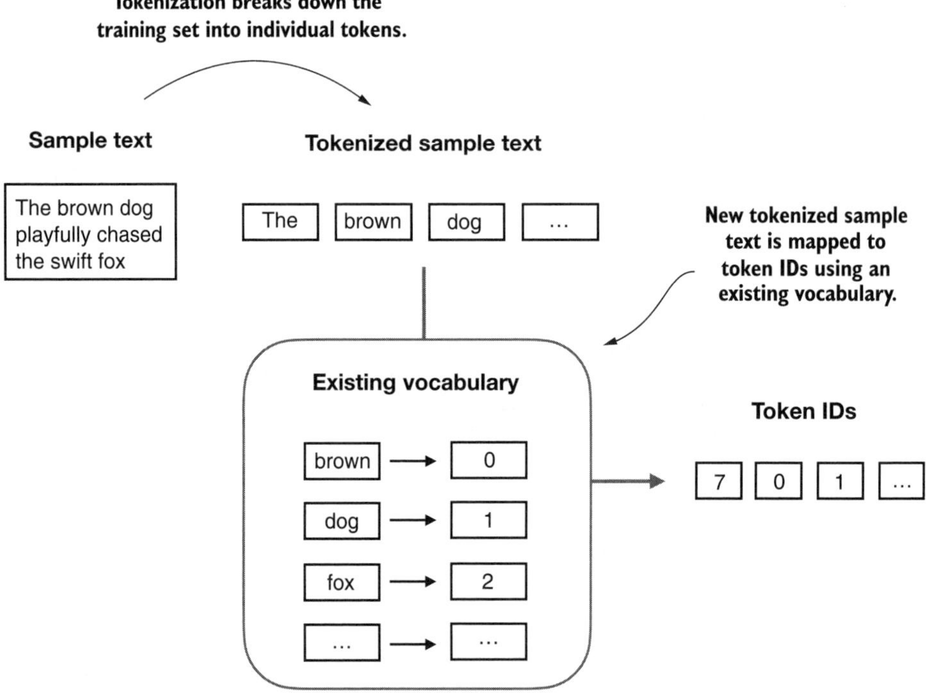

Figure 2.7 Starting with a new text sample, we tokenize the text and use the vocabulary to convert the text tokens into token IDs. The vocabulary is built from the entire training set and can be applied to the training set itself and any new text samples. The depicted vocabulary contains no punctuation or special characters for simplicity.

When we want to convert the outputs of an LLM from numbers back into text, we need a way to turn token IDs into text. For this, we can create an inverse version of the vocabulary that maps token IDs back to the corresponding text tokens.

Let's implement a complete tokenizer class in Python with an `encode` method that splits text into tokens and carries out the string-to-integer mapping to produce token IDs via the vocabulary. In addition, we'll implement a `decode` method that carries out the reverse integer-to-string mapping to convert the token IDs back into text. The following listing shows the code for this tokenizer implementation.

Listing 2.3 Implementing a simple text tokenizer

```
class SimpleTokenizerV1:
    def __init__(self, vocab):
        self.str_to_int = vocab
        self.int_to_str = {i:s for s,i in vocab.items()}

    def encode(self, text):
        preprocessed = re.split(r'([,.?_!"()\']|--|\s)', text)
        preprocessed = [
            item.strip() for item in preprocessed if item.strip()
        ]
        ids = [self.str_to_int[s] for s in preprocessed]
        return ids

    def decode(self, ids):
        text = " ".join([self.int_to_str[i] for i in ids])

        text = re.sub(r'\s+([,.?!"()\'])', r'\1', text)
        return text
```

Stores the vocabulary as a class attribute for access in the encode and decode methods

Creates an inverse vocabulary that maps token IDs back to the original text tokens

Processes input text into token IDs

Converts token IDs back into text

Removes spaces before the specified punctuation

Using the `SimpleTokenizerV1` Python class, we can now instantiate new tokenizer objects via an existing vocabulary, which we can then use to encode and decode text, as illustrated in figure 2.8.

Let's instantiate a new tokenizer object from the `SimpleTokenizerV1` class and tokenize a passage from Edith Wharton's short story to try it out in practice:

```
tokenizer = SimpleTokenizerV1(vocab)
text = """"It's the last he painted, you know,"
       Mrs. Gisburn said with pardonable pride."""
ids = tokenizer.encode(text)
print(ids)
```

The preceding code prints the following token IDs:

```
[1, 56, 2, 850, 988, 602, 533, 746, 5, 1126, 596, 5, 1, 67, 7, 38, 851, 1108,
754, 793, 7]
```

Next, let's see whether we can turn these token IDs back into text using the decode method:

```
print(tokenizer.decode(ids))
```

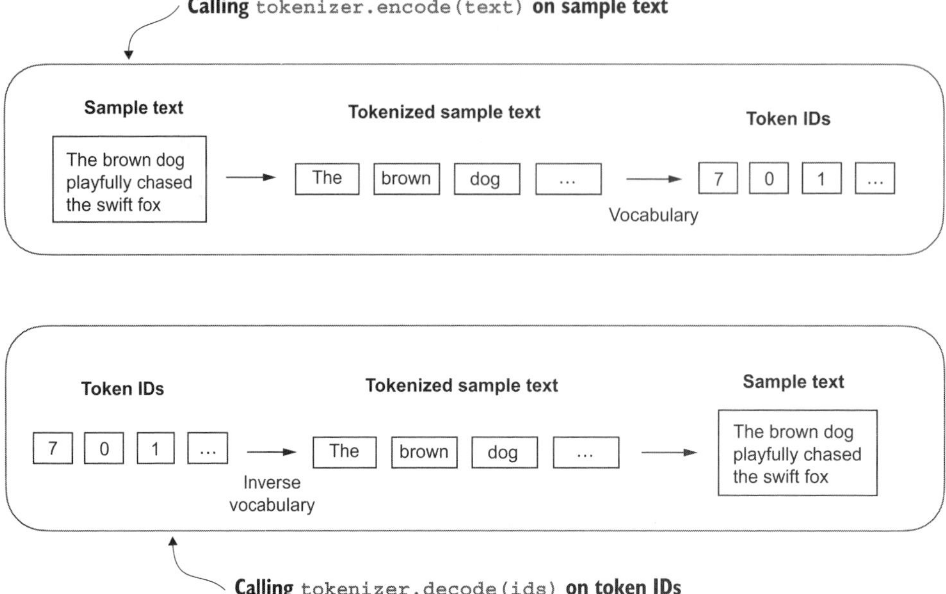

Figure 2.8 Tokenizer implementations share two common methods: an encode method and a decode method. The encode method takes in the sample text, splits it into individual tokens, and converts the tokens into token IDs via the vocabulary. The decode method takes in token IDs, converts them back into text tokens, and concatenates the text tokens into natural text.

This outputs:

```
'" It\' s the last he painted, you know," Mrs. Gisburn said with
pardonable pride.'
```

Based on this output, we can see that the decode method successfully converted the token IDs back into the original text.

So far, so good. We implemented a tokenizer capable of tokenizing and detokenizing text based on a snippet from the training set. Let's now apply it to a new text sample not contained in the training set:

```
text = "Hello, do you like tea?"
print(tokenizer.encode(text))
```

Executing this code will result in the following error:

```
KeyError: 'Hello'
```

The problem is that the word "Hello" was not used in the "The Verdict" short story. Hence, it is not contained in the vocabulary. This highlights the need to consider large and diverse training sets to extend the vocabulary when working on LLMs.

Next, we will test the tokenizer further on text that contains unknown words and discuss additional special tokens that can be used to provide further context for an LLM during training.

2.4 Adding special context tokens

We need to modify the tokenizer to handle unknown words. We also need to address the usage and addition of special context tokens that can enhance a model's understanding of context or other relevant information in the text. These special tokens can include markers for unknown words and document boundaries, for example. In particular, we will modify the vocabulary and tokenizer, `SimpleTokenizerV2`, to support two new tokens, `<|unk|>` and `<|endoftext|>`, as illustrated in figure 2.9.

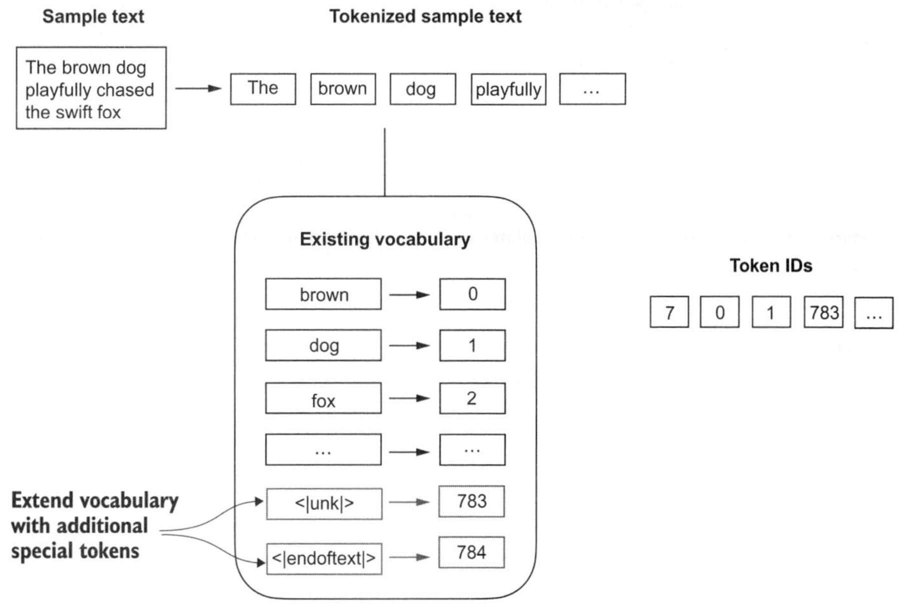

Figure 2.9 We add special tokens to a vocabulary to deal with certain contexts. For instance, we add an `<|unk|>` token to represent new and unknown words that were not part of the training data and thus not part of the existing vocabulary. Furthermore, we add an `<|endoftext|>` token that we can use to separate two unrelated text sources.

We can modify the tokenizer to use an `<|unk|>` token if it encounters a word that is not part of the vocabulary. Furthermore, we add a token between unrelated texts. For example, when training GPT-like LLMs on multiple independent documents or books, it is common to insert a token before each document or book that follows a previous text source, as illustrated in figure 2.10. This helps the LLM understand that although these text sources are concatenated for training, they are, in fact, unrelated.

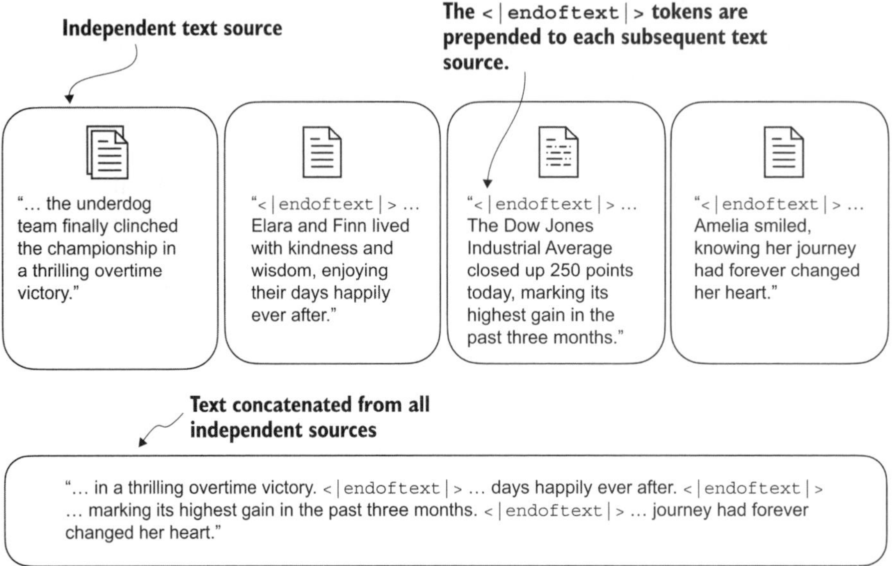

Figure 2.10 When working with multiple independent text source, we add <|endoftext|> tokens between these texts. These <|endoftext|> tokens act as markers, signaling the start or end of a particular segment, allowing for more effective processing and understanding by the LLM.

Let's now modify the vocabulary to include these two special tokens, `<unk>` and `<|endoftext|>`, by adding them to our list of all unique words:

```
all_tokens = sorted(list(set(preprocessed)))
all_tokens.extend(["<|endoftext|>", "<|unk|>"])
vocab = {token:integer for integer,token in enumerate(all_tokens)}

print(len(vocab.items()))
```

Based on the output of this print statement, the new vocabulary size is 1,132 (the previous vocabulary size was 1,130).

As an additional quick check, let's print the last five entries of the updated vocabulary:

```
for i, item in enumerate(list(vocab.items())[-5:]):
    print(item)
```

The code prints

```
('younger', 1127)
('your', 1128)
('yourself', 1129)
('<|endoftext|>', 1130)
('<|unk|>', 1131)
```

Based on the code output, we can confirm that the two new special tokens were indeed successfully incorporated into the vocabulary. Next, we adjust the tokenizer from code listing 2.3 accordingly as shown in the following listing.

Listing 2.4 A simple text tokenizer that handles unknown words

```
class SimpleTokenizerV2:
    def __init__(self, vocab):
        self.str_to_int = vocab
        self.int_to_str = { i:s for s,i in vocab.items()}

    def encode(self, text):
        preprocessed = re.split(r'([,.:;?_!"()\']|--|\s)', text)
        preprocessed = [
            item.strip() for item in preprocessed if item.strip()
        ]
        preprocessed = [item if item in self.str_to_int
                        else "<|unk|>" for item in preprocessed]

        ids = [self.str_to_int[s] for s in preprocessed]
        return ids

    def decode(self, ids):
        text = " ".join([self.int_to_str[i] for i in ids])

        text = re.sub(r'\s+([,.:;?!"()\'])', r'\1', text)
        return text
```

Replaces unknown words by <|unk|> tokens

Replaces spaces before the specified punctuations

Compared to the `SimpleTokenizerV1` we implemented in listing 2.3, the new `SimpleTokenizerV2` replaces unknown words with `<|unk|>` tokens.

Let's now try this new tokenizer out in practice. For this, we will use a simple text sample that we concatenate from two independent and unrelated sentences:

```
text1 = "Hello, do you like tea?"
text2 = "In the sunlit terraces of the palace."
text = " <|endoftext|> ".join((text1, text2))
print(text)
```

The output is

```
Hello, do you like tea? <|endoftext|> In the sunlit terraces of
the palace.
```

Next, let's tokenize the sample text using the `SimpleTokenizerV2` on the vocab we previously created in listing 2.2:

```
tokenizer = SimpleTokenizerV2(vocab)
print(tokenizer.encode(text))
```

This prints the following token IDs:

```
[1131, 5, 355, 1126, 628, 975, 10, 1130, 55, 988, 956, 984, 722, 988, 1131, 7]
```

We can see that the list of token IDs contains `1130` for the `<|endoftext|>` separator token as well as two `1131` tokens, which are used for unknown words.

Let's detokenize the text for a quick sanity check:

```
print(tokenizer.decode(tokenizer.encode(text)))
```

The output is

```
<|unk|>, do you like tea? <|endoftext|> In the sunlit terraces of
the <|unk|>.
```

Based on comparing this detokenized text with the original input text, we know that the training dataset, Edith Wharton's short story "The Verdict," does not contain the words "Hello" and "palace."

Depending on the LLM, some researchers also consider additional special tokens such as the following:

- `[BOS]` *(beginning of sequence)*—This token marks the start of a text. It signifies to the LLM where a piece of content begins.
- `[EOS]` *(end of sequence)*—This token is positioned at the end of a text and is especially useful when concatenating multiple unrelated texts, similar to `<|endoftext|>`. For instance, when combining two different Wikipedia articles or books, the `[EOS]` token indicates where one ends and the next begins.
- `[PAD]` *(padding)*—When training LLMs with batch sizes larger than one, the batch might contain texts of varying lengths. To ensure all texts have the same length, the shorter texts are extended or "padded" using the `[PAD]` token, up to the length of the longest text in the batch.

The tokenizer used for GPT models does not need any of these tokens; it only uses an `<|endoftext|>` token for simplicity. `<|endoftext|>` is analogous to the `[EOS]` token. `<|endoftext|>` is also used for padding. However, as we'll explore in subsequent chapters, when training on batched inputs, we typically use a mask, meaning we don't attend to padded tokens. Thus, the specific token chosen for padding becomes inconsequential.

Moreover, the tokenizer used for GPT models also doesn't use an `<|unk|>` token for out-of-vocabulary words. Instead, GPT models use a *byte pair encoding* tokenizer, which breaks words down into subword units, which we will discuss next.

2.5 Byte pair encoding

Let's look at a more sophisticated tokenization scheme based on a concept called byte pair encoding (BPE). The BPE tokenizer was used to train LLMs such as GPT-2, GPT-3, and the original model used in ChatGPT.

Since implementing BPE can be relatively complicated, we will use an existing Python open source library called *tiktoken* (https://github.com/openai/tiktoken), which implements the BPE algorithm very efficiently based on source code in Rust. Similar to other Python libraries, we can install the tiktoken library via Python's `pip` installer from the terminal:

```
pip install tiktoken
```

The code we will use is based on tiktoken 0.7.0. You can use the following code to check the version you currently have installed:

```
from importlib.metadata import version
import tiktoken
print("tiktoken version:", version("tiktoken"))
```

Once installed, we can instantiate the BPE tokenizer from tiktoken as follows:

```
tokenizer = tiktoken.get_encoding("gpt2")
```

The usage of this tokenizer is similar to the `SimpleTokenizerV2` we implemented previously via an `encode` method:

```
text = (
    "Hello, do you like tea? <|endoftext|> In the sunlit terraces"
     "of someunknownPlace."
)
integers = tokenizer.encode(text, allowed_special={"<|endoftext|>"})
print(integers)
```

The code prints the following token IDs:

```
[15496, 11, 466, 345, 588, 8887, 30, 220, 50256, 554, 262, 4252, 18250,
 8812, 2114, 286, 617, 34680, 27271, 13]
```

We can then convert the token IDs back into text using the decode method, similar to our `SimpleTokenizerV2`:

```
strings = tokenizer.decode(integers)
print(strings)
```

The code prints

```
Hello, do you like tea? <|endoftext|> In the sunlit terraces of
 someunknownPlace.
```

We can make two noteworthy observations based on the token IDs and decoded text. First, the `<|endoftext|>` token is assigned a relatively large token ID, namely, `50256`. In fact, the BPE tokenizer, which was used to train models such as GPT-2, GPT-3, and the original model used in ChatGPT, has a total vocabulary size of 50,257, with `<|endoftext|>` being assigned the largest token ID.

Second, the BPE tokenizer encodes and decodes unknown words, such as `someunknownPlace`, correctly. The BPE tokenizer can handle any unknown word. How does it achieve this without using `<|unk|>` tokens?

The algorithm underlying BPE breaks down words that aren't in its predefined vocabulary into smaller subword units or even individual characters, enabling it to handle out-of-vocabulary words. So, thanks to the BPE algorithm, if the tokenizer encounters an unfamiliar word during tokenization, it can represent it as a sequence of subword tokens or characters, as illustrated in figure 2.11.

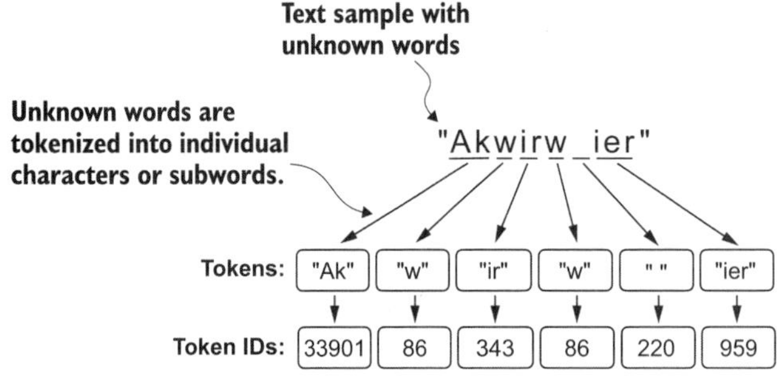

Figure 2.11 BPE tokenizers break down unknown words into subwords and individual characters. This way, a BPE tokenizer can parse any word and doesn't need to replace unknown words with special tokens, such as `<|unk|>`.

The ability to break down unknown words into individual characters ensures that the tokenizer and, consequently, the LLM that is trained with it can process any text, even if it contains words that were not present in its training data.

Exercise 2.1 Byte pair encoding of unknown words

Try the BPE tokenizer from the tiktoken library on the unknown words "Akwirw ier" and print the individual token IDs. Then, call the `decode` function on each of the resulting integers in this list to reproduce the mapping shown in figure 2.11. Lastly, call the decode method on the token IDs to check whether it can reconstruct the original input, "Akwirw ier."

A detailed discussion and implementation of BPE is out of the scope of this book, but in short, it builds its vocabulary by iteratively merging frequent characters into subwords and frequent subwords into words. For example, BPE starts with adding all individual single characters to its vocabulary ("a," "b," etc.). In the next stage, it merges character combinations that frequently occur together into subwords. For example, "d" and "e" may be merged into the subword "de," which is common in many English words like "define," "depend," "made," and "hidden." The merges are determined by a frequency cutoff.

2.6 Data sampling with a sliding window

The next step in creating the embeddings for the LLM is to generate the input–target pairs required for training an LLM. What do these input–target pairs look like? As we already learned, LLMs are pretrained by predicting the next word in a text, as depicted in figure 2.12.

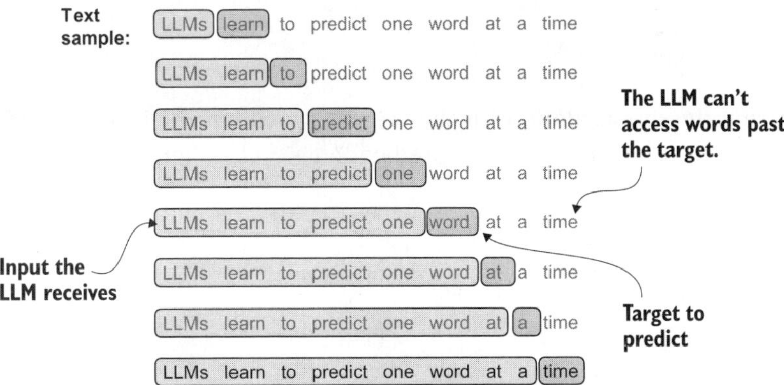

Figure 2.12 Given a text sample, extract input blocks as subsamples that serve as input to the LLM, and the LLM's prediction task during training is to predict the next word that follows the input block. During training, we mask out all words that are past the target. Note that the text shown in this figure must undergo tokenization before the LLM can process it; however, this figure omits the tokenization step for clarity.

Let's implement a data loader that fetches the input–target pairs in figure 2.12 from the training dataset using a sliding window approach. To get started, we will tokenize the whole "The Verdict" short story using the BPE tokenizer:

```
with open("the-verdict.txt", "r", encoding="utf-8") as f:
    raw_text = f.read()

enc_text = tokenizer.encode(raw_text)
print(len(enc_text))
```

Executing this code will return `5145`, the total number of tokens in the training set, after applying the BPE tokenizer.

Next, we remove the first 50 tokens from the dataset for demonstration purposes, as it results in a slightly more interesting text passage in the next steps:

```
enc_sample = enc_text[50:]
```

One of the easiest and most intuitive ways to create the input–target pairs for the next-word prediction task is to create two variables, `x` and `y`, where `x` contains the input tokens and `y` contains the targets, which are the inputs shifted by 1:

```
context_size = 4
x = enc_sample[:context_size]
y = enc_sample[1:context_size+1]
print(f"x: {x}")
print(f"y:      {y}")
```

The context size determines how many tokens are included in the input.

Running the previous code prints the following output:

```
x: [290, 4920, 2241, 287]
y:      [4920, 2241, 287, 257]
```

By processing the inputs along with the targets, which are the inputs shifted by one position, we can create the next-word prediction tasks (see figure 2.12), as follows:

```
for i in range(1, context_size+1):
    context = enc_sample[:i]
    desired = enc_sample[i]
    print(context, "---->", desired)
```

The code prints

```
[290] ----> 4920
[290, 4920] ----> 2241
[290, 4920, 2241] ----> 287
[290, 4920, 2241, 287] ----> 257
```

Everything left of the arrow (`---->`) refers to the input an LLM would receive, and the token ID on the right side of the arrow represents the target token ID that the LLM is supposed to predict. Let's repeat the previous code but convert the token IDs into text:

```
for i in range(1, context_size+1):
    context = enc_sample[:i]
    desired = enc_sample[i]
    print(tokenizer.decode(context), "---->", tokenizer.decode([desired]))
```

The following outputs show how the input and outputs look in text format:

```
 and ---->  established
 and established ---->  himself
 and established himself ---->  in
 and established himself in ---->  a
```

We've now created the input–target pairs that we can use for LLM training.

There's only one more task before we can turn the tokens into embeddings: implementing an efficient data loader that iterates over the input dataset and returns the inputs and targets as PyTorch tensors, which can be thought of as multidimensional arrays. In particular, we are interested in returning two tensors: an input tensor containing the text that the LLM sees and a target tensor that includes the targets for the LLM to predict, as depicted in figure 2.13. While the figure shows the tokens in string format for illustration purposes, the code implementation will operate on token IDs directly since the `encode` method of the BPE tokenizer performs both tokenization and conversion into token IDs as a single step.

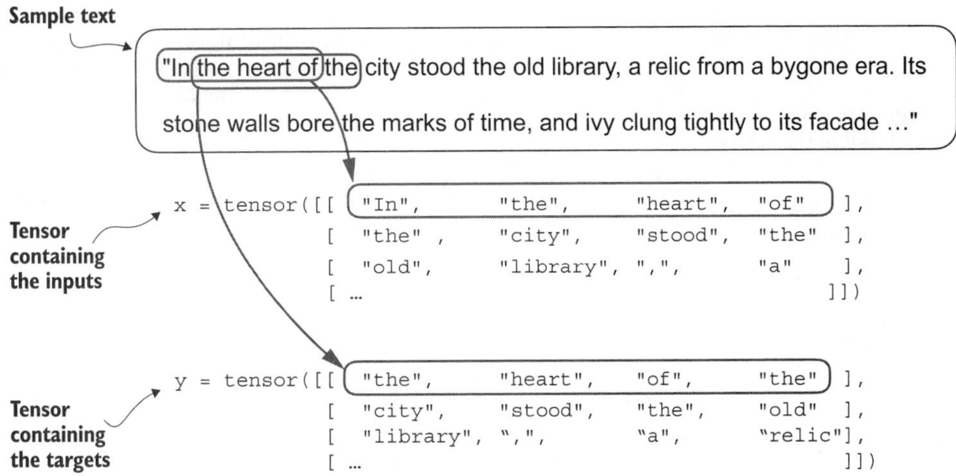

Figure 2.13 To implement efficient data loaders, we collect the inputs in a tensor, x, where each row represents one input context. A second tensor, y, contains the corresponding prediction targets (next words), which are created by shifting the input by one position.

> **NOTE** For the efficient data loader implementation, we will use PyTorch's built-in `Dataset` and `DataLoader` classes. For additional information and guidance on installing PyTorch, please see section A.2.1.3 in appendix A.

The code for the dataset class is shown in the following listing.

Listing 2.5 A dataset for batched inputs and targets

```
import torch
from torch.utils.data import Dataset, DataLoader

class GPTDatasetV1(Dataset):
    def __init__(self, txt, tokenizer, max_length, stride):
        self.input_ids = []
        self.target_ids = []

        token_ids = tokenizer.encode(txt)          # Tokenizes the entire text
```

```
        for i in range(0, len(token_ids) - max_length, stride):
            input_chunk = token_ids[i:i + max_length]
            target_chunk = token_ids[i + 1: i + max_length + 1]
            self.input_ids.append(torch.tensor(input_chunk))
            self.target_ids.append(torch.tensor(target_chunk))

    def __len__(self):
        return len(self.input_ids)

    def __getitem__(self, idx):
        return self.input_ids[idx], self.target_ids[idx]
```

Uses a sliding window to chunk the book into overlapping sequences of max_length

Returns the total number of rows in the dataset

Returns a single row from the dataset

The `GPTDatasetV1` class is based on the PyTorch `Dataset` class and defines how individual rows are fetched from the dataset, where each row consists of a number of token IDs (based on a `max_length`) assigned to an `input_chunk` tensor. The `target_chunk` tensor contains the corresponding targets. I recommend reading on to see what the data returned from this dataset looks like when we combine the dataset with a PyTorch `DataLoader`—this will bring additional intuition and clarity.

> **NOTE** If you are new to the structure of PyTorch `Dataset` classes, such as shown in listing 2.5, refer to section A.6 in appendix A, which explains the general structure and usage of PyTorch `Dataset` and `DataLoader` classes.

The following code uses the `GPTDatasetV1` to load the inputs in batches via a PyTorch `DataLoader`.

Listing 2.6 A data loader to generate batches with input-with pairs

```
def create_dataloader_v1(txt, batch_size=4, max_length=256,
                         stride=128, shuffle=True, drop_last=True,
                         num_workers=0):
    tokenizer = tiktoken.get_encoding("gpt2")
    dataset = GPTDatasetV1(txt, tokenizer, max_length, stride)
    dataloader = DataLoader(
        dataset,
        batch_size=batch_size,
        shuffle=shuffle,
        drop_last=drop_last,
        num_workers=num_workers
    )

    return dataloader
```

Initializes the tokenizer

Creates dataset

drop_last=True drops the last batch if it is shorter than the specified batch_size to prevent loss spikes during training.

The number of CPU processes to use for preprocessing

Let's test the `dataloader` with a batch size of 1 for an LLM with a context size of 4 to develop an intuition of how the `GPTDatasetV1` class from listing 2.5 and the `create_dataloader_v1` function from listing 2.6 work together:

```
with open("the-verdict.txt", "r", encoding="utf-8") as f:
    raw_text = f.read()

dataloader = create_dataloader_v1(
    raw_text, batch_size=1, max_length=4, stride=1, shuffle=False)
data_iter = iter(dataloader)
first_batch = next(data_iter)
print(first_batch)
```

Converts dataloader into a Python iterator to fetch the next entry via Python's built-in next() function

Executing the preceding code prints the following:

```
[tensor([[  40,   367, 2885, 1464]]), tensor([[ 367, 2885, 1464, 1807]])]
```

The `first_batch` variable contains two tensors: the first tensor stores the input token IDs, and the second tensor stores the target token IDs. Since the `max_length` is set to 4, each of the two tensors contains four token IDs. Note that an input size of 4 is quite small and only chosen for simplicity. It is common to train LLMs with input sizes of at least 256.

To understand the meaning of `stride=1`, let's fetch another batch from this dataset:

```
second_batch = next(data_iter)
print(second_batch)
```

The second batch has the following contents:

```
[tensor([[ 367, 2885, 1464, 1807]]), tensor([[2885, 1464, 1807, 3619]])]
```

If we compare the first and second batches, we can see that the second batch's token IDs are shifted by one position (for example, the second ID in the first batch's input is 367, which is the first ID of the second batch's input). The `stride` setting dictates the number of positions the inputs shift across batches, emulating a sliding window approach, as demonstrated in figure 2.14.

Exercise 2.2 Data loaders with different strides and context sizes

To develop more intuition for how the data loader works, try to run it with different settings such as `max_length=2` and `stride=2`, and `max_length=8` and `stride=2`.

Batch sizes of 1, such as we have sampled from the data loader so far, are useful for illustration purposes. If you have previous experience with deep learning, you may know that small batch sizes require less memory during training but lead to more

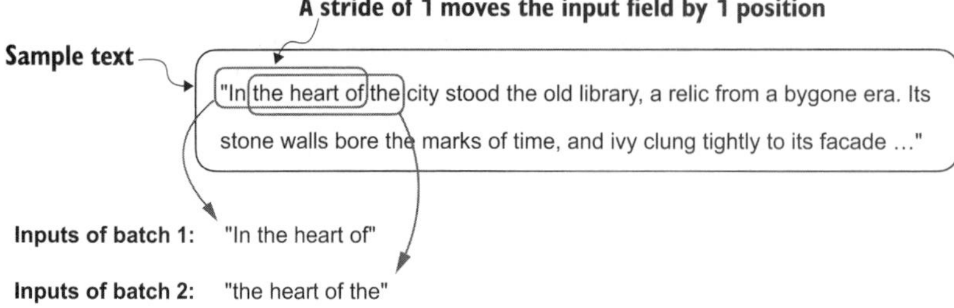

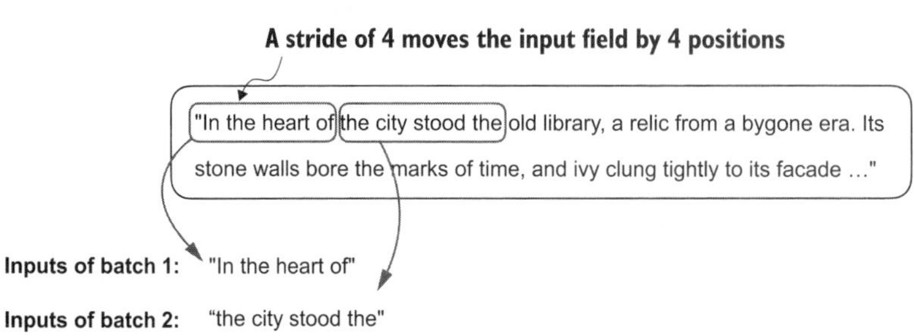

Figure 2.14 When creating multiple batches from the input dataset, we slide an input window across the text. If the stride is set to 1, we shift the input window by one position when creating the next batch. If we set the stride equal to the input window size, we can prevent overlaps between the batches.

noisy model updates. Just like in regular deep learning, the batch size is a tradeoff and a hyperparameter to experiment with when training LLMs.

Let's look briefly at how we can use the data loader to sample with a batch size greater than 1:

```
dataloader = create_dataloader_v1(
    raw_text, batch_size=8, max_length=4, stride=4,
    shuffle=False
)

data_iter = iter(dataloader)
inputs, targets = next(data_iter)
print("Inputs:\n", inputs)
print("\nTargets:\n", targets)
```

This prints

```
Inputs:
 tensor([[   40,   367,  2885,  1464],
        [ 1807,  3619,   402,   271],
        [10899,  2138,   257,  7026],
        [15632,   438,  2016,   257],
        [  922,  5891,  1576,   438],
        [  568,   340,   373,   645],
```

```
        [ 1049,  5975,   284,   502],
        [  284,  3285,   326,    11]])

Targets:
 tensor([[  367,  2885,  1464,  1807],
        [ 3619,   402,   271, 10899],
        [ 2138,   257,  7026, 15632],
        [  438,  2016,   257,   922],
        [ 5891,  1576,   438,   568],
        [  340,   373,   645,  1049],
        [ 5975,   284,   502,   284],
        [ 3285,   326,    11,   287]])
```

Note that we increase the stride to 4 to utilize the data set fully (we don't skip a single word). This avoids any overlap between the batches since more overlap could lead to increased overfitting.

2.7 Creating token embeddings

The last step in preparing the input text for LLM training is to convert the token IDs into embedding vectors, as shown in figure 2.15. As a preliminary step, we must initialize

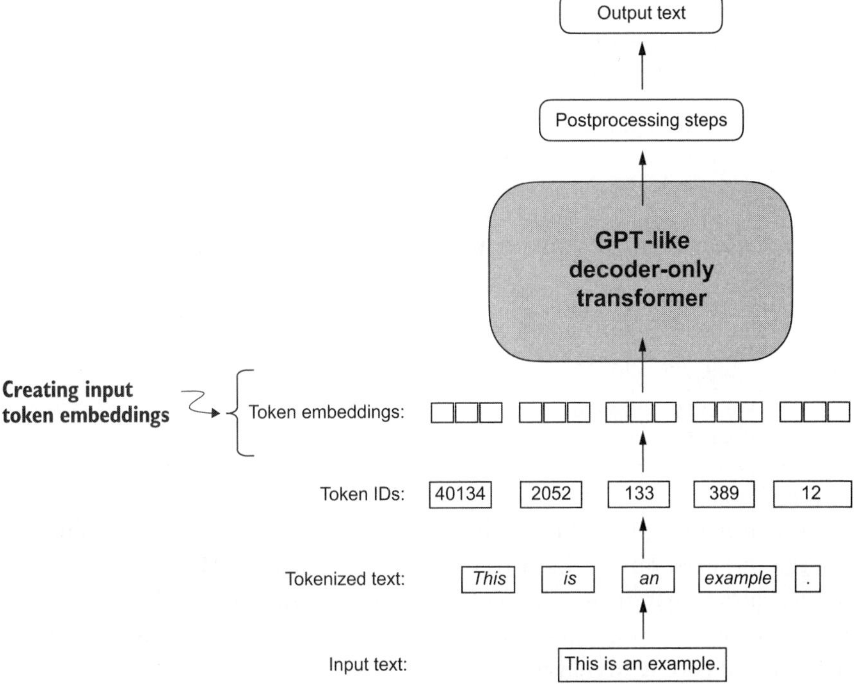

Figure 2.15 Preparation involves tokenizing text, converting text tokens to token IDs, and converting token IDs into embedding vectors. Here, we consider the previously created token IDs to create the token embedding vectors.

these embedding weights with random values. This initialization serves as the starting point for the LLM's learning process. In chapter 5, we will optimize the embedding weights as part of the LLM training.

A continuous vector representation, or embedding, is necessary since GPT-like LLMs are deep neural networks trained with the backpropagation algorithm.

> **NOTE** If you are unfamiliar with how neural networks are trained with backpropagation, please read section B.4 in appendix A.

Let's see how the token ID to embedding vector conversion works with a hands-on example. Suppose we have the following four input tokens with IDs 2, 3, 5, and 1:

```
input_ids = torch.tensor([2, 3, 5, 1])
```

For the sake of simplicity, suppose we have a small vocabulary of only 6 words (instead of the 50,257 words in the BPE tokenizer vocabulary), and we want to create embeddings of size 3 (in GPT-3, the embedding size is 12,288 dimensions):

```
vocab_size = 6
output_dim = 3
```

Using the `vocab_size` and `output_dim`, we can instantiate an embedding layer in PyTorch, setting the random seed to `123` for reproducibility purposes:

```
torch.manual_seed(123)
embedding_layer = torch.nn.Embedding(vocab_size, output_dim)
print(embedding_layer.weight)
```

The print statement prints the embedding layer's underlying weight matrix:

```
Parameter containing:
tensor([[ 0.3374, -0.1778, -0.1690],
        [ 0.9178,  1.5810,  1.3010],
        [ 1.2753, -0.2010, -0.1606],
        [-0.4015,  0.9666, -1.1481],
        [-1.1589,  0.3255, -0.6315],
        [-2.8400, -0.7849, -1.4096]], requires_grad=True)
```

The weight matrix of the embedding layer contains small, random values. These values are optimized during LLM training as part of the LLM optimization itself. Moreover, we can see that the weight matrix has six rows and three columns. There is one row for each of the six possible tokens in the vocabulary, and there is one column for each of the three embedding dimensions.

Now, let's apply it to a token ID to obtain the embedding vector:

```
print(embedding_layer(torch.tensor([3])))
```

The returned embedding vector is

```
tensor([[-0.4015,  0.9666, -1.1481]], grad_fn=<EmbeddingBackward0>)
```

If we compare the embedding vector for token ID 3 to the previous embedding matrix, we see that it is identical to the fourth row (Python starts with a zero index, so it's the row corresponding to index 3). In other words, the embedding layer is essentially a lookup operation that retrieves rows from the embedding layer's weight matrix via a token ID.

> **NOTE** For those who are familiar with one-hot encoding, the embedding layer approach described here is essentially just a more efficient way of implementing one-hot encoding followed by matrix multiplication in a fully connected layer, which is illustrated in the supplementary code on GitHub at https://mng.bz/ZEB5. Because the embedding layer is just a more efficient implementation equivalent to the one-hot encoding and matrix-multiplication approach, it can be seen as a neural network layer that can be optimized via backpropagation.

We've seen how to convert a single token ID into a three-dimensional embedding vector. Let's now apply that to all four input IDs (`torch.tensor([2, 3, 5, 1])`):

```
print(embedding_layer(input_ids))
```

The print output reveals that this results in a 4 × 3 matrix:

```
tensor([[ 1.2753, -0.2010, -0.1606],
        [-0.4015,  0.9666, -1.1481],
        [-2.8400, -0.7849, -1.4096],
        [ 0.9178,  1.5810,  1.3010]], grad_fn=<EmbeddingBackward0>)
```

Each row in this output matrix is obtained via a lookup operation from the embedding weight matrix, as illustrated in figure 2.16.

Having now created embedding vectors from token IDs, next we'll add a small modification to these embedding vectors to encode positional information about a token within a text.

2.8 Encoding word positions

In principle, token embeddings are a suitable input for an LLM. However, a minor shortcoming of LLMs is that their self-attention mechanism (see chapter 3) doesn't have a notion of position or order for the tokens within a sequence. The way the previously introduced embedding layer works is that the same token ID always gets mapped to the same vector representation, regardless of where the token ID is positioned in the input sequence, as shown in figure 2.17.

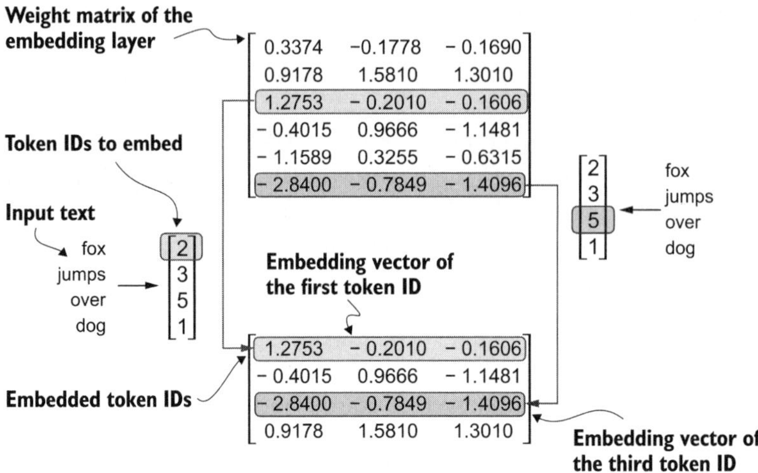

Figure 2.16 Embedding layers perform a lookup operation, retrieving the embedding vector corresponding to the token ID from the embedding layer's weight matrix. For instance, the embedding vector of the token ID 5 is the sixth row of the embedding layer weight matrix (it is the sixth instead of the fifth row because Python starts counting at 0). We assume that the token IDs were produced by the small vocabulary from section 2.3.

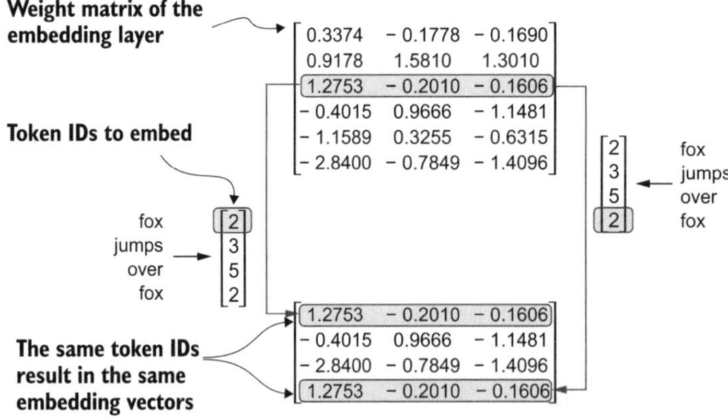

Figure 2.17 The embedding layer converts a token ID into the same vector representation regardless of where it is located in the input sequence. For example, the token ID 5, whether it's in the first or fourth position in the token ID input vector, will result in the same embedding vector.

In principle, the deterministic, position-independent embedding of the token ID is good for reproducibility purposes. However, since the self-attention mechanism of LLMs itself is also position-agnostic, it is helpful to inject additional position information into the LLM.

To achieve this, we can use two broad categories of position-aware embeddings: relative positional embeddings and absolute positional embeddings. Absolute positional embeddings are directly associated with specific positions in a sequence. For each position in the input sequence, a unique embedding is added to the token's embedding to convey its exact location. For instance, the first token will have a specific positional embedding, the second token another distinct embedding, and so on, as illustrated in figure 2.18.

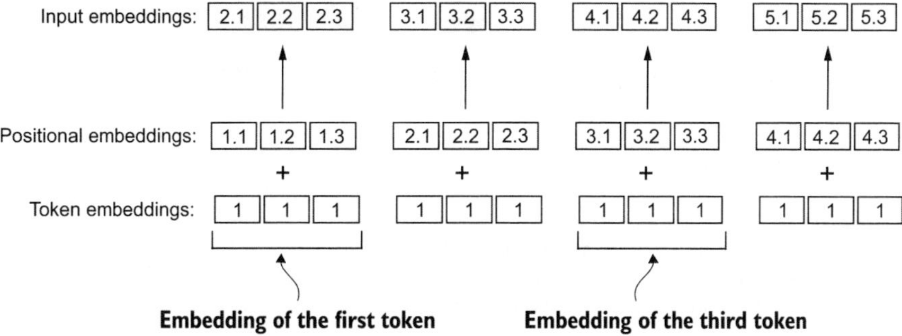

Figure 2.18 Positional embeddings are added to the token embedding vector to create the input embeddings for an LLM. The positional vectors have the same dimension as the original token embeddings. The token embeddings are shown with value 1 for simplicity.

Instead of focusing on the absolute position of a token, the emphasis of relative positional embeddings is on the relative position or distance between tokens. This means the model learns the relationships in terms of "how far apart" rather than "at which exact position." The advantage here is that the model can generalize better to sequences of varying lengths, even if it hasn't seen such lengths during training.

Both types of positional embeddings aim to augment the capacity of LLMs to understand the order and relationships between tokens, ensuring more accurate and context-aware predictions. The choice between them often depends on the specific application and the nature of the data being processed.

OpenAI's GPT models use absolute positional embeddings that are optimized during the training process rather than being fixed or predefined like the positional encodings in the original transformer model. This optimization process is part of the model training itself. For now, let's create the initial positional embeddings to create the LLM inputs.

Previously, we focused on very small embedding sizes for simplicity. Now, let's consider more realistic and useful embedding sizes and encode the input tokens into a 256-dimensional vector representation, which is smaller than what the original GPT-3 model used (in GPT-3, the embedding size is 12,288 dimensions) but still reasonable for experimentation. Furthermore, we assume that the token IDs were created by the BPE tokenizer we implemented earlier, which has a vocabulary size of 50,257:

```
vocab_size = 50257
output_dim = 256
token_embedding_layer = torch.nn.Embedding(vocab_size, output_dim)
```

Using the previous `token_embedding_layer`, if we sample data from the data loader, we embed each token in each batch into a 256-dimensional vector. If we have a batch size of 8 with four tokens each, the result will be an 8 × 4 × 256 tensor.

Let's instantiate the data loader (see section 2.6) first:

```
max_length = 4
dataloader = create_dataloader_v1(
    raw_text, batch_size=8, max_length=max_length,
   stride=max_length, shuffle=False
)
data_iter = iter(dataloader)
inputs, targets = next(data_iter)
print("Token IDs:\n", inputs)
print("\nInputs shape:\n", inputs.shape)
```

This code prints

```
Token IDs:
 tensor([[   40,   367,  2885,  1464],
        [ 1807,  3619,   402,   271],
        [10899,  2138,   257,  7026],
        [15632,   438,  2016,   257],
        [  922,  5891,  1576,   438],
        [  568,   340,   373,   645],
        [ 1049,  5975,   284,   502],
        [  284,  3285,   326,    11]])

Inputs shape:
 torch.Size([8, 4])
```

As we can see, the token ID tensor is 8 × 4 dimensional, meaning that the data batch consists of eight text samples with four tokens each.

Let's now use the embedding layer to embed these token IDs into 256-dimensional vectors:

```
token_embeddings = token_embedding_layer(inputs)
print(token_embeddings.shape)
```

The print function call returns

```
torch.Size([8, 4, 256])
```

The 8 × 4 × 256–dimensional tensor output shows that each token ID is now embedded as a 256-dimensional vector.

For a GPT model's absolute embedding approach, we just need to create another embedding layer that has the same embedding dimension as the `token_embedding_layer`:

```
context_length = max_length
pos_embedding_layer = torch.nn.Embedding(context_length, output_dim)
pos_embeddings = pos_embedding_layer(torch.arange(context_length))
print(pos_embeddings.shape)
```

The input to the `pos_embeddings` is usually a placeholder vector `torch.arange(context_length)`, which contains a sequence of numbers 0, 1, ..., up to the maximum input length –1. The `context_length` is a variable that represents the supported input size of the LLM. Here, we choose it similar to the maximum length of the input text. In practice, input text can be longer than the supported context length, in which case we have to truncate the text.

The output of the print statement is

```
torch.Size([4, 256])
```

As we can see, the positional embedding tensor consists of four 256-dimensional vectors. We can now add these directly to the token embeddings, where PyTorch will add the 4 × 256–dimensional `pos_embeddings` tensor to each 4 × 256–dimensional token embedding tensor in each of the eight batches:

```
input_embeddings = token_embeddings + pos_embeddings
print(input_embeddings.shape)
```

The print output is

```
torch.Size([8, 4, 256])
```

The `input_embeddings` we created, as summarized in figure 2.19, are the embedded input examples that can now be processed by the main LLM modules, which we will begin implementing in the next chapter.

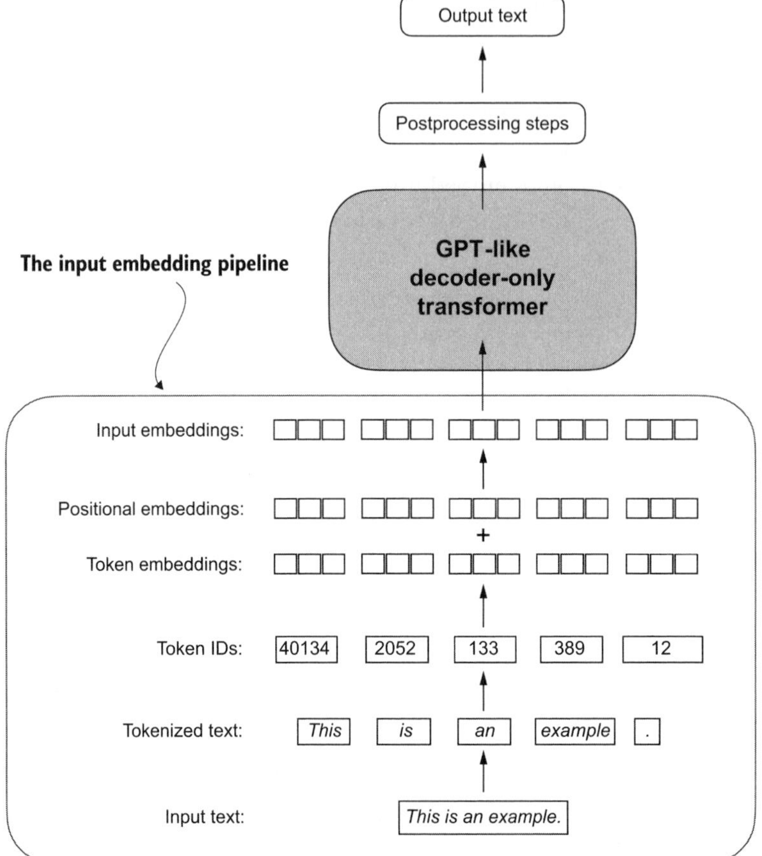

Figure 2.19 As part of the input processing pipeline, input text is first broken up into individual tokens. These tokens are then converted into token IDs using a vocabulary. The token IDs are converted into embedding vectors to which positional embeddings of a similar size are added, resulting in input embeddings that are used as input for the main LLM layers.

Summary

- LLMs require textual data to be converted into numerical vectors, known as embeddings, since they can't process raw text. Embeddings transform discrete data (like words or images) into continuous vector spaces, making them compatible with neural network operations.
- As the first step, raw text is broken into tokens, which can be words or characters. Then, the tokens are converted into integer representations, termed token IDs.
- Special tokens, such as `<|unk|>` and `<|endoftext|>`, can be added to enhance the model's understanding and handle various contexts, such as unknown words or marking the boundary between unrelated texts.

- The byte pair encoding (BPE) tokenizer used for LLMs like GPT-2 and GPT-3 can efficiently handle unknown words by breaking them down into subword units or individual characters.
- We use a sliding window approach on tokenized data to generate input–target pairs for LLM training.
- Embedding layers in PyTorch function as a lookup operation, retrieving vectors corresponding to token IDs. The resulting embedding vectors provide continuous representations of tokens, which is crucial for training deep learning models like LLMs.
- While token embeddings provide consistent vector representations for each token, they lack a sense of the token's position in a sequence. To rectify this, two main types of positional embeddings exist: absolute and relative. OpenAI's GPT models utilize absolute positional embeddings, which are added to the token embedding vectors and are optimized during the model training.

3 Coding attention mechanisms

This chapter covers

- The reasons for using attention mechanisms in neural networks
- A basic self-attention framework, progressing to an enhanced self-attention mechanism
- A causal attention module that allows LLMs to generate one token at a time
- Masking randomly selected attention weights with dropout to reduce overfitting
- Stacking multiple causal attention modules into a multi-head attention module

At this point, you know how to prepare the input text for training LLMs by splitting text into individual word and subword tokens, which can be encoded into vector representations, embeddings, for the LLM.

Now, we will look at an integral part of the LLM architecture itself, attention mechanisms, as illustrated in figure 3.1. We will largely look at attention mechanisms in isolation and focus on them at a mechanistic level. Then we will code the remaining

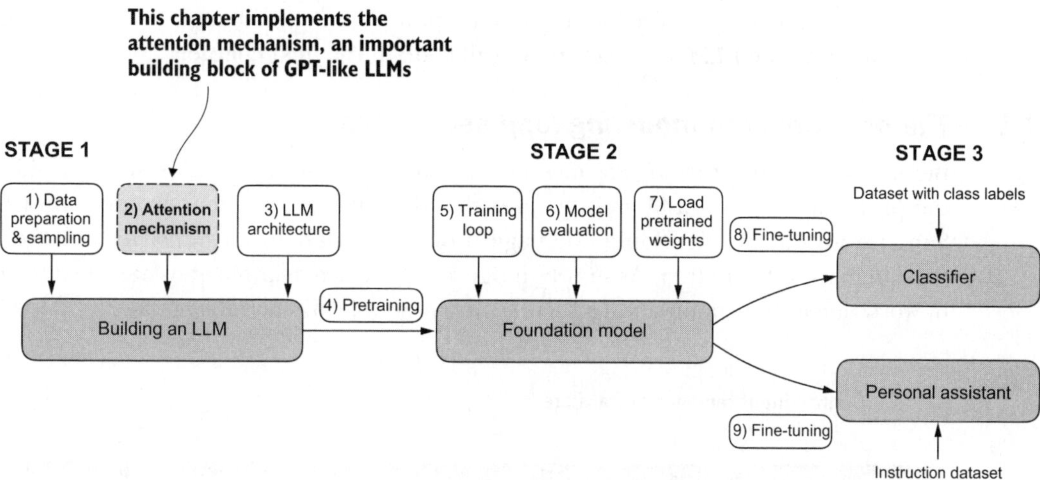

Figure 3.1 The three main stages of coding an LLM. This chapter focuses on step 2 of stage 1: implementing attention mechanisms, which are an integral part of the LLM architecture.

parts of the LLM surrounding the self-attention mechanism to see it in action and to create a model to generate text.

We will implement four different variants of attention mechanisms, as illustrated in figure 3.2. These different attention variants build on each other, and the goal is to

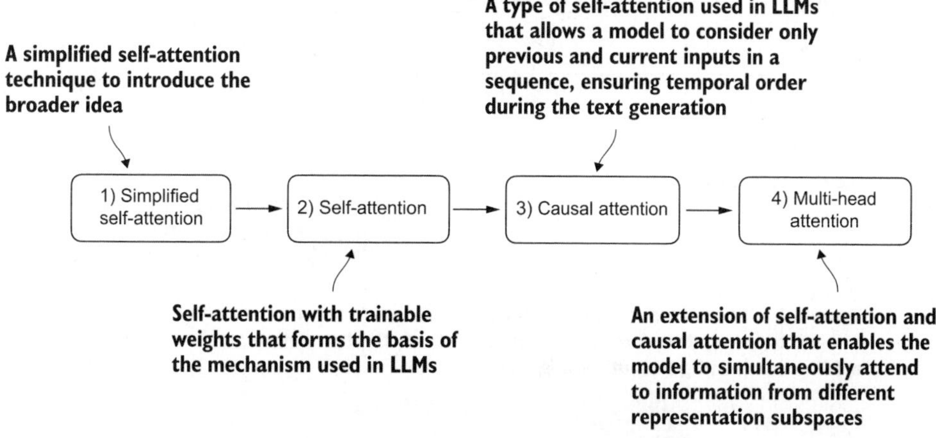

Figure 3.2 The figure depicts different attention mechanisms we will code in this chapter, starting with a simplified version of self-attention before adding the trainable weights. The causal attention mechanism adds a mask to self-attention that allows the LLM to generate one word at a time. Finally, multi-head attention organizes the attention mechanism into multiple heads, allowing the model to capture various aspects of the input data in parallel.

arrive at a compact and efficient implementation of multi-head attention that we can then plug into the LLM architecture we will code in the next chapter.

3.1 The problem with modeling long sequences

Before we dive into the *self-attention* mechanism at the heart of LLMs, let's consider the problem with pre-LLM architectures that do not include attention mechanisms. Suppose we want to develop a language translation model that translates text from one language into another. As shown in figure 3.3, we can't simply translate a text word by word due to the grammatical structures in the source and target language.

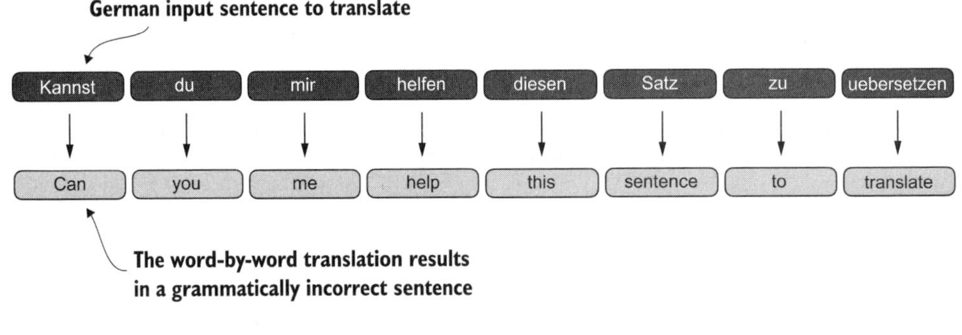

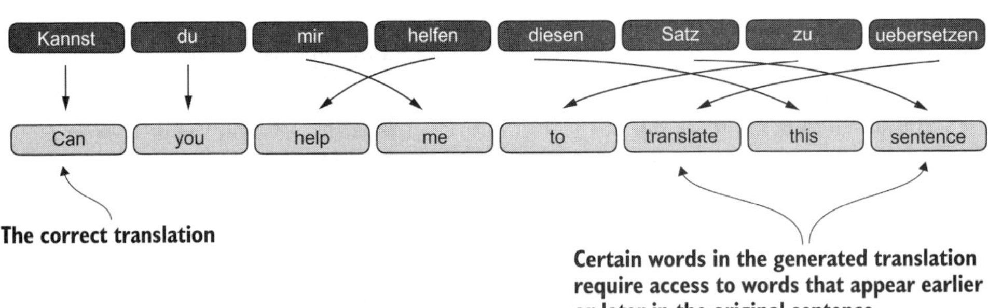

Figure 3.3 When translating text from one language to another, such as German to English, it's not possible to merely translate word by word. Instead, the translation process requires contextual understanding and grammatical alignment.

To address this problem, it is common to use a deep neural network with two submodules, an *encoder* and a *decoder*. The job of the encoder is to first read in and process the entire text, and the decoder then produces the translated text.

Before the advent of transformers, *recurrent neural networks* (RNNs) were the most popular encoder–decoder architecture for language translation. An RNN is a type of neural network where outputs from previous steps are fed as inputs to the current step, making them well-suited for sequential data like text. If you are unfamiliar with RNNs, don't worry—you don't need to know the detailed workings of RNNs to follow this discussion; our focus here is more on the general concept of the encoder–decoder setup.

In an encoder–decoder RNN, the input text is fed into the encoder, which processes it sequentially. The encoder updates its hidden state (the internal values at the hidden layers) at each step, trying to capture the entire meaning of the input sentence in the final hidden state, as illustrated in figure 3.4. The decoder then takes this final hidden state to start generating the translated sentence, one word at a time. It also updates its hidden state at each step, which is supposed to carry the context necessary for the next-word prediction.

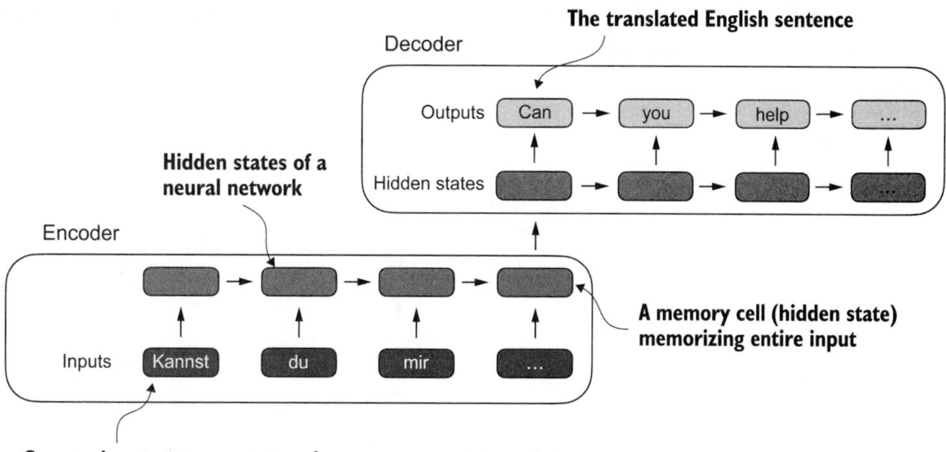

Figure 3.4 Before the advent of transformer models, encoder–decoder RNNs were a popular choice for machine translation. The encoder takes a sequence of tokens from the source language as input, where a hidden state (an intermediate neural network layer) of the encoder encodes a compressed representation of the entire input sequence. Then, the decoder uses its current hidden state to begin the translation, token by token.

While we don't need to know the inner workings of these encoder–decoder RNNs, the key idea here is that the encoder part processes the entire input text into a hidden state (memory cell). The decoder then takes in this hidden state to produce the output. You can think of this hidden state as an embedding vector, a concept we discussed in chapter 2.

The big limitation of encoder–decoder RNNs is that the RNN can't directly access earlier hidden states from the encoder during the decoding phase. Consequently, it relies solely on the current hidden state, which encapsulates all relevant information. This can lead to a loss of context, especially in complex sentences where dependencies might span long distances.

Fortunately, it is not essential to understand RNNs to build an LLM. Just remember that encoder–decoder RNNs had a shortcoming that motivated the design of attention mechanisms.

3.2 Capturing data dependencies with attention mechanisms

Although RNNs work fine for translating short sentences, they don't work well for longer texts as they don't have direct access to previous words in the input. One major shortcoming in this approach is that the RNN must remember the entire encoded input in a single hidden state before passing it to the decoder (figure 3.4).

Hence, researchers developed the *Bahdanau attention* mechanism for RNNs in 2014 (named after the first author of the respective paper; for more information, see appendix B), which modifies the encoder–decoder RNN such that the decoder can selectively access different parts of the input sequence at each decoding step as illustrated in figure 3.5.

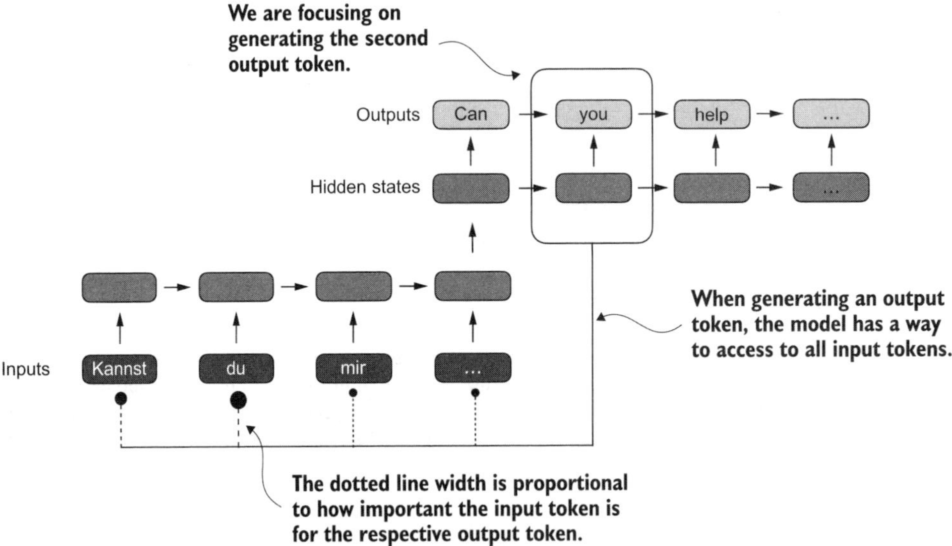

Figure 3.5 Using an attention mechanism, the text-generating decoder part of the network can access all input tokens selectively. This means that some input tokens are more important than others for generating a given output token. The importance is determined by the attention weights, which we will compute later. Note that this figure shows the general idea behind attention and does not depict the exact implementation of the Bahdanau mechanism, which is an RNN method outside this book's scope.

Interestingly, only three years later, researchers found that RNN architectures are not required for building deep neural networks for natural language processing and proposed the original *transformer* architecture (discussed in chapter 1) including a self-attention mechanism inspired by the Bahdanau attention mechanism.

Self-attention is a mechanism that allows each position in the input sequence to consider the relevancy of, or "attend to," all other positions in the same sequence when computing the representation of a sequence. Self-attention is a key component of contemporary LLMs based on the transformer architecture, such as the GPT series.

This chapter focuses on coding and understanding this self-attention mechanism used in GPT-like models, as illustrated in figure 3.6. In the next chapter, we will code the remaining parts of the LLM.

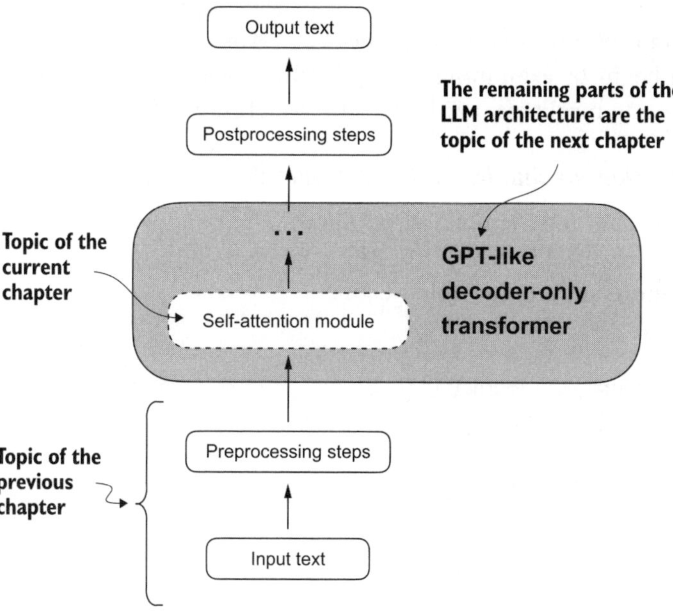

Figure 3.6 Self-attention is a mechanism in transformers used to compute more efficient input representations by allowing each position in a sequence to interact with and weigh the importance of all other positions within the same sequence. In this chapter, we will code this self-attention mechanism from the ground up before we code the remaining parts of the GPT-like LLM in the following chapter.

3.3 Attending to different parts of the input with self-attention

We'll now cover the inner workings of the self-attention mechanism and learn how to code it from the ground up. Self-attention serves as the cornerstone of every LLM based on the transformer architecture. This topic may require a lot of focus and attention (no pun intended), but once you grasp its fundamentals, you will have conquered one of the toughest aspects of this book and LLM implementation in general.

> **The "self" in self-attention**
>
> In self-attention, the "self" refers to the mechanism's ability to compute attention weights by relating different positions within a single input sequence. It assesses and learns the relationships and dependencies between various parts of the input itself, such as words in a sentence or pixels in an image.
>
> This is in contrast to traditional attention mechanisms, where the focus is on the relationships between elements of two different sequences, such as in sequence-to-sequence models where the attention might be between an input sequence and an output sequence, such as the example depicted in figure 3.5.

Since self-attention can appear complex, especially if you are encountering it for the first time, we will begin by examining a simplified version of it. Then we will implement the self-attention mechanism with trainable weights used in LLMs.

3.3.1 A simple self-attention mechanism without trainable weights

Let's begin by implementing a simplified variant of self-attention, free from any trainable weights, as summarized in figure 3.7. The goal is to illustrate a few key concepts in self-attention before adding trainable weights.

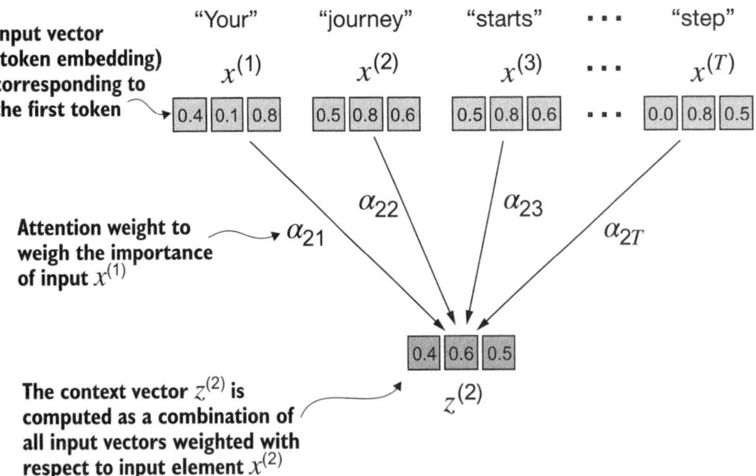

Figure 3.7 The goal of self-attention is to compute a context vector for each input element that combines information from all other input elements. In this example, we compute the context vector $z^{(2)}$. The importance or contribution of each input element for computing $z^{(2)}$ is determined by the attention weights α_{21} to α_{2T}. When computing $z^{(2)}$, the attention weights are calculated with respect to input element $x^{(2)}$ and all other inputs.

Figure 3.7 shows an input sequence, denoted as x, consisting of T elements represented as $x^{(1)}$ to $x^{(T)}$. This sequence typically represents text, such as a sentence, that has already been transformed into token embeddings.

For example, consider an input text like "Your journey starts with one step." In this case, each element of the sequence, such as $x^{(1)}$, corresponds to a d-dimensional embedding vector representing a specific token, like "Your." Figure 3.7 shows these input vectors as three-dimensional embeddings.

In self-attention, our goal is to calculate context vectors $z^{(i)}$ for each element $x^{(i)}$ in the input sequence. A *context vector* can be interpreted as an enriched embedding vector.

To illustrate this concept, let's focus on the embedding vector of the second input element, $x^{(2)}$ (which corresponds to the token "journey"), and the corresponding context vector, $z^{(2)}$, shown at the bottom of figure 3.7. This enhanced context vector, $z^{(2)}$, is an embedding that contains information about $x^{(2)}$ and all other input elements, $x^{(1)}$ to $x^{(T)}$.

Context vectors play a crucial role in self-attention. Their purpose is to create enriched representations of each element in an input sequence (like a sentence) by incorporating information from all other elements in the sequence (figure 3.7). This is essential in LLMs, which need to understand the relationship and relevance of words in a sentence to each other. Later, we will add trainable weights that help an LLM learn to construct these context vectors so that they are relevant for the LLM to generate the next token. But first, let's implement a simplified self-attention mechanism to compute these weights and the resulting context vector one step at a time.

Consider the following input sentence, which has already been embedded into three-dimensional vectors (see chapter 2). I've chosen a small embedding dimension to ensure it fits on the page without line breaks:

```
import torch
inputs = torch.tensor(
  [[0.43, 0.15, 0.89], # Your     (x^1)
   [0.55, 0.87, 0.66], # journey  (x^2)
   [0.57, 0.85, 0.64], # starts   (x^3)
   [0.22, 0.58, 0.33], # with     (x^4)
   [0.77, 0.25, 0.10], # one      (x^5)
   [0.05, 0.80, 0.55]] # step     (x^6)
)
```

The first step of implementing self-attention is to compute the intermediate values ω, referred to as attention scores, as illustrated in figure 3.8. Due to spatial constraints, the figure displays the values of the preceding `inputs` tensor in a truncated version; for example, 0.87 is truncated to 0.8. In this truncated version, the embeddings of the words "journey" and "starts" may appear similar by random chance.

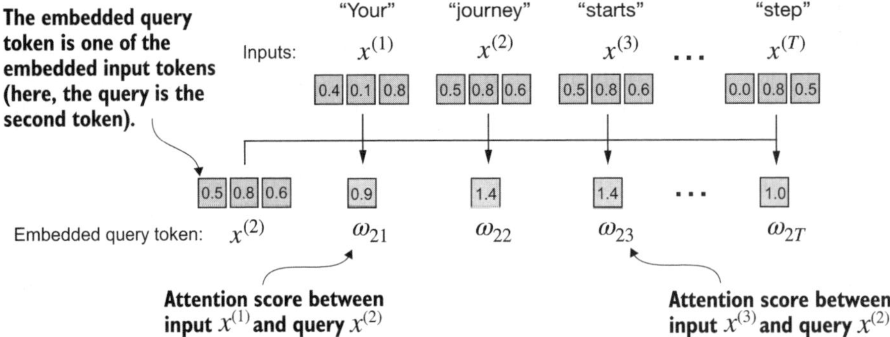

Figure 3.8 The overall goal is to illustrate the computation of the context vector $z^{(2)}$ using the second input element, $x^{(2)}$ as a query. This figure shows the first intermediate step, computing the attention scores ω between the query $x^{(2)}$ and all other input elements as a dot product. (Note that the numbers are truncated to one digit after the decimal point to reduce visual clutter.)

Figure 3.8 illustrates how we calculate the intermediate attention scores between the query token and each input token. We determine these scores by computing the dot product of the query, $x^{(2)}$, with every other input token:

```
query = inputs[1]                              # The second input token serves as the query.
attn_scores_2 = torch.empty(inputs.shape[0])
for i, x_i in enumerate(inputs):
    attn_scores_2[i] = torch.dot(x_i, query)
print(attn_scores_2)
```

The computed attention scores are

```
tensor([0.9544, 1.4950, 1.4754, 0.8434, 0.7070, 1.0865])
```

> **Understanding dot products**
>
> A dot product is essentially a concise way of multiplying two vectors element-wise and then summing the products, which can be demonstrated as follows:
>
> ```
> res = 0.
> for idx, element in enumerate(inputs[0]):
>     res += inputs[0][idx] * query[idx]
> print(res)
> print(torch.dot(inputs[0], query))
> ```
>
> The output confirms that the sum of the element-wise multiplication gives the same results as the dot product:
>
> ```
> tensor(0.9544)
> tensor(0.9544)
> ```

> Beyond viewing the dot product operation as a mathematical tool that combines two vectors to yield a scalar value, the dot product is a measure of similarity because it quantifies how closely two vectors are aligned: a higher dot product indicates a greater degree of alignment or similarity between the vectors. In the context of self-attention mechanisms, the dot product determines the extent to which each element in a sequence focuses on, or "attends to," any other element: the higher the dot product, the higher the similarity and attention score between two elements.

In the next step, as shown in figure 3.9, we normalize each of the attention scores we computed previously. The main goal behind the normalization is to obtain attention weights that sum up to 1. This normalization is a convention that is useful for interpretation and maintaining training stability in an LLM. Here's a straightforward method for achieving this normalization step:

```
attn_weights_2_tmp = attn_scores_2 / attn_scores_2.sum()
print("Attention weights:", attn_weights_2_tmp)
print("Sum:", attn_weights_2_tmp.sum())
```

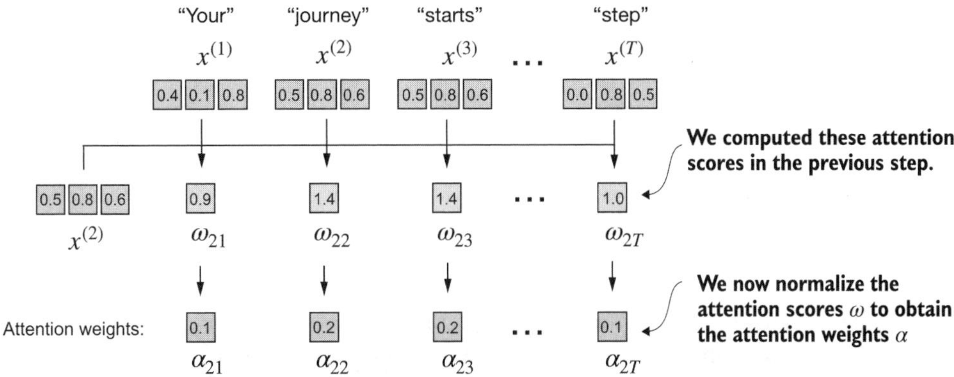

Figure 3.9 After computing the attention scores ω_{21} to ω_{2T} with respect to the input query $x^{(2)}$, the next step is to obtain the attention weights α_{21} to α_{2T} by normalizing the attention scores.

As the output shows, the attention weights now sum to 1:

```
Attention weights: tensor([0.1455, 0.2278, 0.2249, 0.1285, 0.1077, 0.1656])
Sum: tensor(1.0000)
```

In practice, it's more common and advisable to use the softmax function for normalization. This approach is better at managing extreme values and offers more favorable

VE 507 2677

gradient properties during training. The following is a basic implementation of the softmax function for normalizing the attention scores:

```
def softmax_naive(x):
    return torch.exp(x) / torch.exp(x).sum(dim=0)

attn_weights_2_naive = softmax_naive(attn_scores_2)
print("Attention weights:", attn_weights_2_naive)
print("Sum:", attn_weights_2_naive.sum())
```

As the output shows, the softmax function also meets the objective and normalizes the attention weights such that they sum to 1:

```
Attention weights: tensor([0.1385, 0.2379, 0.2333, 0.1240, 0.1082, 0.1581])
Sum: tensor(1.)
```

In addition, the softmax function ensures that the attention weights are always positive. This makes the output interpretable as probabilities or relative importance, where higher weights indicate greater importance.

Note that this naive softmax implementation (`softmax_naive`) may encounter numerical instability problems, such as overflow and underflow, when dealing with large or small input values. Therefore, in practice, it's advisable to use the PyTorch implementation of softmax, which has been extensively optimized for performance:

```
attn_weights_2 = torch.softmax(attn_scores_2, dim=0)
print("Attention weights:", attn_weights_2)
print("Sum:", attn_weights_2.sum())
```

In this case, it yields the same results as our previous `softmax_naive` function:

```
Attention weights: tensor([0.1385, 0.2379, 0.2333, 0.1240, 0.1082, 0.1581])
Sum: tensor(1.)
```

Now that we have computed the normalized attention weights, we are ready for the final step, as shown in figure 3.10: calculating the context vector $z^{(2)}$ by multiplying the embedded input tokens, $x^{(i)}$, with the corresponding attention weights and then summing the resulting vectors. Thus, context vector $z^{(2)}$ is the weighted sum of all input vectors, obtained by multiplying each input vector by its corresponding attention weight:

```
query = inputs[1]                                  <-- The second input token is the query.
context_vec_2 = torch.zeros(query.shape)
for i,x_i in enumerate(inputs):
    context_vec_2 += attn_weights_2[i]*x_i
print(context_vec_2)
```

The results of this computation are

```
tensor([0.4419, 0.6515, 0.5683])
```

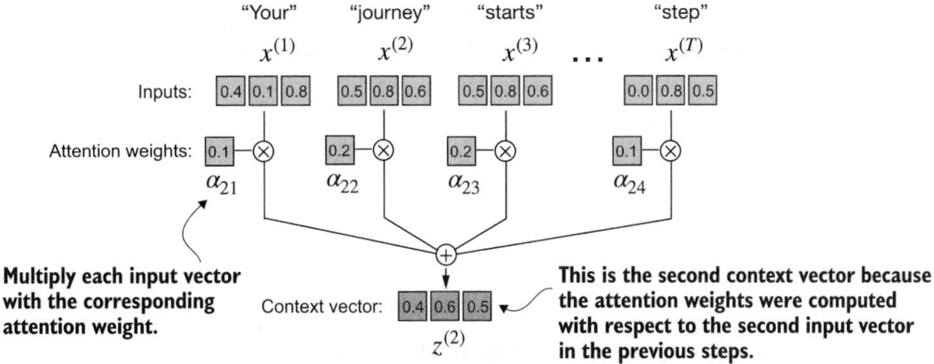

Figure 3.10 The final step, after calculating and normalizing the attention scores to obtain the attention weights for query $x^{(2)}$, is to compute the context vector $z^{(2)}$. This context vector is a combination of all input vectors $x^{(1)}$ *to* $x^{(T)}$ weighted by the attention weights.

Next, we will generalize this procedure for computing context vectors to calculate all context vectors simultaneously.

3.3.2 *Computing attention weights for all input tokens*

So far, we have computed attention weights and the context vector for input 2, as shown in the highlighted row in figure 3.11. Now let's extend this computation to calculate attention weights and context vectors for all inputs.

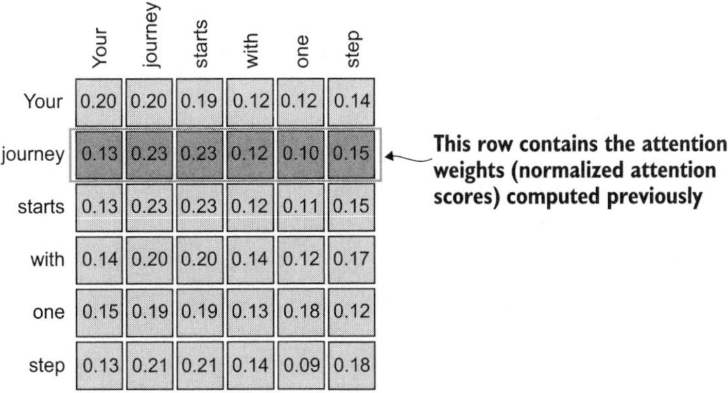

	Your	journey	starts	with	one	step
Your	0.20	0.20	0.19	0.12	0.12	0.14
journey	0.13	0.23	0.23	0.12	0.10	0.15
starts	0.13	0.23	0.23	0.12	0.11	0.15
with	0.14	0.20	0.20	0.14	0.12	0.17
one	0.15	0.19	0.19	0.13	0.18	0.12
step	0.13	0.21	0.21	0.14	0.09	0.18

Figure 3.11 The highlighted row shows the attention weights for the second input element as a query. Now we will generalize the computation to obtain all other attention weights. (Please note that the numbers in this figure are truncated to two digits after the decimal point to reduce visual clutter. The values in each row should add up to 1.0 or 100%.)

We follow the same three steps as before (see figure 3.12), except that we make a few modifications in the code to compute all context vectors instead of only the second one, $z^{(2)}$:

```
attn_scores = torch.empty(6, 6)
for i, x_i in enumerate(inputs):
    for j, x_j in enumerate(inputs):
        attn_scores[i, j] = torch.dot(x_i, x_j)
print(attn_scores)
```

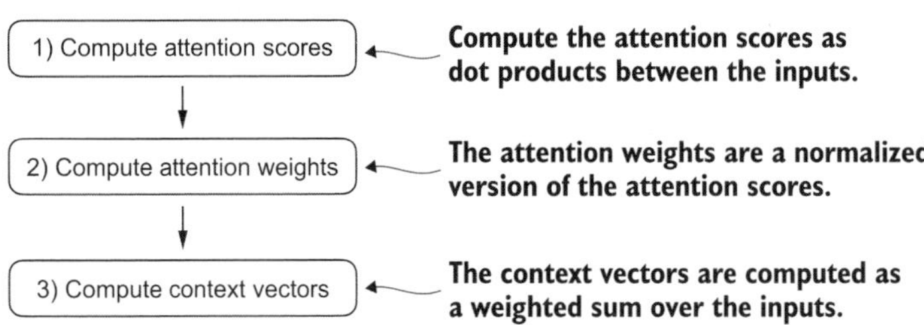

Figure 3.12 In step 1, we add an additional `for` loop to compute the dot products for all pairs of inputs.

The resulting attention scores are as follows:

```
tensor([[0.9995, 0.9544, 0.9422, 0.4753, 0.4576, 0.6310],
        [0.9544, 1.4950, 1.4754, 0.8434, 0.7070, 1.0865],
        [0.9422, 1.4754, 1.4570, 0.8296, 0.7154, 1.0605],
        [0.4753, 0.8434, 0.8296, 0.4937, 0.3474, 0.6565],
        [0.4576, 0.7070, 0.7154, 0.3474, 0.6654, 0.2935],
        [0.6310, 1.0865, 1.0605, 0.6565, 0.2935, 0.9450]])
```

Each element in the tensor represents an attention score between each pair of inputs, as we saw in figure 3.11. Note that the values in that figure are normalized, which is why they differ from the unnormalized attention scores in the preceding tensor. We will take care of the normalization later.

When computing the preceding attention score tensor, we used `for` loops in Python. However, `for` loops are generally slow, and we can achieve the same results using matrix multiplication:

```
attn_scores = inputs @ inputs.T
print(attn_scores)
```

We can visually confirm that the results are the same as before:

```
tensor([[0.9995, 0.9544, 0.9422, 0.4753, 0.4576, 0.6310],
        [0.9544, 1.4950, 1.4754, 0.8434, 0.7070, 1.0865],
        [0.9422, 1.4754, 1.4570, 0.8296, 0.7154, 1.0605],
        [0.4753, 0.8434, 0.8296, 0.4937, 0.3474, 0.6565],
```

```
        [0.4576, 0.7070, 0.7154, 0.3474, 0.6654, 0.2935],
        [0.6310, 1.0865, 1.0605, 0.6565, 0.2935, 0.9450]])
```

In step 2 of figure 3.12, we normalize each row so that the values in each row sum to 1:

```
attn_weights = torch.softmax(attn_scores, dim=-1)
print(attn_weights)
```

This returns the following attention weight tensor that matches the values shown in figure 3.10:

```
tensor([[0.2098, 0.2006, 0.1981, 0.1242, 0.1220, 0.1452],
        [0.1385, 0.2379, 0.2333, 0.1240, 0.1082, 0.1581],
        [0.1390, 0.2369, 0.2326, 0.1242, 0.1108, 0.1565],
        [0.1435, 0.2074, 0.2046, 0.1462, 0.1263, 0.1720],
        [0.1526, 0.1958, 0.1975, 0.1367, 0.1879, 0.1295],
        [0.1385, 0.2184, 0.2128, 0.1420, 0.0988, 0.1896]])
```

In the context of using PyTorch, the dim parameter in functions like `torch.softmax` specifies the dimension of the input tensor along which the function will be computed. By setting `dim=-1`, we are instructing the `softmax` function to apply the normalization along the last dimension of the `attn_scores` tensor. If `attn_scores` is a two-dimensional tensor (for example, with a shape of [rows, columns]), it will normalize across the columns so that the values in each row (summing over the column dimension) sum up to 1.

We can verify that the rows indeed all sum to 1:

```
row_2_sum = sum([0.1385, 0.2379, 0.2333, 0.1240, 0.1082, 0.1581])
print("Row 2 sum:", row_2_sum)
print("All row sums:", attn_weights.sum(dim=-1))
```

The result is

```
Row 2 sum: 1.0
All row sums: tensor([1.0000, 1.0000, 1.0000, 1.0000, 1.0000, 1.0000])
```

In the third and final step of figure 3.12, we use these attention weights to compute all context vectors via matrix multiplication:

```
all_context_vecs = attn_weights @ inputs
print(all_context_vecs)
```

In the resulting output tensor, each row contains a three-dimensional context vector:

```
tensor([[0.4421, 0.5931, 0.5790],
        [0.4419, 0.6515, 0.5683],
        [0.4431, 0.6496, 0.5671],
        [0.4304, 0.6298, 0.5510],
        [0.4671, 0.5910, 0.5266],
        [0.4177, 0.6503, 0.5645]])
```

We can double-check that the code is correct by comparing the second row with the context vector $z^{(2)}$ that we computed in section 3.3.1:

```
print("Previous 2nd context vector:", context_vec_2)
```

Based on the result, we can see that the previously calculated `context_vec_2` matches the second row in the previous tensor exactly:

```
Previous 2nd context vector: tensor([0.4419, 0.6515, 0.5683])
```

This concludes the code walkthrough of a simple self-attention mechanism. Next, we will add trainable weights, enabling the LLM to learn from data and improve its performance on specific tasks.

3.4 Implementing self-attention with trainable weights

Our next step will be to implement the self-attention mechanism used in the original transformer architecture, the GPT models, and most other popular LLMs. This self-attention mechanism is also called *scaled dot-product attention*. Figure 3.13 shows how this self-attention mechanism fits into the broader context of implementing an LLM.

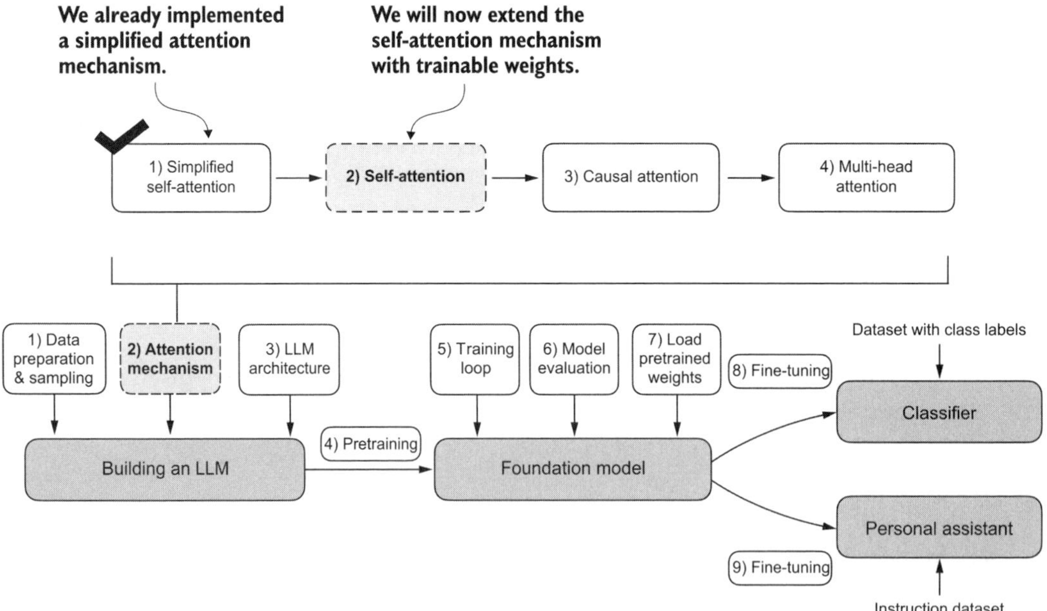

Figure 3.13 Previously, we coded a simplified attention mechanism to understand the basic mechanism behind attention mechanisms. Now, we add trainable weights to this attention mechanism. Later, we will extend this self-attention mechanism by adding a causal mask and multiple heads.

As illustrated in figure 3.13, the self-attention mechanism with trainable weights builds on the previous concepts: we want to compute context vectors as weighted sums over the input vectors specific to a certain input element. As you will see, there are only slight differences compared to the basic self-attention mechanism we coded earlier.

The most notable difference is the introduction of weight matrices that are updated during model training. These trainable weight matrices are crucial so that the model (specifically, the attention module inside the model) can learn to produce "good" context vectors. (We will train the LLM in chapter 5.)

We will tackle this self-attention mechanism in the two subsections. First, we will code it step by step as before. Second, we will organize the code into a compact Python class that can be imported into the LLM architecture.

3.4.1 Computing the attention weights step by step

We will implement the self-attention mechanism step by step by introducing the three trainable weight matrices W_q, W_k, and W_v. These three matrices are used to project the embedded input tokens, $x^{(i)}$, into query, key, and value vectors, respectively, as illustrated in figure 3.14.

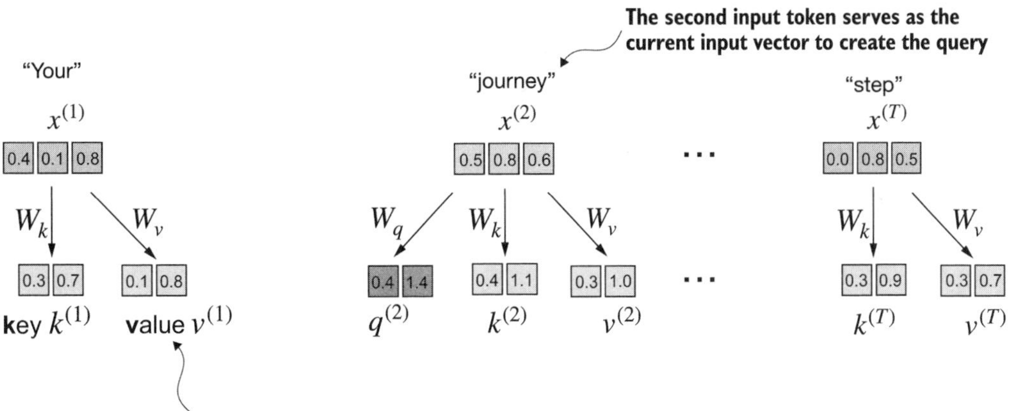

Figure 3.14 In the first step of the self-attention mechanism with trainable weight matrices, we compute query (q), key (k), and value (v) vectors for input elements x. Similar to previous sections, we designate the second input, $x^{(2)}$, as the query input. The query vector $q^{(2)}$ is obtained via matrix multiplication between the input $x^{(2)}$ and the weight matrix W_q. Similarly, we obtain the key and value vectors via matrix multiplication involving the weight matrices W_k and W_v.

Earlier, we defined the second input element $x^{(2)}$ as the query when we computed the simplified attention weights to compute the context vector $z^{(2)}$. Then we generalized this to compute all context vectors $z^{(1)}$ ... $z^{(T)}$ for the six-word input sentence "Your journey starts with one step."

Similarly, we start here by computing only one context vector, $z^{(2)}$, for illustration purposes. We will then modify this code to calculate all context vectors.

Let's begin by defining a few variables:

```
x_2 - inputs[1]          # The second input element
d_in = inputs.shape[1]   # The input embedding size, d=3
d_out = 2                # The output embedding size, d_out=2
```

Note that in GPT-like models, the input and output dimensions are usually the same, but to better follow the computation, we'll use different input (`d_in=3`) and output (`d_out=2`) dimensions here.

Next, we initialize the three weight matrices W_q, W_k, and W_v shown in figure 3.14:

```
torch.manual_seed(123)
W_query = torch.nn.Parameter(torch.rand(d_in, d_out), requires_grad=False)
W_key   = torch.nn.Parameter(torch.rand(d_in, d_out), requires_grad=False)
W_value = torch.nn.Parameter(torch.rand(d_in, d_out), requires_grad=False)
```

We set `requires_grad=False` to reduce clutter in the outputs, but if we were to use the weight matrices for model training, we would set `requires_grad=True` to update these matrices during model training.

Next, we compute the query, key, and value vectors:

```
query_2 = x_2 @ W_query
key_2 = x_2 @ W_key
value_2 = x_2 @ W_value
print(query_2)
```

The output for the query results in a two-dimensional vector since we set the number of columns of the corresponding weight matrix, via `d_out`, to 2:

```
tensor([0.4306, 1.4551])
```

> **Weight parameters vs. attention weights**
>
> In the weight matrices *W*, the term "weight" is short for "weight parameters," the values of a neural network that are optimized during training. This is not to be confused with the attention weights. As we already saw, attention weights determine the extent to which a context vector depends on the different parts of the input (i.e., to what extent the network focuses on different parts of the input).
>
> In summary, weight parameters are the fundamental, learned coefficients that define the network's connections, while attention weights are dynamic, context-specific values.

Even though our temporary goal is only to compute the one context vector, $z^{(2)}$, we still require the key and value vectors for all input elements as they are involved in computing the attention weights with respect to the query $q^{(2)}$ (see figure 3.14).

We can obtain all keys and values via matrix multiplication:

```
keys = inputs @ W_key
values = inputs @ W_value
print("keys.shape:", keys.shape)
print("values.shape:", values.shape)
```

As we can tell from the outputs, we successfully projected the six input tokens from a three-dimensional onto a two-dimensional embedding space:

```
keys.shape: torch.Size([6, 2])
values.shape: torch.Size([6, 2])
```

The second step is to compute the attention scores, as shown in figure 3.15.

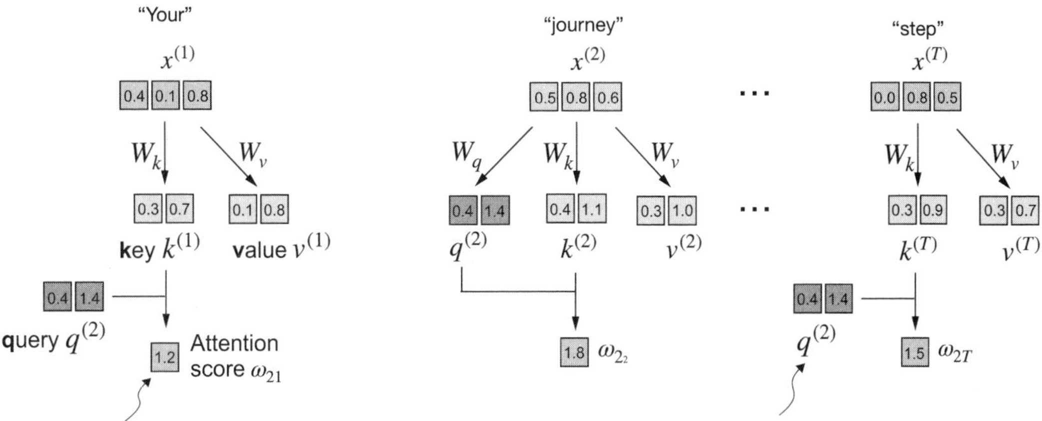

Figure 3.15 The attention score computation is a dot-product computation similar to what we used in the simplified self-attention mechanism in section 3.3. The new aspect here is that we are not directly computing the dot-product between the input elements but using the query and key obtained by transforming the inputs via the respective weight matrices.

First, let's compute the attention score ω_{22}:

```
keys_2 = keys[1]                        # Remember that Python starts indexing at 0.
attn_score_22 = query_2.dot(keys_2)
print(attn_score_22)
```

The result for the unnormalized attention score is

```
tensor(1.8524)
```

Again, we can generalize this computation to all attention scores via matrix multiplication:

```
attn_scores_2 = query_2 @ keys.T
print(attn_scores_2)
```

All attention scores for given query

As we can see, as a quick check, the second element in the output matches the `attn_score_22` we computed previously:

```
tensor([1.2705, 1.8524, 1.8111, 1.0795, 0.5577, 1.5440])
```

Now, we want to go from the attention scores to the attention weights, as illustrated in figure 3.16. We compute the attention weights by scaling the attention scores and using the softmax function. However, now we scale the attention scores by dividing them by the square root of the embedding dimension of the keys (taking the square root is mathematically the same as exponentiating by 0.5):

```
d_k = keys.shape[-1]
attn_weights_2 = torch.softmax(attn_scores_2 / d_k**0.5, dim=-1)
print(attn_weights_2)
```

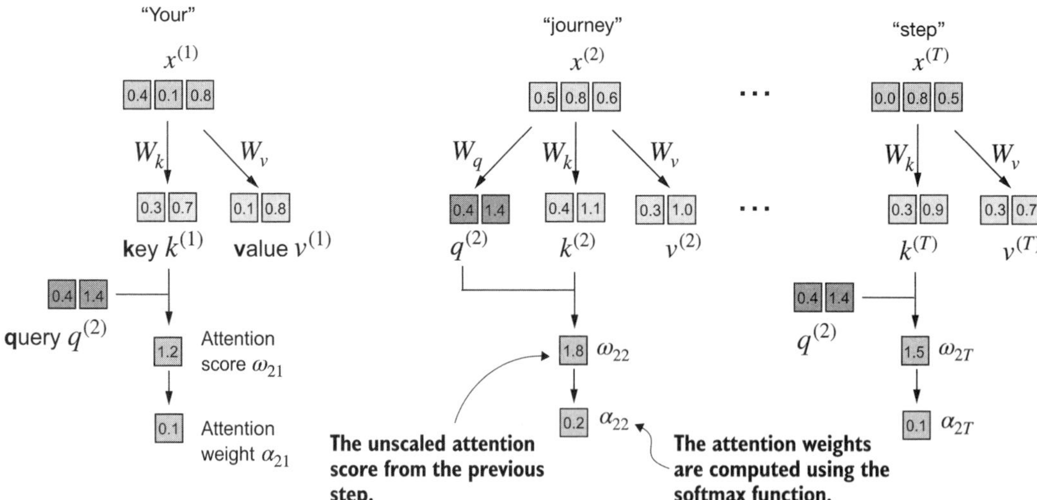

Figure 3.16 After computing the attention scores ω, the next step is to normalize these scores using the softmax function to obtain the attention weights α.

The resulting attention weights are

```
tensor([0.1500, 0.2264, 0.2199, 0.1311, 0.0906, 0.1820])
```

> **The rationale behind scaled-dot product attention**
>
> The reason for the normalization by the embedding dimension size is to improve the training performance by avoiding small gradients. For instance, when scaling up the embedding dimension, which is typically greater than 1,000 for GPT-like LLMs, large dot products can result in very small gradients during backpropagation due to the softmax function applied to them. As dot products increase, the softmax function behaves more like a step function, resulting in gradients nearing zero. These small gradients can drastically slow down learning or cause training to stagnate.
>
> The scaling by the square root of the embedding dimension is the reason why this self-attention mechanism is also called scaled-dot product attention.

Now, the final step is to compute the context vectors, as illustrated in figure 3.17.

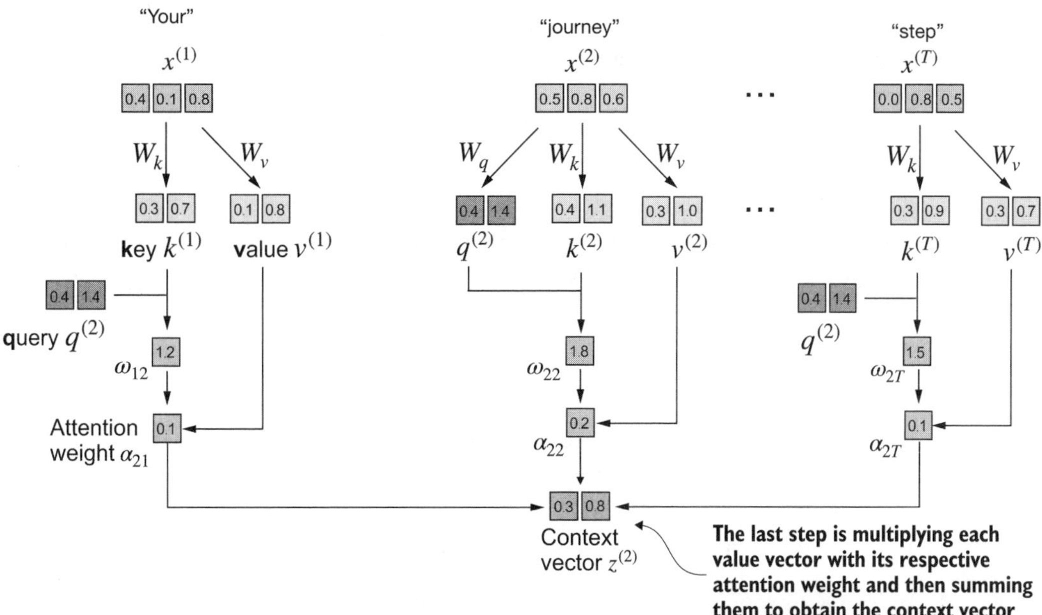

Figure 3.17 In the final step of the self-attention computation, we compute the context vector by combining all value vectors via the attention weights.

Similar to when we computed the context vector as a weighted sum over the input vectors (see section 3.3), we now compute the context vector as a weighted sum over the value vectors. Here, the attention weights serve as a weighting factor that weighs the respective importance of each value vector. Also as before, we can use matrix multiplication to obtain the output in one step:

```
context_vec_2 = attn_weights_2 @ values
print(context_vec_2)
```

The contents of the resulting vector are as follows:

```
tensor([0.3061, 0.8210])
```

So far, we've only computed a single context vector, $z^{(2)}$. Next, we will generalize the code to compute all context vectors in the input sequence, $z^{(1)}$ to $z^{(T)}$.

Why query, key, and value?

The terms "key," "query," and "value" in the context of attention mechanisms are borrowed from the domain of information retrieval and databases, where similar concepts are used to store, search, and retrieve information.

A *query* is analogous to a search query in a database. It represents the current item (e.g., a word or token in a sentence) the model focuses on or tries to understand. The query is used to probe the other parts of the input sequence to determine how much attention to pay to them.

The *key* is like a database key used for indexing and searching. In the attention mechanism, each item in the input sequence (e.g., each word in a sentence) has an associated key. These keys are used to match the query.

The *value* in this context is similar to the value in a key-value pair in a database. It represents the actual content or representation of the input items. Once the model determines which keys (and thus which parts of the input) are most relevant to the query (the current focus item), it retrieves the corresponding values.

3.4.2 Implementing a compact self-attention Python class

At this point, we have gone through a lot of steps to compute the self-attention outputs. We did so mainly for illustration purposes so we could go through one step at a time. In practice, with the LLM implementation in the next chapter in mind, it is helpful to organize this code into a Python class, as shown in the following listing.

Listing 3.1 A compact self-attention class

```
import torch.nn as nn
class SelfAttention_v1(nn.Module):
    def __init__(self, d_in, d_out):
        super().__init__()
        self.W_query = nn.Parameter(torch.rand(d_in, d_out))
        self.W_key   = nn.Parameter(torch.rand(d_in, d_out))
        self.W_value = nn.Parameter(torch.rand(d_in, d_out))
```

```
    def forward(self, x):
        keys = x @ self.W_key
        queries = x @ self.W_query
        values = x @ self.W_value
        attn_scores = queries @ keys.T # omega
        attn_weights = torch.softmax(
            attn_scores / keys.shape[-1]**0.5, dim=-1
        )
        context_vec = attn_weights @ values
        return context_vec
```

In this PyTorch code, `SelfAttention_v1` is a class derived from `nn.Module`, which is a fundamental building block of PyTorch models that provides necessary functionalities for model layer creation and management.

The `__init__` method initializes trainable weight matrices (`W_query`, `W_key`, and `W_value`) for queries, keys, and values, each transforming the input dimension `d_in` to an output dimension `d_out`.

During the forward pass, using the forward method, we compute the attention scores (`attn_scores`) by multiplying queries and keys, normalizing these scores using softmax. Finally, we create a context vector by weighting the values with these normalized attention scores.

We can use this class as follows:

```
torch.manual_seed(123)
sa_v1 = SelfAttention_v1(d_in, d_out)
print(sa_v1(inputs))
```

Since `inputs` contains six embedding vectors, this results in a matrix storing the six context vectors:

```
tensor([[0.2996, 0.8053],
        [0.3061, 0.8210],
        [0.3058, 0.8203],
        [0.2948, 0.7939],
        [0.2927, 0.7891],
        [0.2990, 0.8040]], grad_fn=<MmBackward0>)
```

As a quick check, notice that the second row (`[0.3061, 0.8210]`) matches the contents of `context_vec_2` in the previous section. Figure 3.18 summarizes the self-attention mechanism we just implemented.

Self-attention involves the trainable weight matrices W_q, W_k, and W_v. These matrices transform input data into queries, keys, and values, respectively, which are crucial components of the attention mechanism. As the model is exposed to more data during training, it adjusts these trainable weights, as we will see in upcoming chapters.

We can improve the `SelfAttention_v1` implementation further by utilizing PyTorch's `nn.Linear` layers, which effectively perform matrix multiplication when the bias units are disabled. Additionally, a significant advantage of using `nn.Linear`

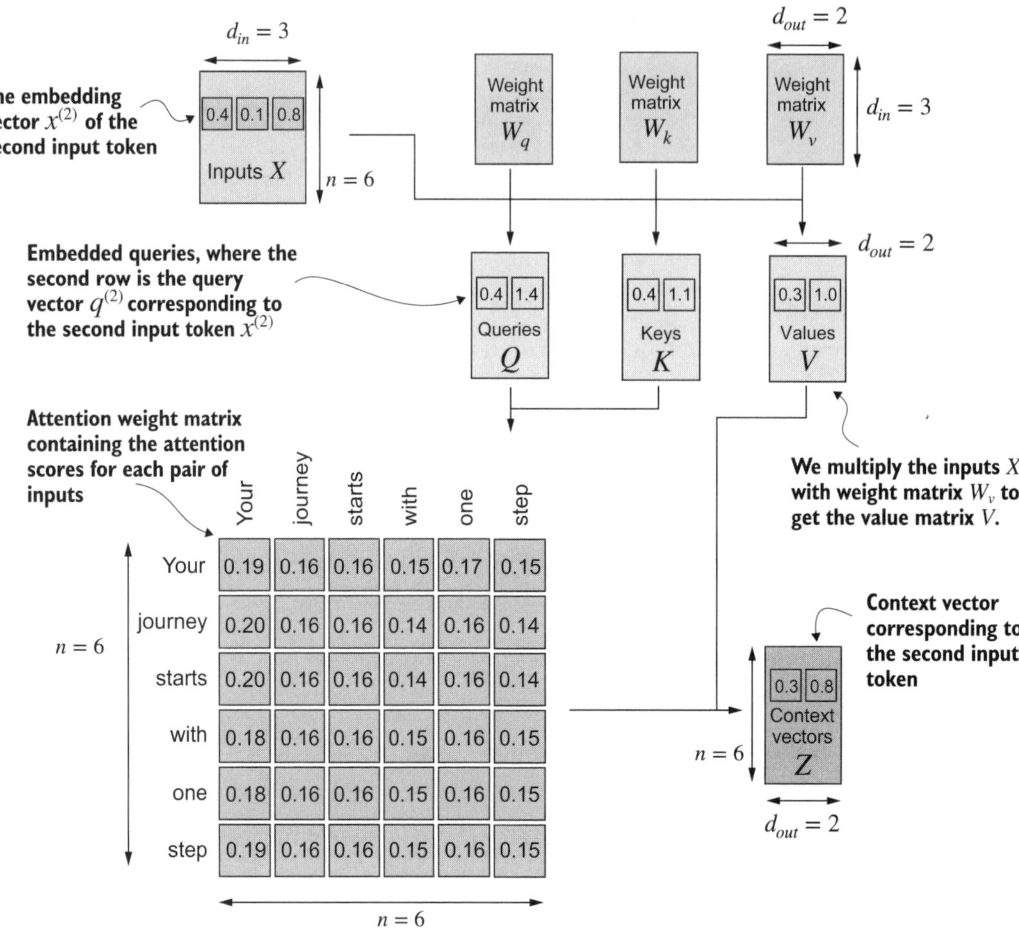

Figure 3.18 In self-attention, we transform the input vectors in the input matrix X with the three weight matrices, W_q, W_k, and W_v. The new compute the attention weight matrix based on the resulting queries (Q) and keys (K). Using the attention weights and values (V), we then compute the context vectors (Z). For visual clarity, we focus on a single input text with *n* tokens, not a batch of multiple inputs. Consequently, the three-dimensional input tensor is simplified to a two-dimensional matrix in this context. This approach allows for a more straightforward visualization and understanding of the processes involved. For consistency with later figures, the values in the attention matrix do not depict the real attention weights. (The numbers in this figure are truncated to two digits after the decimal point to reduce visual clutter. The values in each row should add up to 1.0 or 100%.)

instead of manually implementing `nn.Parameter(torch.rand(...))` is that `nn.Linear` has an optimized weight initialization scheme, contributing to more stable and effective model training.

Listing 3.2 A self-attention class using PyTorch's Linear layers

```
class SelfAttention_v2(nn.Module):
    def __init__(self, d_in, d_out, qkv_bias=False):
```

```
        super().__init__()
        self.W_query = nn.Linear(d_in, d_out, bias=qkv_bias)
        self.W_key   = nn.Linear(d_in, d_out, bias=qkv_bias)
        self.W_value = nn.Linear(d_in, d_out, bias=qkv_bias)

    def forward(self, x):
        keys = self.W_key(x)
        queries = self.W_query(x)
        values = self.W_value(x)
        attn_scores = queries @ keys.T
        attn_weights = torch.softmax(
            attn_scores / keys.shape[-1]**0.5, dim=-1
        )
        context_vec = attn_weights @ values
        return context_vec
```

You can use the `SelfAttention_v2` similar to `SelfAttention_v1`:

```
torch.manual_seed(789)
sa_v2 = SelfAttention_v2(d_in, d_out)
print(sa_v2(inputs))
```

The output is

```
tensor([[-0.0739,  0.0713],
        [-0.0748,  0.0703],
        [-0.0749,  0.0702],
        [-0.0760,  0.0685],
        [-0.0763,  0.0679],
        [-0.0754,  0.0693]], grad_fn=<MmBackward0>)
```

Note that `SelfAttention_v1` and `SelfAttention_v2` give different outputs because they use different initial weights for the weight matrices since `nn.Linear` uses a more sophisticated weight initialization scheme.

Exercise 3.1 Comparing SelfAttention_v1 and SelfAttention_v2

Note that `nn.Linear` in `SelfAttention_v2` uses a different weight initialization scheme as `nn.Parameter(torch.rand(d_in, d_out))` used in `SelfAttention_v1`, which causes both mechanisms to produce different results. To check that both implementations, `SelfAttention_v1` and `SelfAttention_v2`, are otherwise similar, we can transfer the weight matrices from a `SelfAttention_v2` object to a `SelfAttention_v1`, such that both objects then produce the same results.

Your task is to correctly assign the weights from an instance of `SelfAttention_v2` to an instance of `SelfAttention_v1`. To do this, you need to understand the relationship between the weights in both versions. (Hint: `nn.Linear` stores the weight matrix in a transposed form.) After the assignment, you should observe that both instances produce the same outputs.

Next, we will make enhancements to the self-attention mechanism, focusing specifically on incorporating causal and multi-head elements. The causal aspect involves modifying the attention mechanism to prevent the model from accessing future information in the sequence, which is crucial for tasks like language modeling, where each word prediction should only depend on previous words.

The multi-head component involves splitting the attention mechanism into multiple "heads." Each head learns different aspects of the data, allowing the model to simultaneously attend to information from different representation subspaces at different positions. This improves the model's performance in complex tasks.

3.5 Hiding future words with causal attention

For many LLM tasks, you will want the self-attention mechanism to consider only the tokens that appear prior to the current position when predicting the next token in a sequence. Causal attention, also known as *masked attention*, is a specialized form of self-attention. It restricts a model to only consider previous and current inputs in a sequence when processing any given token when computing attention scores. This is in contrast to the standard self-attention mechanism, which allows access to the entire input sequence at once.

Now, we will modify the standard self-attention mechanism to create a *causal attention* mechanism, which is essential for developing an LLM in the subsequent chapters. To achieve this in GPT-like LLMs, for each token processed, we mask out the future tokens, which come after the current token in the input text, as illustrated in figure 3.19. We mask out the attention weights above the diagonal, and we

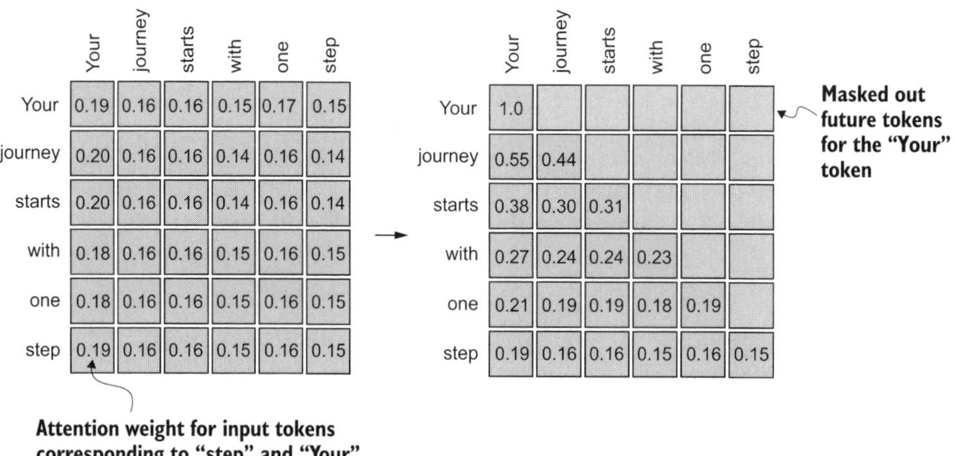

Figure 3.19 In causal attention, we mask out the attention weights above the diagonal such that for a given input, the LLM can't access future tokens when computing the context vectors using the attention weights. For example, for the word "journey" in the second row, we only keep the attention weights for the words before ("Your") and in the current position ("journey").

normalize the nonmasked attention weights such that the attention weights sum to 1 in each row. Later, we will implement this masking and normalization procedure in code.

3.5.1 Applying a causal attention mask

Our next step is to implement the causal attention mask in code. To implement the steps to apply a causal attention mask to obtain the masked attention weights, as summarized in figure 3.20, let's work with the attention scores and weights from the previous section to code the causal attention mechanism.

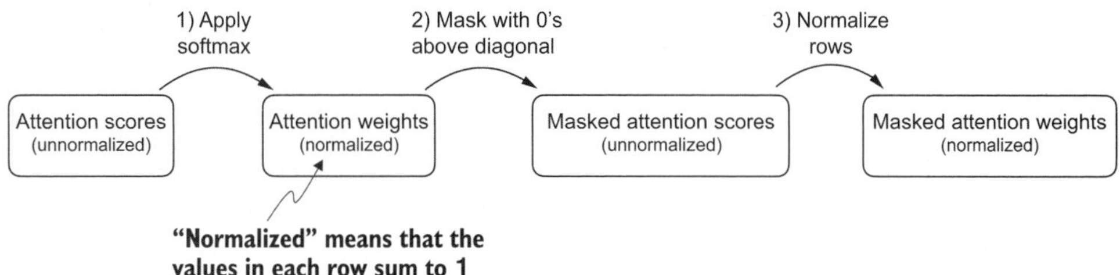

Figure 3.20 One way to obtain the masked attention weight matrix in causal attention is to apply the softmax function to the attention scores, zeroing out the elements above the diagonal and normalizing the resulting matrix.

In the first step, we compute the attention weights using the softmax function as we have done previously:

```
queries = sa_v2.W_query(inputs)
keys = sa_v2.W_key(inputs)
attn_scores = queries @ keys.T
attn_weights = torch.softmax(attn_scores / keys.shape[-1]**0.5, dim=-1)
print(attn_weights)
```

Reuses the query and key weight matrices of the SelfAttention_v2 object from the previous section for convenience

This results in the following attention weights:

```
tensor([[0.1921, 0.1646, 0.1652, 0.1550, 0.1721, 0.1510],
        [0.2041, 0.1659, 0.1662, 0.1496, 0.1665, 0.1477],
        [0.2036, 0.1659, 0.1662, 0.1498, 0.1664, 0.1480],
        [0.1869, 0.1667, 0.1668, 0.1571, 0.1661, 0.1564],
        [0.1830, 0.1669, 0.1670, 0.1588, 0.1658, 0.1585],
        [0.1935, 0.1663, 0.1666, 0.1542, 0.1666, 0.1529]],
       grad_fn=<SoftmaxBackward0>)
```

We can implement the second step using PyTorch's `tril` function to create a mask where the values above the diagonal are zero:

```
context_length = attn_scores.shape[0]
mask_simple = torch.tril(torch.ones(context_length, context_length))
print(mask_simple)
```

The resulting mask is

```
tensor([[1., 0., 0., 0., 0., 0.],
        [1., 1., 0., 0., 0., 0.],
        [1., 1., 1., 0., 0., 0.],
        [1., 1., 1., 1., 0., 0.],
        [1., 1., 1., 1., 1., 0.],
        [1., 1., 1., 1., 1., 1.]])
```

Now, we can multiply this mask with the attention weights to zero-out the values above the diagonal:

```
masked_simple = attn_weights*mask_simple
print(masked_simple)
```

As we can see, the elements above the diagonal are successfully zeroed out:

```
tensor([[0.1921, 0.0000, 0.0000, 0.0000, 0.0000, 0.0000],
        [0.2041, 0.1659, 0.0000, 0.0000, 0.0000, 0.0000],
        [0.2036, 0.1659, 0.1662, 0.0000, 0.0000, 0.0000],
        [0.1869, 0.1667, 0.1668, 0.1571, 0.0000, 0.0000],
        [0.1830, 0.1669, 0.1670, 0.1588, 0.1658, 0.0000],
        [0.1935, 0.1663, 0.1666, 0.1542, 0.1666, 0.1529]],
       grad_fn=<MulBackward0>)
```

The third step is to renormalize the attention weights to sum up to 1 again in each row. We can achieve this by dividing each element in each row by the sum in each row:

```
row_sums = masked_simple.sum(dim=-1, keepdim=True)
masked_simple_norm = masked_simple / row_sums
print(masked_simple_norm)
```

The result is an attention weight matrix where the attention weights above the diagonal are zeroed-out, and the rows sum to 1:

```
tensor([[1.0000, 0.0000, 0.0000, 0.0000, 0.0000, 0.0000],
        [0.5517, 0.4483, 0.0000, 0.0000, 0.0000, 0.0000],
        [0.3800, 0.3097, 0.3103, 0.0000, 0.0000, 0.0000],
        [0.2758, 0.2460, 0.2462, 0.2319, 0.0000, 0.0000],
        [0.2175, 0.1983, 0.1984, 0.1888, 0.1971, 0.0000],
        [0.1935, 0.1663, 0.1666, 0.1542, 0.1666, 0.1529]],
       grad_fn=<DivBackward0>)
```

Information leakage

When we apply a mask and then renormalize the attention weights, it might initially appear that information from future tokens (which we intend to mask) could still influence the current token because their values are part of the softmax calculation. However, the key insight is that when we renormalize the attention weights after masking, what we're essentially doing is recalculating the softmax over a smaller subset (since masked positions don't contribute to the softmax value).

The mathematical elegance of softmax is that despite initially including all positions in the denominator, after masking and renormalizing, the effect of the masked positions is nullified—they don't contribute to the softmax score in any meaningful way.

In simpler terms, after masking and renormalization, the distribution of attention weights is as if it was calculated only among the unmasked positions to begin with. This ensures there's no information leakage from future (or otherwise masked) tokens as we intended.

While we could wrap up our implementation of causal attention at this point, we can still improve it. Let's take a mathematical property of the softmax function and implement the computation of the masked attention weights more efficiently in fewer steps, as shown in figure 3.21.

Figure 3.21 A more efficient way to obtain the masked attention weight matrix in causal attention is to mask the attention scores with negative infinity values before applying the softmax function.

The softmax function converts its inputs into a probability distribution. When negative infinity values ($-\infty$) are present in a row, the softmax function treats them as zero probability. (Mathematically, this is because $e^{-\infty}$ approaches 0.)

We can implement this more efficient masking "trick" by creating a mask with 1s above the diagonal and then replacing these 1s with negative infinity (`-inf`) values:

```
mask = torch.triu(torch.ones(context_length, context_length), diagonal=1)
masked = attn_scores.masked_fill(mask.bool(), -torch.inf)
print(masked)
```

This results in the following mask:

```
tensor([[0.2899,   -inf,   -inf,   -inf,   -inf,   -inf],
        [0.4656, 0.1723,   -inf,   -inf,   -inf,   -inf],
        [0.4594, 0.1703, 0.1731,   -inf,   -inf,   -inf],
        [0.2642, 0.1024, 0.1036, 0.0186,   -inf,   -inf],
        [0.2183, 0.0874, 0.0882, 0.0177, 0.0786,   -inf],
        [0.3408, 0.1270, 0.1290, 0.0198, 0.1290, 0.0078]],
       grad_fn=<MaskedFillBackward0>)
```

Now all we need to do is apply the softmax function to these masked results, and we are done:

```
attn_weights = torch.softmax(masked / keys.shape[-1]**0.5, dim=1)
print(attn_weights)
```

As we can see based on the output, the values in each row sum to 1, and no further normalization is necessary:

```
tensor([[1.0000, 0.0000, 0.0000, 0.0000, 0.0000, 0.0000],
        [0.5517, 0.4483, 0.0000, 0.0000, 0.0000, 0.0000],
        [0.3800, 0.3097, 0.3103, 0.0000, 0.0000, 0.0000],
        [0.2758, 0.2460, 0.2462, 0.2319, 0.0000, 0.0000],
        [0.2175, 0.1983, 0.1984, 0.1888, 0.1971, 0.0000],
        [0.1935, 0.1663, 0.1666, 0.1542, 0.1666, 0.1529]],
       grad_fn=<SoftmaxBackward0>)
```

We could now use the modified attention weights to compute the context vectors via `context_vec = attn_weights @ values`, as in section 3.4. However, we will first cover another minor tweak to the causal attention mechanism that is useful for reducing overfitting when training LLMs.

3.5.2 Masking additional attention weights with dropout

Dropout in deep learning is a technique where randomly selected hidden layer units are ignored during training, effectively "dropping" them out. This method helps prevent overfitting by ensuring that a model does not become overly reliant on any specific set of hidden layer units. It's important to emphasize that dropout is only used during training and is disabled afterward.

In the transformer architecture, including models like GPT, dropout in the attention mechanism is typically applied at two specific times: after calculating the attention weights or after applying the attention weights to the value vectors. Here we will apply the dropout mask after computing the attention weights, as illustrated in figure 3.22, because it's the more common variant in practice.

In the following code example, we use a dropout rate of 50%, which means masking out half of the attention weights. (When we train the GPT model in later chapters, we will use a lower dropout rate, such as 0.1 or 0.2.) We apply PyTorch's dropout implementation first to a 6 × 6 tensor consisting of 1s for simplicity:

```
torch.manual_seed(123)
dropout = torch.nn.Dropout(0.5)      # We choose a dropout rate of 50%.
example = torch.ones(6, 6)           # Here, we create a matrix of 1s.
print(dropout(example))
```

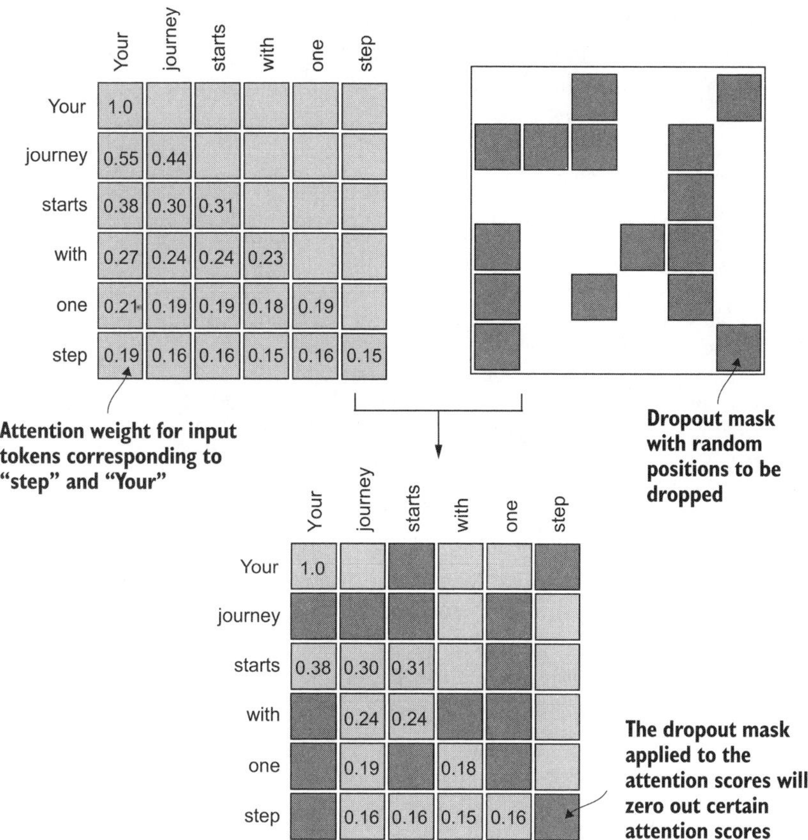

Figure 3.22 Using the causal attention mask (upper left), we apply an additional dropout mask (upper right) to zero out additional attention weights to reduce overfitting during training.

As we can see, approximately half of the values are zeroed out:

```
tensor([[2., 2., 0., 2., 2., 0.],
        [0., 0., 0., 2., 0., 2.],
        [2., 2., 2., 2., 0., 2.],
        [0., 2., 2., 0., 0., 2.],
        [0., 2., 0., 2., 0., 2.],
        [0., 2., 2., 2., 2., 0.]])
```

When applying dropout to an attention weight matrix with a rate of 50%, half of the elements in the matrix are randomly set to zero. To compensate for the reduction in active elements, the values of the remaining elements in the matrix are scaled up by a factor of 1/0.5 = 2. This scaling is crucial to maintain the overall balance of the attention weights, ensuring that the average influence of the attention mechanism remains consistent during both the training and inference phases.

Now let's apply dropout to the attention weight matrix itself:

```
torch.manual_seed(123)
print(dropout(attn_weights))
```

The resulting attention weight matrix now has additional elements zeroed out and the remaining 1s rescaled:

```
tensor([[2.0000, 0.0000, 0 .0000, 0.0000, 0.0000, 0.0000],
        [0.0000, 0.0000, 0.0000, 0.0000, 0.0000, 0.0000],
        [0.7599, 0.6194, 0.6206, 0.0000, 0.0000, 0.0000],
        [0.0000, 0.4921, 0.4925, 0.0000, 0.0000, 0.0000],
        [0.0000, 0.3966, 0.0000, 0.3775, 0.0000, 0.0000],
        [0.0000, 0.3327, 0.3331, 0.3084, 0.3331, 0.0000]],
       grad_fn=<MulBackward0>
```

Note that the resulting dropout outputs may look different depending on your operating system; you can read more about this inconsistency here on the PyTorch issue tracker at https://github.com/pytorch/pytorch/issues/121595.

Having gained an understanding of causal attention and dropout masking, we can now develop a concise Python class. This class is designed to facilitate the efficient application of these two techniques.

3.5.3 Implementing a compact causal attention class

We will now incorporate the causal attention and dropout modifications into the `SelfAttention` Python class we developed in section 3.4. This class will then serve as a template for developing *multi-head attention*, which is the final attention class we will implement.

But before we begin, let's ensure that the code can handle batches consisting of more than one input so that the `CausalAttention` class supports the batch outputs produced by the data loader we implemented in chapter 2.

For simplicity, to simulate such batch inputs, we duplicate the input text example:

```
batch = torch.stack((inputs, inputs), dim=0)
print(batch.shape)
```

Two inputs with six tokens each; each token has embedding dimension 3.

This results in a three-dimensional tensor consisting of two input texts with six tokens each, where each token is a three-dimensional embedding vector:

```
torch.Size([2, 6, 3])
```

The following `CausalAttention` class is similar to the `SelfAttention` class we implemented earlier, except that we added the dropout and causal mask components.

Listing 3.3 A compact causal attention class

```
class CausalAttention(nn.Module):
    def __init__(self, d_in, d_out, context_length,
                dropout, qkv_bias=False):
        super().__init__()
        self.d_out = d_out
        self.W_query = nn.Linear(d_in, d_out, bias=qkv_bias)
        self.W_key   = nn.Linear(d_in, d_out, bias=qkv_bias)
        self.W_value = nn.Linear(d_in, d_out, bias=qkv_bias)
        self.dropout = nn.Dropout(dropout)
        self.register_buffer(
           'mask',
           torch.triu(torch.ones(context_length, context_length),
           diagonal=1)
        )

    def forward(self, x):
        b, num_tokens, d_in = x.shape
        keys = self.W_key(x)
        queries = self.W_query(x)
        values = self.W_value(x)

        attn_scores = queries @ keys.transpose(1, 2)
        attn_scores.masked_fill_(
            self.mask.bool()[:num_tokens, :num_tokens], -torch.inf)
        attn_weights = torch.softmax(
            attn_scores / keys.shape[-1]**0.5, dim=-1
        )
        attn_weights = self.dropout(attn_weights)

        context_vec = attn_weights @ values
        return context_vec
```

Compared to the previous SelfAttention_v1 class, we added a dropout layer.

The register_buffer call is also a new addition (more information is provided in the following text).

We transpose dimensions 1 and 2, keeping the batch dimension at the first position (0).

In PyTorch, operations with a trailing underscore are performed in-place, avoiding unnecessary memory copies.

While all added code lines should be familiar at this point, we now added a `self.register_buffer()` call in the `__init__` method. The use of `register_buffer` in PyTorch is not strictly necessary for all use cases but offers several advantages here. For instance, when we use the `CausalAttention` class in our LLM, buffers are automatically moved to the appropriate device (CPU or GPU) along with our model, which will be relevant when training our LLM. This means we don't need to manually ensure these tensors are on the same device as your model parameters, avoiding device mismatch errors.

We can use the `CausalAttention` class as follows, similar to `SelfAttention` previously:

```
torch.manual_seed(123)
context_length = batch.shape[1]
ca = CausalAttention(d_in, d_out, context_length, 0.0)
context_vecs = ca(batch)
print("context_vecs.shape:", context_vecs.shape)
```

The resulting context vector is a three-dimensional tensor where each token is now represented by a two-dimensional embedding:

```
context_vecs.shape: torch.Size([2, 6, 2])
```

Figure 3.23 summarizes what we have accomplished so far. We have focused on the concept and implementation of causal attention in neural networks. Next, we will expand on this concept and implement a multi-head attention module that implements several causal attention mechanisms in parallel.

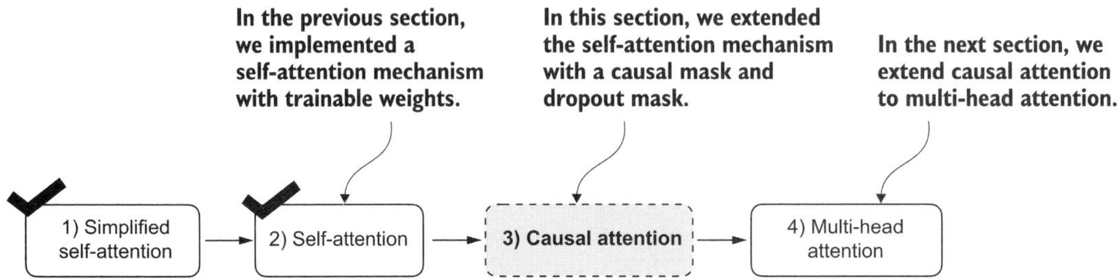

Figure 3.23 Here's what we've done so far. We began with a simplified attention mechanism, added trainable weights, and then added a causal attention mask. Next, we will extend the causal attention mechanism and code multi-head attention, which we will use in our LLM.

3.6 *Extending single-head attention to multi-head attention*

Our final step will be to extend the previously implemented causal attention class over multiple heads. This is also called *multi-head attention.*

The term "multi-head" refers to dividing the attention mechanism into multiple "heads," each operating independently. In this context, a single causal attention module can be considered single-head attention, where there is only one set of attention weights processing the input sequentially.

We will tackle this expansion from causal attention to multi-head attention. First, we will intuitively build a multi-head attention module by stacking multiple `CausalAttention` modules. Then we will then implement the same multi-head attention module in a more complicated but more computationally efficient way.

3.6.1 *Stacking multiple single-head attention layers*

In practical terms, implementing multi-head attention involves creating multiple instances of the self-attention mechanism (see figure 3.18), each with its own weights, and then combining their outputs. Using multiple instances of the self-attention mechanism can be computationally intensive, but it's crucial for the kind of complex pattern recognition that models like transformer-based LLMs are known for.

Figure 3.24 illustrates the structure of a multi-head attention module, which consists of multiple single-head attention modules, as previously depicted in figure 3.18, stacked on top of each other.

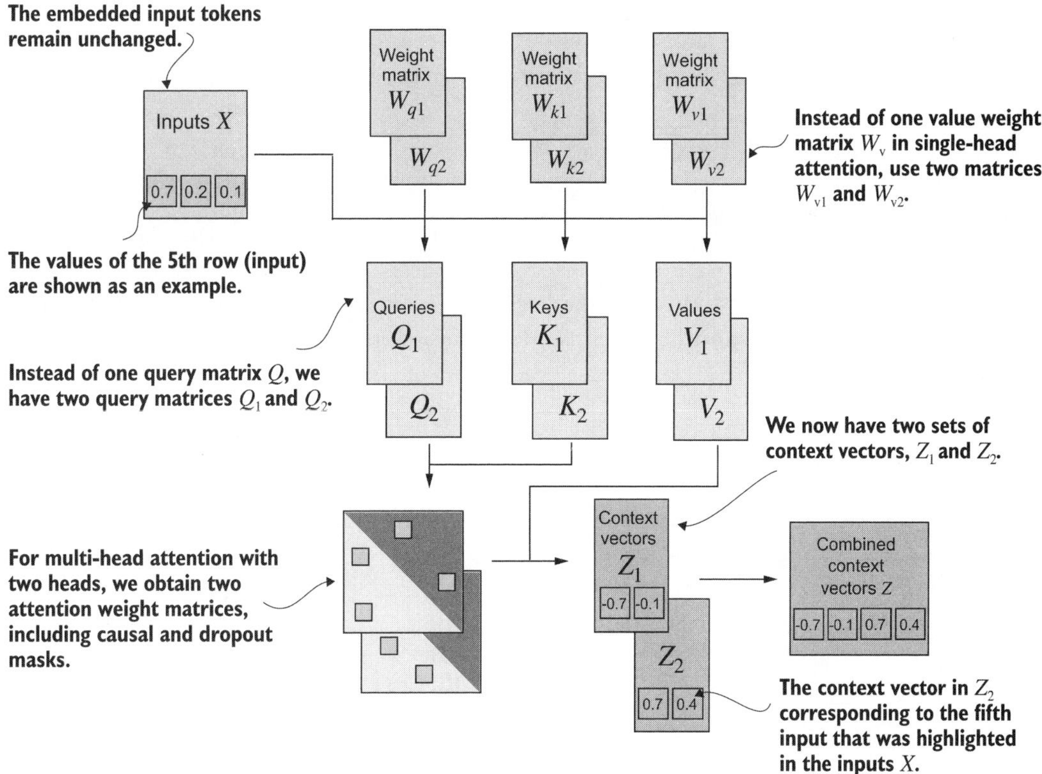

Figure 3.24 The multi-head attention module includes two single-head attention modules stacked on top of each other. So, instead of using a single matrix W_v for computing the value matrices, in a multi-head attention module with two heads, we now have two value weight matrices: W_{v1} and W_{v2}. The same applies to the other weight matrices, W_Q and W_k. We obtain two sets of context vectors Z_1 and Z_2 that we can combine into a single context vector matrix Z.

As mentioned before, the main idea behind multi-head attention is to run the attention mechanism multiple times (in parallel) with different, learned linear projections—the results of multiplying the input data (like the query, key, and value vectors in attention mechanisms) by a weight matrix. In code, we can achieve this by implementing a simple `MultiHeadAttentionWrapper` class that stacks multiple instances of our previously implemented `CausalAttention` module.

Listing 3.4 A wrapper class to implement multi-head attention

```
class MultiHeadAttentionWrapper(nn.Module):
    def __init__(self, d_in, d_out, context_length,
                 dropout, num_heads, qkv_bias=False):
        super().__init__()
        self.heads = nn.ModuleList(
            [CausalAttention(
                 d_in, d_out, context_length, dropout, qkv_bias
             )
             for _ in range(num_heads)]
        )

    def forward(self, x):
        return torch.cat([head(x) for head in self.heads], dim=-1)
```

For example, if we use this `MultiHeadAttentionWrapper` class with two attention heads (via `num_heads=2`) and `CausalAttention` output dimension `d_out=2`, we get a four-dimensional context vector (`d_out*num_heads=4`), as depicted in figure 3.25.

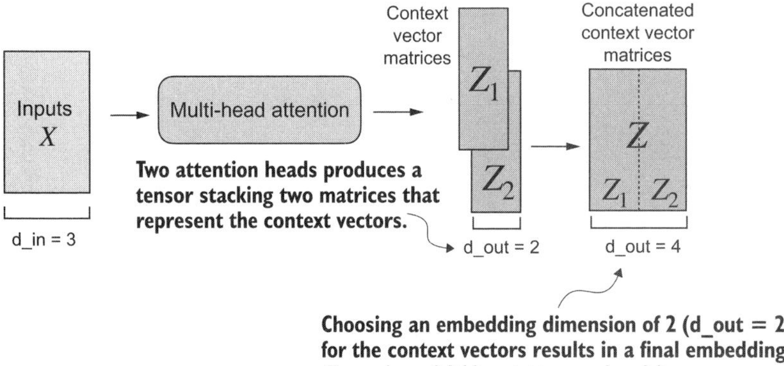

Figure 3.25 Using the `MultiHeadAttentionWrapper`, we specified the number of attention heads (`num_heads`). If we set `num_heads=2`, as in this example, we obtain a tensor with two sets of context vector matrices. In each context vector matrix, the rows represent the context vectors corresponding to the tokens, and the columns correspond to the embedding dimension specified via `d_out=4`. We concatenate these context vector matrices along the column dimension. Since we have two attention heads and an embedding dimension of 2, the final embedding dimension is 2 × 2 = 4.

To illustrate this further with a concrete example, we can use the `MultiHeadAttentionWrapper` class similar to the `CausalAttention` class before:

```
torch.manual_seed(123)
context_length = batch.shape[1] # This is the number of tokens
d_in, d_out = 3, 2
```

```
mha = MultiHeadAttentionWrapper(
    d_in, d_out, context_length, 0.0, num_heads=2
)
context_vecs = mha(batch)

print(context_vecs)
print("context_vecs.shape:", context_vecs.shape)
```

This results in the following tensor representing the context vectors:

```
tensor([[[-0.4519,  0.2216,  0.4772,  0.1063],
         [-0.5874,  0.0058,  0.5891,  0.3257],
         [-0.6300, -0.0632,  0.6202,  0.3860],
         [-0.5675, -0.0843,  0.5478,  0.3589],
         [-0.5526, -0.0981,  0.5321,  0.3428],
         [-0.5299, -0.1081,  0.5077,  0.3493]],

        [[-0.4519,  0.2216,  0.4772,  0.1063],
         [-0.5874,  0.0058,  0.5891,  0.3257],
         [-0.6300, -0.0632,  0.6202,  0.3860],
         [-0.5675, -0.0843,  0.5478,  0.3589],
         [-0.5526, -0.0981,  0.5321,  0.3428],
         [-0.5299, -0.1081,  0.5077,  0.3493]]], grad_fn=<CatBackward0>)
context_vecs.shape: torch.Size([2, 6, 4])
```

The first dimension of the resulting `context_vecs` tensor is 2 since we have two input texts (the input texts are duplicated, which is why the context vectors are exactly the same for those). The second dimension refers to the 6 tokens in each input. The third dimension refers to the four-dimensional embedding of each token.

> **Exercise 3.2 Returning two-dimensional embedding vectors**
>
> Change the input arguments for the `MultiHeadAttentionWrapper(..., num_heads=2)` call such that the output context vectors are two-dimensional instead of four dimensional while keeping the setting `num_heads=2`. Hint: You don't have to modify the class implementation; you just have to change one of the other input arguments.

Up to this point, we have implemented a `MultiHeadAttentionWrapper` that combined multiple single-head attention modules. However, these are processed sequentially via `[head(x) for head in self.heads]` in the forward method. We can improve this implementation by processing the heads in parallel. One way to achieve this is by computing the outputs for all attention heads simultaneously via matrix multiplication.

3.6.2 Implementing multi-head attention with weight splits

So far, we have created a `MultiHeadAttentionWrapper` to implement multi-head attention by stacking multiple single-head attention modules. This was done by instantiating and combining several `CausalAttention` objects.

Instead of maintaining two separate classes, `MultiHeadAttentionWrapper` and `CausalAttention`, we can combine these concepts into a single `MultiHeadAttention` class. Also, in addition to merging the `MultiHeadAttentionWrapper` with the `CausalAttention` code, we will make some other modifications to implement multi-head attention more efficiently.

In the `MultiHeadAttentionWrapper`, multiple heads are implemented by creating a list of `CausalAttention` objects (`self.heads`), each representing a separate attention head. The `CausalAttention` class independently performs the attention mechanism, and the results from each head are concatenated. In contrast, the following `MultiHeadAttention` class integrates the multi-head functionality within a single class. It splits the input into multiple heads by reshaping the projected query, key, and value tensors and then combines the results from these heads after computing attention.

Let's take a look at the `MultiHeadAttention` class before we discuss it further.

Listing 3.5 An efficient multi-head attention class

```
class MultiHeadAttention(nn.Module):
    def __init__(self, d_in, d_out,
                 context_length, dropout, num_heads, qkv_bias=False):
        super().__init__()
        assert (d_out % num_heads == 0), \
            "d_out must be divisible by num_heads"

        self.d_out = d_out
        self.num_heads = num_heads
        self.head_dim = d_out // num_heads
        self.W_query = nn.Linear(d_in, d_out, bias=qkv_bias)
        self.W_key = nn.Linear(d_in, d_out, bias=qkv_bias)
        self.W_value = nn.Linear(d_in, d_out, bias=qkv_bias)
        self.out_proj = nn.Linear(d_out, d_out)
        self.dropout = nn.Dropout(dropout)
        self.register_buffer(
            "mask",
            torch.triu(torch.ones(context_length, context_length),
                       diagonal=1)
        )

    def forward(self, x):
        b, num_tokens, d_in = x.shape
        keys = self.W_key(x)
        queries = self.W_query(x)
        values = self.W_value(x)
```

Reduces the projection dim to match the desired output dim

Uses a Linear layer to combine head outputs

Tensor shape: (b, num_tokens, d_out)

```
        keys = keys.view(b, num_tokens, self.num_heads, self.head_dim)
        values = values.view(b, num_tokens, self.num_heads, self.head_dim)
        queries = queries.view(
            b, num_tokens, self.num_heads, self.head_dim
        )

        keys = keys.transpose(1, 2)
        queries = queries.transpose(1, 2)
        values = values.transpose(1, 2)

        attn_scores = queries @ keys.transpose(2, 3)
        mask_bool = self.mask.bool()[:num_tokens, :num_tokens]

        attn_scores.masked_fill_(mask_bool, -torch.inf)

        attn_weights = torch.softmax(
            attn_scores / keys.shape[-1]**0.5, dim=-1)
        attn_weights = self.dropout(attn_weights)

        context_vec = (attn_weights @ values).transpose(1, 2)

        context_vec = context_vec.contiguous().view(
            b, num_tokens, self.d_out
        )
        context_vec = self.out_proj(context_vec)
        return context_vec
```

We implicitly split the matrix by adding a num_heads dimension. Then we unroll the last dim: (b, num_tokens, d_out) -> (b, num_tokens, num_heads, head_dim).

Transposes from shape (b, num_tokens, num_heads, head_dim) to (b, num_heads, num_tokens, head_dim)

Computes dot product for each head

Masks truncated to the number of tokens

Uses the mask to fill attention scores

Tensor shape: (b, num_tokens, n_heads, head_dim)

Combines heads, where self.d_out = self.num_heads * self.head_dim

Adds an optional linear projection

Even though the reshaping (`.view`) and transposing (`.transpose`) of tensors inside the `MultiHeadAttention` class looks very mathematically complicated, the `MultiHeadAttention` class implements the same concept as the `MultiHeadAttentionWrapper` earlier.

On a big-picture level, in the previous `MultiHeadAttentionWrapper`, we stacked multiple single-head attention layers that we combined into a multi-head attention layer. The `MultiHeadAttention` class takes an integrated approach. It starts with a multi-head layer and then internally splits this layer into individual attention heads, as illustrated in figure 3.26.

The splitting of the query, key, and value tensors is achieved through tensor reshaping and transposing operations using PyTorch's `.view` and `.transpose` methods. The input is first transformed (via linear layers for queries, keys, and values) and then reshaped to represent multiple heads.

The key operation is to split the `d_out` dimension into `num_heads` and `head_dim`, where `head_dim = d_out / num_heads`. This splitting is then achieved using the `.view` method: a tensor of dimensions `(b, num_tokens, d_out)` is reshaped to dimension `(b, num_tokens, num_heads, head_dim)`.

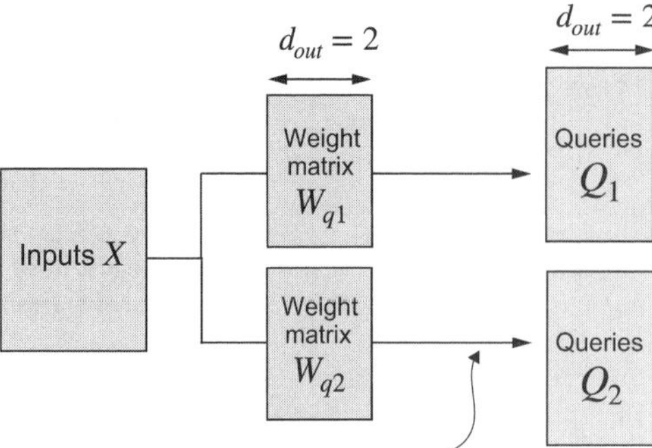

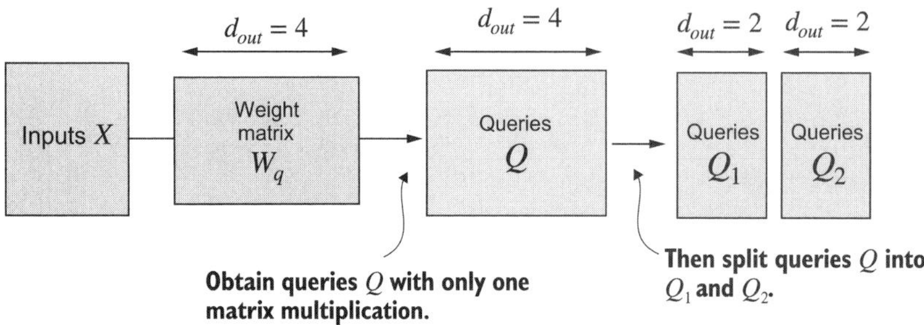

Figure 3.26 In the `MultiHeadAttentionWrapper` class with two attention heads, we initialized two weight matrices, W_{q1} and W_{q2}, and computed two query matrices, Q_1 and Q_2 (top). In the `MultiheadAttention` class, we initialize one larger weight matrix W_q, only perform one matrix multiplication with the inputs to obtain a query matrix Q, and then split the query matrix into Q_1 and Q_2 (bottom). We do the same for the keys and values, which are not shown to reduce visual clutter.

The tensors are then transposed to bring the `num_heads` dimension before the `num_tokens` dimension, resulting in a shape of `(b, num_heads, num_tokens, head_dim)`. This transposition is crucial for correctly aligning the queries, keys, and values across the different heads and performing batched matrix multiplications efficiently.

To illustrate this batched matrix multiplication, suppose we have the following tensor:

```
a = torch.tensor([[[[0.2745, 0.6584, 0.2775, 0.8573],
                    [0.8993, 0.0390, 0.9268, 0.7388],
                    [0.7179, 0.7058, 0.9156, 0.4340]],

                   [[0.0772, 0.3565, 0.1479, 0.5331],
                    [0.4066, 0.2318, 0.4545, 0.9737],
                    [0.4606, 0.5159, 0.4220, 0.5786]]]])
```

The shape of this tensor is (b, num_heads, num_tokens, head_dim) = (1, 2, 3, 4).

Now we perform a batched matrix multiplication between the tensor itself and a view of the tensor where we transposed the last two dimensions, `num_tokens` and `head_dim`:

```
print(a @ a.transpose(2, 3))
```

The result is

```
tensor([[[[1.3208, 1.1631, 1.2879],
          [1.1631, 2.2150, 1.8424],
          [1.2879, 1.8424, 2.0402]],

         [[0.4391, 0.7003, 0.5903],
          [0.7003, 1.3737, 1.0620],
          [0.5903, 1.0620, 0.9912]]]])
```

In this case, the matrix multiplication implementation in PyTorch handles the four-dimensional input tensor so that the matrix multiplication is carried out between the two last dimensions `(num_tokens, head_dim)` and then repeated for the individual heads.

For instance, the preceding becomes a more compact way to compute the matrix multiplication for each head separately:

```
first_head = a[0, 0, :, :]
first_res = first_head @ first_head.T
print("First head:\n", first_res)

second_head = a[0, 1, :, :]
second_res = second_head @ second_head.T
print("\nSecond head:\n", second_res)
```

The results are exactly the same results as those we obtained when using the batched matrix multiplication `print(a @ a.transpose(2, 3))`:

```
First head:
 tensor([[1.3208, 1.1631, 1.2879],
        [1.1631, 2.2150, 1.8424],
        [1.2879, 1.8424, 2.0402]])

Second head:
 tensor([[0.4391, 0.7003, 0.5903],
        [0.7003, 1.3737, 1.0620],
        [0.5903, 1.0620, 0.9912]])
```

Continuing with `MultiHeadAttention`, after computing the attention weights and context vectors, the context vectors from all heads are transposed back to the shape `(b, num_tokens, num_heads, head_dim)`. These vectors are then reshaped (flattened) into the shape `(b, num_tokens, d_out)`, effectively combining the outputs from all heads.

Additionally, we added an output projection layer (`self.out_proj`) to `MultiHeadAttention` after combining the heads, which is not present in the `CausalAttention` class. This output projection layer is not strictly necessary (see appendix B for more details), but it is commonly used in many LLM architectures, which is why I added it here for completeness.

Even though the `MultiHeadAttention` class looks more complicated than the `MultiHeadAttentionWrapper` due to the additional reshaping and transposition of tensors, it is more efficient. The reason is that we only need one matrix multiplication to compute the keys, for instance, `keys = self.W_key(x)` (the same is true for the queries and values). In the `MultiHeadAttentionWrapper`, we needed to repeat this matrix multiplication, which is computationally one of the most expensive steps, for each attention head.

The `MultiHeadAttention` class can be used similar to the `SelfAttention` and `CausalAttention` classes we implemented earlier:

```
torch.manual_seed(123)
batch_size, context_length, d_in = batch.shape
d_out = 2
mha = MultiHeadAttention(d_in, d_out, context_length, 0.0, num_heads=2)
context_vecs = mha(batch)
print(context_vecs)
print("context_vecs.shape:", context_vecs.shape)
```

The results show that the output dimension is directly controlled by the `d_out` argument:

```
tensor([[[0.3190, 0.4858],
         [0.2943, 0.3897],
         [0.2856, 0.3593],
         [0.2693, 0.3873],
         [0.2639, 0.3928],
         [0.2575, 0.4028]],

        [[0.3190, 0.4858],
         [0.2943, 0.3897],
         [0.2856, 0.3593],
         [0.2693, 0.3873],
         [0.2639, 0.3928],
         [0.2575, 0.4028]]], grad_fn=<ViewBackward0>)
context_vecs.shape: torch.Size([2, 6, 2])
```

We have now implemented the `MultiHeadAttention` class that we will use when we implement and train the LLM. Note that while the code is fully functional, I used relatively small embedding sizes and numbers of attention heads to keep the outputs readable.

For comparison, the smallest GPT-2 model (117 million parameters) has 12 attention heads and a context vector embedding size of 768. The largest GPT-2 model (1.5 billion parameters) has 25 attention heads and a context vector embedding size of 1,600. The embedding sizes of the token inputs and context embeddings are the same in GPT models (`d_in = d_out`).

Exercise 3.3 Initializing GPT-2 size attention modules

Using the `MultiHeadAttention` class, initialize a multi-head attention module that has the same number of attention heads as the smallest GPT-2 model (12 attention heads). Also ensure that you use the respective input and output embedding sizes similar to GPT-2 (768 dimensions). Note that the smallest GPT-2 model supports a context length of 1,024 tokens.

Summary

- Attention mechanisms transform input elements into enhanced context vector representations that incorporate information about all inputs.
- A self-attention mechanism computes the context vector representation as a weighted sum over the inputs.
- In a simplified attention mechanism, the attention weights are computed via dot products.
- A dot product is a concise way of multiplying two vectors element-wise and then summing the products.
- Matrix multiplications, while not strictly required, help us implement computations more efficiently and compactly by replacing nested `for` loops.
- In self-attention mechanisms used in LLMs, also called scaled-dot product attention, we include trainable weight matrices to compute intermediate transformations of the inputs: queries, values, and keys.
- When working with LLMs that read and generate text from left to right, we add a causal attention mask to prevent the LLM from accessing future tokens.
- In addition to causal attention masks to zero-out attention weights, we can add a dropout mask to reduce overfitting in LLMs.
- The attention modules in transformer-based LLMs involve multiple instances of causal attention, which is called multi-head attention.
- We can create a multi-head attention module by stacking multiple instances of causal attention modules.
- A more efficient way of creating multi-head attention modules involves batched matrix multiplications.

4 Implementing a GPT model from scratch to generate text

This chapter covers

- Coding a GPT-like large language model (LLM) that can be trained to generate human-like text
- Normalizing layer activations to stabilize neural network training
- Adding shortcut connections in deep neural networks
- Implementing transformer blocks to create GPT models of various sizes
- Computing the number of parameters and storage requirements of GPT models

You've already learned and coded the *multi-head attention* mechanism, one of the core components of LLMs. Now, we will code the other building blocks of an LLM and assemble them into a GPT-like model that we will train in the next chapter to generate human-like text.

The LLM architecture referenced in figure 4.1, consists of several building blocks. We will begin with a top-down view of the model architecture before covering the individual components in more detail.

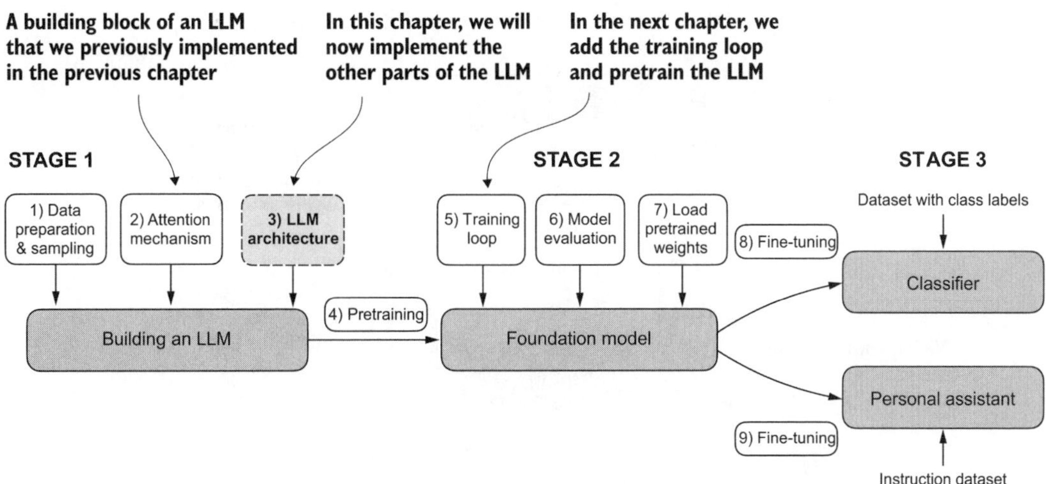

Figure 4.1 The three main stages of coding an LLM. This chapter focuses on step 3 of stage 1: implementing the LLM architecture.

4.1 Coding an LLM architecture

LLMs, such as GPT (which stands for *generative pretrained transformer*), are large deep neural network architectures designed to generate new text one word (or token) at a time. However, despite their size, the model architecture is less complicated than you might think, since many of its components are repeated, as we will see later. Figure 4.2 provides a top-down view of a GPT-like LLM, with its main components highlighted.

We have already covered several aspects of the LLM architecture, such as input tokenization and embedding and the masked multi-head attention module. Now, we will implement the core structure of the GPT model, including its *transformer blocks*, which we will later train to generate human-like text.

Previously, we used smaller embedding dimensions for simplicity, ensuring that the concepts and examples could comfortably fit on a single page. Now, we are scaling up to the size of a small GPT-2 model, specifically the smallest version with 124 million parameters, as described in "Language Models Are Unsupervised Multitask Learners," by Radford et al. (https://mng.bz/yoBq). Note that while the original report mentions 117 million parameters, this was later corrected. In chapter 6, we will focus on loading pretrained weights into our implementation and adapting it for larger GPT-2 models with 345, 762, and 1,542 million parameters.

In the context of deep learning and LLMs like GPT, the term "parameters" refers to the trainable weights of the model. These weights are essentially the internal variables of the model that are adjusted and optimized during the training process to minimize a specific loss function. This optimization allows the model to learn from the training data.

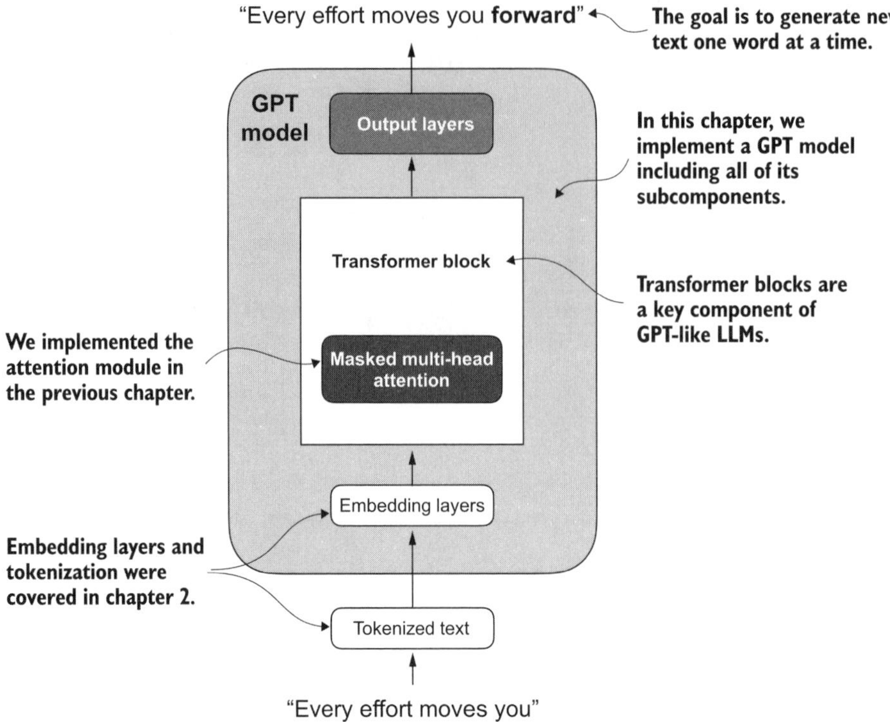
"Every effort moves you **forward**"
The goal is to generate new text one word at a time.
GPT model
Output layers
In this chapter, we implement a GPT model including all of its subcomponents.
Transformer block
Transformer blocks are a key component of GPT-like LLMs.
We implemented the attention module in the previous chapter.
Masked multi-head attention
Embedding layers
Embedding layers and tokenization were covered in chapter 2.
Tokenized text
"Every effort moves you"

Figure 4.2 A GPT model. In addition to the embedding layers, it consists of one or more transformer blocks containing the masked multi-head attention module we previously implemented.

For example, in a neural network layer that is represented by a 2,048 × 2,048–dimensional matrix (or tensor) of weights, each element of this matrix is a parameter. Since there are 2,048 rows and 2,048 columns, the total number of parameters in this layer is 2,048 multiplied by 2,048, which equals 4,194,304 parameters.

GPT-2 vs. GPT-3

Note that we are focusing on GPT-2 because OpenAI has made the weights of the pretrained model publicly available, which we will load into our implementation in chapter 6. GPT-3 is fundamentally the same in terms of model architecture, except that it is scaled up from 1.5 billion parameters in GPT-2 to 175 billion parameters in GPT-3, and it is trained on more data. As of this writing, the weights for GPT-3 are not publicly available. GPT-2 is also a better choice for learning how to implement LLMs, as it can be run on a single laptop computer, whereas GPT-3 requires a GPU cluster for training and inference. According to Lambda Labs (https://lambdalabs.com/), it would take 355 years to train GPT-3 on a single V100 datacenter GPU and 665 years on a consumer RTX 8000 GPU.

We specify the configuration of the small GPT-2 model via the following Python dictionary, which we will use in the code examples later:

```
GPT_CONFIG_124M = {
    "vocab_size": 50257,     # Vocabulary size
    "context_length": 1024,  # Context length
    "emb_dim": 768,          # Embedding dimension
    "n_heads": 12,           # Number of attention heads
    "n_layers": 12,          # Number of layers
    "drop_rate": 0.1,        # Dropout rate
    "qkv_bias": False        # Query-Key-Value bias
}
```

In the `GPT_CONFIG_124M` dictionary, we use concise variable names for clarity and to prevent long lines of code:

- `vocab_size` refers to a vocabulary of 50,257 words, as used by the BPE tokenizer (see chapter 2).
- `context_length` denotes the maximum number of input tokens the model can handle via the positional embeddings (see chapter 2).
- `emb_dim` represents the embedding size, transforming each token into a 768-dimensional vector.
- `n_heads` indicates the count of attention heads in the multi-head attention mechanism (see chapter 3).
- `n_layers` specifies the number of transformer blocks in the model, which we will cover in the upcoming discussion.
- `drop_rate` indicates the intensity of the dropout mechanism (0.1 implies a 10% random drop out of hidden units) to prevent overfitting (see chapter 3).
- `qkv_bias` determines whether to include a bias vector in the `Linear` layers of the multi-head attention for query, key, and value computations. We will initially disable this, following the norms of modern LLMs, but we will revisit it in chapter 6 when we load pretrained GPT-2 weights from OpenAI into our model (see chapter 6).

Using this configuration, we will implement a GPT placeholder architecture (`DummyGPTModel`), as shown in figure 4.3. This will provide us with a big-picture view of how everything fits together and what other components we need to code to assemble the full GPT model architecture.

The numbered boxes in figure 4.3 illustrate the order in which we tackle the individual concepts required to code the final GPT architecture. We will start with step 1, a placeholder GPT backbone we will call `DummyGPTModel`.

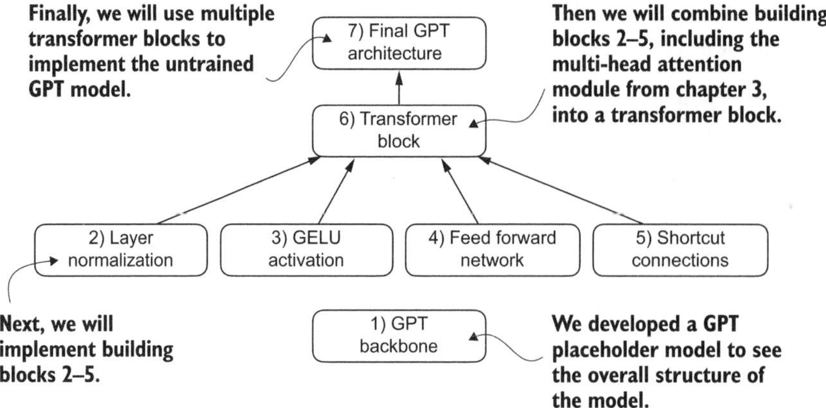
Finally, we will use multiple transformer blocks to implement the untrained GPT model.
7) Final GPT architecture
Then we will combine building blocks 2–5, including the multi-head attention module from chapter 3, into a transformer block.
6) Transformer block
2) Layer normalization
3) GELU activation
4) Feed forward network
5) Shortcut connections
Next, we will implement building blocks 2–5.
1) GPT backbone
We developed a GPT placeholder model to see the overall structure of the model.

Figure 4.3 The order in which we code the GPT architecture. We start with the GPT backbone, a placeholder architecture, before getting to the individual core pieces and eventually assembling them in a transformer block for the final GPT architecture.

Listing 4.1 A placeholder GPT model architecture class

```
import torch
import torch.nn as nn

class DummyGPTModel(nn.Module):
    def __init__(self, cfg):
        super().__init__()
        self.tok_emb = nn.Embedding(cfg["vocab_size"], cfg["emb_dim"])
        self.pos_emb = nn.Embedding(cfg["context_length"], cfg["emb_dim"])
        self.drop_emb = nn.Dropout(cfg["drop_rate"])
        self.trf_blocks = nn.Sequential(
            *[DummyTransformerBlock(cfg)
              for _ in range(cfg["n_layers"])]
        )
        self.final_norm = DummyLayerNorm(cfg["emb_dim"])
        self.out_head = nn.Linear(
            cfg["emb_dim"], cfg["vocab_size"], bias=False
        )

    def forward(self, in_idx):
        batch_size, seq_len = in_idx.shape
        tok_embeds = self.tok_emb(in_idx)
        pos_embeds = self.pos_emb(
            torch.arange(seq_len, device=in_idx.device)
        )
        x = tok_embeds + pos_embeds
        x = self.drop_emb(x)
        x = self.trf_blocks(x)
        x = self.final_norm(x)
        logits = self.out_head(x)
        return logits
```

Uses a placeholder for TransformerBlock

Uses a placeholder for LayerNorm

```
class DummyTransformerBlock(nn.Module):          # A simple placeholder class that will be replaced by a real TransformerBlock later
    def __init__(self, cfg):
        super().__init__()

    def forward(self, x):                         # This block does nothing and just returns its input.
        return x

class DummyLayerNorm(nn.Module):                  # A simple placeholder class that will be replaced by a real LayerNorm later
    def __init__(self, normalized_shape, eps=1e-5):   # The parameters here are just to mimic the LayerNorm interface.
        super().__init__()

    def forward(self, x):
        return x
```

The `DummyGPTModel` class in this code defines a simplified version of a GPT-like model using PyTorch's neural network module (`nn.Module`). The model architecture in the `DummyGPTModel` class consists of token and positional embeddings, dropout, a series of transformer blocks (`DummyTransformerBlock`), a final layer normalization (`DummyLayerNorm`), and a linear output layer (`out_head`). The configuration is passed in via a Python dictionary, for instance, the `GPT_CONFIG_124M` dictionary we created earlier.

The `forward` method describes the data flow through the model: it computes token and positional embeddings for the input indices, applies dropout, processes the data through the transformer blocks, applies normalization, and finally produces logits with the linear output layer.

The code in listing 4.1 is already functional. However, for now, note that we use placeholders (`DummyLayerNorm` and `DummyTransformerBlock`) for the transformer block and layer normalization, which we will develop later.

Next, we will prepare the input data and initialize a new GPT model to illustrate its usage. Building on our coding of the tokenizer (see chapter 2), let's now consider a high-level overview of how data flows in and out of a GPT model, as shown in figure 4.4.

To implement these steps, we tokenize a batch consisting of two text inputs for the GPT model using the tiktoken tokenizer from chapter 2:

```
import tiktoken

tokenizer = tiktoken.get_encoding("gpt2")
batch = []
txt1 = "Every effort moves you"
txt2 = "Every day holds a"

batch.append(torch.tensor(tokenizer.encode(txt1)))
batch.append(torch.tensor(tokenizer.encode(txt2)))
batch = torch.stack(batch, dim=0)
print(batch)
```

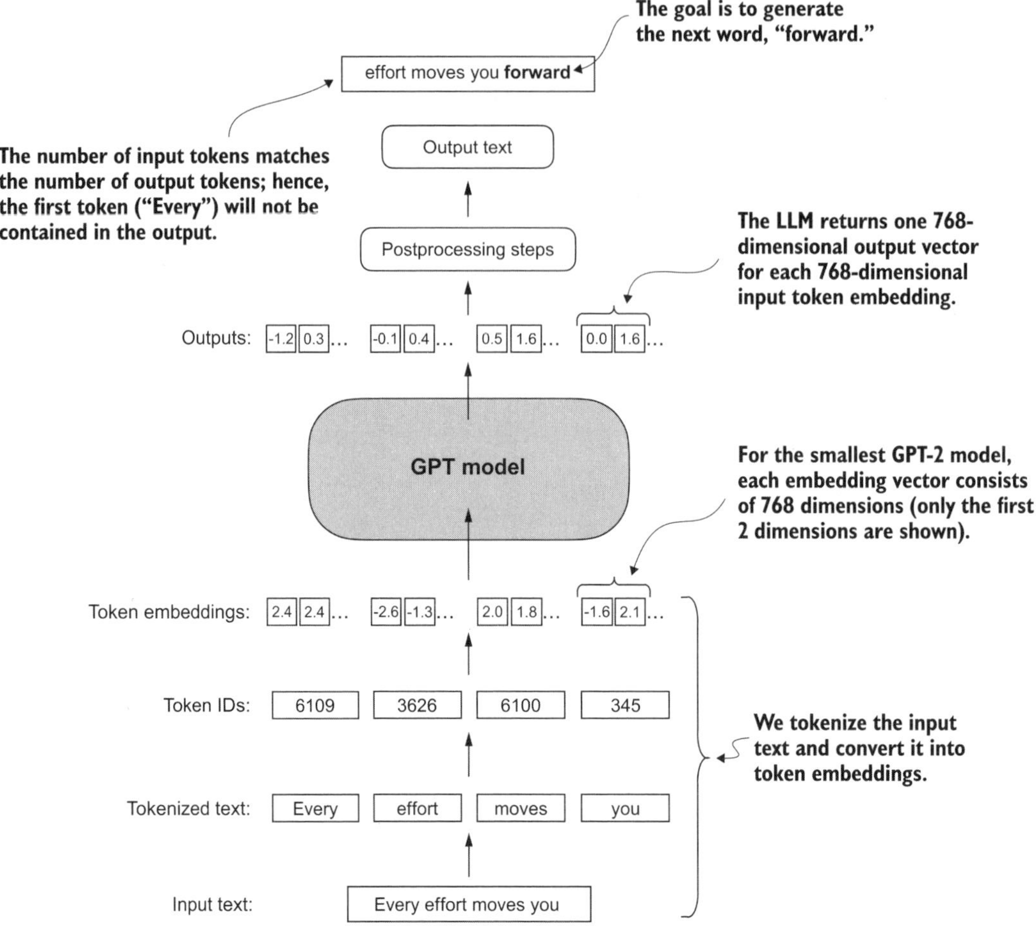

Figure 4.4 A big-picture overview showing how the input data is tokenized, embedded, and fed to the GPT model. Note that in our `DummyGPTClass` coded earlier, the token embedding is handled inside the GPT model. In LLMs, the embedded input token dimension typically matches the output dimension. The output embeddings here represent the context vectors (see chapter 3).

The resulting token IDs for the two texts are as follows:

```
tensor([[6109,  3626,  6100,   345],
        [6109,  1110,  6622,   257]])
```

The first row corresponds to the first text, and the second row corresponds to the second text.

Next, we initialize a new 124-million-parameter `DummyGPTModel` instance and feed it the tokenized `batch`:

```
torch.manual_seed(123)
model = DummyGPTModel(GPT_CONFIG_124M)
logits = model(batch)
print("Output shape:", logits.shape)
print(logits)
```

The model outputs, which are commonly referred to as logits, are as follows:

```
Output shape: torch.Size([2, 4, 50257])
tensor([[[-1.2034,  0.3201, -0.7130,  ..., -1.5548, -0.2390, -0.4667],
         [-0.1192,  0.4539, -0.4432,  ...,  0.2392,  1.3469,  1.2430],
         [ 0.5307,  1.6720, -0.4695,  ...,  1.1966,  0.0111,  0.5835],
         [ 0.0139,  1.6755, -0.3388,  ...,  1.1586, -0.0435, -1.0400]],

        [[-1.0908,  0.1798, -0.9484,  ..., -1.6047,  0.2439, -0.4530],
         [-0.7860,  0.5581, -0.0610,  ...,  0.4835, -0.0077,  1.6621],
         [ 0.3567,  1.2698, -0.6398,  ..., -0.0162, -0.1296,  0.3717],
         [-0.2407, -0.7349, -0.5102,  ...,  2.0057, -0.3694,  0.1814]]],
       grad_fn=<UnsafeViewBackward0>)
```

The output tensor has two rows corresponding to the two text samples. Each text sample consists of four tokens; each token is a 50,257-dimensional vector, which matches the size of the tokenizer's vocabulary.

The embedding has 50,257 dimensions because each of these dimensions refers to a unique token in the vocabulary. When we implement the postprocessing code, we will convert these 50,257-dimensional vectors back into token IDs, which we can then decode into words.

Now that we have taken a top-down look at the GPT architecture and its inputs and outputs, we will code the individual placeholders, starting with the real layer normalization class that will replace the `DummyLayerNorm` in the previous code.

4.2 Normalizing activations with layer normalization

Training deep neural networks with many layers can sometimes prove challenging due to problems like vanishing or exploding gradients. These problems lead to unstable training dynamics and make it difficult for the network to effectively adjust its weights, which means the learning process struggles to find a set of parameters (weights) for the neural network that minimizes the loss function. In other words, the network has difficulty learning the underlying patterns in the data to a degree that would allow it to make accurate predictions or decisions.

> **NOTE** If you are new to neural network training and the concepts of gradients, a brief introduction to these concepts can be found in section A.4 in appendix A. However, a deep mathematical understanding of gradients is not required to follow the contents of this book.

Let's now implement *layer normalization* to improve the stability and efficiency of neural network training. The main idea behind layer normalization is to adjust the activations (outputs) of a neural network layer to have a mean of 0 and a variance of 1, also known as unit variance. This adjustment speeds up the convergence to effective weights and ensures consistent, reliable training. In GPT-2 and modern transformer architectures, layer normalization is typically applied before and after the multi-head attention module, and, as we have seen with the `DummyLayerNorm` placeholder, before the final output layer. Figure 4.5 provides a visual overview of how layer normalization functions.

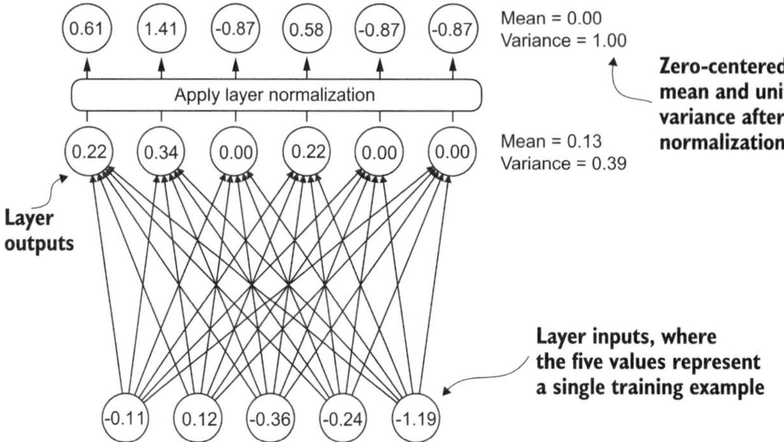

Figure 4.5 An illustration of layer normalization where the six outputs of the layer, also called activations, are normalized such that they have a 0 mean and a variance of 1.

We can recreate the example shown in figure 4.5 via the following code, where we implement a neural network layer with five inputs and six outputs that we apply to two input examples:

```
torch.manual_seed(123)
batch_example = torch.randn(2, 5)        # Creates two training examples with five dimensions (features) each
layer = nn.Sequential(nn.Linear(5, 6), nn.ReLU())
out = layer(batch_example)
print(out)
```

This prints the following tensor, where the first row lists the layer outputs for the first input and the second row lists the layer outputs for the second row:

```
tensor([[0.2260, 0.3470, 0.0000, 0.2216, 0.0000, 0.0000],
        [0.2133, 0.2394, 0.0000, 0.5198, 0.3297, 0.0000]],
       grad_fn=<ReluBackward0>)
```

The neural network layer we have coded consists of a `Linear` layer followed by a non-linear activation function, `ReLU` (short for rectified linear unit), which is a standard activation function in neural networks. If you are unfamiliar with `ReLU`, it simply thresholds negative inputs to 0, ensuring that a layer outputs only positive values, which explains why the resulting layer output does not contain any negative values. Later, we will use another, more sophisticated activation function in GPT.

Before we apply layer normalization to these outputs, let's examine the mean and variance:

```
mean = out.mean(dim=-1, keepdim=True)
var = out.var(dim=-1, keepdim=True)
print("Mean:\n", mean)
print("Variance:\n", var)
```

The output is

```
Mean:
  tensor([[0.1324],
          [0.2170]], grad_fn=<MeanBackward1>)
Variance:
  tensor([[0.0231],
          [0.0398]], grad_fn=<VarBackward0>)
```

The first row in the mean tensor here contains the mean value for the first input row, and the second output row contains the mean for the second input row.

Using `keepdim=True` in operations like mean or variance calculation ensures that the output tensor retains the same number of dimensions as the input tensor, even though the operation reduces the tensor along the dimension specified via `dim`. For instance, without `keepdim=True`, the returned mean tensor would be a two-dimensional vector `[0.1324, 0.2170]` instead of a 2 × 1–dimensional matrix `[[0.1324], [0.2170]]`.

The `dim` parameter specifies the dimension along which the calculation of the statistic (here, mean or variance) should be performed in a tensor. As figure 4.6 explains, for

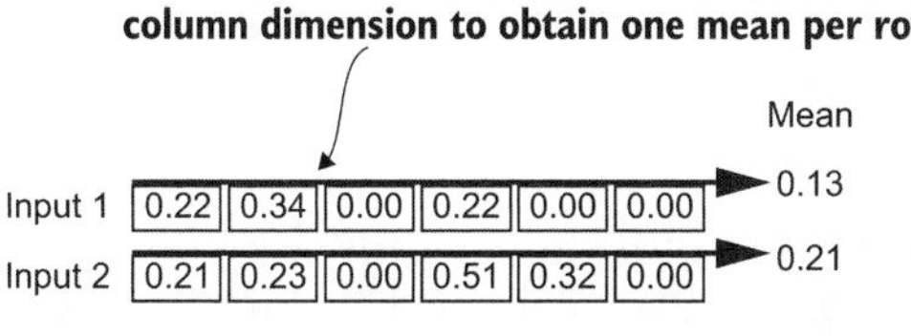

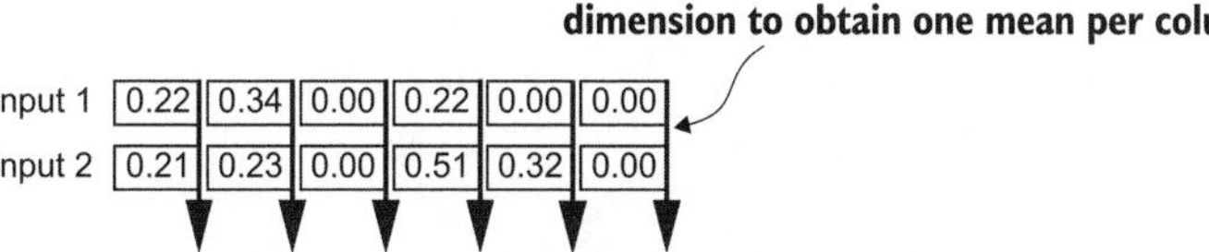

Figure 4.6 An illustration of the dim parameter when calculating the mean of a tensor. For instance, if we have a two-dimensional tensor (matrix) with dimensions `[rows, columns]`, using `dim=0` will perform the operation across rows (vertically, as shown at the bottom), resulting in an output that aggregates the data for each column. Using `dim=1` or `dim=-1` will perform the operation across columns (horizontally, as shown at the top), resulting in an output aggregating the data for each row.

a two-dimensional tensor (like a matrix), using `dim=-1` for operations such as mean or variance calculation is the same as using `dim=1`. This is because `-1` refers to the tensor's last dimension, which corresponds to the columns in a two-dimensional tensor. Later, when adding layer normalization to the GPT model, which produces three-dimensional tensors with the shape `[batch_size, num_tokens, embedding_size]`, we can still use `dim=-1` for normalization across the last dimension, avoiding a change from `dim=1` to `dim=2`.

Next, let's apply layer normalization to the layer outputs we obtained earlier. The operation consists of subtracting the mean and dividing by the square root of the variance (also known as the standard deviation):

```
out_norm = (out - mean) / torch.sqrt(var)
mean = out_norm.mean(dim=-1, keepdim=True)
var = out_norm.var(dim=-1, keepdim=True)
print("Normalized layer outputs:\n", out_norm)
print("Mean:\n", mean)
print("Variance:\n", var)
```

As we can see based on the results, the normalized layer outputs, which now also contain negative values, have 0 mean and a variance of 1:

```
Normalized layer outputs:
 tensor([[ 0.6159,  1.4126, -0.8719,  0.5872, -0.8719, -0.8719],
        [-0.0189,  0.1121, -1.0876,  1.5173,  0.5647, -1.0876]],
       grad_fn=<DivBackward0>)
Mean:
 tensor([[-5.9605e-08],
        [1.9868e-08]], grad_fn=<MeanBackward1>)
Variance:
 tensor([[1.],
        [1.]], grad_fn=<VarBackward0>)
```

Note that the value –5.9605e-08 in the output tensor is the scientific notation for -5.9605×10^{-8}, which is –0.000000059605 in decimal form. This value is very close to 0, but it is not exactly 0 due to small numerical errors that can accumulate because of the finite precision with which computers represent numbers.

To improve readability, we can also turn off the scientific notation when printing tensor values by setting `sci_mode` to `False`:

```
torch.set_printoptions(sci_mode=False)
print("Mean:\n", mean)
print("Variance:\n", var)
```

The output is

```
Mean:
 tensor([[    0.0000],
        [    0.0000]], grad_fn=<MeanBackward1>)
```

```
Variance:
 tensor([[1.],
        [1.]], grad_fn=<VarBackward0>)
```

So far, we have coded and applied layer normalization in a step-by-step process. Let's now encapsulate this process in a PyTorch module that we can use in the GPT model later.

Listing 4.2 A layer normalization class

```
class LayerNorm(nn.Module):
    def __init__(self, emb_dim):
        super().__init__()
        self.eps = 1e-5
        self.scale = nn.Parameter(torch.ones(emb_dim))
        self.shift = nn.Parameter(torch.zeros(emb_dim))

    def forward(self, x):
        mean = x.mean(dim=-1, keepdim=True)
        var = x.var(dim=-1, keepdim=True, unbiased=False)
        norm_x = (x - mean) / torch.sqrt(var + self.eps)
        return self.scale * norm_x + self.shift
```

This specific implementation of layer normalization operates on the last dimension of the input tensor x, which represents the embedding dimension (`emb_dim`). The variable `eps` is a small constant (epsilon) added to the variance to prevent division by zero during normalization. The `scale` and `shift` are two trainable parameters (of the same dimension as the input) that the LLM automatically adjusts during training if it is determined that doing so would improve the model's performance on its training task. This allows the model to learn appropriate scaling and shifting that best suit the data it is processing.

Biased variance

In our variance calculation method, we use an implementation detail by setting `unbiased=False`. For those curious about what this means, in the variance calculation, we divide by the number of inputs n in the variance formula. This approach does not apply Bessel's correction, which typically uses $n - 1$ instead of n in the denominator to adjust for bias in sample variance estimation. This decision results in a so-called biased estimate of the variance. For LLMs, where the embedding dimension n is significantly large, the difference between using n and $n - 1$ is practically negligible. I chose this approach to ensure compatibility with the GPT-2 model's normalization layers and because it reflects TensorFlow's default behavior, which was used to implement the original GPT-2 model. Using a similar setting ensures our method is compatible with the pretrained weights we will load in chapter 6.

Let's now try the `LayerNorm` module in practice and apply it to the batch input:

```
ln = LayerNorm(emb_dim=5)
out_ln = ln(batch_example)
mean = out_ln.mean(dim=-1, keepdim=True)
var = out_ln.var(dim=-1, unbiased=False, keepdim=True)
print("Mean:\n", mean)
print("Variance:\n", var)
```

The results show that the layer normalization code works as expected and normalizes the values of each of the two inputs such that they have a mean of 0 and a variance of 1:

```
Mean:
 tensor([[    -0.0000],
        [     0.0000]], grad_fn=<MeanBackward1>)
Variance:
 tensor([[1.0000],
        [1.0000]], grad_fn=<VarBackward0>)
```

We have now covered two of the building blocks we will need to implement the GPT architecture, as shown in figure 4.7. Next, we will look at the GELU activation function, which is one of the activation functions used in LLMs, instead of the traditional ReLU function we used previously.

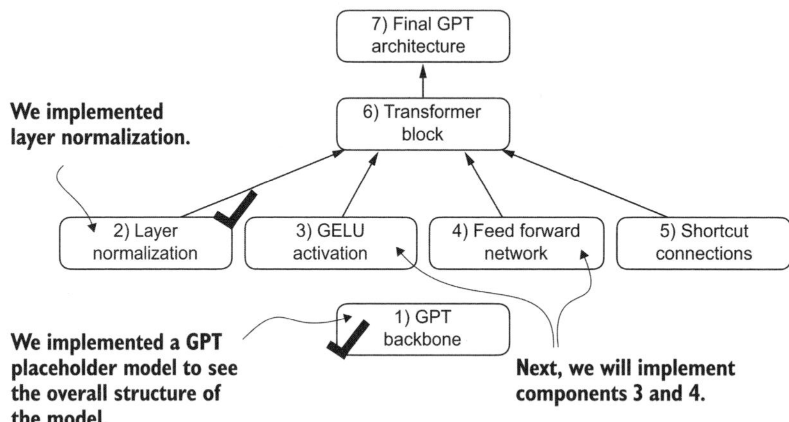

Figure 4.7 The building blocks necessary to build the GPT architecture. So far, we have completed the GPT backbone and layer normalization. Next, we will focus on GELU activation and the feed forward network.

Layer normalization vs. batch normalization

If you are familiar with batch normalization, a common and traditional normalization method for neural networks, you may wonder how it compares to layer normalization. Unlike batch normalization, which normalizes across the batch dimension, layer normalization normalizes across the feature dimension. LLMs often require significant computational resources, and the available hardware or the specific use case can dictate the batch size during training or inference. Since layer normalization normalizes each input independently of the batch size, it offers more flexibility and stability in these scenarios. This is particularly beneficial for distributed training or when deploying models in environments where resources are constrained.

4.3 Implementing a feed forward network with GELU activations

Next, we will implement a small neural network submodule used as part of the transformer block in LLMs. We begin by implementing the *GELU* activation function, which plays a crucial role in this neural network submodule.

NOTE For additional information on implementing neural networks in PyTorch, see section A.5 in appendix A.

Historically, the ReLU activation function has been commonly used in deep learning due to its simplicity and effectiveness across various neural network architectures. However, in LLMs, several other activation functions are employed beyond the traditional ReLU. Two notable examples are GELU (*Gaussian error linear unit*) and SwiGLU (*Swish-gated linear unit*).

GELU and SwiGLU are more complex and smooth activation functions incorporating Gaussian and sigmoid-gated linear units, respectively. They offer improved performance for deep learning models, unlike the simpler ReLU.

The GELU activation function can be implemented in several ways; the exact version is defined as GELU(x) = x⋅Φ(x), where Φ(x) is the cumulative distribution function of the standard Gaussian distribution. In practice, however, it's common to implement a computationally cheaper approximation (the original GPT-2 model was also trained with this approximation, which was found via curve fitting):

$$GELU(x) \approx 0.5 \cdot x \cdot \left(1 + tanh\left[\sqrt{\frac{2}{\pi}} \cdot \left(x + 0.044715 \cdot x^3\right)\right]\right)$$

In code, we can implement this function as a PyTorch module.

Listing 4.3 An implementation of the GELU activation function

```
class GELU(nn.Module):
    def __init__(self):
        super().__init__()

    def forward(self, x):
        return 0.5 * x * (1 + torch.tanh(
            torch.sqrt(torch.tensor(2.0 / torch.pi)) *
            (x + 0.044715 * torch.pow(x, 3))
        ))
```

Next, to get an idea of what this GELU function looks like and how it compares to the ReLU function, let's plot these functions side by side:

```
import matplotlib.pyplot as plt
gelu, relu = GELU(), nn.ReLU()

x = torch.linspace(-3, 3, 100)
y_gelu, y_relu = gelu(x), relu(x)
plt.figure(figsize=(8, 3))
for i, (y, label) in enumerate(zip([y_gelu, y_relu], ["GELU", "ReLU"]), 1):
    plt.subplot(1, 2, i)
    plt.plot(x, y)
    plt.title(f"{label} activation function")
    plt.xlabel("x")
    plt.ylabel(f"{label}(x)")
    plt.grid(True)
plt.tight_layout()
plt.show()
```

Creates 100 sample data points in the range –3 to 3

As we can see in the resulting plot in figure 4.8, ReLU (right) is a piecewise linear function that outputs the input directly if it is positive; otherwise, it outputs zero. GELU (left) is a smooth, nonlinear function that approximates ReLU but with a non-zero gradient for almost all negative values (except at approximately $x = -0.75$).

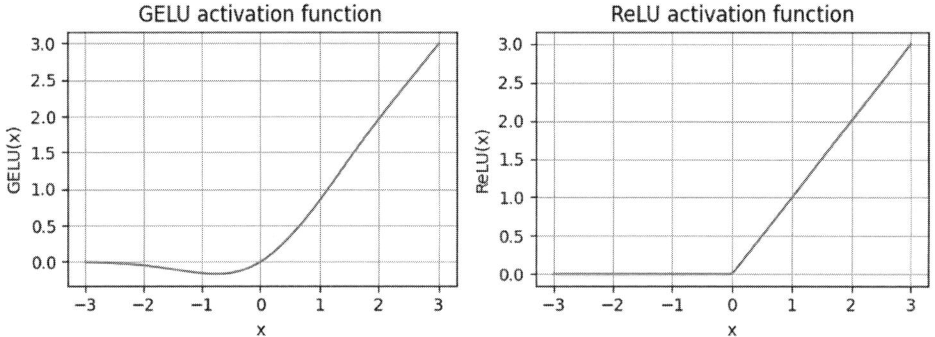

Figure 4.8 The output of the GELU and ReLU plots using matplotlib. The x-axis shows the function inputs and the y-axis shows the function outputs.

The smoothness of GELU can lead to better optimization properties during training, as it allows for more nuanced adjustments to the model's parameters. In contrast, ReLU has a sharp corner at zero (figure 4.18, right), which can sometimes make optimization harder, especially in networks that are very deep or have complex architectures. Moreover, unlike ReLU, which outputs zero for any negative input, GELU allows for a small, non-zero output for negative values. This characteristic means that during the training process, neurons that receive negative input can still contribute to the learning process, albeit to a lesser extent than positive inputs.

Next, let's use the GELU function to implement the small neural network module, `FeedForward`, that we will be using in the LLM's transformer block later.

Listing 4.4 A feed forward neural network module

```
class FeedForward(nn.Module):
    def __init__(self, cfg):
        super().__init__()
        self.layers = nn.Sequential(
            nn.Linear(cfg["emb_dim"], 4 * cfg["emb_dim"]),
            GELU(),
            nn.Linear(4 * cfg["emb_dim"], cfg["emb_dim"]),
        )

    def forward(self, x):
        return self.layers(x)
```

As we can see, the `FeedForward` module is a small neural network consisting of two `Linear` layers and a `GELU` activation function. In the 124-million-parameter GPT model, it receives the input batches with tokens that have an embedding size of 768 each via the `GPT_CONFIG_124M` dictionary where `GPT_CONFIG_ 124M["emb_dim"] = 768`. Figure 4.9 shows how the embedding size is manipulated inside this small feed forward neural network when we pass it some inputs.

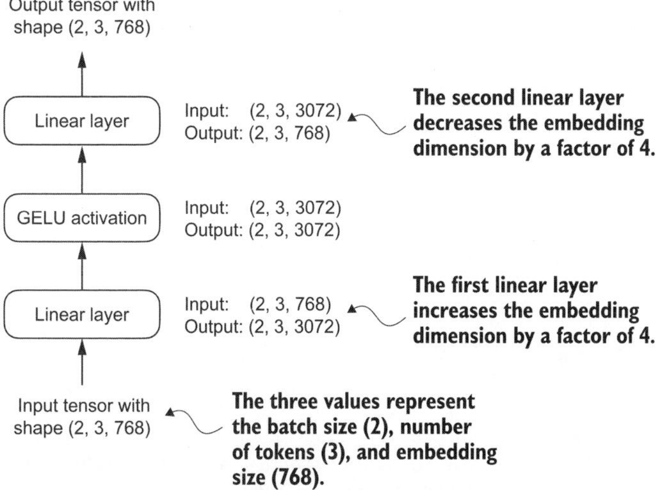

Figure 4.9 An overview of the connections between the layers of the feed forward neural network. This neural network can accommodate variable batch sizes and numbers of tokens in the input. However, the embedding size for each token is determined and fixed when initializing the weights.

Following the example in figure 4.9, let's initialize a new `FeedForward` module with a token embedding size of 768 and feed it a batch input with two samples and three tokens each:

```
ffn = FeedForward(GPT_CONFIG_124M)
x = torch.rand(2, 3, 768)          # Creates sample input with batch dimension 2
out = ffn(x)
print(out.shape)
```

As we can see, the shape of the output tensor is the same as that of the input tensor:

```
torch.Size([2, 3, 768])
```

The `FeedForward` module plays a crucial role in enhancing the model's ability to learn from and generalize the data. Although the input and output dimensions of this module are the same, it internally expands the embedding dimension into a higher-dimensional space through the first linear layer, as illustrated in figure 4.10. This expansion is followed by a nonlinear GELU activation and then a contraction back to the original dimension with the second linear transformation. Such a design allows for the exploration of a richer representation space.

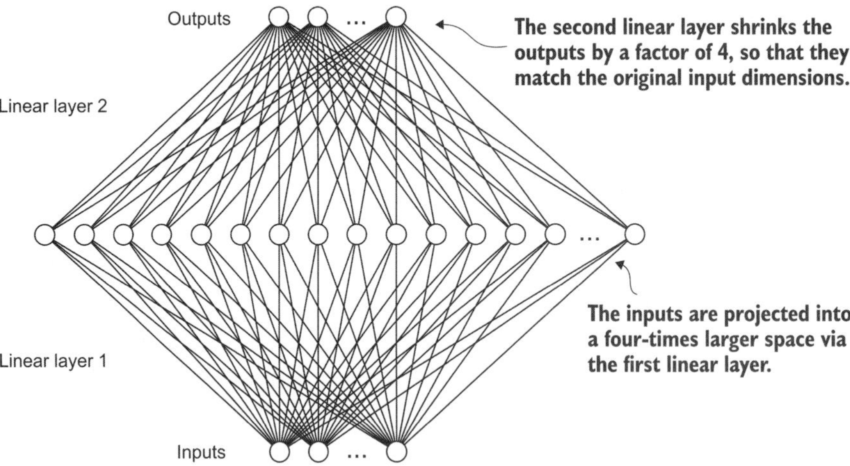

Figure 4.10 An illustration of the expansion and contraction of the layer outputs in the feed forward neural network. First, the inputs expand by a factor of 4 from 768 to 3,072 values. Then, the second layer compresses the 3,072 values back into a 768-dimensional representation.

Moreover, the uniformity in input and output dimensions simplifies the architecture by enabling the stacking of multiple layers, as we will do later, without the need to adjust dimensions between them, thus making the model more scalable.

As figure 4.11 shows, we have now implemented most of the LLM's building blocks. Next, we will go over the concept of shortcut connections that we insert between different layers of a neural network, which are important for improving the training performance in deep neural network architectures.

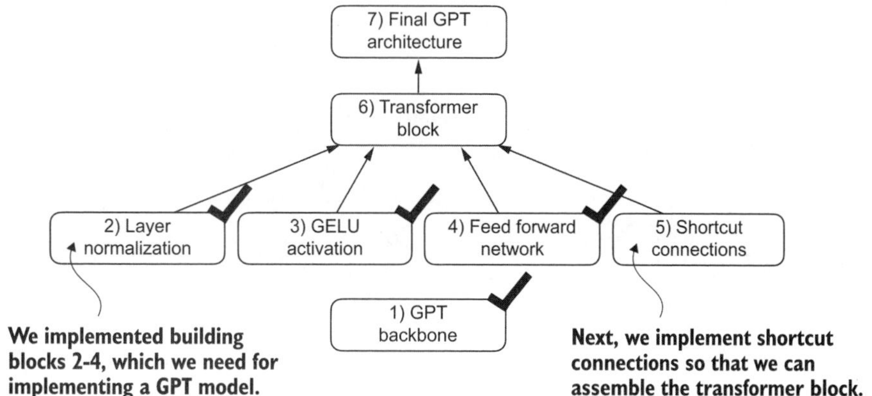

Figure 4.11 The building blocks necessary to build the GPT architecture. The black checkmarks indicating those we have already covered.

4.4 Adding shortcut connections

Let's discuss the concept behind *shortcut connections*, also known as skip or residual connections. Originally, shortcut connections were proposed for deep networks in computer vision (specifically, in residual networks) to mitigate the challenge of vanishing gradients. The vanishing gradient problem refers to the issue where gradients (which guide weight updates during training) become progressively smaller as they propagate backward through the layers, making it difficult to effectively train earlier layers.

Figure 4.12 shows that a shortcut connection creates an alternative, shorter path for the gradient to flow through the network by skipping one or more layers, which is achieved by adding the output of one layer to the output of a later layer. This is why these connections are also known as skip connections. They play a crucial role in preserving the flow of gradients during the backward pass in training.

In the following list, we implement the neural network in figure 4.12 to see how we can add shortcut connections in the `forward` method.

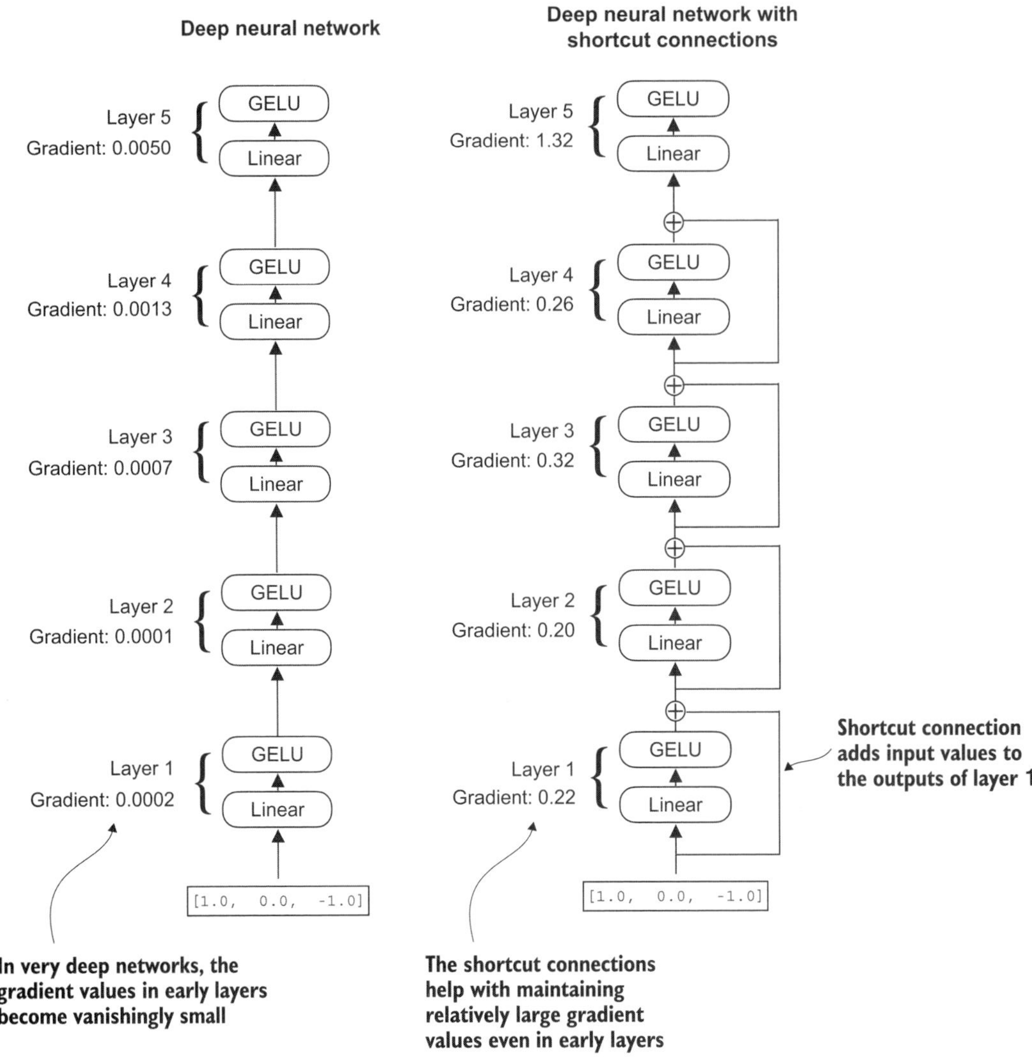

Figure 4.12 A comparison between a deep neural network consisting of five layers without (left) and with shortcut connections (right). Shortcut connections involve adding the inputs of a layer to its outputs, effectively creating an alternate path that bypasses certain layers. The gradients denote the mean absolute gradient at each layer, which we compute in listing 4.5.

Listing 4.5 A neural network to illustrate shortcut connections

```
class ExampleDeepNeuralNetwork(nn.Module):
    def __init__(self, layer_sizes, use_shortcut):
        super().__init__()
        self.use_shortcut = use_shortcut
        self.layers = nn.ModuleList([          # Implements five layers
```

```
            nn.Sequential(nn.Linear(layer_sizes[0], layer_sizes[1]),
                          GELU()),
            nn.Sequential(nn.Linear(layer_sizes[1], layer_sizes[2]),
                          GELU()),
            nn.Sequential(nn.Linear(layer_sizes[2], layer_sizes[3]),
                          GELU()),
            nn.Sequential(nn.Linear(layer_sizes[3], layer_sizes[4]),
                          GELU()),
            nn.Sequential(nn.Linear(layer_sizes[4], layer_sizes[5]),
                          GELU())
        ])

    def forward(self, x):
        for layer in self.layers:
            layer_output = layer(x)          # Compute the output of the current layer
            if self.use_shortcut and x.shape == layer_output.shape:    # Check if shortcut can be applied
                x = x + layer_output
            else:
                x = layer_output
        return x
```

The code implements a deep neural network with five layers, each consisting of a `Linear` layer and a `GELU` activation function. In the forward pass, we iteratively pass the input through the layers and optionally add the shortcut connections if the `self.use_shortcut` attribute is set to `True`.

Let's use this code to initialize a neural network without shortcut connections. Each layer will be initialized such that it accepts an example with three input values and returns three output values. The last layer returns a single output value:

```
layer_sizes = [3, 3, 3, 3, 3, 1]
sample_input = torch.tensor([[1., 0., -1.]])
torch.manual_seed(123)        # Specifies random seed for the initial weights for reproducibility
model_without_shortcut = ExampleDeepNeuralNetwork(
    layer_sizes, use_shortcut=False
)
```

Next, we implement a function that computes the gradients in the model's backward pass:

```
def print_gradients(model, x):
    output = model(x)         # Forward pass
    target = torch.tensor([[0.]])

    loss = nn.MSELoss()
    loss = loss(output, target)       # Calculates loss based on how close the target and output are

    loss.backward()        # Backward pass to calculate the gradients
```

```
    for name, param in model.named_parameters():
        if 'weight' in name:
            print(f"{name} has gradient mean of {param.grad.abs().mean().item()}")
```

This code specifies a loss function that computes how close the model output and a user-specified target (here, for simplicity, the value 0) are. Then, when calling `loss.backward()`, PyTorch computes the loss gradient for each layer in the model. We can iterate through the weight parameters via `model.named_parameters()`. Suppose we have a 3 × 3 weight parameter matrix for a given layer. In that case, this layer will have 3 × 3 gradient values, and we print the mean absolute gradient of these 3 × 3 gradient values to obtain a single gradient value per layer to compare the gradients between layers more easily.

In short, the `.backward()` method is a convenient method in PyTorch that computes loss gradients, which are required during model training, without implementing the math for the gradient calculation ourselves, thereby making working with deep neural networks much more accessible.

NOTE If you are unfamiliar with the concept of gradients and neural network training, I recommend reading sections A.4 and A.7 in appendix A.

Let's now use the `print_gradients` function and apply it to the model without skip connections:

```
print_gradients(model_without_shortcut, sample_input)
```

The output is

```
layers.0.0.weight has gradient mean of 0.00020173587836325169
layers.1.0.weight has gradient mean of 0.0001201116101583466
layers.2.0.weight has gradient mean of 0.0007152041653171182
layers.3.0.weight has gradient mean of 0.001398873864673078
layers.4.0.weight has gradient mean of 0.005049646366387606
```

The output of the `print_gradients` function shows, the gradients become smaller as we progress from the last layer (`layers.4`) to the first layer (`layers.0`), which is a phenomenon called the *vanishing gradient problem*.

Let's now instantiate a model with skip connections and see how it compares:

```
torch.manual_seed(123)
model_with_shortcut = ExampleDeepNeuralNetwork(
    layer_sizes, use_shortcut=True
)
print_gradients(model_with_shortcut, sample_input)
```

The output is

```
layers.0.0.weight has gradient mean of 0.22169792652130127
layers.1.0.weight has gradient mean of 0.20694105327129364
layers.2.0.weight has gradient mean of 0.32896995544433594
layers.3.0.weight has gradient mean of 0.2665732502937317
layers.4.0.weight has gradient mean of 1.3258541822433472
```

The last layer (`layers.4`) still has a larger gradient than the other layers. However, the gradient value stabilizes as we progress toward the first layer (`layers.0`) and doesn't shrink to a vanishingly small value.

In conclusion, shortcut connections are important for overcoming the limitations posed by the vanishing gradient problem in deep neural networks. Shortcut connections are a core building block of very large models such as LLMs, and they will help facilitate more effective training by ensuring consistent gradient flow across layers when we train the GPT model in the next chapter.

Next, we'll connect all of the previously covered concepts (layer normalization, GELU activations, feed forward module, and shortcut connections) in a transformer block, which is the final building block we need to code the GPT architecture.

4.5 Connecting attention and linear layers in a transformer block

Now, let's implement the *transformer block*, a fundamental building block of GPT and other LLM architectures. This block, which is repeated a dozen times in the 124-million-parameter GPT-2 architecture, combines several concepts we have previously covered: multi-head attention, layer normalization, dropout, feed forward layers, and GELU activations. Later, we will connect this transformer block to the remaining parts of the GPT architecture.

Figure 4.13 shows a transformer block that combines several components, including the masked multi-head attention module (see chapter 3) and the `FeedForward` module we previously implemented (see section 4.3). When a transformer block processes an input sequence, each element in the sequence (for example, a word or subword token) is represented by a fixed-size vector (in this case, 768 dimensions). The operations within the transformer block, including multi-head attention and feed forward layers, are designed to transform these vectors in a way that preserves their dimensionality.

The idea is that the self-attention mechanism in the multi-head attention block identifies and analyzes relationships between elements in the input sequence. In contrast, the feed forward network modifies the data individually at each position. This combination not only enables a more nuanced understanding and processing of the input but also enhances the model's overall capacity for handling complex data patterns.

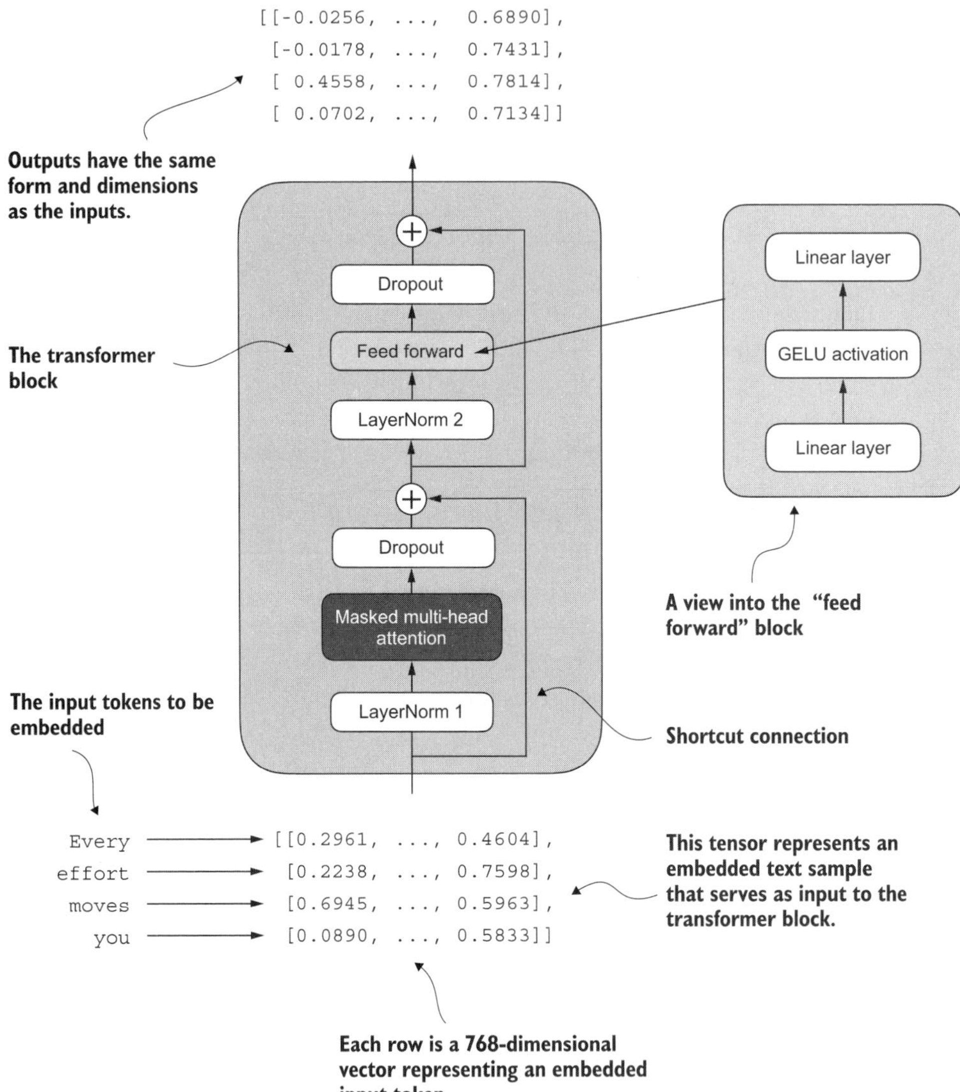

Figure 4.13 An illustration of a transformer block. Input tokens have been embedded into 768-dimensional vectors. Each row corresponds to one token's vector representation. The outputs of the transformer block are vectors of the same dimension as the input, which can then be fed into subsequent layers in an LLM.

We can create the `TransformerBlock` in code.

Listing 4.6 The transformer block component of GPT

```
from chapter03 import MultiHeadAttention

class TransformerBlock(nn.Module):
    def __init__(self, cfg):
        super().__init__()
        self.att = MultiHeadAttention(
            d_in=cfg["emb_dim"],
            d_out=cfg["emb_dim"],
            context_length=cfg["context_length"],
            num_heads=cfg["n_heads"],
            dropout=cfg["drop_rate"],
            qkv_bias=cfg["qkv_bias"])
        self.ff = FeedForward(cfg)
        self.norm1 = LayerNorm(cfg["emb_dim"])
        self.norm2 = LayerNorm(cfg["emb_dim"])
        self.drop_shortcut = nn.Dropout(cfg["drop_rate"])

    def forward(self, x):
                                            # Shortcut connection for attention block
        shortcut = x
        x = self.norm1(x)
        x = self.att(x)
        x = self.drop_shortcut(x)
        x = x + shortcut                    # Add the original input back

        shortcut = x                        # Shortcut connection for feed forward block
        x = self.norm2(x)
        x = self.ff(x)
        x = self.drop_shortcut(x)
        x = x + shortcut                    # Adds the original input back
        return x
```

The given code defines a `TransformerBlock` class in PyTorch that includes a multi-head attention mechanism (`MultiHeadAttention`) and a feed forward network (`FeedForward`), both configured based on a provided configuration dictionary (`cfg`), such as `GPT_CONFIG_124M`.

Layer normalization (`LayerNorm`) is applied before each of these two components, and dropout is applied after them to regularize the model and prevent overfitting. This is also known as *Pre-LayerNorm*. Older architectures, such as the original transformer model, applied layer normalization after the self-attention and feed forward networks instead, known as *Post-LayerNorm*, which often leads to worse training dynamics.

The class also implements the forward pass, where each component is followed by a shortcut connection that adds the input of the block to its output. This critical feature helps gradients flow through the network during training and improves the learning of deep models (see section 4.4).

Using the `GPT_CONFIG_124M` dictionary we defined earlier, let's instantiate a transformer block and feed it some sample data:

```
torch.manual_seed(123)
x = torch.rand(2, 4, 768)
block = TransformerBlock(GPT_CONFIG_124M)
output = block(x)

print("Input shape:", x.shape)
print("Output shape:", output.shape)
```

Creates sample input of shape [batch_size, num_tokens, emb_dim]

The output is

```
Input shape: torch.Size([2, 4, 768])
Output shape: torch.Size([2, 4, 768])
```

As we can see, the transformer block maintains the input dimensions in its output, indicating that the transformer architecture processes sequences of data without altering their shape throughout the network.

The preservation of shape throughout the transformer block architecture is not incidental but a crucial aspect of its design. This design enables its effective application across a wide range of sequence-to-sequence tasks, where each output vector directly corresponds to an input vector, maintaining a one-to-one relationship. However, the output is a context vector that encapsulates information from the entire input sequence (see chapter 3). This means that while the physical dimensions of the sequence (length and feature size) remain unchanged as it passes through the transformer block, the content of each output vector is re-encoded to integrate contextual information from across the entire input sequence.

With the transformer block implemented, we now have all the building blocks needed to implement the GPT architecture. As illustrated in figure 4.14, the transformer block combines layer normalization, the feed forward network, GELU activations, and shortcut connections. As we will eventually see, this transformer block will make up the main component of the GPT architecture.

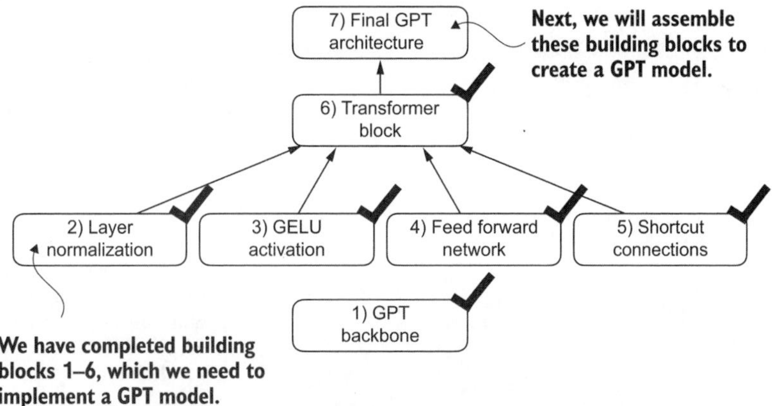

Figure 4.14 The building blocks necessary to build the GPT architecture. The black checks indicate the blocks we have completed.

4.6 Coding the GPT model

We started this chapter with a big-picture overview of a GPT architecture that we called `DummyGPTModel`. In this `DummyGPTModel` code implementation, we showed the input and outputs to the GPT model, but its building blocks remained a black box using a `DummyTransformerBlock` and `DummyLayerNorm` class as placeholders.

Let's now replace the `DummyTransformerBlock` and `DummyLayerNorm` placeholders with the real `TransformerBlock` and `LayerNorm` classes we coded previously to assemble a fully working version of the original 124-million-parameter version of GPT-2. In chapter 5, we will pretrain a GPT-2 model, and in chapter 6, we will load in the pretrained weights from OpenAI.

Before we assemble the GPT-2 model in code, let's look at its overall structure, as shown in figure 4.15, which includes all the concepts we have covered so far. As we can see, the transformer block is repeated many times throughout a GPT model architecture. In the case of the 124-million-parameter GPT-2 model, it's repeated 12 times, which we specify via the `n_layers` entry in the `GPT_CONFIG_124M` dictionary. This transform block is repeated 48 times in the largest GPT-2 model with 1,542 million parameters.

The output from the final transformer block then goes through a final layer normalization step before reaching the linear output layer. This layer maps the transformer's output to a high-dimensional space (in this case, 50,257 dimensions, corresponding to the model's vocabulary size) to predict the next token in the sequence.

Let's now code the architecture in figure 4.15.

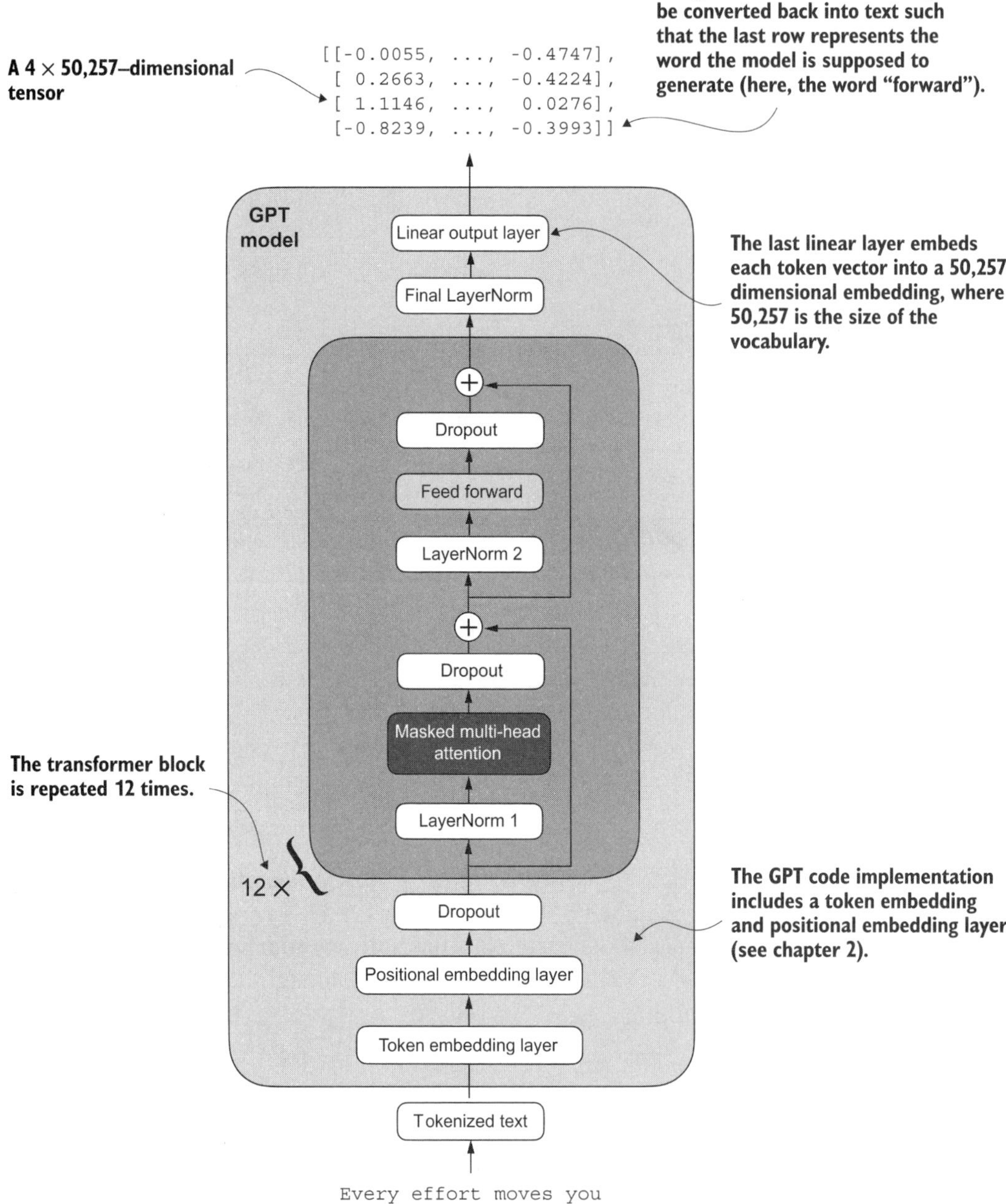
A 4 × 50,257–dimensional tensor
[[-0.0055, ..., -0.4747],
[0.2663, ..., -0.4224],
[1.1146, ..., 0.0276],
[-0.8239, ..., -0.3993]]
The goal is for these embeddings to be converted back into text such that the last row represents the word the model is supposed to generate (here, the word "forward").
GPT model
Linear output layer
The last linear layer embeds each token vector into a 50,257-dimensional embedding, where 50,257 is the size of the vocabulary.
Final LayerNorm
Dropout
Feed forward
LayerNorm 2
Dropout
Masked multi-head attention
LayerNorm 1
The transformer block is repeated 12 times.
12 ×
Dropout
The GPT code implementation includes a token embedding and positional embedding layer (see chapter 2).
Positional embedding layer
Token embedding layer
Tokenized text
Every effort moves you

Figure 4.15 An overview of the GPT model architecture showing the flow of data through the GPT model. Starting from the bottom, tokenized text is first converted into token embeddings, which are then augmented with positional embeddings. This combined information forms a tensor that is passed through a series of transformer blocks shown in the center (each containing multi-head attention and feed forward neural network layers with dropout and layer normalization), which are stacked on top of each other and repeated 12 times.

Listing 4.7 The GPT model architecture implementation

```
class GPTModel(nn.Module):
    def __init__(self, cfg):
        super().__init__()
        self.tok_emb = nn.Embedding(cfg["vocab_size"], cfg["emb_dim"])
        self.pos_emb = nn.Embedding(cfg["context_length"], cfg["emb_dim"])
        self.drop_emb = nn.Dropout(cfg["drop_rate"])

        self.trf_blocks = nn.Sequential(
            *[TransformerBlock(cfg) for _ in range(cfg["n_layers"])])

        self.final_norm = LayerNorm(cfg["emb_dim"])
        self.out_head = nn.Linear(
            cfg["emb_dim"], cfg["vocab_size"], bias=False
        )

    def forward(self, in_idx):
        batch_size, seq_len = in_idx.shape
        tok_embeds = self.tok_emb(in_idx)

        pos_embeds = self.pos_emb(
            torch.arange(seq_len, device=in_idx.device)
        )
        x = tok_embeds + pos_embeds
        x = self.drop_emb(x)
        x = self.trf_blocks(x)
        x = self.final_norm(x)
        logits = self.out_head(x)
        return logits
```

The device setting will allow us to train the model on a CPU or GPU, depending on which device the input data sits on.

Thanks to the `TransformerBlock` class, the `GPTModel` class is relatively small and compact.

The `__init__` constructor of this `GPTModel` class initializes the token and positional embedding layers using the configurations passed in via a Python dictionary, `cfg`. These embedding layers are responsible for converting input token indices into dense vectors and adding positional information (see chapter 2).

Next, the `__init__` method creates a sequential stack of `TransformerBlock` modules equal to the number of layers specified in `cfg`. Following the transformer blocks, a `LayerNorm` layer is applied, standardizing the outputs from the transformer blocks to stabilize the learning process. Finally, a linear output head without bias is defined, which projects the transformer's output into the vocabulary space of the tokenizer to generate logits for each token in the vocabulary.

The forward method takes a batch of input token indices, computes their embeddings, applies the positional embeddings, passes the sequence through the transformer blocks, normalizes the final output, and then computes the logits, representing the next token's unnormalized probabilities. We will convert these logits into tokens and text outputs in the next section.

Let's now initialize the 124-million-parameter GPT model using the `GPT_CONFIG_124M` dictionary we pass into the `cfg` parameter and feed it with the batch text input we previously created:

```
torch.manual_seed(123)
model = GPTModel(GPT_CONFIG_124M)

out = model(batch)
print("Input batch:\n", batch)
print("\nOutput shape:", out.shape)
print(out)
```

This code prints the contents of the input batch followed by the output tensor:

```
Input batch:
 tensor([[6109,  3626,  6100,   345],      <-- Token IDs of text 1
         [6109,  1110,  6622,   257]])     <-- Token IDs of text 2

Output shape: torch.Size([2, 4, 50257])
tensor([[[ 0.3613,  0.4222, -0.0711,  ...,  0.3483,  0.4661, -0.2838],
         [-0.1792, -0.5660, -0.9485,  ...,  0.0477,  0.5181, -0.3168],
         [ 0.7120,  0.0332,  0.1085,  ...,  0.1018, -0.4327, -0.2553],
         [-1.0076,  0.3418, -0.1190,  ...,  0.7195,  0.4023,  0.0532]],

        [[-0.2564,  0.0900,  0.0335,  ...,  0.2659,  0.4454, -0.6806],
         [ 0.1230,  0.3653, -0.2074,  ...,  0.7705,  0.2710,  0.2246],
         [ 1.0558,  1.0318, -0.2800,  ...,  0.6936,  0.3205, -0.3178],
         [-0.1565,  0.3926,  0.3288,  ...,  1.2630, -0.1858,  0.0388]]],
       grad_fn=<UnsafeViewBackward0>)
```

As we can see, the output tensor has the shape `[2, 4, 50257]`, since we passed in two input texts with four tokens each. The last dimension, `50257`, corresponds to the vocabulary size of the tokenizer. Later, we will see how to convert each of these 50,257-dimensional output vectors back into tokens.

Before we move on to coding the function that converts the model outputs into text, let's spend a bit more time with the model architecture itself and analyze its size. Using the `numel()` method, short for "number of elements," we can collect the total number of parameters in the model's parameter tensors:

```
total_params = sum(p.numel() for p in model.parameters())
print(f"Total number of parameters: {total_params:,}")
```

The result is

```
Total number of parameters: 163,009,536
```

Now, a curious reader might notice a discrepancy. Earlier, we spoke of initializing a 124-million-parameter GPT model, so why is the actual number of parameters 163 million?

The reason is a concept called *weight tying*, which was used in the original GPT-2 architecture. It means that the original GPT-2 architecture reuses the weights from the token embedding layer in its output layer. To understand better, let's take a look at the shapes of the token embedding layer and linear output layer that we initialized on the `model` via the `GPTModel` earlier:

```
print("Token embedding layer shape:", model.tok_emb.weight.shape)
print("Output layer shape:", model.out_head.weight.shape)
```

As we can see from the print outputs, the weight tensors for both these layers have the same shape:

```
Token embedding layer shape: torch.Size([50257, 768])
Output layer shape: torch.Size([50257, 768])
```

The token embedding and output layers are very large due to the number of rows for the 50,257 in the tokenizer's vocabulary. Let's remove the output layer parameter count from the total GPT-2 model count according to the weight tying:

```
total_params_gpt2 = (
    total_params - sum(p.numel()
    for p in model.out_head.parameters())
)
print(f"Number of trainable parameters "
      f"considering weight tying: {total_params_gpt2:,}"
)
```

The output is

```
Number of trainable parameters considering weight tying: 124,412,160
```

As we can see, the model is now only 124 million parameters large, matching the original size of the GPT-2 model.

Weight tying reduces the overall memory footprint and computational complexity of the model. However, in my experience, using separate token embedding and output layers results in better training and model performance; hence, we use separate layers in our `GPTModel` implementation. The same is true for modern LLMs. However, we will revisit and implement the weight tying concept later in chapter 6 when we load the pretrained weights from OpenAI.

Exercise 4.1 Number of parameters in feed forward and attention modules

Calculate and compare the number of parameters that are contained in the feed forward module and those that are contained in the multi-head attention module.

Lastly, let's compute the memory requirements of the 163 million parameters in our `GPTModel` object:

```
total_size_bytes = total_params * 4
total_size_mb = total_size_bytes / (1024 * 1024)
print(f"Total size of the model: {total_size_mb:.2f} MB")
```

Calculates the total size in bytes (assuming float32, 4 bytes per parameter)

Converts to megabytes

The result is

```
Total size of the model: 621.83 MB
```

In conclusion, by calculating the memory requirements for the 163 million parameters in our `GPTModel` object and assuming each parameter is a 32-bit float taking up 4 bytes, we find that the total size of the model amounts to 621.83 MB, illustrating the relatively large storage capacity required to accommodate even relatively small LLMs.

Now that we've implemented the `GPTModel` architecture and saw that it outputs numeric tensors of shape `[batch_size, num_tokens, vocab_size]`, let's write the code to convert these output tensors into text.

Exercise 4.2 Initializing larger GPT models

We initialized a 124-million-parameter GPT model, which is known as "GPT-2 small." Without making any code modifications besides updating the configuration file, use the `GPTModel` class to implement GPT-2 medium (using 1,024-dimensional embeddings, 24 transformer blocks, 16 multi-head attention heads), GPT-2 large (1,280-dimensional embeddings, 36 transformer blocks, 20 multi-head attention heads), and GPT-2 XL (1,600-dimensional embeddings, 48 transformer blocks, 25 multi-head attention heads). As a bonus, calculate the total number of parameters in each GPT model.

4.7 Generating text

We will now implement the code that converts the tensor outputs of the GPT model back into text. Before we get started, let's briefly review how a generative model like an LLM generates text one word (or token) at a time.

Figure 4.16 illustrates the step-by-step process by which a GPT model generates text given an input context, such as "Hello, I am." With each iteration, the input context grows, allowing the model to generate coherent and contextually appropriate text. By the sixth iteration, the model has constructed a complete sentence: "Hello, I am a model ready to help." We've seen that our current `GPTModel` implementation outputs tensors with shape `[batch_size, num_token, vocab_size]`. Now the question is: How does a GPT model go from these output tensors to the generated text?

The process by which a GPT model goes from output tensors to generated text involves several steps, as illustrated in figure 4.17. These steps include decoding the

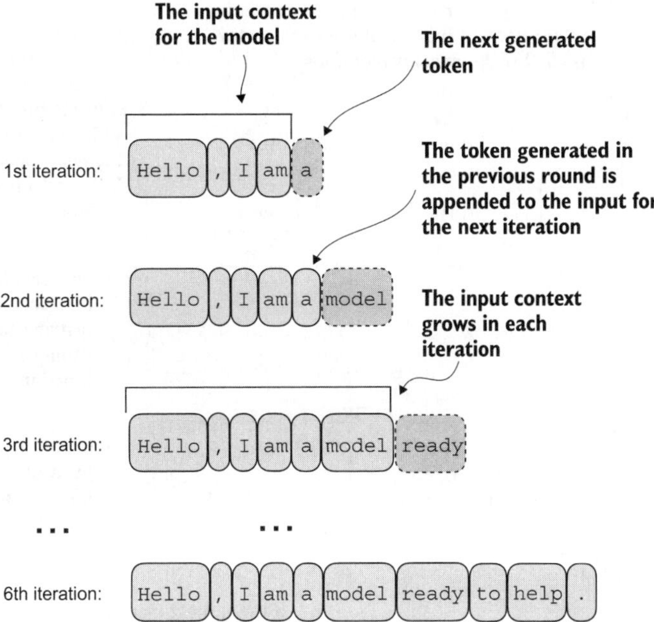

Figure 4.16 The step-by-step process by which an LLM generates text, one token at a time. Starting with an initial input context ("Hello, I am"), the model predicts a subsequent token during each iteration, appending it to the input context for the next round of prediction. As shown, the first iteration adds "a," the second "model," and the third "ready," progressively building the sentence.

output tensors, selecting tokens based on a probability distribution, and converting these tokens into human-readable text.

The next-token generation process detailed in figure 4.17 illustrates a single step where the GPT model generates the next token given its input. In each step, the model outputs a matrix with vectors representing potential next tokens. The vector corresponding to the next token is extracted and converted into a probability distribution via the `softmax` function. Within the vector containing the resulting probability scores, the index of the highest value is located, which translates to the token ID. This token ID is then decoded back into text, producing the next token in the sequence. Finally, this token is appended to the previous inputs, forming a new input sequence for the subsequent iteration. This step-by-step process enables the model to generate text sequentially, building coherent phrases and sentences from the initial input context.

In practice, we repeat this process over many iterations, such as shown in figure 4.16, until we reach a user-specified number of generated tokens. In code, we can implement the token-generation process as shown in the following listing.

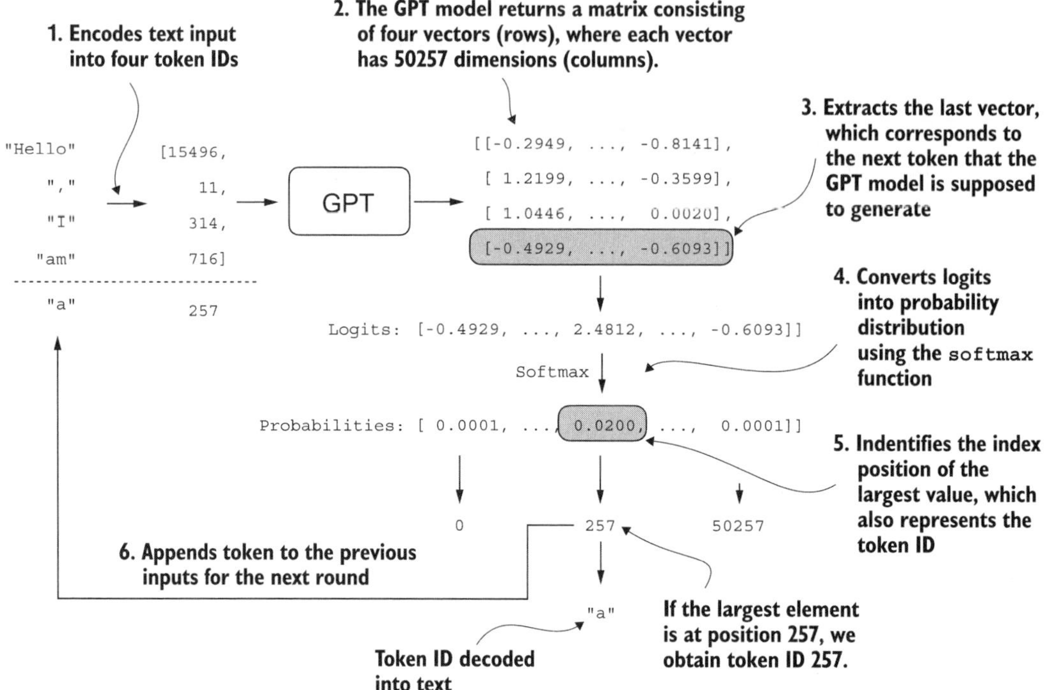

Figure 4.17 The mechanics of text generation in a GPT model by showing a single iteration in the token generation process. The process begins by encoding the input text into token IDs, which are then fed into the GPT model. The outputs of the model are then converted back into text and appended to the original input text.

Listing 4.8 A function for the GPT model to generate text

```
def generate_text_simple(model, idx,
                         max_new_tokens, context_size):
    for _ in range(max_new_tokens):
        idx_cond = idx[:, -context_size:]
        with torch.no_grad():
            logits = model(idx_cond)

        logits = logits[:, -1, :]
        probas = torch.softmax(logits, dim=-1)
        idx_next = torch.argmax(probas, dim=-1, keepdim=True)
        idx = torch.cat((idx, idx_next), dim=1)

    return idx
```

- idx is a (batch, n_tokens) array of indices in the current context.
- Crops current context if it exceeds the supported context size, e.g., if LLM supports only 5 tokens, and the context size is 10, then only the last 5 tokens are used as context
- Focuses only on the last time step, so that (batch, n_token, vocab_size) becomes (batch, vocab_size)
- probas has shape (batch, vocab_size).
- idx_next has shape (batch, 1).
- Appends sampled index to the running sequence, where idx has shape (batch, n_tokens+1)

This code demonstrates a simple implementation of a generative loop for a language model using PyTorch. It iterates for a specified number of new tokens to be generated, crops the current context to fit the model's maximum context size, computes predictions, and then selects the next token based on the highest probability prediction.

To code the `generate_text_simple` function, we use a `softmax` function to convert the logits into a probability distribution from which we identify the position with the highest value via `torch.argmax`. The `softmax` function is monotonic, meaning it preserves the order of its inputs when transformed into outputs. So, in practice, the softmax step is redundant since the position with the highest score in the softmax output tensor is the same position in the logit tensor. In other words, we could apply the `torch.argmax` function to the logits tensor directly and get identical results. However, I provide the code for the conversion to illustrate the full process of transforming logits to probabilities, which can add additional intuition so that the model generates the most likely next token, which is known as *greedy decoding*.

When we implement the GPT training code in the next chapter, we will use additional sampling techniques to modify the softmax outputs such that the model doesn't always select the most likely token. This introduces variability and creativity in the generated text.

This process of generating one token ID at a time and appending it to the context using the `generate_text_simple` function is further illustrated in figure 4.18. (The token ID generation process for each iteration is detailed in figure 4.17.) We generate the token IDs in an iterative fashion. For instance, in iteration 1, the model is provided with the tokens corresponding to "Hello, I am," predicts the next token (with ID 257, which is "a"), and appends it to the input. This process is repeated until the model produces the complete sentence "Hello, I am a model ready to help" after six iterations.

Let's now try out the `generate_text_simple` function with the `"Hello, I am"` context as model input. First, we encode the input context into token IDs:

```
start_context = "Hello, I am"
encoded = tokenizer.encode(start_context)
print("encoded:", encoded)
encoded_tensor = torch.tensor(encoded).unsqueeze(0)    # Adds batch dimension
print("encoded_tensor.shape:", encoded_tensor.shape)
```

The encoded IDs are

```
encoded: [15496, 11, 314, 716]
encoded_tensor.shape: torch.Size([1, 4])
```

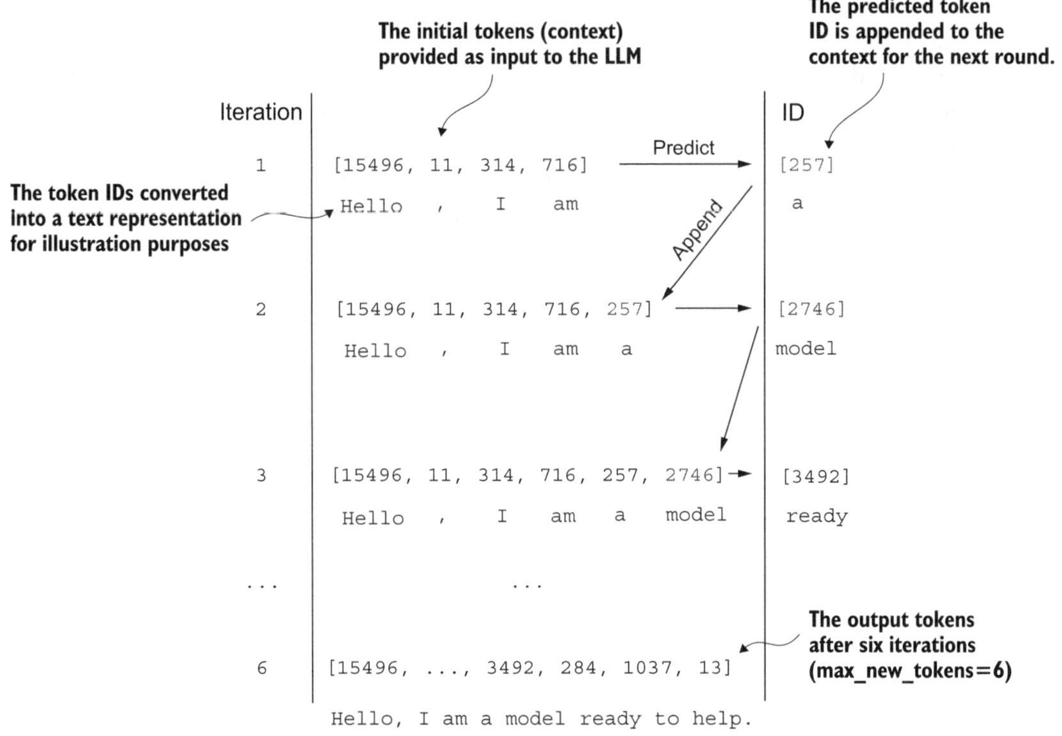

Figure 4.18 The six iterations of a token prediction cycle, where the model takes a sequence of initial token IDs as input, predicts the next token, and appends this token to the input sequence for the next iteration. (The token IDs are also translated into their corresponding text for better understanding.)

Next, we put the model into `.eval()` mode. This disables random components like dropout, which are only used during training, and use the `generate_text_simple` function on the encoded input tensor:

```
model.eval()                                    # Disables dropout since we are not training the model
out = generate_text_simple(
    model=model,
    idx=encoded_tensor,
    max_new_tokens=6,
    context_size=GPT_CONFIG_124M["context_length"]
)
print("Output:", out)
print("Output length:", len(out[0]))
```

The resulting output token IDs are

```
Output: tensor([[15496,    11,   314,   716, 27018, 24086, 47843,
30961, 42348,  7267]])
Output length: 10
```

Using the `.decode` method of the tokenizer, we can convert the IDs back into text:

```
decoded_text = tokenizer.decode(out.squeeze(0).tolist())
print(decoded_text)
```

The model output in text format is

```
Hello, I am Featureiman Byeswickattribute argue
```

As we can see, the model generated gibberish, which is not at all like the coherent text `Hello, I am a model ready to help`. What happened? The reason the model is unable to produce coherent text is that we haven't trained it yet. So far, we have only implemented the GPT architecture and initialized a GPT model instance with initial random weights. Model training is a large topic in itself, and we will tackle it in the next chapter.

Exercise 4.3 Using separate dropout parameters

At the beginning of this chapter, we defined a global `drop_rate` setting in the `GPT_CONFIG_124M` dictionary to set the dropout rate in various places throughout the `GPTModel` architecture. Change the code to specify a separate dropout value for the various dropout layers throughout the model architecture. (Hint: there are three distinct places where we used dropout layers: the embedding layer, shortcut layer, and multi-head attention module.)

Summary

- Layer normalization stabilizes training by ensuring that each layer's outputs have a consistent mean and variance.
- Shortcut connections are connections that skip one or more layers by feeding the output of one layer directly to a deeper layer, which helps mitigate the vanishing gradient problem when training deep neural networks, such as LLMs.
- Transformer blocks are a core structural component of GPT models, combining masked multi-head attention modules with fully connected feed forward networks that use the GELU activation function.
- GPT models are LLMs with many repeated transformer blocks that have millions to billions of parameters.
- GPT models come in various sizes, for example, 124, 345, 762, and 1,542 million parameters, which we can implement with the same `GPTModel` Python class.
- The text-generation capability of a GPT-like LLM involves decoding output tensors into human-readable text by sequentially predicting one token at a time based on a given input context.
- Without training, a GPT model generates incoherent text, which underscores the importance of model training for coherent text generation.

5 Pretraining on unlabeled data

This chapter covers

- Computing the training and validation set losses to assess the quality of LLM-generated text during training
- Implementing a training function and pretraining the LLM
- Saving and loading model weights to continue training an LLM
- Loading pretrained weights from OpenAI

Thus far, we have implemented the data sampling and attention mechanism and coded the LLM architecture. It is now time to implement a training function and pretrain the LLM. We will learn about basic model evaluation techniques to measure the quality of the generated text, which is a requirement for optimizing the LLM during the training process. Moreover, we will discuss how to load pretrained weights, giving our LLM a solid starting point for fine-tuning. Figure 5.1 lays out our overall plan, highlighting what we will discuss in this chapter.

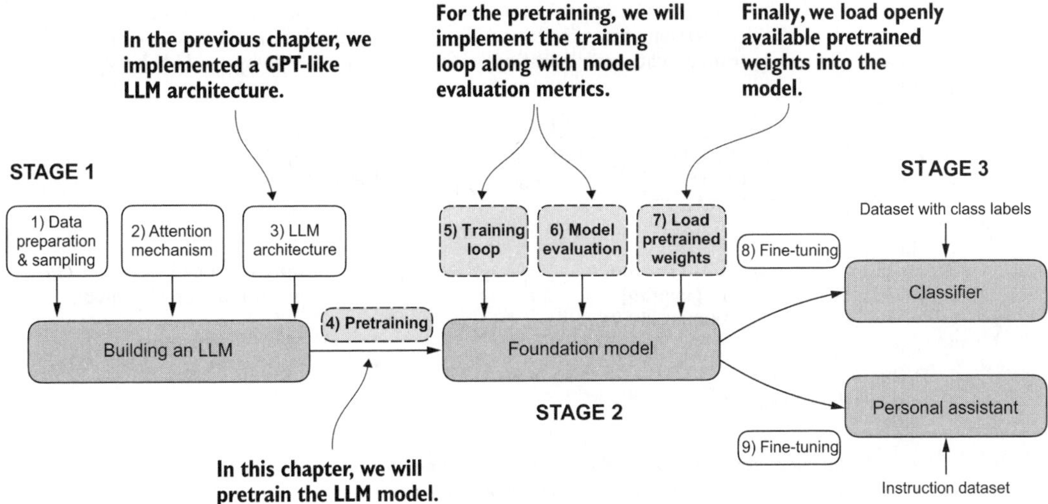

Figure 5.1 The three main stages of coding an LLM. This chapter focuses on stage 2: pretraining the LLM (step 4), which includes implementing the training code (step 5), evaluating the performance (step 6), and saving and loading model weights (step 7).

> **Weight parameters**
>
> In the context of LLMs and other deep learning models, *weights* refer to the trainable parameters that the learning process adjusts. These weights are also known as *weight parameters* or simply *parameters*. In frameworks like PyTorch, these weights are stored in linear layers; we used these to implement the multi-head attention module in chapter 3 and the `GPTModel` in chapter 4. After initializing a layer (`new_layer = torch.nn.Linear(...)`), we can access its weights through the `.weight` attribute, `new_layer.weight`. Additionally, for convenience, PyTorch allows direct access to all a model's trainable parameters, including weights and biases, through the method `model.parameters()`, which we will use later when implementing the model training.

5.1 Evaluating generative text models

After briefly recapping the text generation from chapter 4, we will set up our LLM for text generation and then discuss basic ways to evaluate the quality of the generated text. We will then calculate the training and validation losses. Figure 5.2 shows the topics covered in this chapter, with these first three steps highlighted.

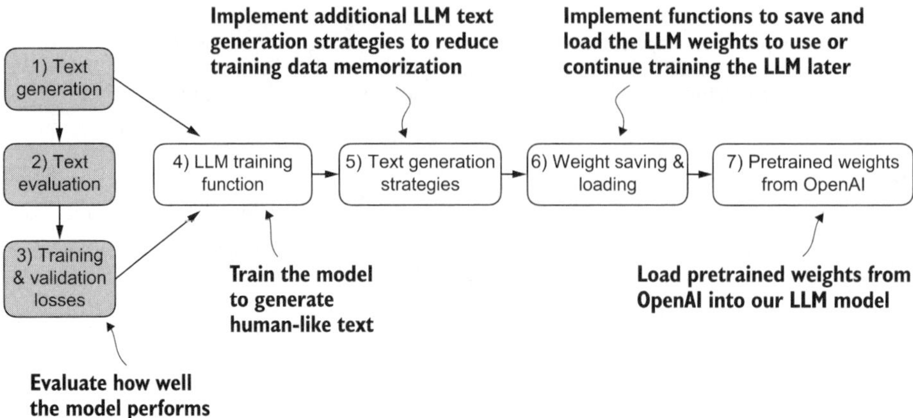

Figure 5.2 An overview of the topics covered in this chapter. We begin by recapping text generation (step 1) before moving on to discuss basic model evaluation techniques (step 2) and training and validation losses (step 3).

5.1.1 Using GPT to generate text

Let's set up the LLM and briefly recap the text generation process we implemented in chapter 4. We begin by initializing the GPT model that we will later evaluate and train using the `GPTModel` class and `GPT_CONFIG_124M` dictionary (see chapter 4):

```
import torch
from chapter04 import GPTModel

GPT_CONFIG_124M = {
    "vocab_size": 50257,
    "context_length": 256,       # We shorten the context length from 1,024 to 256 tokens.
    "emb_dim": 768,
    "n_heads": 12,
    "n_layers": 12,
    "drop_rate": 0.1,            # It's possible and common to set dropout to 0.
    "qkv_bias": False
}
torch.manual_seed(123)
model = GPTModel(GPT_CONFIG_124M)
model.eval()
```

Considering the `GPT_CONFIG_124M` dictionary, the only adjustment we have made compared to the previous chapter is that we have reduced the context length (`context_length`) to 256 tokens. This modification reduces the computational demands of training the model, making it possible to carry out the training on a standard laptop computer.

Originally, the GPT-2 model with 124 million parameters was configured to handle up to 1,024 tokens. After the training process, we will update the context size setting and load pretrained weights to work with a model configured for a 1,024-token context length.

Using the `GPTModel` instance, we adopt the `generate_text_simple` function from chapter 4 and introduce two handy functions: `text_to_token_ids` and `token_ids_to_text`. These functions facilitate the conversion between text and token representations, a technique we will utilize throughout this chapter.

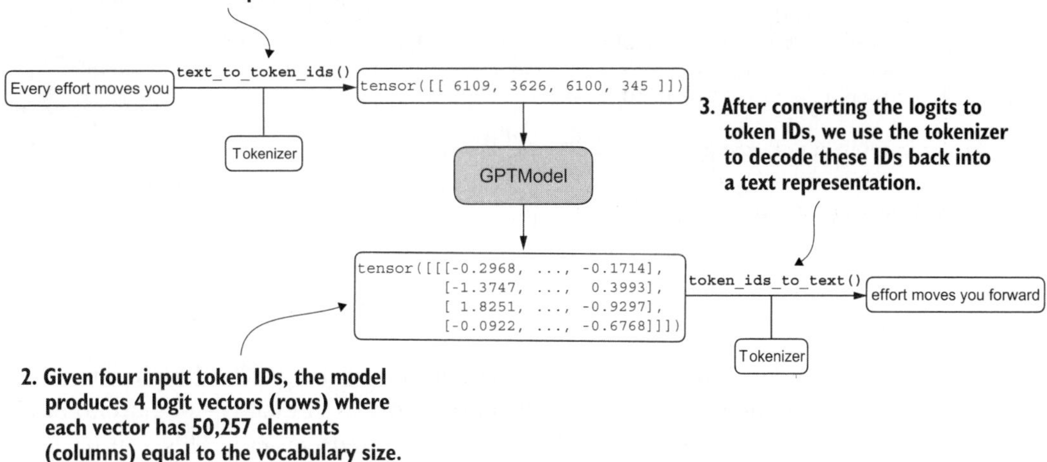
1. Use the tokenizer to encode input text into a token ID representation.
Every effort moves you
text_to_token_ids()
Tokenizer
tensor([[6109, 3626, 6100, 345]])
GPTModel
3. After converting the logits to token IDs, we use the tokenizer to decode these IDs back into a text representation.
tensor([[[-0.2968, ..., -0.1714],
[-1.3747, ..., 0.3993],
[1.8251, ..., -0.9297],
[-0.0922, ..., -0.6768]]])
token_ids_to_text()
effort moves you forward
Tokenizer
2. Given four input token IDs, the model produces 4 logit vectors (rows) where each vector has 50,257 elements (columns) equal to the vocabulary size.

Figure 5.3 Generating text involves encoding text into token IDs that the LLM processes into logit vectors. The logit vectors are then converted back into token IDs, detokenized into a text representation.

Figure 5.3 illustrates a three-step text generation process using a GPT model. First, the tokenizer converts input text into a series of token IDs (see chapter 2). Second, the model receives these token IDs and generates corresponding logits, which are vectors representing the probability distribution for each token in the vocabulary (see chapter 4). Third, these logits are converted back into token IDs, which the tokenizer decodes into human-readable text, completing the cycle from textual input to textual output.

We can implement the text generation process, as shown in the following listing.

Listing 5.1 Utility functions for text to token ID conversion

```
import tiktoken
from chapter04 import generate_text_simple

def text_to_token_ids(text, tokenizer):
    encoded = tokenizer.encode(text, allowed_special={'<|endoftext|>'})
```

```
    encoded_tensor = torch.tensor(encoded).unsqueeze(0)    # .unsqueeze(0) adds the batch dimension
    return encoded_tensor

def token_ids_to_text(token_ids, tokenizer):
    flat = token_ids.squeeze(0)                            # Removes batch dimension
    return tokenizer.decode(flat.tolist())

start_context = "Every effort moves you"
tokenizer = tiktoken.get_encoding("gpt2")

token_ids = generate_text_simple(
    model=model,
    idx=text_to_token_ids(start_context, tokenizer),
    max_new_tokens=10,
    context_size=GPT_CONFIG_124M["context_length"]
)
print("Output text:\n", token_ids_to_text(token_ids, tokenizer))
```

Using this code, the `model` generates the following text:

```
Output text:
 Every effort moves you rentingetic wasn? refres RexMeCHicular stren
```

Clearly, the model isn't yet producing coherent text because it hasn't undergone training. To define what makes text "coherent" or "high quality," we have to implement a numerical method to evaluate the generated content. This approach will enable us to monitor and enhance the model's performance throughout its training process.

Next, we will calculate a *loss metric* for the generated outputs. This loss serves as a progress and success indicator of the training progress. Furthermore, in later chapters, when we fine-tune our LLM, we will review additional methodologies for assessing model quality.

5.1.2 Calculating the text generation loss

Next, let's explore techniques for numerically assessing text quality generated during training by calculating a *text generation loss*. We will go over this topic step by step with a practical example to make the concepts clear and applicable, beginning with a short recap of how the data is loaded and how the text is generated via the `generate_text_simple` function.

Figure 5.4 illustrates the overall flow from input text to LLM-generated text using a five-step procedure. This text-generation process shows what the `generate_text_simple` function does internally. We need to perform these same initial steps before we can compute a loss that measures the generated text quality later in this section.

Figure 5.4 outlines the text generation process with a small seven-token vocabulary to fit this image on a single page. However, our `GPTModel` works with a much larger

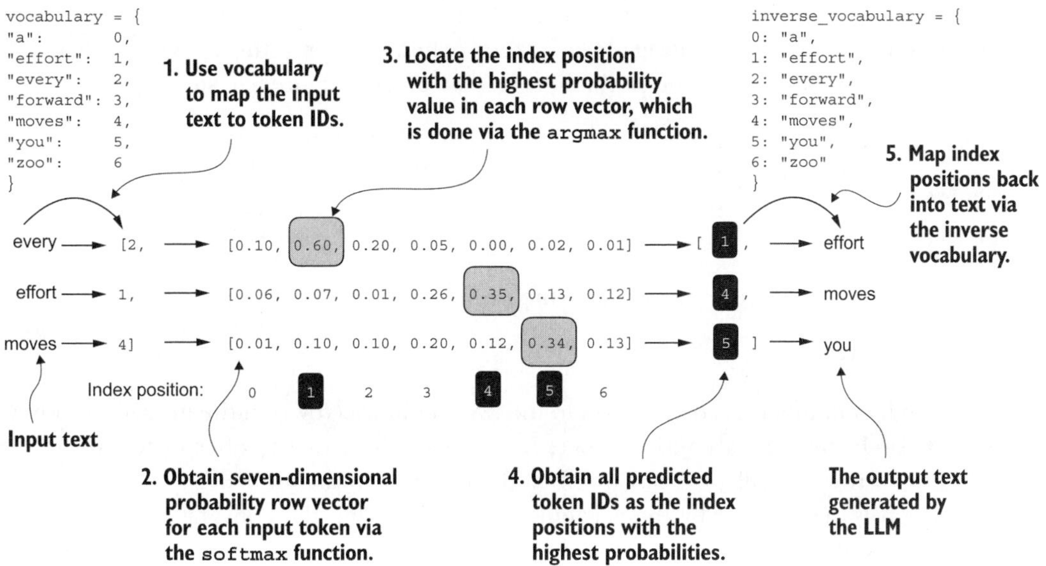

Figure 5.4 For each of the three input tokens, shown on the left, we compute a vector containing probability scores corresponding to each token in the vocabulary. The index position of the highest probability score in each vector represents the most likely next token ID. These token IDs associated with the highest probability scores are selected and mapped back into a text that represents the text generated by the model.

vocabulary consisting of 50,257 words; hence, the token IDs in the following code will range from 0 to 50,256 rather than 0 to 6.

Also, figure 5.4 only shows a single text example (`"every effort moves"`) for simplicity. In the following hands-on code example that implements the steps in the figure, we will work with two input examples for the GPT model (`"every effort moves"` and `"I really like"`).

Consider these two input examples, which have already been mapped to token IDs (figure 5.4, step 1):

```
inputs = torch.tensor([[16833, 3626, 6100],   # ["every effort moves",
                       [40,    1107, 588]])   #  "I really like"]
```

Matching these inputs, the `targets` contain the token IDs we want the model to produce:

```
targets = torch.tensor([[3626, 6100, 345  ],  # [" effort moves you",
                        [1107, 588, 11311]])  #  " really like chocolate"]
```

Note that the targets are the inputs but shifted one position forward, a concept we covered in chapter 2 during the implementation of the data loader. This shifting strategy is crucial for teaching the model to predict the next token in a sequence.

Now we feed the inputs into the model to calculate logits vectors for the two input examples, each comprising three tokens. Then we apply the `softmax` function to transform these logits into probability scores (`probas`; figure 5.4, step 2):

```
with torch.no_grad():                       # Disables gradient tracking since we are not training yet
    logits = model(inputs)
probas = torch.softmax(logits, dim=-1)      # Probability of each token in vocabulary
print(probas.shape)
```

The resulting tensor dimension of the probability score (`probas`) tensor is

```
torch.Size([2, 3, 50257])
```

The first number, 2, corresponds to the two examples (rows) in the inputs, also known as batch size. The second number, 3, corresponds to the number of tokens in each input (row). Finally, the last number corresponds to the embedding dimensionality, which is determined by the vocabulary size. Following the conversion from logits to probabilities via the `softmax` function, the `generate_text_simple` function then converts the resulting probability scores back into text (figure 5.4, steps 3–5).

We can complete steps 3 and 4 by applying the `argmax` function to the probability scores to obtain the corresponding token IDs:

```
token_ids = torch.argmax(probas, dim=-1, keepdim=True)
print("Token IDs:\n", token_ids)
```

Given that we have two input batches, each containing three tokens, applying the `argmax` function to the probability scores (figure 5.4, step 3) yields two sets of outputs, each with three predicted token IDs:

```
Token IDs:
 tensor([[[16657],          # First batch
         [  339],
         [42826]],
        [[49906],           # Second batch
         [29669],
         [41751]]])
```

Finally, step 5 converts the token IDs back into text:

```
print(f"Targets batch 1: {token_ids_to_text(targets[0], tokenizer)}")
print(f"Outputs batch 1:"
      f" {token_ids_to_text(token_ids[0].flatten(), tokenizer)}")
```

When we decode these tokens, we find that these output tokens are quite different from the target tokens we want the model to generate:

```
Targets batch 1:  effort moves you
Outputs batch 1:  Armed heNetflix
```

The model produces random text that is different from the target text because it has not been trained yet. We now want to evaluate the performance of the model's generated text numerically via a loss (figure 5.5). Not only is this useful for measuring the quality of the generated text, but it's also a building block for implementing the training function, which we will use to update the model's weight to improve the generated text.

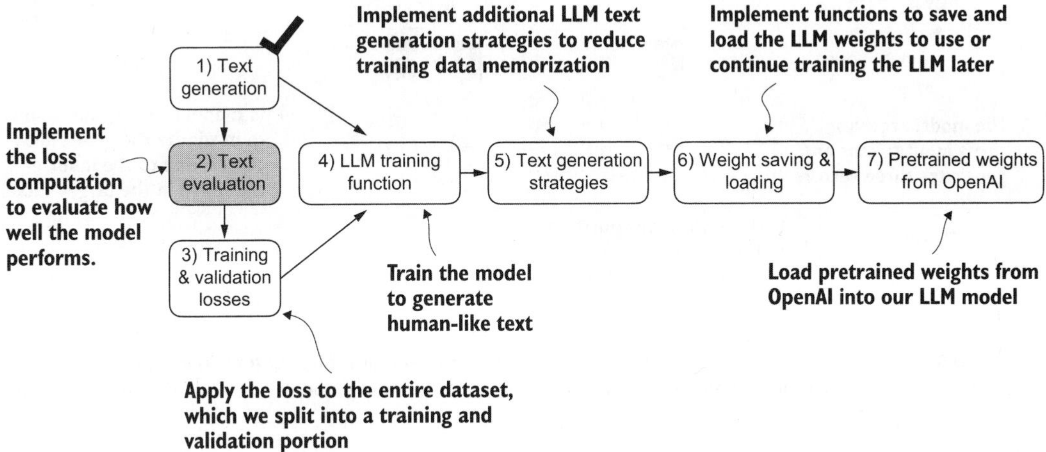

Figure 5.5 An overview of the topics covered in this chapter. We have completed step 1. We are now ready to implement the text evaluation function (step 2).

Part of the text evaluation process that we implement, as shown in figure 5.5, is to measure "how far" the generated tokens are from the correct predictions (targets). The training function we implement later will use this information to adjust the model weights to generate text that is more similar to (or, ideally, matches) the target text.

The model training aims to increase the softmax probability in the index positions corresponding to the correct target token IDs, as illustrated in figure 5.6. This softmax probability is also used in the evaluation metric we will implement next to numerically assess the model's generated outputs: the higher the probability in the correct positions, the better.

Remember that figure 5.6 displays the softmax probabilities for a compact seven-token vocabulary to fit everything into a single figure. This implies that the starting random values will hover around 1/7, which equals approximately 0.14. However, the vocabulary we are using for our GPT-2 model has 50,257 tokens, so most of the initial probabilities will hover around 0.00002 (1/50,257).

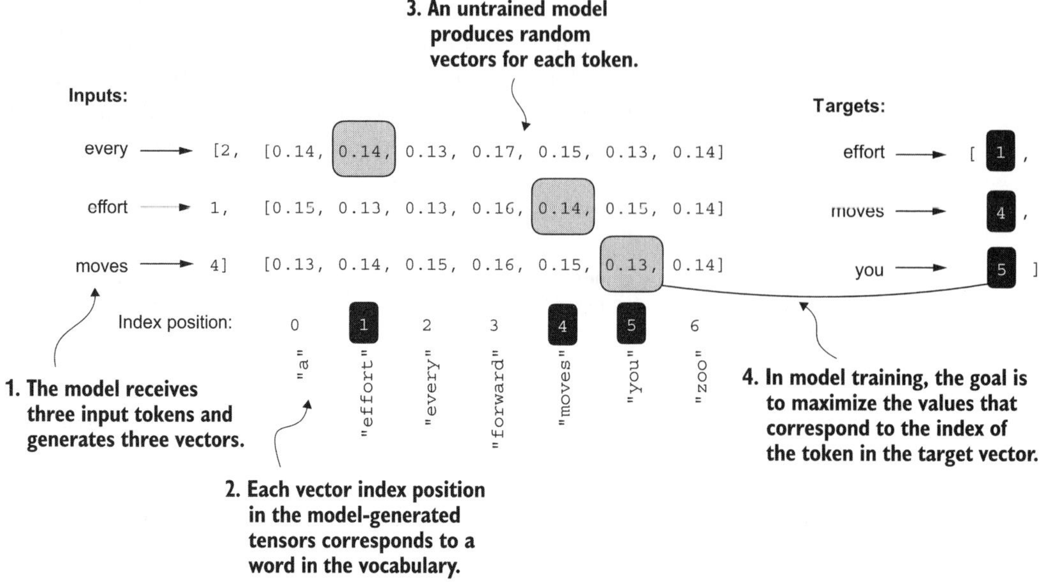

Figure 5.6 Before training, the model produces random next-token probability vectors. The goal of model training is to ensure that the probability values corresponding to the highlighted target token IDs are maximized.

For each of the two input texts, we can print the initial softmax probability scores corresponding to the target tokens using the following code:

```
text_idx = 0
target_probas_1 = probas[text_idx, [0, 1, 2], targets[text_idx]]
print("Text 1:", target_probas_1)

text_idx = 1
target_probas_2 = probas[text_idx, [0, 1, 2], targets[text_idx]]
print("Text 2:", target_probas_2)
```

The three target token ID probabilities for each batch are

```
Text 1: tensor([7.4541e-05, 3.1061e-05, 1.1563e-05])
Text 2: tensor([1.0337e-05, 5.6776e-05, 4.7559e-06])
```

The goal of training an LLM is to maximize the likelihood of the correct token, which involves increasing its probability relative to other tokens. This way, we ensure the LLM consistently picks the target token—essentially the next word in the sentence—as the next token it generates.

> **Backpropagation**
>
> How do we maximize the softmax probability values corresponding to the target tokens? The big picture is that we update the model weights so that the model outputs higher values for the respective token IDs we want to generate. The weight update is done via a process called *backpropagation*, a standard technique for training deep neural networks (see sections A.3 to A.7 in appendix A for more details about backpropagation and model training).
>
> Backpropagation requires a loss function, which calculates the difference between the model's predicted output (here, the probabilities corresponding to the target token IDs) and the actual desired output. This loss function measures how far off the model's predictions are from the target values.

Next, we will calculate the loss for the probability scores of the two example batches, `target_probas_1` and `target_probas_2`. The main steps are illustrated in figure 5.7. Since we already applied steps 1 to 3 to obtain `target_probas_1` and `target_probas_2`, we proceed with step 4, applying the *logarithm* to the probability scores:

```
log_probas = torch.log(torch.cat((target_probas_1, target_probas_2)))
print(log_probas)
```

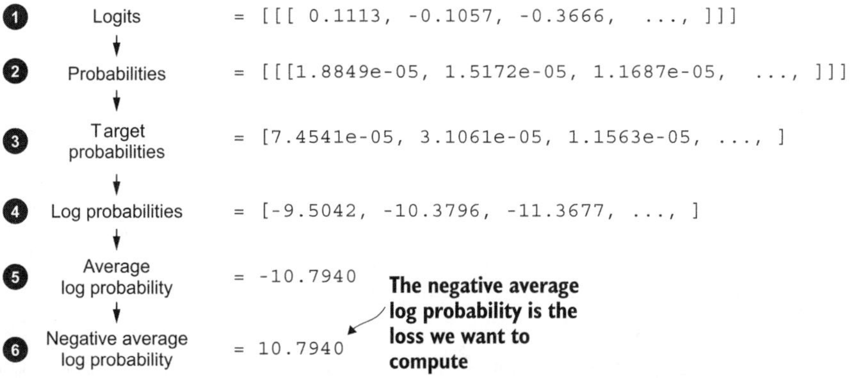

Figure 5.7 Calculating the loss involves several steps. Steps 1 to 3, which we have already completed, calculate the token probabilities corresponding to the target tensors. These probabilities are then transformed via a logarithm and averaged in steps 4 to 6.

This results in the following values:

```
tensor([ -9.5042, -10.3796, -11.3677, -11.4798,  -9.7764, -12.2561])
```

Working with logarithms of probability scores is more manageable in mathematical optimization than handling the scores directly. This topic is outside the scope of this book, but I've detailed it further in a lecture, which can be found in appendix B.

Next, we combine these log probabilities into a single score by computing the average (step 5 in figure 5.7):

```
avg_log_probas = torch.mean(log_probas)
print(avg_log_probas)
```

The resulting average log probability score is

```
tensor(-10.7940)
```

The goal is to get the average log probability as close to 0 as possible by updating the model's weights as part of the training process. However, in deep learning, the common practice isn't to push the average log probability up to 0 but rather to bring the negative average log probability down to 0. The negative average log probability is simply the average log probability multiplied by –1, which corresponds to step 6 in figure 5.7:

```
neg_avg_log_probas = avg_log_probas * -1
print(neg_avg_log_probas)
```

This prints `tensor(10.7940)`. In deep learning, the term for turning this negative value, –10.7940, into 10.7940, is known as the *cross entropy* loss. PyTorch comes in handy here, as it already has a built-in `cross_entropy` function that takes care of all these six steps in figure 5.7 for us.

Cross entropy loss

At its core, the cross entropy loss is a popular measure in machine learning and deep learning that measures the difference between two probability distributions—typically, the true distribution of labels (here, tokens in a dataset) and the predicted distribution from a model (for instance, the token probabilities generated by an LLM).

In the context of machine learning and specifically in frameworks like PyTorch, the `cross_entropy` function computes this measure for discrete outcomes, which is similar to the negative average log probability of the target tokens given the model's generated token probabilities, making the terms "cross entropy" and "negative average log probability" related and often used interchangeably in practice.

Before we apply the `cross_entropy` function, let's briefly recall the shape of the logits and target tensors:

```
print("Logits shape:", logits.shape)
print("Targets shape:", targets.shape)
```

The resulting shapes are

```
Logits shape: torch.Size([2, 3, 50257])
Targets shape: torch.Size([2, 3])
```

As we can see, the `logits` tensor has three dimensions: batch size, number of tokens, and vocabulary size. The `targets` tensor has two dimensions: batch size and number of tokens.

For the `cross_entropy` loss function in PyTorch, we want to flatten these tensors by combining them over the batch dimension:

```
logits_flat = logits.flatten(0, 1)
targets_flat = targets.flatten()
print("Flattened logits:", logits_flat.shape)
print("Flattened targets:", targets_flat.shape)
```

The resulting tensor dimensions are

```
Flattened logits: torch.Size([6, 50257])
Flattened targets: torch.Size([6])
```

Remember that the `targets` are the token IDs we want the LLM to generate, and the `logits` contain the unscaled model outputs before they enter the `softmax` function to obtain the probability scores.

Previously, we applied the `softmax` function, selected the probability scores corresponding to the target IDs, and computed the negative average log probabilities. PyTorch's `cross_entropy` function will take care of all these steps for us:

```
loss = torch.nn.functional.cross_entropy(logits_flat, targets_flat)
print(loss)
```

The resulting loss is the same that we obtained previously when applying the individual steps in figure 5.7 manually:

```
tensor(10.7940)
```

Perplexity

Perplexity is a measure often used alongside cross entropy loss to evaluate the performance of models in tasks like language modeling. It can provide a more interpretable way to understand the uncertainty of a model in predicting the next token in a sequence.

Perplexity measures how well the probability distribution predicted by the model matches the actual distribution of the words in the dataset. Similar to the loss, a lower perplexity indicates that the model predictions are closer to the actual distribution.

> ***(continued)***
>
> Perplexity can be calculated as `perplexity = torch.exp(loss)`, which returns `tensor(48725.8203)` when applied to the previously calculated loss.
>
> Perplexity is often considered more interpretable than the raw loss value because it signifies the effective vocabulary size about which the model is uncertain at each step. In the given example, this would translate to the model being unsure about which among 48,725 tokens in the vocabulary to generate as the next token.

We have now calculated the loss for two small text inputs for illustration purposes. Next, we will apply the loss computation to the entire training and validation sets.

5.1.3 Calculating the training and validation set losses

We must first prepare the training and validation datasets that we will use to train the LLM. Then, as highlighted in figure 5.8, we will calculate the cross entropy for the training and validation sets, which is an important component of the model training process.

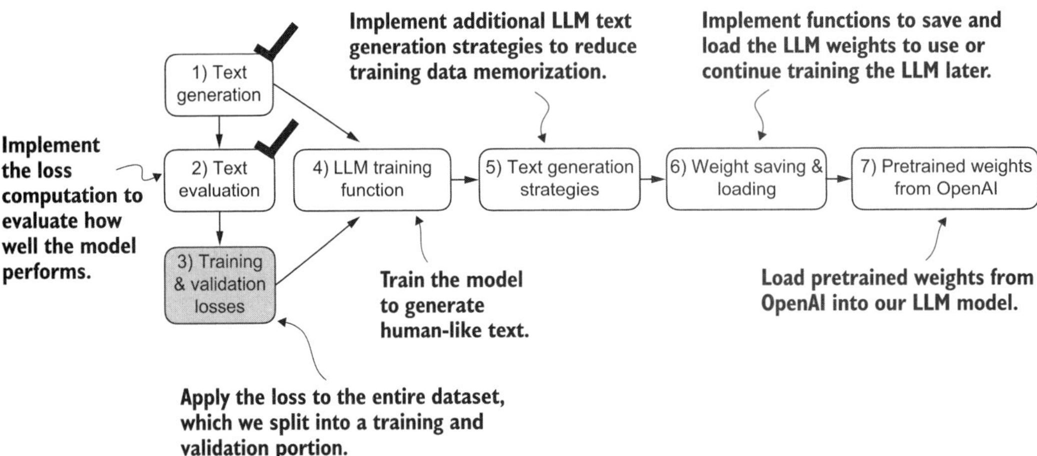

Figure 5.8 Having completed steps 1 and 2, including computing the cross entropy loss, we can now apply this loss computation to the entire text dataset that we will use for model training.

To compute the loss on the training and validation datasets, we use a very small text dataset, the "The Verdict" short story by Edith Wharton, which we have already worked with in chapter 2. By selecting a text from the public domain, we circumvent any concerns related to usage rights. Additionally, using such a small dataset allows for the execution of code examples on a standard laptop computer in a matter of minutes, even without a high-end GPU, which is particularly advantageous for educational purposes.

NOTE Interested readers can also use the supplementary code for this book to prepare a larger-scale dataset consisting of more than 60,000 public domain books from Project Gutenberg and train an LLM on these (see appendix D for details).

The cost of pretraining LLMs

To put the scale of our project into perspective, consider the training of the 7 billion parameter Llama 2 model, a relatively popular openly available LLM. This model required 184,320 GPU hours on expensive A100 GPUs, processing 2 trillion tokens. At the time of writing, running an 8 × A100 cloud server on AWS costs around $30 per hour. A rough estimate puts the total training cost of such an LLM at around $690,000 (calculated as 184,320 hours divided by 8, then multiplied by $30).

The following code loads the "The Verdict" short story:

```
file_path = "the-verdict.txt"
with open(file_path, "r", encoding="utf-8") as file:
    text_data = file.read()
```

After loading the dataset, we can check the number of characters and tokens in the dataset:

```
total_characters = len(text_data)
total_tokens = len(tokenizer.encode(text_data))
print("Characters:", total_characters)
print("Tokens:", total_tokens)
```

The output is

```
Characters: 20479
Tokens: 5145
```

With just 5,145 tokens, the text might seem too small to train an LLM, but as mentioned earlier, it's for educational purposes so that we can run the code in minutes instead of weeks. Plus, later we will load pretrained weights from OpenAI into our `GPTModel` code.

Next, we divide the dataset into a training and a validation set and use the data loaders from chapter 2 to prepare the batches for LLM training. This process is visualized in figure 5.9. Due to spatial constraints, we use a `max_length=6`. However, for the actual data loaders, we set the `max_length` equal to the 256-token context length that the LLM supports so that the LLM sees longer texts during training.

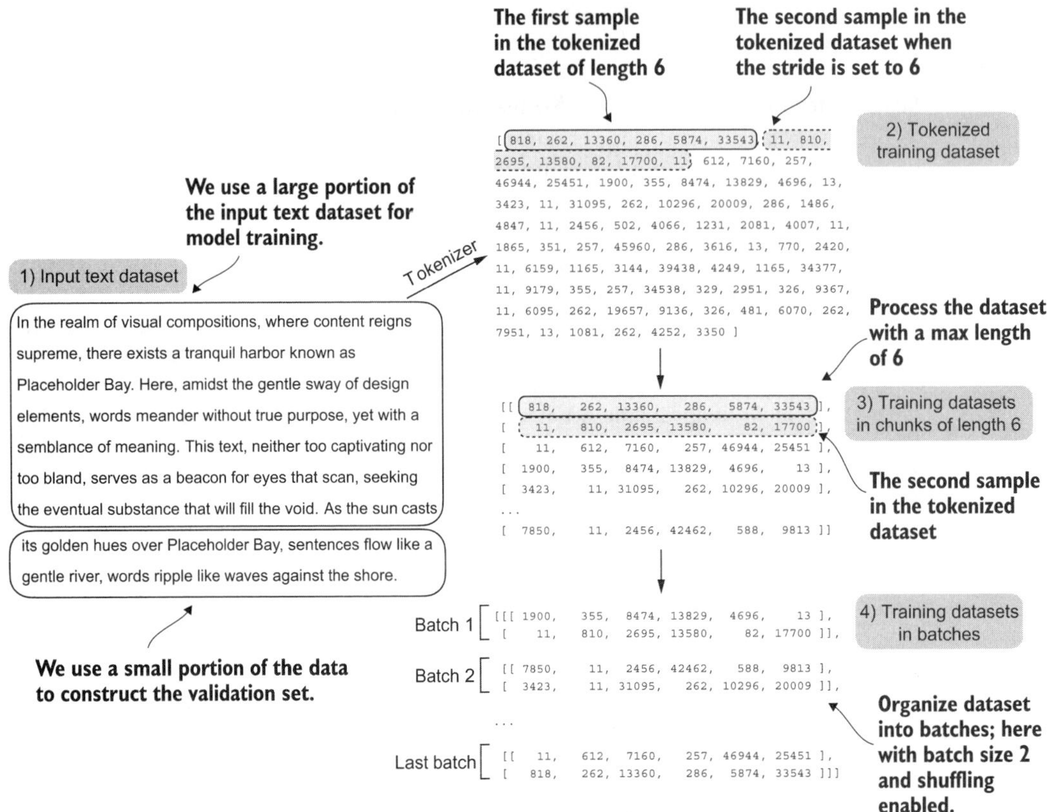

Figure 5.9 When preparing the data loaders, we split the input text into training and validation set portions. Then we tokenize the text (only shown for the training set portion for simplicity) and divide the tokenized text into chunks of a user-specified length (here, 6). Finally, we shuffle the rows and organize the chunked text into batches (here, batch size 2), which we can use for model training.

NOTE We are training the model with training data presented in similarly sized chunks for simplicity and efficiency. However, in practice, it can also be beneficial to train an LLM with variable-length inputs to help the LLM to better generalize across different types of inputs when it is being used.

To implement the data splitting and loading, we first define a `train_ratio` to use 90% of the data for training and the remaining 10% as validation data for model evaluation during training:

```
train_ratio = 0.90
split_idx = int(train_ratio * len(text_data))
train_data = text_data[:split_idx]
val_data = text_data[split_idx:]
```

Using the `train_data` and `val_data` subsets, we can now create the respective data loader reusing the `create_dataloader_v1` code from chapter 2:

```
from chapter02 import create_dataloader_v1
torch.manual_seed(123)

train_loader = create_dataloader_v1(
    train_data,
    batch_size=2,
    max_length=GPT_CONFIG_124M["context_length"],
    stride=GPT_CONFIG_124M["context_length"],
    drop_last=True,
    shuffle=True,
    num_workers=0
)
val_loader = create_dataloader_v1(
    val_data,
    batch_size=2,
    max_length=GPT_CONFIG_124M["context_length"],
    stride=GPT_CONFIG_124M["context_length"],
    drop_last=False,
    shuffle=False,
    num_workers=0
)
```

We used a relatively small batch size to reduce the computational resource demand because we were working with a very small dataset. In practice, training LLMs with batch sizes of 1,024 or larger is not uncommon.

As an optional check, we can iterate through the data loaders to ensure that they were created correctly:

```
print("Train loader:")
for x, y in train_loader:
    print(x.shape, y.shape)

print("\nValidation loader:")
for x, y in val_loader:
    print(x.shape, y.shape)
```

We should see the following outputs:

```
Train loader:
torch.Size([2, 256]) torch.Size([2, 256])
torch.Size([2, 256]) torch.Size([2, 256])
torch.Size([2, 256]) torch.Size([2, 256])
torch.Size([2, 256]) torch.Size([2, 256])
torch.Size([2, 256]) torch.Size([2, 256])
torch.Size([2, 256]) torch.Size([2, 256])
torch.Size([2, 256]) torch.Size([2, 256])
torch.Size([2, 256]) torch.Size([2, 256])
torch.Size([2, 256]) torch.Size([2, 256])
```

BQ 208 5897

```
Validation loader:
torch.Size([2, 256]) torch.Size([2, 256])
```

Based on the preceding code output, we have nine training set batches with two samples and 256 tokens each. Since we allocated only 10% of the data for validation, there is only one validation batch consisting of two input examples. As expected, the input data (x) and target data (y) have the same shape (the batch size times the number of tokens in each batch) since the targets are the inputs shifted by one position, as discussed in chapter 2.

Next, we implement a utility function to calculate the cross entropy loss of a given batch returned via the training and validation loader:

```
def calc_loss_batch(input_batch, target_batch, model, device):
    input_batch = input_batch.to(device)
    target_batch = target_batch.to(device)
    logits = model(input_batch)
    loss = torch.nn.functional.cross_entropy(
        logits.flatten(0, 1), target_batch.flatten()
    )
    return loss
```

The transfer to a given device allows us to transfer the data to a GPU.

We can now use this `calc_loss_batch` utility function, which computes the loss for a single batch, to implement the following `calc_loss_loader` function that computes the loss over all the batches sampled by a given data loader.

Listing 5.2 Function to compute the training and validation loss

```
def calc_loss_loader(data_loader, model, device, num_batches=None):
    total_loss = 0.
    if len(data_loader) == 0:
        return float("nan")
    elif num_batches is None:
        num_batches = len(data_loader)
    else:
        num_batches = min(num_batches, len(data_loader))
    for i, (input_batch, target_batch) in enumerate(data_loader):
        if i < num_batches:
            loss = calc_loss_batch(
                input_batch, target_batch, model, device
            )
            total_loss += loss.item()
        else:
            break
    return total_loss / num_batches
```

Iteratives over all batches if no fixed num_batches is specified

Reduces the number of batches to match the total number of batches in the data loader if num_batches exceeds the number of batches in the data loader

Sums loss for each batch

Averages the loss over all batches

By default, the `calc_loss_loader` function iterates over all batches in a given data loader, accumulates the loss in the `total_loss` variable, and then computes and averages the loss over the total number of batches. Alternatively, we can specify a smaller number of batches via `num_batches` to speed up the evaluation during model training.

Let's now see this `calc_loss_loader` function in action, applying it to the training and validation set loaders:

If you have a machine with a CUDA-supported GPU, the LLM will train on the GPU without making any changes to the code.

Disables gradient tracking for efficiency because we are not training yet

```
device = torch.device("cuda" if torch.cuda.is_available() else "cpu")
model.to(device)
with torch.no_grad():
    train_loss = calc_loss_loader(train_loader, model, device)
    val_loss = calc_loss_loader(val_loader, model, device)
print("Training loss:", train_loss)
print("Validation loss:", val_loss)
```

Via the "device" setting, we ensure the data is loaded onto the same device as the LLM model.

The resulting loss values are

```
Training loss: 10.98758347829183
Validation loss: 10.98110580444336
```

The loss values are relatively high because the model has not yet been trained. For comparison, the loss approaches 0 if the model learns to generate the next tokens as they appear in the training and validation sets.

Now that we have a way to measure the quality of the generated text, we will train the LLM to reduce this loss so that it becomes better at generating text, as illustrated in figure 5.10.

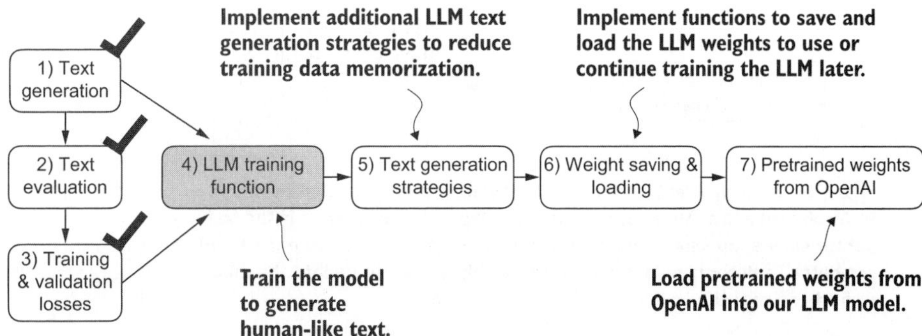

Figure 5.10 We have recapped the text generation process (step 1) and implemented basic model evaluation techniques (step 2) to compute the training and validation set losses (step 3). Next, we will go to the training functions and pretrain the LLM (step 4).

Next, we will focus on pretraining the LLM. After model training, we will implement alternative text generation strategies and save and load pretrained model weights.

5.2 Training an LLM

It is finally time to implement the code for pretraining the LLM, our `GPTModel`. For this, we focus on a straightforward training loop to keep the code concise and readable.

> **NOTE** Interested readers can learn about more advanced techniques, including *learning rate warmup*, *cosine annealing*, and *gradient clipping*, in appendix D.

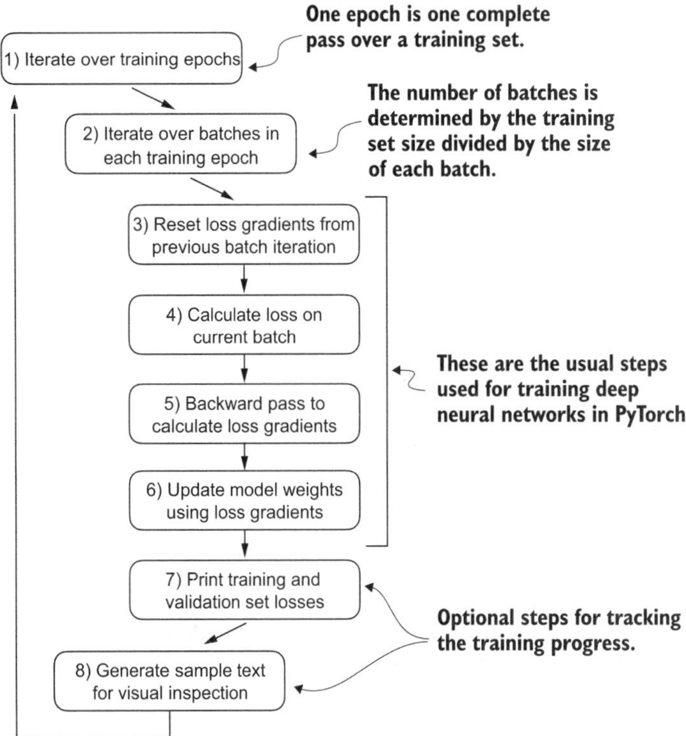

Figure 5.11 A typical training loop for training deep neural networks in PyTorch consists of numerous steps, iterating over the batches in the training set for several epochs. In each loop, we calculate the loss for each training set batch to determine loss gradients, which we use to update the model weights so that the training set loss is minimized.

The flowchart in figure 5.11 depicts a typical PyTorch neural network training workflow, which we use for training an LLM. It outlines eight steps, starting with iterating over each epoch, processing batches, resetting gradients, calculating the loss and new gradients, and updating weights and concluding with monitoring steps like printing losses and generating text samples.

> **NOTE** If you are relatively new to training deep neural networks with PyTorch and any of these steps are unfamiliar, consider reading sections A.5 to A.8 in appendix A.

We can implement this training flow via the `train_model_simple` function in code.

Listing 5.3 The main function for pretraining LLMs

```
def train_model_simple(model, train_loader, val_loader,
                       optimizer, device, num_epochs,
                       eval_freq, eval_iter, start_context, tokenizer):
    train_losses, val_losses, track_tokens_seen = [], [], []    # Initializes lists to track losses and tokens seen
    tokens_seen, global_step = 0, -1

    for epoch in range(num_epochs):    # Starts the main training loop
        model.train()
        for input_batch, target_batch in train_loader:
            optimizer.zero_grad()    # Resets loss gradients from the previous batch iteration
            loss = calc_loss_batch(
                input_batch, target_batch, model, device
            )
            loss.backward()    # Calculates loss gradients
            optimizer.step()    # Updates model weights using loss gradients
            tokens_seen += input_batch.numel()
            global_step += 1

            if global_step % eval_freq == 0:    # Optional evaluation step
                train_loss, val_loss = evaluate_model(
                    model, train_loader, val_loader, device, eval_iter)
                train_losses.append(train_loss)
                val_losses.append(val_loss)
                track_tokens_seen.append(tokens_seen)
                print(f"Ep {epoch+1} (Step {global_step:06d}): "
                      f"Train loss {train_loss:.3f}, "
                      f"Val loss {val_loss:.3f}"
                )

        generate_and_print_sample(    # Prints a sample text after each epoch
            model, tokenizer, device, start_context
        )
    return train_losses, val_losses, track_tokens_seen
```

Note that the `train_model_simple` function we just created uses two functions we have not defined yet: `evaluate_model` and `generate_and_print_sample`.

The `evaluate_model` function corresponds to step 7 in figure 5.11. It prints the training and validation set losses after each model update so we can evaluate whether the training improves the model. More specifically, the `evaluate_model` function calculates the loss over the training and validation set while ensuring the model is in evaluation mode with gradient tracking and dropout disabled when calculating the loss over the training and validation sets:

Dropout is disabled during evaluation for stable, reproducible results.

Disables gradient tracking, which is not required during evaluation, to reduce the computational overhead

```
def evaluate_model(model, train_loader, val_loader, device, eval_iter):
    model.eval()
    with torch.no_grad():
        train_loss = calc_loss_loader(
            train_loader, model, device, num_batches=eval_iter
        )
        val_loss = calc_loss_loader(
            val_loader, model, device, num_batches=eval_iter
        )
    model.train()
    return train_loss, val_loss
```

Similar to `evaluate_model`, the `generate_and_print_sample` function is a convenience function that we use to track whether the model improves during the training. In particular, the `generate_and_print_sample` function takes a text snippet (`start_context`) as input, converts it into token IDs, and feeds it to the LLM to generate a text sample using the `generate_text_simple` function we used earlier:

```
def generate_and_print_sample(model, tokenizer, device, start_context):
    model.eval()
    context_size = model.pos_emb.weight.shape[0]
    encoded = text_to_token_ids(start_context, tokenizer).to(device)
    with torch.no_grad():
        token_ids = generate_text_simple(
            model=model, idx=encoded,
            max_new_tokens=50, context_size=context_size
        )
    decoded_text = token_ids_to_text(token_ids, tokenizer)
    print(decoded_text.replace("\n", " "))
    model.train()
```

Compact print format

While the `evaluate_model` function gives us a numeric estimate of the model's training progress, this `generate_and_print_sample` text function provides a concrete text example generated by the model to judge its capabilities during training.

AdamW

Adam optimizers are a popular choice for training deep neural networks. However, in our training loop, we opt for the *AdamW* optimizer. AdamW is a variant of Adam that improves the weight decay approach, which aims to minimize model complexity and prevent overfitting by penalizing larger weights. This adjustment allows AdamW to achieve more effective regularization and better generalization; thus, AdamW is frequently used in the training of LLMs.

Let's see this all in action by training a `GPTModel` instance for 10 epochs using an `AdamW` optimizer and the `train_model_simple` function we defined earlier:

```
torch.manual_seed(123)
model = GPTModel(GPT_CONFIG_124M)
model.to(device)
optimizer = torch.optim.AdamW(
     model.parameters(),
    lr=0.0004, weight_decay=0.1
)
num_epochs = 10
train_losses, val_losses, tokens_seen = train_model_simple(
    model, train_loader, val_loader, optimizer, device,
    num_epochs=num_epochs, eval_freq=5, eval_iter=5,
    start_context="Every effort moves you", tokenizer=tokenizer
)
```

The .parameters() method returns all trainable weight parameters of the model.

Executing the `train_model_simple` function starts the training process, which takes about 5 minutes to complete on a MacBook Air or a similar laptop. The output printed during this execution is as follows:

```
Ep 1 (Step 000000): Train loss 9.781, Val loss 9.933
Ep 1 (Step 000005): Train loss 8.111, Val loss 8.339
Every effort moves you,,,,,,,,,,,,.
Ep 2 (Step 000010): Train loss 6.661, Val loss 7.048
Ep 2 (Step 000015): Train loss 5.961, Val loss 6.616
Every effort moves you, and, and, and, and, and, and, and, and, and, and,
 and, and, and, and, and, and, and, and, and, and, and, and,, and, and,
[...]
Ep 9 (Step 000080): Train loss 0.541, Val loss 6.393
Every effort moves you?"  "Yes--quite insensible to the irony. She wanted
him vindicated--and by me!"  He laughed again, and threw back the
window-curtains, I had the donkey. "There were days when I
Ep 10 (Step 000085): Train loss 0.391, Val loss 6.452
Every effort moves you know," was one of the axioms he laid down across the
Sevres and silver of an exquisitely appointed luncheon-table, when, on a
later day, I had again run over from Monte Carlo; and Mrs. Gis
```

Intermediate results removed to save space

As we can see, the training loss improves drastically, starting with a value of 9.781 and converging to 0.391. The language skills of the model have improved quite a lot. In the beginning, the model is only able to append commas to the start context (`Every effort moves you,,,,,,,,,,,,`) or repeat the word `and`. At the end of the training, it can generate grammatically correct text.

Similar to the training set loss, we can see that the validation loss starts high (9.933) and decreases during the training. However, it never becomes as small as the training set loss and remains at 6.452 after the 10th epoch.

Before discussing the validation loss in more detail, let's create a simple plot that shows the training and validation set losses side by side:

```
import matplotlib.pyplot as plt
from matplotlib.ticker import MaxNLocator
def plot_losses(epochs_seen, tokens_seen, train_losses, val_losses):
    fig, ax1 = plt.subplots(figsize=(5, 3))
    ax1.plot(epochs_seen, train_losses, label="Training loss")
    ax1.plot(
        epochs_seen, val_losses, linestyle="-.", label="Validation loss"
    )
    ax1.set_xlabel("Epochs")
    ax1.set_ylabel("Loss")
    ax1.legend(loc="upper right")
    ax1.xaxis.set_major_locator(MaxNLocator(integer=True))
    ax2 = ax1.twiny()                                      # Creates a second x-axis that shares the same y-axis
    ax2.plot(tokens_seen, train_losses, alpha=0)           # Invisible plot for aligning ticks
    ax2.set_xlabel("Tokens seen")
    fig.tight_layout()
    plt.show()

epochs_tensor = torch.linspace(0, num_epochs, len(train_losses))
plot_losses(epochs_tensor, tokens_seen, train_losses, val_losses)
```

The resulting training and validation loss plot is shown in figure 5.12. As we can see, both the training and validation losses start to improve for the first epoch. However, the losses start to diverge past the second epoch. This divergence and the fact that the validation loss is much larger than the training loss indicate that the model is overfitting to the training data. We can confirm that the model memorizes the training data verbatim by searching for the generated text snippets, such as `quite insensible to the irony` in the "The Verdict" text file.

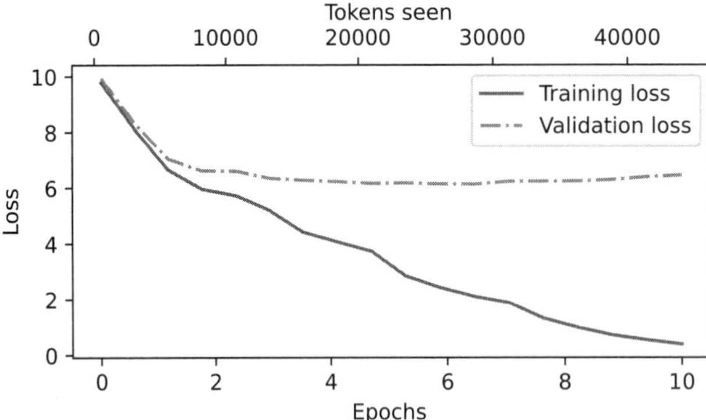

Figure 5.12 At the beginning of the training, both the training and validation set losses sharply decrease, which is a sign that the model is learning. However, the training set loss continues to decrease past the second epoch, whereas the validation loss stagnates. This is a sign that the model is still learning, but it's overfitting to the training set past epoch 2.

This memorization is expected since we are working with a very, very small training dataset and training the model for multiple epochs. Usually, it's common to train a model on a much larger dataset for only one epoch.

NOTE As mentioned earlier, interested readers can try to train the model on 60,000 public domain books from Project Gutenberg, where this overfitting does not occur; see appendix B for details.

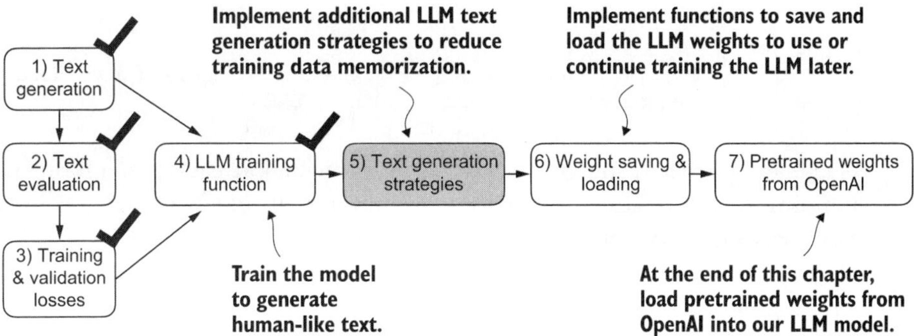

Figure 5.13 Our model can generate coherent text after implementing the training function. However, it often memorizes passages from the training set verbatim. Next, we will discuss strategies to generate more diverse output texts.

As illustrated in figure 5.13, we have completed four of our objectives for this chaper. Next, we will cover text generation strategies for LLMs to reduce training data memorization and increase the originality of the LLM-generated text before we cover weight loading and saving and loading pretrained weights from OpenAI's GPT model.

5.3 Decoding strategies to control randomness

Let's look at text generation strategies (also called decoding strategies) to generate more original text. First, we will briefly revisit the `generate_text_simple` function that we used inside `generate_and_print_sample` earlier. Then we will cover two techniques, *temperature scaling* and *top-k sampling*, to improve this function.

We begin by transferring the model back from the GPU to the CPU since inference with a relatively small model does not require a GPU. Also, after training, we put the model into evaluation mode to turn off random components such as dropout:

```
model.to("cpu")
model.eval()
```

Next, we plug the `GPTModel` instance (`model`) into the `generate_text_simple` function, which uses the LLM to generate one token at a time:

```
tokenizer = tiktoken.get_encoding("gpt2")
token_ids = generate_text_simple(
    model=model,
    idx=text_to_token_ids("Every effort moves you", tokenizer),
    max_new_tokens=25,
    context_size=GPT_CONFIG_124M["context_length"]
)
print("Output text:\n", token_ids_to_text(token_ids, tokenizer))
```

The generated text is

```
Output text:
Every effort moves you know," was one of the axioms he laid down across the
Sevres and silver of an exquisitely appointed lun
```

As explained earlier, the generated token is selected at each generation step corresponding to the largest probability score among all tokens in the vocabulary. This means that the LLM will always generate the same outputs even if we run the preceding `generate_text_simple` function multiple times on the same start context (`Every effort moves you`).

5.3.1 Temperature scaling

Let's now look at temperature scaling, a technique that adds a probabilistic selection process to the next-token generation task. Previously, inside the `generate_text_simple` function, we always sampled the token with the highest probability as the next token using `torch.argmax`, also known as *greedy decoding*. To generate text with more variety, we can replace `argmax` with a function that samples from a probability distribution (here, the probability scores the LLM generates for each vocabulary entry at each token generation step).

To illustrate the probabilistic sampling with a concrete example, let's briefly discuss the next-token generation process using a very small vocabulary for illustration purposes:

```
vocab = {
    "closer": 0,
    "every": 1,
    "effort": 2,
    "forward": 3,
    "inches": 4,
    "moves": 5,
    "pizza": 6,
    "toward": 7,
    "you": 8,
}
inverse_vocab = {v: k for k, v in vocab.items()}
```

Next, assume the LLM is given the start context "every effort moves you" and generates the following next-token logits:

```
next_token_logits = torch.tensor(
    [4.51, 0.89, -1.90, 6.75, 1.63, -1.62, -1.89, 6.28, 1.79]
)
```

As discussed in chapter 4, inside generate_text_simple, we convert the logits into probabilities via the softmax function and obtain the token ID corresponding to the generated token via the argmax function, which we can then map back into text via the inverse vocabulary:

```
probas = torch.softmax(next_token_logits, dim=0)
next_token_id = torch.argmax(probas).item()
print(inverse_vocab[next_token_id])
```

Since the largest logit value and, correspondingly, the largest softmax probability score are in the fourth position (index position 3 since Python uses 0 indexing), the generated word is "forward".

To implement a probabilistic sampling process, we can now replace argmax with the multinomial function in PyTorch:

```
torch.manual_seed(123)
next_token_id = torch.multinomial(probas, num_samples=1).item()
print(inverse_vocab[next_token_id])
```

The printed output is "forward" just like before. What happened? The multinomial function samples the next token proportional to its probability score. In other words, "forward" is still the most likely token and will be selected by multinomial most of the time but not all the time. To illustrate this, let's implement a function that repeats this sampling 1,000 times:

```
def print_sampled_tokens(probas):
    torch.manual_seed(123)
    sample = [torch.multinomial(probas, num_samples=1).item()
              for i in range(1_000)]
    sampled_ids = torch.bincount(torch.tensor(sample))
    for i, freq in enumerate(sampled_ids):
        print(f"{freq} x {inverse_vocab[i]}")

print_sampled_tokens(probas)
```

The sampling output is

```
73 x closer
0 x every
0 x effort
582 x forward
2 x inches
```

```
0 x moves
0 x pizza
343 x toward
```

As we can see, the word `forward` is sampled most of the time (582 out of 1,000 times), but other tokens such as `closer`, `inches`, and `toward` will also be sampled some of the time. This means that if we replaced the `argmax` function with the `multinomial` function inside the `generate_and_print_sample` function, the LLM would sometimes generate texts such as `every effort moves you toward`, `every effort moves you inches`, and `every effort moves you closer` instead of `every effort moves you forward`.

We can further control the distribution and selection process via a concept called *temperature scaling*. Temperature scaling is just a fancy description for dividing the logits by a number greater than 0:

```
def softmax_with_temperature(logits, temperature):
    scaled_logits = logits / temperature
    return torch.softmax(scaled_logits, dim=0)
```

Temperatures greater than 1 result in more uniformly distributed token probabilities, and temperatures smaller than 1 will result in more confident (sharper or more peaky) distributions. Let's illustrate this by plotting the original probabilities alongside probabilities scaled with different temperature values:

```
temperatures = [1, 0.1, 5]                                          # Original, lower, and higher confidence
scaled_probas = [softmax_with_temperature(next_token_logits, T)
                for T in temperatures]
x = torch.arange(len(vocab))
bar_width = 0.15
fig, ax = plt.subplots(figsize=(5, 3))
for i, T in enumerate(temperatures):
    rects = ax.bar(x + i * bar_width, scaled_probas[i],
                   bar_width, label=f'Temperature = {T}')
ax.set_ylabel('Probability')
ax.set_xticks(x)
ax.set_xticklabels(vocab.keys(), rotation=90)
ax.legend()
plt.tight_layout()
plt.show()
```

The resulting plot is shown in figure 5.14.

A temperature of 1 divides the logits by 1 before passing them to the `softmax` function to compute the probability scores. In other words, using a temperature of 1 is the same as not using any temperature scaling. In this case, the tokens are selected with a probability equal to the original softmax probability scores via the `multinomial` sampling function in PyTorch. For example, for the temperature setting 1, the token corresponding to "forward" would be selected about 60% of the time, as we can see in figure 5.14.

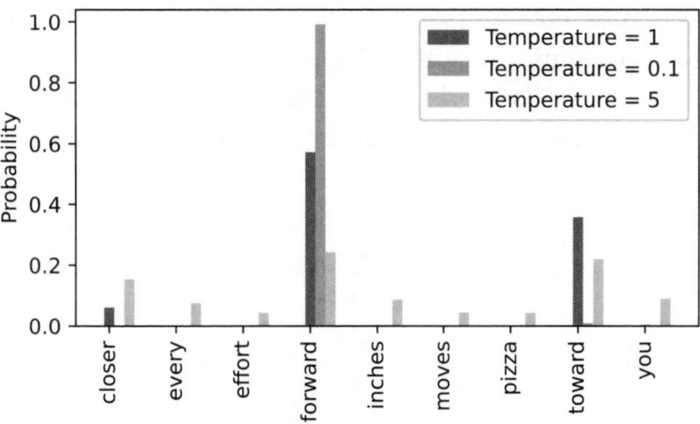

Figure 5.14 A temperature of 1 represents the unscaled probability scores for each token in the vocabulary. Decreasing the temperature to 0.1 sharpens the distribution, so the most likely token (here, "forward") will have an even higher probability score. Likewise, increasing the temperature to 5 makes the distribution more uniform.

Also, as we can see in figure 5.14, applying very small temperatures, such as 0.1, will result in sharper distributions such that the behavior of the `multinomial` function selects the most likely token (here, `"forward"`) almost 100% of the time, approaching the behavior of the `argmax` function. Likewise, a temperature of 5 results in a more uniform distribution where other tokens are selected more often. This can add more variety to the generated texts but also more often results in nonsensical text. For example, using the temperature of 5 results in texts such as `every effort moves you pizza` about 4% of the time.

> **Exercise 5.1**
>
> Use the `print_sampled_tokens` function to print the sampling frequencies of the softmax probabilities scaled with the temperatures shown in figure 5.14. How often is the word `pizza` sampled in each case? Can you think of a faster and more accurate way to determine how often the word `pizza` is sampled?

5.3.2 *Top-k sampling*

We've now implemented a probabilistic sampling approach coupled with temperature scaling to increase the diversity of the outputs. We saw that higher temperature values result in more uniformly distributed next-token probabilities, which result in more diverse outputs as it reduces the likelihood of the model repeatedly selecting the most probable token. This method allows for the exploring of less likely but potentially more interesting and creative paths in the generation process. However, one downside of this approach is that it sometimes leads to grammatically incorrect or completely nonsensical outputs such as `every effort moves you pizza`.

Top-k sampling, when combined with probabilistic sampling and temperature scaling, can improve the text generation results. In top-k sampling, we can restrict the sampled tokens to the top-k most likely tokens and exclude all other tokens from the selection process by masking their probability scores, as illustrated in figure 5.15.

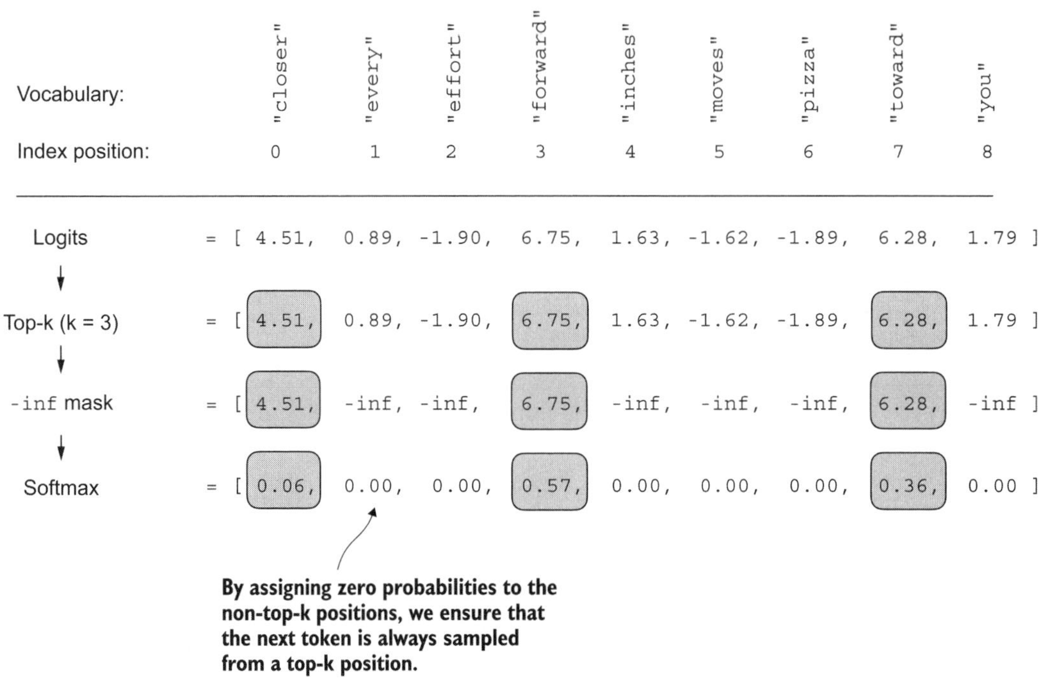

Figure 5.15 Using top-k sampling with k = 3, we focus on the three tokens associated with the highest logits and mask out all other tokens with negative infinity (`-inf`) before applying the `softmax` function. This results in a probability distribution with a probability value 0 assigned to all non-top-k tokens. (The numbers in this figure are truncated to two digits after the decimal point to reduce visual clutter. The values in the "Softmax" row should add up to 1.0.)

The top-k approach replaces all nonselected logits with negative infinity value (`-inf`), such that when computing the softmax values, the probability scores of the non-top-k tokens are 0, and the remaining probabilities sum up to 1. (Careful readers may remember this masking trick from the causal attention module we implemented in chapter 3, section 3.5.1.)

In code, we can implement the top-k procedure in figure 5.15 as follows, starting with the selection of the tokens with the largest logit values:

```
top_k = 3
top_logits, top_pos = torch.topk(next_token_logits, top_k)
print("Top logits:", top_logits)
print("Top positions:", top_pos)
```

The logits values and token IDs of the top three tokens, in descending order, are

```
Top logits: tensor([6.7500, 6.2800, 4.5100])
Top positions: tensor([3, 7, 0])
```

Subsequently, we apply PyTorch's `where` function to set the logit values of tokens that are below the lowest logit value within our top-three selection to negative infinity (`-inf`):

```
new_logits = torch.where(
    condition=next_token_logits < top_logits[-1],
    input=torch.tensor(float('-inf')),
    other=next_token_logits
)
print(new_logits)
```

Identifies logits less than the minimum in the top 3

Assigns –inf to these lower logits

Retains the original logits for all other tokens

The resulting logits for the next token in the nine-token vocabulary are

```
tensor([4.5100,    -inf,    -inf, 6.7500,    -inf,    -inf,    -inf, 6.2800,
     -inf])
```

Lastly, let's apply the `softmax` function to turn these into next-token probabilities:

```
topk_probas = torch.softmax(new_logits, dim=0)
print(topk_probas)
```

As we can see, the result of this top-three approach are three non-zero probability scores:

```
tensor([0.0615, 0.0000, 0.0000, 0.5775, 0.0000, 0.0000, 0.0000, 0.3610,
        0.0000])
```

We can now apply the temperature scaling and multinomial function for probabilistic sampling to select the next token among these three non-zero probability scores to generate the next token. We do this next by modifying the text generation function.

5.3.3 Modifying the text generation function

Now, let's combine temperature sampling and top-k sampling to modify the `generate_text_simple` function we used to generate text via the LLM earlier, creating a new `generate` function.

Listing 5.4 A modified text generation function with more diversity

```
def generate(model, idx, max_new_tokens, context_size,
             temperature=0.0, top_k=None, eos_id=None):
    for _ in range(max_new_tokens):
        idx_cond = idx[:, -context_size:]
        with torch.no_grad():
            logits = model(idx_cond)
        logits = logits[:, -1, :]
```

The for loop is the same as before: gets logits and only focuses on the last time step.

```
        if top_k is not None:                              # Filters logits with top_k sampling
            top_logits, _ = torch.topk(logits, top_k)
            min_val = top_logits[:, -1]
            logits = torch.where(
                logits < min_val,
                torch.tensor(float('-inf')).to(logits.device),
                logits
            )
        if temperature > 0.0:                              # Applies temperature scaling
            logits = logits / temperature
            probs = torch.softmax(logits, dim=-1)
            idx_next = torch.multinomial(probs, num_samples=1)
        else:                                              # Carries out greedy next-token selection as before when temperature scaling is disabled
            idx_next = torch.argmax(logits, dim=-1, keepdim=True)
        if idx_next == eos_id:                             # Stops generating early if end-of-sequence token is encountered
            break
        idx = torch.cat((idx, idx_next), dim=1)
    return idx
```

Let's now see this new `generate` function in action:

```
torch.manual_seed(123)
token_ids = generate(
    model=model,
    idx=text_to_token_ids("Every effort moves you", tokenizer),
    max_new_tokens=15,
    context_size=GPT_CONFIG_124M["context_length"],
    top_k=25,
    temperature=1.4
)
print("Output text:\n", token_ids_to_text(token_ids, tokenizer))
```

The generated text is

```
Output text:
 Every effort moves you stand to work on surprise, a one of us had gone
 with random-
```

As we can see, the generated text is very different from the one we previously generated via the `generate_simple` function in section 5.3 (`"Every effort moves you know," was one of the axioms he laid...!`), which was a memorized passage from the training set.

> **Exercise 5.2**
>
> Play around with different temperatures and top-k settings. Based on your observations, can you think of applications where lower temperature and top-k settings are desired? Likewise, can you think of applications where higher temperature and top-k settings are preferred? (It's recommended to also revisit this exercise at the end of the chapter after loading the pretrained weights from OpenAI.)

> **Exercise 5.3**
>
> What are the different combinations of settings for the `generate` function to force deterministic behavior, that is, disabling the random sampling such that it always produces the same outputs similar to the `generate_simple` function?

5.4 Loading and saving model weights in PyTorch

Thus far, we have discussed how to numerically evaluate the training progress and pretrain an LLM from scratch. Even though both the LLM and dataset were relatively small, this exercise showed that pretraining LLMs is computationally expensive. Thus, it is important to be able to save the LLM so that we don't have to rerun the training every time we want to use it in a new session.

So, let's discuss how to save and load a pretrained model, as highlighted in figure 5.16. Later, we will load a more capable pretrained GPT model from OpenAI into our `GPTModel` instance.

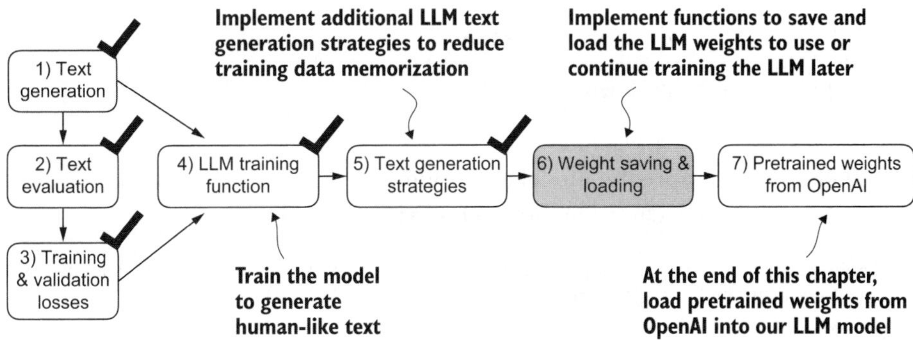

Figure 5.16 After training and inspecting the model, it is often helpful to save the model so that we can use or continue training it later (step 6).

Fortunately, saving a PyTorch model is relatively straightforward. The recommended way is to save a model's `state_dict`, a dictionary mapping each layer to its parameters, using the `torch.save` function:

```
torch.save(model.state_dict(), "model.pth")
```

`"model.pth"` is the filename where the `state_dict` is saved. The `.pth` extension is a convention for PyTorch files, though we could technically use any file extension.

Then, after saving the model weights via the `state_dict`, we can load the model weights into a new `GPTModel` model instance:

```
model = GPTModel(GPT_CONFIG_124M)
model.load_state_dict(torch.load("model.pth", map_location=device))
model.eval()
```

As discussed in chapter 4, dropout helps prevent the model from overfitting to the training data by randomly "dropping out" of a layer's neurons during training. However, during inference, we don't want to randomly drop out any of the information the network has learned. Using `model.eval()` switches the model to evaluation mode for inference, disabling the dropout layers of the `model`. If we plan to continue pretraining a model later—for example, using the `train_model_simple` function we defined earlier in this chapter—saving the optimizer state is also recommended.

Adaptive optimizers such as AdamW store additional parameters for each model weight. AdamW uses historical data to adjust learning rates for each model parameter dynamically. Without it, the optimizer resets, and the model may learn suboptimally or even fail to converge properly, which means it will lose the ability to generate coherent text. Using `torch.save`, we can save both the model and optimizer `state_dict` contents:

```
torch.save({
    "model_state_dict": model.state_dict(),
    "optimizer_state_dict": optimizer.state_dict(),
    },
    "model_and_optimizer.pth"
)
```

Then we can restore the model and optimizer states by first loading the saved data via `torch.load` and then using the `load_state_dict` method:

```
checkpoint = torch.load("model_and_optimizer.pth", map_location=device)
model = GPTModel(GPT_CONFIG_124M)
model.load_state_dict(checkpoint["model_state_dict"])
optimizer = torch.optim.AdamW(model.parameters(), lr=5e-4, weight_decay=0.1)
optimizer.load_state_dict(checkpoint["optimizer_state_dict"])
model.train();
```

Exercise 5.4

After saving the weights, load the model and optimizer in a new Python session or Jupyter notebook file and continue pretraining it for one more epoch using the `train_model_simple` function.

5.5 Loading pretrained weights from OpenAI

Previously, we trained a small GPT-2 model using a limited dataset comprising a short-story book. This approach allowed us to focus on the fundamentals without the need for extensive time and computational resources.

Fortunately, OpenAI openly shared the weights of their GPT-2 models, thus eliminating the need to invest tens to hundreds of thousands of dollars in retraining the model on a large corpus ourselves. So, let's load these weights into our `GPTModel` class and use the model for text generation. Here, *weights* refer to the weight parameters stored in the `.weight` attributes of PyTorch's `Linear` and `Embedding` layers, for example. We accessed them earlier via `model.parameters()` when training the model. In chapter 6, will reuse these pretrained weights to fine-tune the model for a text classification task and follow instructions similar to ChatGPT.

Note that OpenAI originally saved the GPT-2 weights via TensorFlow, which we have to install to load the weights in Python. The following code will use a progress bar tool called `tqdm` to track the download process, which we also have to install.

You can install these libraries by executing the following command in your terminal:

```
pip install tensorflow>=2.15.0  tqdm>=4.66
```

The download code is relatively long, mostly boilerplate, and not very interesting. Hence, instead of devoting precious space to discussing Python code for fetching files from the internet, we download the `gpt_download.py` Python module directly from this chapter's online repository:

```
import urllib.request
url = (
    "https://raw.githubusercontent.com/rasbt/"
    "LLMs-from-scratch/main/ch05/"
    "01_main-chapter-code/gpt_download.py"
)
filename = url.split('/')[-1]
urllib.request.urlretrieve(url, filename)
```

Next, after downloading this file to the local directory of your Python session, you should briefly inspect the contents of this file to ensure that it was saved correctly and contains valid Python code.

We can now import the `download_and_load_gpt2` function from the `gpt_download.py` file as follows, which will load the GPT-2 architecture settings (`settings`) and weight parameters (`params`) into our Python session:

```
from gpt_download import download_and_load_gpt2
settings, params = download_and_load_gpt2(
    model_size="124M", models_dir="gpt2"
)
```

Executing this code downloads the following seven files associated with the `124M` parameter GPT-2 model:

```
checkpoint: 100%|██████████████████████████| 77.0/77.0 [00:00<00:00,
                                                         63.9kiB/s]
encoder.json: 100%|████████████████████████| 1.04M/1.04M [00:00<00:00,
                                                         2.20MiB/s]
```

```
hprams.json: 100%|██████████████████████████| 90.0/90.0 [00:00<00:00,
                                                          78.3kiB/s]
model.ckpt.data-00000-of-00001: 100%|███████| 498M/498M [01:09<00:00,
                                                          7.16MiB/s]
model.ckpt.index: 100%|█████████████████████| 5.21k/5.21k [00:00<00:00,
                                                          3.24MiB/s]
model.ckpt.meta: 100%|██████████████████████| 471k/471k [00:00<00:00,
                                                          2.46MiB/s]
vocab.bpe: 100%|████████████████████████████| 456k/456k [00:00<00:00,
                                                          1.70MiB/s]
```

NOTE If the download code does not work for you, it could be due to intermittent internet connection, server problems, or changes in how OpenAI shares the weights of the open-source GPT-2 model. In this case, please visit this chapter's online code repository at https://github.com/rasbt/LLMs-from-scratch for alternative and updated instructions, and reach out via the Manning Forum for further questions.

Assuming the execution of the previous code has completed, let's inspect the contents of `settings` and `params`:

```
print("Settings:", settings)
print("Parameter dictionary keys:", params.keys())
```

The contents are

```
Settings: {'n_vocab': 50257, 'n_ctx': 1024, 'n_embd': 768, 'n_head': 12,
           'n_layer': 12}
Parameter dictionary keys: dict_keys(['blocks', 'b', 'g', 'wpe', 'wte'])
```

Both `settings` and `params` are Python dictionaries. The `settings` dictionary stores the LLM architecture settings similarly to our manually defined `GPT_CONFIG_124M` settings. The `params` dictionary contains the actual weight tensors. Note that we only printed the dictionary keys because printing the weight contents would take up too much screen space; however, we can inspect these weight tensors by printing the whole dictionary via `print(params)` or by selecting individual tensors via the respective dictionary keys, for example, the embedding layer weights:

```
print(params["wte"])
print("Token embedding weight tensor dimensions:", params["wte"].shape)
```

The weights of the token embedding layer are

```
[[-0.11010301 ... -0.1363697   0.01506208   0.04531523]
 [ 0.04034033 ...  0.08605453  0.00253983   0.04318958]
 [-0.12746179  ...  0.08991534 -0.12972379 -0.08785918]
 ...
 [-0.04453601 ...   0.10435229  0.09783269 -0.06952604]
 [ 0.1860082  ...  -0.09625227  0.07847701 -0.02245961]
```

```
 [ 0.05135201 ...   0.00704835  0.15519823  0.12067825]]
Token embedding weight tensor dimensions: (50257, 768)
```

We downloaded and loaded the weights of the smallest GPT-2 model via the `download_and_load_gpt2(model_size="124M", ...)` setting. OpenAI also shares the weights of larger models: `355M`, `774M`, and `1558M`. The overall architecture of these differently sized GPT models is the same, as illustrated in figure 5.17, except that different

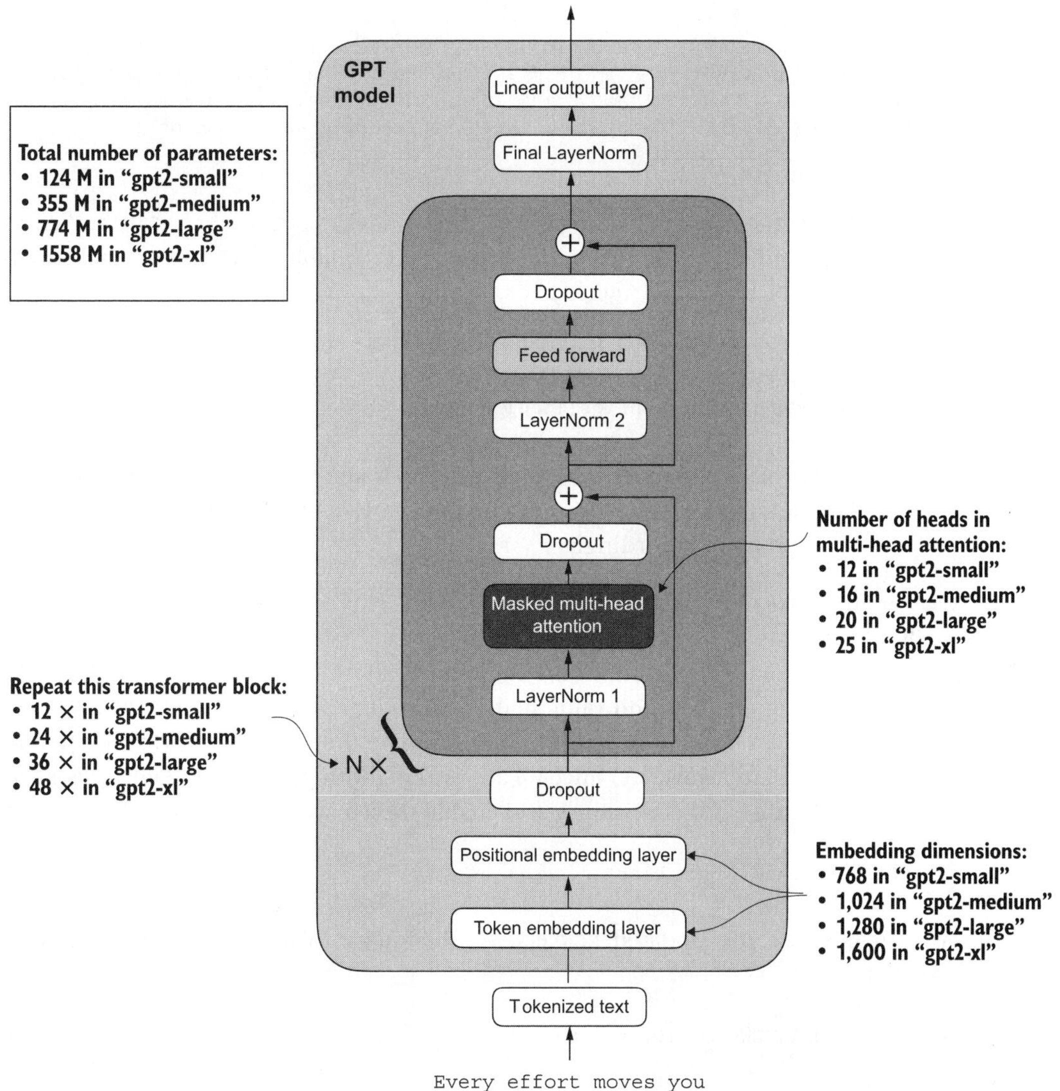

Figure 5.17 GPT-2 LLMs come in several different model sizes, ranging from 124 million to 1,558 million parameters. The core architecture is the same, with the only difference being the embedding sizes and the number of times individual components like the attention heads and transformer blocks are repeated.

architectural elements are repeated different numbers of times and the embedding size differs. The remaining code in this chapter is also compatible with these larger models.

After loading the GPT-2 model weights into Python, we still need to transfer them from the `settings` and `params` dictionaries into our `GPTModel` instance. First, we create a dictionary that lists the differences between the different GPT model sizes in figure 5.17:

```
model_configs = {
    "gpt2-small (124M)": {"emb_dim": 768, "n_layers": 12, "n_heads": 12},
    "gpt2-medium (355M)": {"emb_dim": 1024, "n_layers": 24, "n_heads": 16},
    "gpt2-large (774M)": {"emb_dim": 1280, "n_layers": 36, "n_heads": 20},
    "gpt2-xl (1558M)": {"emb_dim": 1600, "n_layers": 48, "n_heads": 25},
}
```

Suppose we are interested in loading the smallest model, `"gpt2-small (124M)"`. We can use the corresponding settings from the `model_configs` table to update our full-length `GPT_CONFIG_124M` we defined and used earlier:

```
model_name = "gpt2-small (124M)"
NEW_CONFIG = GPT_CONFIG_124M.copy()
NEW_CONFIG.update(model_configs[model_name])
```

Careful readers may remember that we used a 256-token length earlier, but the original GPT-2 models from OpenAI were trained with a 1,024-token length, so we have to update the `NEW_CONFIG` accordingly:

```
NEW_CONFIG.update({"context_length": 1024})
```

Also, OpenAI used bias vectors in the multi-head attention module's linear layers to implement the query, key, and value matrix computations. Bias vectors are not commonly used in LLMs anymore as they don't improve the modeling performance and are thus unnecessary. However, since we are working with pretrained weights, we need to match the settings for consistency and enable these bias vectors:

```
NEW_CONFIG.update({"qkv_bias": True})
```

We can now use the updated `NEW_CONFIG` dictionary to initialize a new `GPTModel` instance:

```
gpt = GPTModel(NEW_CONFIG)
gpt.eval()
```

By default, the `GPTModel` instance is initialized with random weights for pretraining. The last step to using OpenAI's model weights is to override these random weights with the weights we loaded into the `params` dictionary. For this, we will first define a small `assign` utility function that checks whether two tensors or arrays (`left` and `right`) have the same dimensions or shape and returns the right tensor as trainable PyTorch parameters:

```
def assign(left, right):
    if left.shape != right.shape:
        raise ValueError(f"Shape mismatch. Left: {left.shape}, "
                          "Right: {right.shape}"
        )
    return torch.nn.Parameter(torch.tensor(right))
```

Next, we define a `load_weights_into_gpt` function that loads the weights from the `params` dictionary into a `GPTModel` instance `gpt`.

Listing 5.5 Loading OpenAI weights into our GPT model code

```
import numpy as np

def load_weights_into_gpt(gpt, params):
    gpt.pos_emb.weight = assign(gpt.pos_emb.weight, params['wpe'])
    gpt.tok_emb.weight = assign(gpt.tok_emb.weight, params['wte'])

    for b in range(len(params["blocks"])):
        q_w, k_w, v_w = np.split(
            (params["blocks"][b]["attn"]["c_attn"])["w"], 3, axis=-1)
        gpt.trf_blocks[b].att.W_query.weight = assign(
            gpt.trf_blocks[b].att.W_query.weight, q_w.T)
        gpt.trf_blocks[b].att.W_key.weight = assign(
            gpt.trf_blocks[b].att.W_key.weight, k_w.T)
        gpt.trf_blocks[b].att.W_value.weight = assign(
            gpt.trf_blocks[b].att.W_value.weight, v_w.T)

        q_b, k_b, v_b = np.split(
            (params["blocks"][b]["attn"]["c_attn"])["b"], 3, axis=-1)
        gpt.trf_blocks[b].att.W_query.bias = assign(
            gpt.trf_blocks[b].att.W_query.bias, q_b)
        gpt.trf_blocks[b].att.W_key.bias = assign(
            gpt.trf_blocks[b].att.W_key.bias, k_b)
        gpt.trf_blocks[b].att.W_value.bias = assign(
            gpt.trf_blocks[b].att.W_value.bias, v_b)

        gpt.trf_blocks[b].att.out_proj.weight = assign(
            gpt.trf_blocks[b].att.out_proj.weight,
            params["blocks"][b]["attn"]["c_proj"]["w"].T)
```

Sets the model's positional and token embedding weights to those specified in params.

The np.split function is used to divide the attention and bias weights into three equal parts for the query, key, and value components.

Iterates over each transformer block in the model

```
        gpt.trf_blocks[b].att.out_proj.bias = assign(
            gpt.trf_blocks[b].att.out_proj.bias,
            params["blocks"][b]["attn"]["c_proj"]["b"])

        gpt.trf_blocks[b].ff.layers[0].weight = assign(
            gpt.trf_blocks[b].ff.layers[0].weight,
            params["blocks"][b]["mlp"]["c_fc"]["w"].T)
        gpt.trf_blocks[b].ff.layers[0].bias = assign(
            gpt.trf_blocks[b].ff.layers[0].bias,
            params["blocks"][b]["mlp"]["c_fc"]["b"])
        gpt.trf_blocks[b].ff.layers[2].weight = assign(
            gpt.trf_blocks[b].ff.layers[2].weight,
            params["blocks"][b]["mlp"]["c_proj"]["w"].T)
        gpt.trf_blocks[b].ff.layers[2].bias = assign(
            gpt.trf_blocks[b].ff.layers[2].bias,
            params["blocks"][b]["mlp"]["c_proj"]["b"])

        gpt.trf_blocks[b].norm1.scale = assign(
            gpt.trf_blocks[b].norm1.scale,
            params["blocks"][b]["ln_1"]["g"])
        gpt.trf_blocks[b].norm1.shift = assign(
            gpt.trf_blocks[b].norm1.shift,
            params["blocks"][b]["ln_1"]["b"])
        gpt.trf_blocks[b].norm2.scale = assign(
            gpt.trf_blocks[b].norm2.scale,
            params["blocks"][b]["ln_2"]["g"])
        gpt.trf_blocks[b].norm2.shift = assign(
            gpt.trf_blocks[b].norm2.shift,
            params["blocks"][b]["ln_2"]["b"])

    gpt.final_norm.scale = assign(gpt.final_norm.scale, params["g"])
    gpt.final_norm.shift = assign(gpt.final_norm.shift, params["b"])
    gpt.out_head.weight = assign(gpt.out_head.weight, params["wte"])
```

The original GPT-2 model by OpenAI reused the token embedding weights in the output layer to reduce the total number of parameters, which is a concept known as weight tying.

In the `load_weights_into_gpt` function, we carefully match the weights from OpenAI's implementation with our `GPTModel` implementation. To pick a specific example, OpenAI stored the weight tensor for the output projection layer for the first transformer block as `params["blocks"][0]["attn"]["c_proj"]["w"]`. In our implementation, this weight tensor corresponds to `gpt.trf_blocks[b].att.out_proj.weight`, where `gpt` is a `GPTModel` instance.

Developing the `load_weights_into_gpt` function took a lot of guesswork since OpenAI used a slightly different naming convention from ours. However, the `assign` function would alert us if we try to match two tensors with different dimensions. Also, if we made a mistake in this function, we would notice this, as the resulting GPT model would be unable to produce coherent text.

Let's now try the `load_weights_into_gpt` out in practice and load the OpenAI model weights into our `GPTModel` instance `gpt`:

```
load_weights_into_gpt(gpt, params)
gpt.to(device)
```

If the model is loaded correctly, we can now use it to generate new text using our previous `generate` function:

```
torch.manual_seed(123)
token_ids = generate(
    model=gpt,
    idx=text_to_token_ids("Every effort moves you", tokenizer).to(device),
    max_new_tokens=25,
    context_size=NEW_CONFIG["context_length"],
    top_k=50,
    temperature=1.5
)
print("Output text:\n", token_ids_to_text(token_ids, tokenizer))
```

The resulting text is as follows:

```
Output text:
 Every effort moves you toward finding an ideal new way to practice
     something!
What makes us want to be on top of that?
```

We can be confident that we loaded the model weights correctly because the model can produce coherent text. A tiny mistake in this process would cause the model to fail. In the following chapters, we will work further with this pretrained model and fine-tune it to classify text and follow instructions.

> **Exercise 5.5**
> Calculate the training and validation set losses of the `GPTModel` with the pretrained weights from OpenAI on the "The Verdict" dataset.

> **Exercise 5.6**
> Experiment with GPT-2 models of different sizes—for example, the largest 1,558 million parameter model—and compare the generated text to the 124 million model.

Summary

- When LLMs generate text, they output one token at a time.
- By default, the next token is generated by converting the model outputs into probability scores and selecting the token from the vocabulary that corresponds to the highest probability score, which is known as "greedy decoding."
- Using probabilistic sampling and temperature scaling, we can influence the diversity and coherence of the generated text.
- Training and validation set losses can be used to gauge the quality of text generated by LLM during training.

- Pretraining an LLM involves changing its weights to minimize the training loss.
- The training loop for LLMs itself is a standard procedure in deep learning, using a conventional cross entropy loss and AdamW optimizer.
- Pretraining an LLM on a large text corpus is time- and resource-intensive, so we can load openly available weights as an alternative to pretraining the model on a large dataset ourselves.

6 Fine-tuning for classification

This chapter covers

- Introducing different LLM fine-tuning approaches
- Preparing a dataset for text classification
- Modifying a pretrained LLM for fine-tuning
- Fine-tuning an LLM to identify spam messages
- Evaluating the accuracy of a fine-tuned LLM classifier
- Using a fine-tuned LLM to classify new data

So far, we have coded the LLM architecture, pretrained it, and learned how to import pretrained weights from an external source, such as OpenAI, into our model. Now we will reap the fruits of our labor by fine-tuning the LLM on a specific target task, such as classifying text. The concrete example we examine is classifying text messages as "spam" or "not spam." Figure 6.1 highlights the two main ways of fine-tuning an LLM: fine-tuning for classification (step 8) and fine-tuning to follow instructions (step 9).

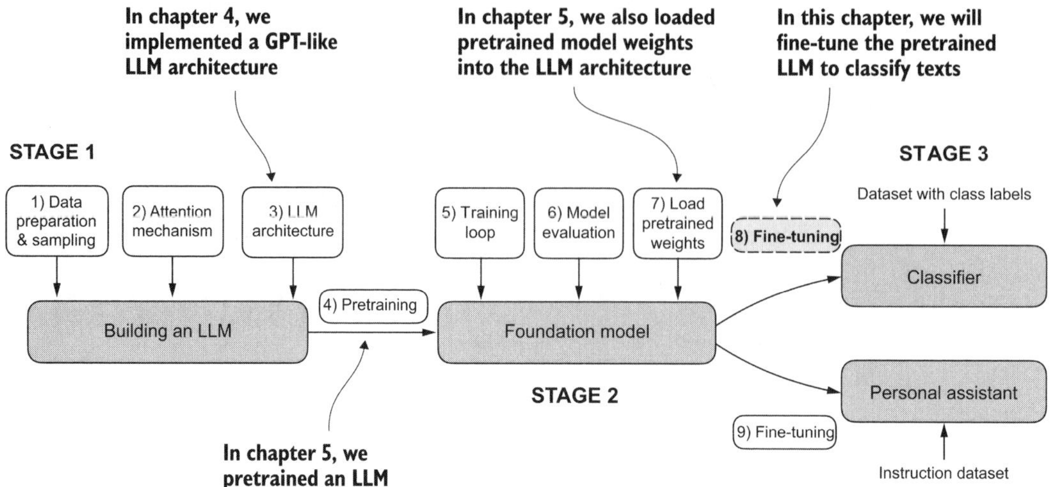

Figure 6.1 The three main stages of coding an LLM. This chapter focus on stage 3 (step 8): fine-tuning a pretrained LLM as a classifier.

6.1 Different categories of fine-tuning

The most common ways to fine-tune language models are *instruction fine-tuning* and *classification fine-tuning*. Instruction fine-tuning involves training a language model on a set of tasks using specific instructions to improve its ability to understand and execute tasks described in natural language prompts, as illustrated in figure 6.2.

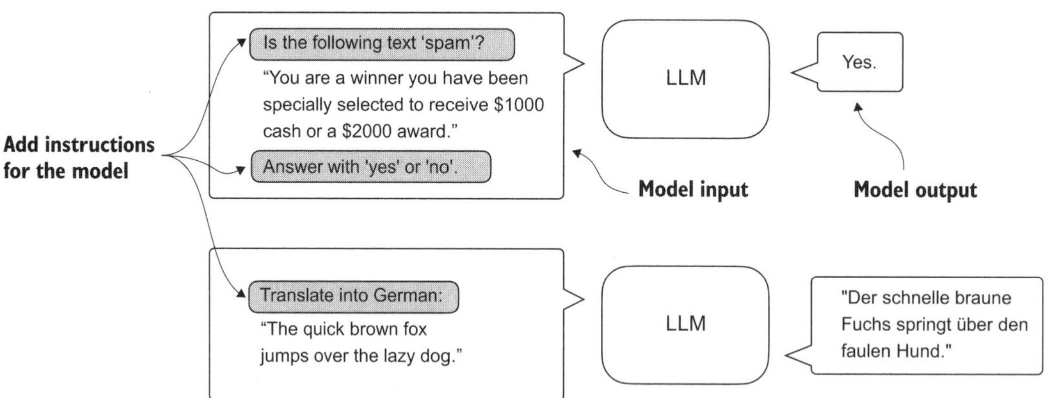

Figure 6.2 Two different instruction fine-tuning scenarios. At the top, the model is tasked with determining whether a given text is spam. At the bottom, the model is given an instruction on how to translate an English sentence into German.

In classification fine-tuning, a concept you might already be acquainted with if you have a background in machine learning, the model is trained to recognize a specific set of class labels, such as "spam" and "not spam." Examples of classification tasks extend beyond LLMs and email filtering: they include identifying different species of plants from images; categorizing news articles into topics like sports, politics, and technology; and distinguishing between benign and malignant tumors in medical imaging.

The key point is that a classification fine-tuned model is restricted to predicting classes it has encountered during its training. For instance, it can determine whether something is "spam" or "not spam," as illustrated in figure 6.3, but it can't say anything else about the input text.

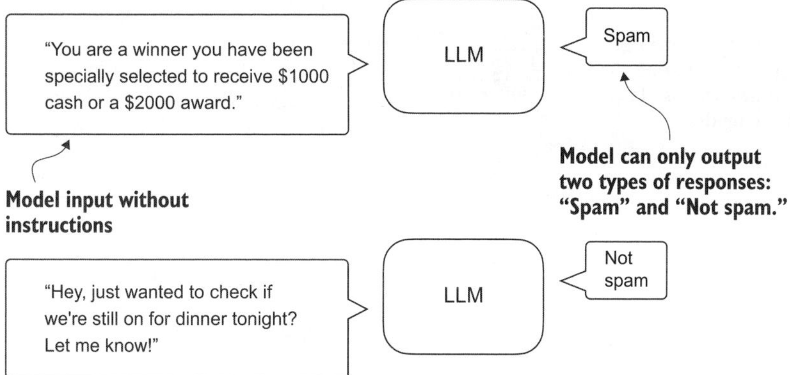

Figure 6.3 A text classification scenario using an LLM. A model fine-tuned for spam classification does not require further instruction alongside the input. In contrast to an instruction fine-tuned model, it can only respond with "spam" or "not spam."

In contrast to the classification fine-tuned model depicted in figure 6.3, an instruction fine-tuned model typically can undertake a broader range of tasks. We can view a classification fine-tuned model as highly specialized, and generally, it is easier to develop a specialized model than a generalist model that works well across various tasks.

Choosing the right approach

Instruction fine-tuning improves a model's ability to understand and generate responses based on specific user instructions. Instruction fine-tuning is best suited for models that need to handle a variety of tasks based on complex user instructions, improving flexibility and interaction quality. Classification fine-tuning is ideal for projects requiring precise categorization of data into predefined classes, such as sentiment analysis or spam detection.

While instruction fine-tuning is more versatile, it demands larger datasets and greater computational resources to develop models proficient in various tasks. In contrast, classification fine-tuning requires less data and compute power, but its use is confined to the specific classes on which the model has been trained.

6.2 Preparing the dataset

We will modify and classification fine-tune the GPT model we previously implemented and pretrained. We begin by downloading and preparing the dataset, as highlighted in figure 6.4. To provide an intuitive and useful example of classification fine-tuning, we will work with a text message dataset that consists of spam and non-spam messages.

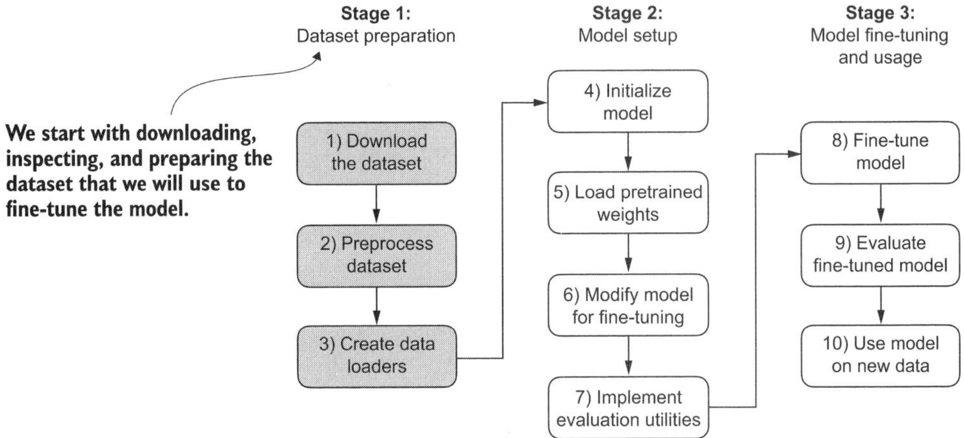

Figure 6.4 The three-stage process for classification fine-tuning an LLM. Stage 1 involves dataset preparation. Stage 2 focuses on model setup. Stage 3 covers fine-tuning and evaluating the model.

> **NOTE** Text messages typically sent via phone, not email. However, the same steps also apply to email classification, and interested readers can find links to email spam classification datasets in appendix B.

The first step is to download the dataset.

Listing 6.1 Downloading and unzipping the dataset

```
import urllib.request
import zipfile
import os
from pathlib import Path

url = "https://archive.ics.uci.edu/static/public/228/sms+spam+collection.zip"
zip_path = "sms_spam_collection.zip"
extracted_path = "sms_spam_collection"
data_file_path = Path(extracted_path) / "SMSSpamCollection.tsv"


def download_and_unzip_spam_data(
        url, zip_path, extracted_path, data_file_path):
    if data_file_path.exists():
```

```
        print(f"{data_file_path} already exists. Skipping download "
              "and extraction."
        )
        return

    with urllib.request.urlopen(url) as response:     # Downloads the file
        with open(zip_path, "wb") as out_file:
            out_file.write(response.read())

    with zipfile.ZipFile(zip_path, "r") as zip_ref:    # Unzips the file
        zip_ref.extractall(extracted_path)

    original_file_path = Path(extracted_path) / "SMSSpamCollection"
    os.rename(original_file_path, data_file_path)           # Adds a .tsv file extension
    print(f"File downloaded and saved as {data_file_path}")

download_and_unzip_spam_data(url, zip_path, extracted_path, data_file_path)
```

After executing the preceding code, the dataset is saved as a tab-separated text file, `SMSSpamCollection.tsv`, in the `sms_spam_collection` folder. We can load it into a pandas `DataFrame` as follows:

```
import pandas as pd
df = pd.read_csv(
    data_file_path, sep="\t", header=None, names=["Label", "Text"]
)
df          # Renders the data frame in a Jupyter notebook. Alternatively, use print(df).
```

Figure 6.5 shows the resulting data frame of the spam dataset.

	Label	Text
0	ham	Go until jurong point, crazy.. Available only ...
1	ham	Ok lar... Joking wif u oni...
2	spam	Free entry in 2 a wkly comp to win FA Cup fina...
3	ham	U dun say so early hor... U c already then say...
4	ham	Nah I don't think he goes to usf, he lives aro...
...	...	...
5571	ham	Rofl. Its true to its name

5572 rows × 2 columns

Figure 6.5 Preview of the `SMSSpamCollection` dataset in a pandas `DataFrame`, showing class labels ("ham" or "spam") and corresponding text messages. The dataset consists of 5,572 rows (text messages and labels).

Let's examine the class label distribution:

```
print(df["Label"].value_counts())
```

Executing the previous code, we find that the data contains "ham" (i.e., not spam) far more frequently than "spam":

```
Label
ham     4825
spam     747
Name: count, dtype: int64
```

For simplicity, and because we prefer a small dataset (which will facilitate faster fine-tuning of the LLM), we choose to undersample the dataset to include 747 instances from each class.

NOTE There are several other methods to handle class imbalances, but these are beyond the scope of this book. Readers interested in exploring methods for dealing with imbalanced data can find additional information in appendix B.

We can use the code in the following listing to undersample and create a balanced dataset.

Listing 6.2 Creating a balanced dataset

```
def create_balanced_dataset(df):
    num_spam = df[df["Label"] == "spam"].shape[0]        # Counts the instances of "spam"
    ham_subset = df[df["Label"] == "ham"].sample(
        num_spam, random_state=123
    )                                                    # Randomly samples "ham" instances to match the number of "spam" instances
    balanced_df = pd.concat([
        ham_subset, df[df["Label"] == "spam"]
    ])                                                   # Combines ham subset with "spam"
    return balanced_df

balanced_df = create_balanced_dataset(df)
print(balanced_df["Label"].value_counts())
```

After executing the previous code to balance the dataset, we can see that we now have equal amounts of spam and non-spam messages:

```
Label
ham     747
spam    747
Name: count, dtype: int64
```

Next, we convert the "string" class labels `"ham"` and `"spam"` into integer class labels 0 and 1, respectively:

```
balanced_df["Label"] = balanced_df["Label"].map({"ham": 0, "spam": 1})
```

This process is similar to converting text into token IDs. However, instead of using the GPT vocabulary, which consists of more than 50,000 words, we are dealing with just two token IDs: 0 and 1.

Next, we create a `random_split` function to split the dataset into three parts: 70% for training, 10% for validation, and 20% for testing. (These ratios are common in machine learning to train, adjust, and evaluate models.)

Listing 6.3 Splitting the dataset

```
def random_split(df, train_frac, validation_frac):

    df = df.sample(
        frac=1, random_state=123
    ).reset_index(drop=True)                     # Shuffles the entire DataFrame
    train_end = int(len(df) * train_frac)        # Calculates split indices
    validation_end = train_end + int(len(df) * validation_frac)

                                                 # Splits the DataFrame
    train_df = df[:train_end]
    validation_df = df[train_end:validation_end]
    test_df = df[validation_end:]

    return train_df, validation_df, test_df

train_df, validation_df, test_df = random_split(
    balanced_df, 0.7, 0.1)                       # Test size is implied to be 0.2 as the remainder.
```

Let's save the dataset as CSV (comma-separated value) files so we can reuse it later:

```
train_df.to_csv("train.csv", index=None)
validation_df.to_csv("validation.csv", index=None)
test_df.to_csv("test.csv", index=None)
```

Thus far, we have downloaded the dataset, balanced it, and split it into training and evaluation subsets. Now we will set up the PyTorch data loaders that will be used to train the model.

6.3 Creating data loaders

We will develop PyTorch data loaders conceptually similar to those we implemented while working with text data. Previously, we utilized a sliding window technique to generate uniformly sized text chunks, which we then grouped into batches for more efficient model training. Each chunk functioned as an individual training instance. However, we are now working with a spam dataset that contains text messages of varying lengths. To batch these messages as we did with the text chunks, we have two primary options:

- Truncate all messages to the length of the shortest message in the dataset or batch.
- Pad all messages to the length of the longest message in the dataset or batch.

The first option is computationally cheaper, but it may result in significant information loss if shorter messages are much smaller than the average or longest messages, potentially reducing model performance. So, we opt for the second option, which preserves the entire content of all messages.

To implement batching, where all messages are padded to the length of the longest message in the dataset, we add padding tokens to all shorter messages. For this purpose, we use `"<|endoftext|>"` as a padding token.

However, instead of appending the string `"<|endoftext|>"` to each of the text messages directly, we can add the token ID corresponding to `"<|endoftext|>"` to the encoded text messages, as illustrated in figure 6.6. `50256` is the token ID of the padding token `"<|endoftext|>"`. We can double-check whether the token ID is correct by encoding the `"<|endoftext|>"` using the *GPT-2 tokenizer* from the `tiktoken` package that we used previously:

```
import tiktoken
tokenizer = tiktoken.get_encoding("gpt2")
print(tokenizer.encode("<|endoftext|>", allowed_special={"<|endoftext|>"}))
```

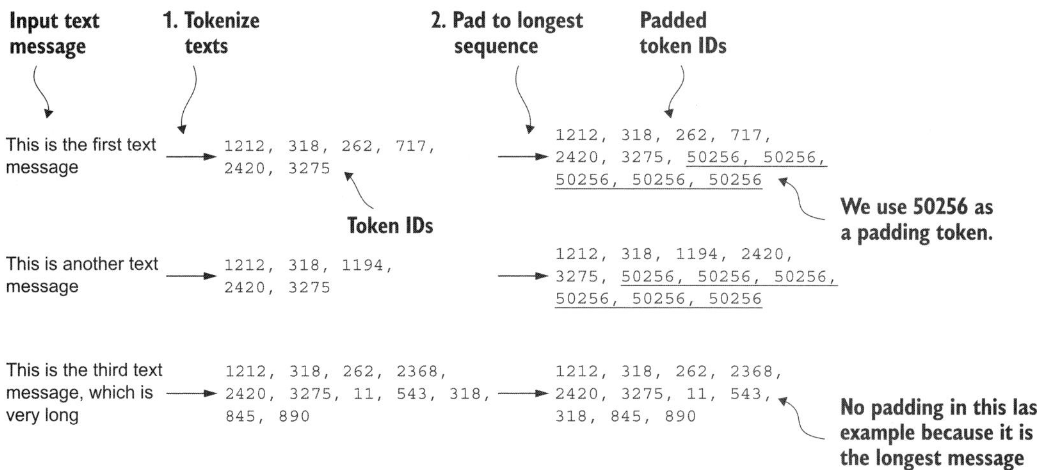

Figure 6.6 The input text preparation process. First, each input text message is converted into a sequence of token IDs. Then, to ensure uniform sequence lengths, shorter sequences are padded with a padding token (in this case, token ID 50256) to match the length of the longest sequence.

Indeed, executing the preceding code returns `[50256]`.

We first need to implement a PyTorch `Dataset`, which specifies how the data is loaded and processed before we can instantiate the data loaders. For this purpose, we define the `SpamDataset` class, which implements the concepts in figure 6.6. This `SpamDataset` class handles several key tasks: it identifies the longest sequence in the training dataset, encodes the text messages, and ensures that all other sequences are padded with a *padding token* to match the length of the longest sequence.

Listing 6.4 Setting up a Pytorch `Dataset` class

```
import torch
from torch.utils.data import Dataset

class SpamDataset(Dataset):
    def __init__(self, csv_file, tokenizer, max_length=None,
                 pad_token_id=50256):
        self.data = pd.read_csv(csv_file)
                                                    # Pretokenizes texts
        self.encoded_texts = [
            tokenizer.encode(text) for text in self.data["Text"]
        ]

        if max_length is None:
            self.max_length = self._longest_encoded_length()
        else:
            self.max_length = max_length
                                                    # Truncates sequences if they
            self.encoded_texts = [                  # are longer than max_length
                encoded_text[:self.max_length]
                for encoded_text in self.encoded_texts
            ]
                                                    # Pads sequences to
        self.encoded_texts = [                      # the longest sequence
            encoded_text + [pad_token_id] *
            (self.max_length - len(encoded_text))
            for encoded_text in self.encoded_texts
        ]


    def __getitem__(self, index):
        encoded = self.encoded_texts[index]
        label = self.data.iloc[index]["Label"]
        return (
            torch.tensor(encoded, dtype=torch.long),
            torch.tensor(label, dtype=torch.long)
        )

    def __len__(self):
        return len(self.data)

    def _longest_encoded_length(self):
        max_length = 0
        for encoded_text in self.encoded_texts:
            encoded_length = len(encoded_text)
            if encoded_length > max_length:
                max_length = encoded_length
        return max_length
```

The `SpamDataset` class loads data from the CSV files we created earlier, tokenizes the text using the GPT-2 tokenizer from `tiktoken`, and allows us to *pad* or *truncate* the sequences to a uniform length determined by either the longest sequence or a predefined maximum length. This ensures each input tensor is of the same size, which is necessary to create the batches in the training data loader we implement next:

```
train_dataset = SpamDataset(
    csv_file="train.csv",
    max_length=None,
    tokenizer=tokenizer
)
```

The longest sequence length is stored in the dataset's `max_length` attribute. If you are curious to see the number of tokens in the longest sequence, you can use the following code:

```
print(train_dataset.max_length)
```

The code outputs `120`, showing that the longest sequence contains no more than 120 tokens, a common length for text messages. The model can handle sequences of up to 1,024 tokens, given its context length limit. If your dataset includes longer texts, you can pass `max_length=1024` when creating the training dataset in the preceding code to ensure that the data does not exceed the model's supported input (context) length.

Next, we pad the validation and test sets to match the length of the longest training sequence. Importantly, any validation and test set samples exceeding the length of the longest training example are truncated using `encoded_text[:self.max_length]` in the `SpamDataset` code we defined earlier. This truncation is optional; you can set `max_length=None` for both validation and test sets, provided there are no sequences exceeding 1,024 tokens in these sets:

```
val_dataset = SpamDataset(
    csv_file="validation.csv",
    max_length=train_dataset.max_length,
    tokenizer=tokenizer
)
test_dataset = SpamDataset(
    csv_file="test.csv",
    max_length=train_dataset.max_length,
    tokenizer=tokenizer
)
```

> **Exercise 6.1 Increasing the context length**
>
> Pad the inputs to the maximum number of tokens the model supports and observe how it affects the predictive performance.

Using the datasets as inputs, we can instantiate the data loaders similarly to when we were working with text data. However, in this case, the targets represent class labels rather than the next tokens in the text. For instance, if we choose a batch size of 8, each batch will consist of eight training examples of length 120 and the corresponding class label of each example, as illustrated in figure 6.7.

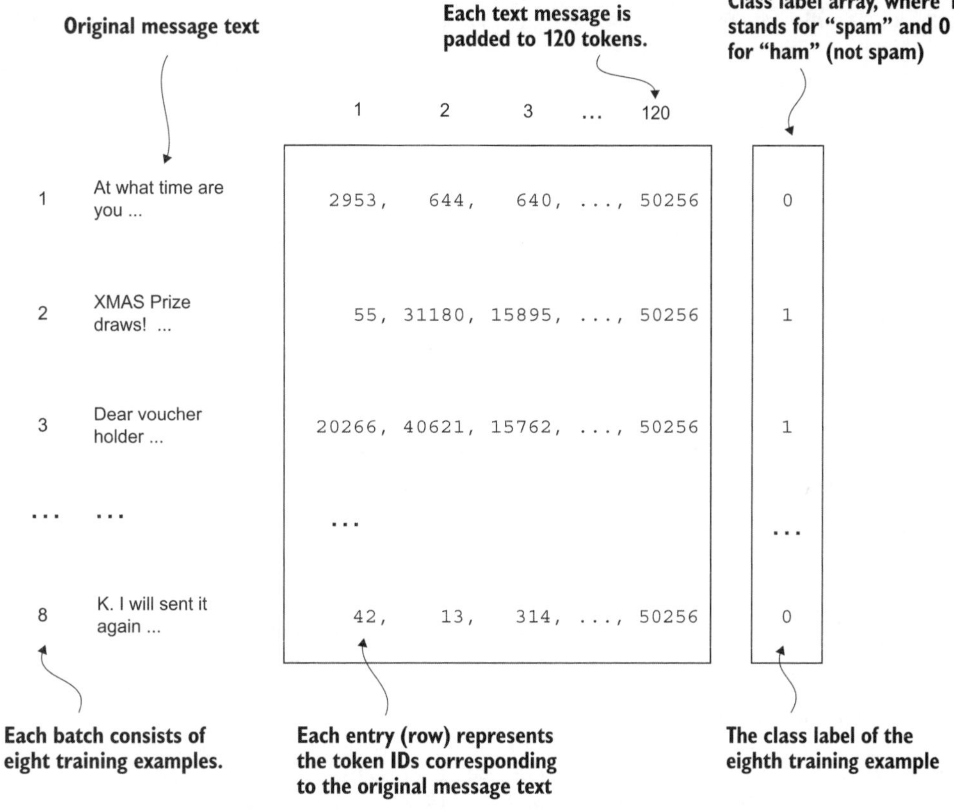

Figure 6.7 A single training batch consisting of eight text messages represented as token IDs. Each text message consists of 120 token IDs. A class label array stores the eight class labels corresponding to the text messages, which can be either `0` ("not spam") or `1` ("spam").

The code in the following listing creates the training, validation, and test set data loaders that load the text messages and labels in batches of size 8.

Listing 6.5 Creating PyTorch data loaders

```
from torch.utils.data import DataLoader

num_workers = 0
batch_size = 8
torch.manual_seed(123)

train_loader = DataLoader(
    dataset=train_dataset,
    batch_size=batch_size,
    shuffle=True,
    num_workers=num_workers,
    drop_last=True,
)
val_loader = DataLoader(
    dataset=val_dataset,
    batch_size=batch_size,
    num_workers=num_workers,
    drop_last=False,
)
test_loader = DataLoader(
    dataset=test_dataset,
    batch_size=batch_size,
    num_workers=num_workers,
    drop_last=False,
)
```

This setting ensures compatibility with most computers.

To ensure that the data loaders are working and are, indeed, returning batches of the expected size, we iterate over the training loader and then print the tensor dimensions of the last batch:

```
for input_batch, target_batch in train_loader:
    pass
print("Input batch dimensions:", input_batch.shape)
print("Label batch dimensions", target_batch.shape)
```

The output is

```
Input batch dimensions: torch.Size([8, 120])
Label batch dimensions torch.Size([8])
```

As we can see, the input batches consist of eight training examples with 120 tokens each, as expected. The label tensor stores the class labels corresponding to the eight training examples.

Lastly, to get an idea of the dataset size, let's print the total number of batches in each dataset:

```
print(f"{len(train_loader)} training batches")
print(f"{len(val_loader)} validation batches")
print(f"{len(test_loader)} test batches")
```

The number of batches in each dataset are

```
130 training batches
19 validation batches
38 test batches
```

Now that we've prepared the data, we need to prepare the model for fine-tuning.

6.4 Initializing a model with pretrained weights

We must prepare the model for classification fine-tuning to identify spam messages. We start by initializing our pretrained model, as highlighted in figure 6.8.

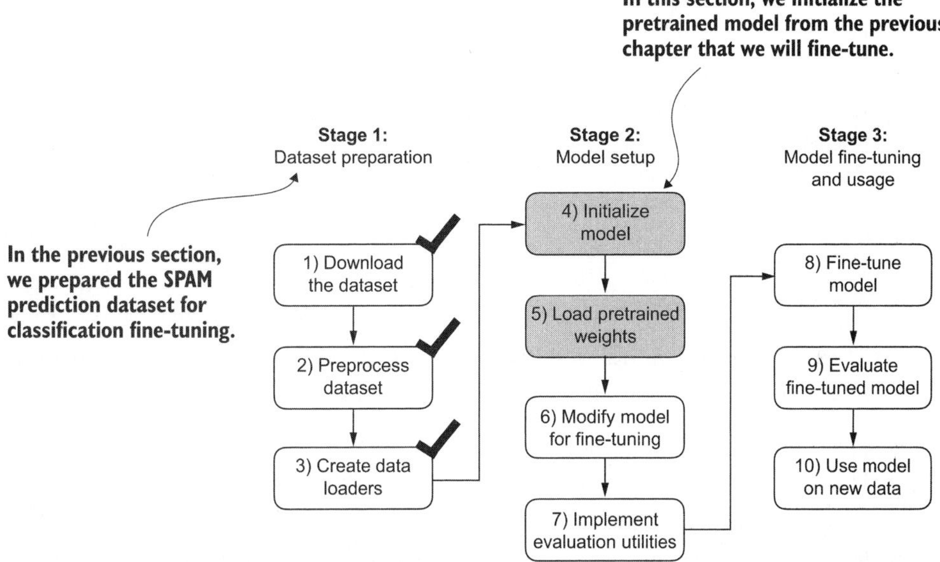

Figure 6.8 The three-stage process for classification fine-tuning the LLM. Having completed stage 1, preparing the dataset, we now must initialize the LLM, which we will then fine-tune to classify spam messages.

To begin the model preparation process, we employ the same configurations we used to pretrain unlabeled data:

```
CHOOSE_MODEL = "gpt2-small (124M)"
INPUT_PROMPT = "Every effort moves"
```

```
BASE_CONFIG = {
    "vocab_size": 50257,          # Vocabulary size
    "context_length": 1024,       # Context length
    "drop_rate": 0.0,             # Dropout rate
    "qkv_bias": True              # Query-key-value bias
}
model_configs = {
    "gpt2-small (124M)": {"emb_dim": 768, "n_layers": 12, "n_heads": 12},
    "gpt2-medium (355M)": {"emb_dim": 1024, "n_layers": 24, "n_heads": 16},
    "gpt2-large (774M)": {"emb_dim": 1280, "n_layers": 36, "n_heads": 20},
    "gpt2-xl (1558M)": {"emb_dim": 1600, "n_layers": 48, "n_heads": 25},
}
BASE_CONFIG.update(model_configs[CHOOSE_MODEL])
```

Next, we import the `download_and_load_gpt2` function from the `gpt_download.py` file and reuse the `GPTModel` class and `load_weights_into_gpt` function from pretraining (see chapter 5) to load the downloaded weights into the GPT model.

Listing 6.6 Loading a pretrained GPT model

```
from gpt_download import download_and_load_gpt2
from chapter05 import GPTModel, load_weights_into_gpt

model_size = CHOOSE_MODEL.split(" ")[-1].lstrip("(").rstrip(")")
settings, params = download_and_load_gpt2(
    model_size=model_size, models_dir="gpt2"
)

model = GPTModel(BASE_CONFIG)
load_weights_into_gpt(model, params)
model.eval()
```

After loading the model weights into the `GPTModel`, we reuse the text generation utility function from chapters 4 and 5 to ensure that the model generates coherent text:

```
from chapter04 import generate_text_simple
from chapter05 import text_to_token_ids, token_ids_to_text

text_1 = "Every effort moves you"
token_ids = generate_text_simple(
    model=model,
    idx=text_to_token_ids(text_1, tokenizer),
    max_new_tokens=15,
    context_size=BASE_CONFIG["context_length"]
)
print(token_ids_to_text(token_ids, tokenizer))
```

The following output shows the model generates coherent text, which is indicates that the model weights have been loaded correctly:

```
Every effort moves you forward.
The first step is to understand the importance of your work
```

Before we start fine-tuning the model as a spam classifier, let's see whether the model already classifies spam messages by prompting it with instructions:

```
text_2 = (
    "Is the following text 'spam'? Answer with 'yes' or 'no':"
    " 'You are a winner you have been specially"
    " selected to receive $1000 cash or a $2000 award.'"
)
token_ids = generate_text_simple(
    model=model,
    idx=text_to_token_ids(text_2, tokenizer),
    max_new_tokens=23,
    context_size=BASE_CONFIG["context_length"]
)
print(token_ids_to_text(token_ids, tokenizer))
```

The model output is

```
Is the following text 'spam'? Answer with 'yes' or 'no': 'You are a winner
you have been specially selected to receive $1000 cash
or a $2000 award.'
The following text 'spam'? Answer with 'yes' or 'no': 'You are a winner
```

Based on the output, it's apparent that the model is struggling to follow instructions. This result is expected, as it has only undergone pretraining and lacks instruction fine-tuning. So, let's prepare the model for classification fine-tuning.

6.5 Adding a classification head

We must modify the pretrained LLM to prepare it for classification fine-tuning. To do so, we replace the original output layer, which maps the hidden representation to a vocabulary of 50,257, with a smaller output layer that maps to two classes: `0` ("not spam") and `1` ("spam"), as shown in figure 6.9. We use the same model as before, except we replace the output layer.

> **Output layer nodes**
>
> We could technically use a single output node since we are dealing with a binary classification task. However, it would require modifying the loss function, as I discuss in "Losses Learned—Optimizing Negative Log-Likelihood and Cross-Entropy in PyTorch" (https://mng.bz/NRZ2). Therefore, we choose a more general approach, where the number of output nodes matches the number of classes. For example, for a three-class problem, such as classifying news articles as "Technology," "Sports," or "Politics," we would use three output nodes, and so forth.

JU 914 4748

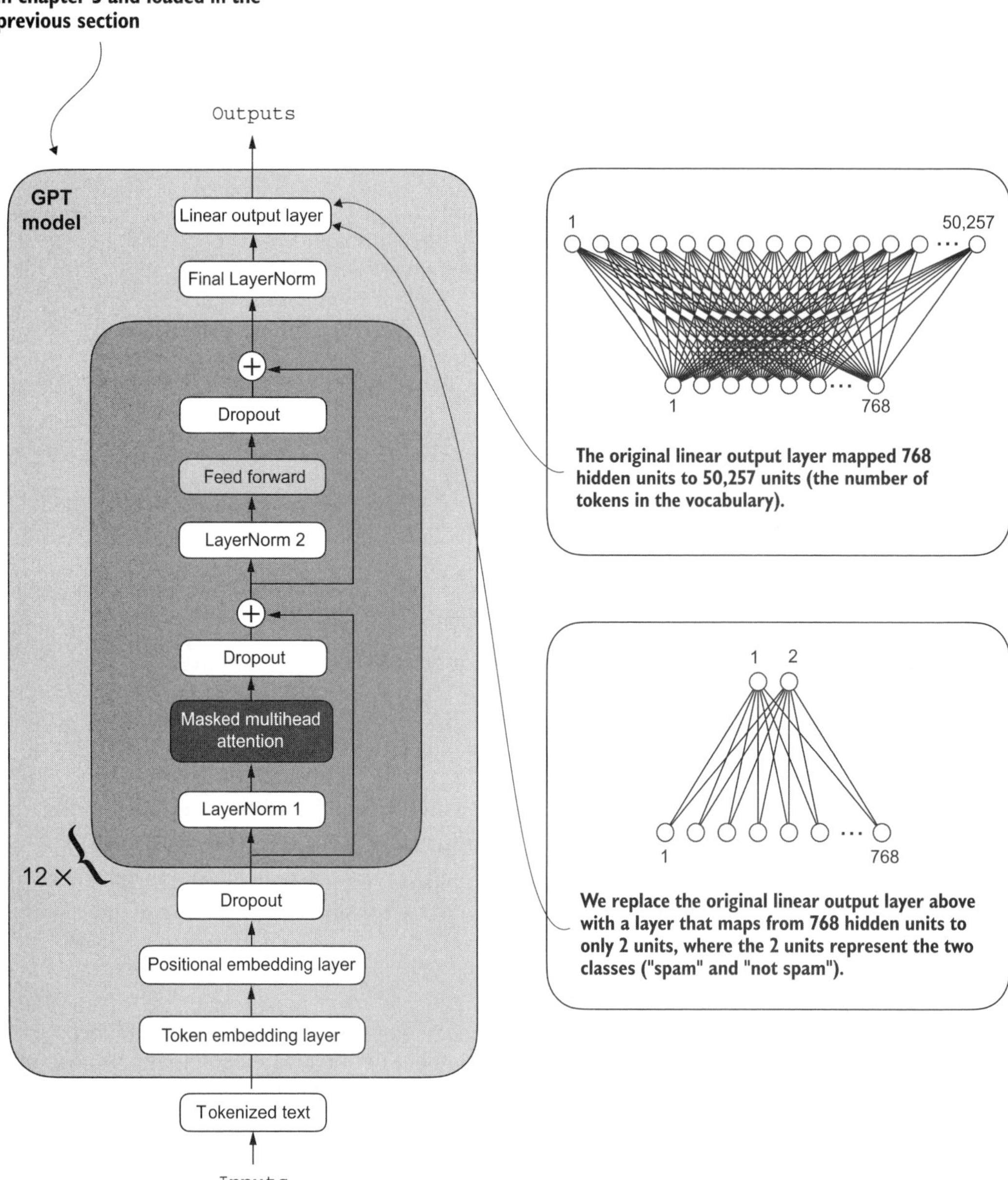

Figure 6.9 Adapting a GPT model for spam classification by altering its architecture. Initially, the model's linear output layer mapped 768 hidden units to a vocabulary of 50,257 tokens. To detect spam, we replace this layer with a new output layer that maps the same 768 hidden units to just two classes, representing "spam" and "not spam."

Before we attempt the modification shown in figure 6.9, let's print the model architecture via `print(model)`:

```
GPTModel(
  (tok_emb): Embedding(50257, 768)
  (pos_emb): Embedding(1024, 768)
  (drop_emb): Dropout(p=0.0, inplace=False)
  (trf_blocks): Sequential(
...
    (11): TransformerBlock(
      (att): MultiHeadAttention(
        (W_query): Linear(in_features=768, out_features=768, bias=True)
        (W_key): Linear(in_features=768, out_features=768, bias=True)
        (W_value): Linear(in_features=768, out_features=768, bias=True)
        (out_proj): Linear(in_features=768, out_features=768, bias=True)
        (dropout): Dropout(p=0.0, inplace=False)
      )
      (ff): FeedForward(
        (layers): Sequential(
          (0): Linear(in_features=768, out_features=3072, bias=True)
          (1): GELU()
          (2): Linear(in_features=3072, out_features=768, bias=True)
        )
      )
      (norm1): LayerNorm()
      (norm2): LayerNorm()
      (drop_resid): Dropout(p=0.0, inplace=False)
    )
  )
  (final_norm): LayerNorm()
  (out_head): Linear(in_features=768, out_features=50257, bias=False)
)
```

This output neatly lays out the architecture we laid out in chapter 4. As previously discussed, the `GPTModel` consists of embedding layers followed by 12 identical *transformer blocks* (only the last block is shown for brevity), followed by a final `LayerNorm` and the output layer, `out_head`.

Next, we replace the `out_head` with a new output layer (see figure 6.9) that we will fine-tune.

Fine-tuning selected layers vs. all layers

Since we start with a pretrained model, it's not necessary to fine-tune all model layers. In neural network-based language models, the lower layers generally capture basic language structures and semantics applicable across a wide range of tasks and datasets. So, fine-tuning only the last layers (i.e., layers near the output), which are more specific to nuanced linguistic patterns and task-specific features, is often sufficient to adapt the model to new tasks. A nice side effect is that it is computationally more efficient to fine-tune only a small number of layers. Interested readers can find more information, including experiments, on which layers to fine-tune in appendix B.

To get the model ready for classification fine-tuning, we first *freeze* the model, meaning that we make all layers nontrainable:

```
for param in model.parameters():
    param.requires_grad = False
```

Then, we replace the output layer (`model.out_head`), which originally maps the layer inputs to 50,257 dimensions, the size of the vocabulary (see figure 6.9).

Listing 6.7 Adding a classification layer

```
torch.manual_seed(123)
num_classes = 2
model.out_head = torch.nn.Linear(
    in_features=BASE_CONFIG["emb_dim"],
    out_features=num_classes
)
```

To keep the code more general, we use `BASE_CONFIG["emb_dim"]`, which is equal to 768 in the `"gpt2-small (124M)"` model. Thus, we can also use the same code to work with the larger GPT-2 model variants.

This new `model.out_head` output layer has its `requires_grad` attribute set to `True` by default, which means that it's the only layer in the model that will be updated during training. Technically, training the output layer we just added is sufficient. However, as I found in experiments, fine-tuning additional layers can noticeably improve the predictive performance of the model. (For more details, refer to appendix B.) We also configure the last transformer block and the final `LayerNorm` module, which connects this block to the output layer, to be trainable, as depicted in figure 6.10.

To make the final `LayerNorm` and last transformer block trainable, we set their respective `requires_grad` to `True`:

```
for param in model.trf_blocks[-1].parameters():
    param.requires_grad = True
for param in model.final_norm.parameters():
    param.requires_grad = True
```

Exercise 6.2 Fine-tuning the whole model

Instead of fine-tuning just the final transformer block, fine-tune the entire model and assess the effect on predictive performance.

Even though we added a new output layer and marked certain layers as trainable or nontrainable, we can still use this model similarly to how we have previously. For

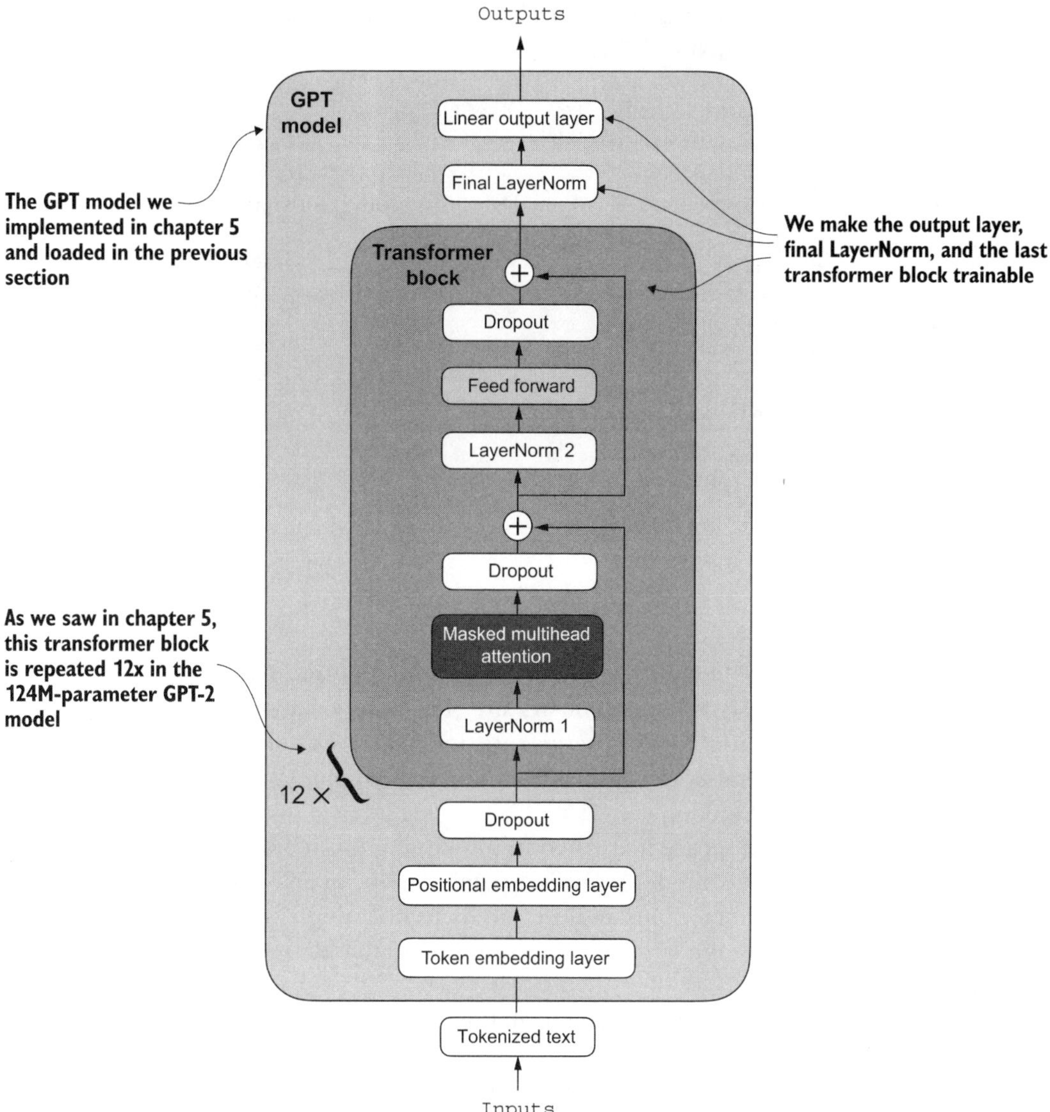

Figure 6.10 The GPT model includes 12 repeated transformer blocks. Alongside the output layer, we set the final `LayerNorm` and the last transformer block as trainable. The remaining 11 transformer blocks and the embedding layers are kept nontrainable.

instance, we can feed it an example text identical to our previously used example text:

```
inputs = tokenizer.encode("Do you have time")
inputs = torch.tensor(inputs).unsqueeze(0)
print("Inputs:", inputs)
print("Inputs dimensions:", inputs.shape)
```

shape: (batch_size, num_tokens)

The print output shows that the preceding code encodes the inputs into a tensor consisting of four input tokens:

```
Inputs: tensor([[5211,  345,  423,  640]])
Inputs dimensions: torch.Size([1, 4])
```

Then, we can pass the encoded token IDs to the model as usual:

```
with torch.no_grad():
    outputs = model(inputs)
print("Outputs:\n", outputs)
print("Outputs dimensions:", outputs.shape)
```

The output tensor looks like the following:

```
Outputs:
 tensor([[[-1.5854,  0.9904],
         [-3.7235,  7.4548],
         [-2.2661,  6.6049],
         [-3.5983,  3.9902]]])
Outputs dimensions: torch.Size([1, 4, 2])
```

A similar input would have previously produced an output tensor of `[1, 4, 50257]`, where `50257` represents the vocabulary size. The number of output rows corresponds to the number of input tokens (in this case, four). However, each output's embedding dimension (the number of columns) is now 2 instead of 50,257 since we replaced the output layer of the model.

Remember that we are interested in fine-tuning this model to return a class label indicating whether a model input is "spam" or "not spam." We don't need to fine-tune all four output rows; instead, we can focus on a single output token. In particular, we will focus on the last row corresponding to the last output token, as shown in figure 6.11.

To extract the last output token from the output tensor, we use the following code:

```
print("Last output token:", outputs[:, -1, :])
```

This prints

```
Last output token: tensor([[-3.5983,  3.9902]])
```

We still need to convert the values into a class-label prediction. But first, let's understand why we are particularly interested in the last output token only.

We have already explored the attention mechanism, which establishes a relationship between each input token and every other input token, and the concept of a *causal attention mask*, commonly used in GPT-like models (see chapter 3). This mask restricts a

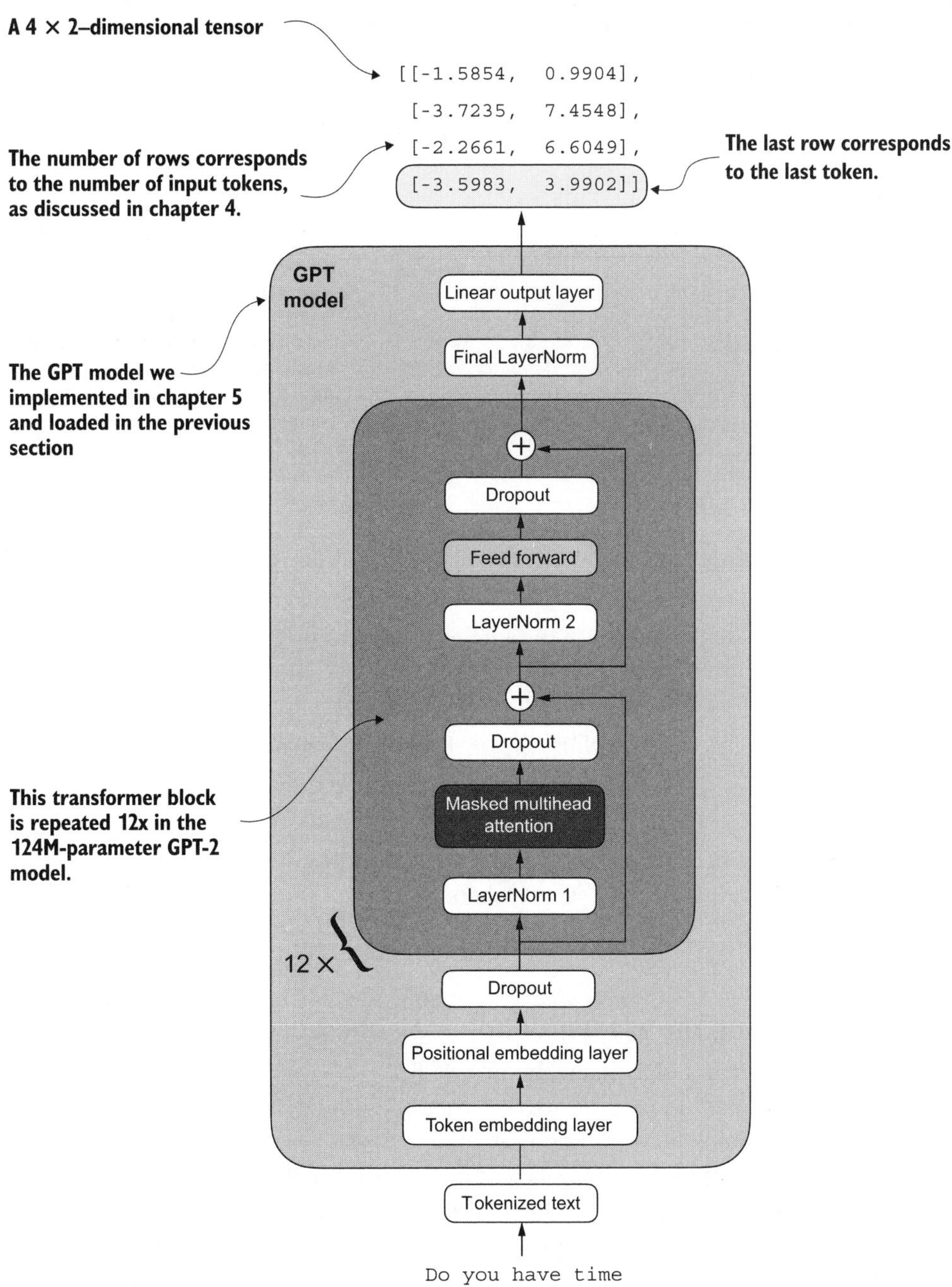

Figure 6.11 The GPT model with a four-token example input and output. The output tensor consists of two columns due to the modified output layer. We are only interested in the last row corresponding to the last token when fine-tuning the model for spam classification.

token's focus to its current position and the those before it, ensuring that each token can only be influenced by itself and the preceding tokens, as illustrated in figure 6.12.

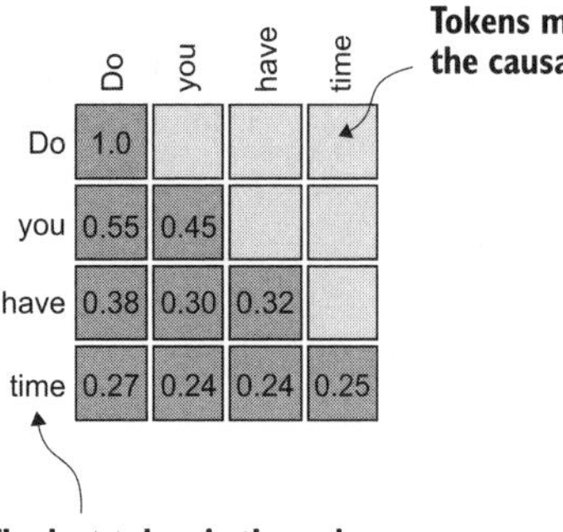

Figure 6.12 The causal attention mechanism, where the attention scores between input tokens are displayed in a matrix format. The empty cells indicate masked positions due to the causal attention mask, preventing tokens from attending to future tokens. The values in the cells represent attention scores; the last token, `time`, is the only one that computes attention scores for all preceding tokens.

Given the causal attention mask setup in figure 6.12, the last token in a sequence accumulates the most information since it is the only token with access to data from all the previous tokens. Therefore, in our spam classification task, we focus on this last token during the fine-tuning process.

We are now ready to transform the last token into class label predictions and calculate the model's initial prediction accuracy. Subsequently, we will fine-tune the model for the spam classification task.

> **Exercise 6.3 Fine-tuning the first vs. last token**
>
> Try fine-tuning the first output token. Notice the changes in predictive performance compared to fine-tuning the last output token.

6.6 Calculating the classification loss and accuracy

Only one small task remains before we fine-tune the model: we must implement the model evaluation functions used during fine-tuning, as illustrated in figure 6.13.

Before implementing the evaluation utilities, let's briefly discuss how we convert the model outputs into class label predictions. We previously computed the token ID of the next token generated by the LLM by converting the 50,257 outputs into probabilities via the `softmax` function and then returning the position of the highest probability via the `argmax` function. We take the same approach here to calculate whether the model outputs a "spam" or "not spam" prediction for a given input, as shown in figure 6.14. The only difference is that we work with 2-dimensional instead of 50,257-dimensional outputs.

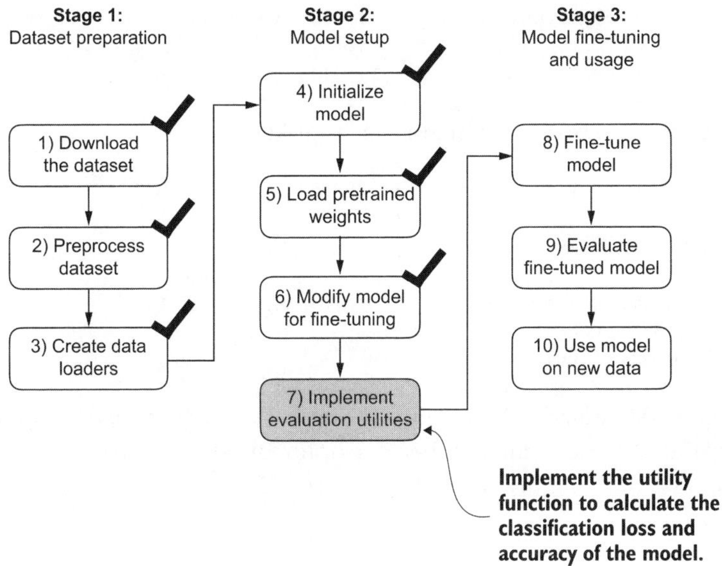

Figure 6.13 The three-stage process for classification fine-tuning the LLM. We've completed the first six steps. We are now ready to undertake the last step of stage 2: implementing the functions to evaluate the model's performance to classify spam messages before, during, and after the fine-tuning.

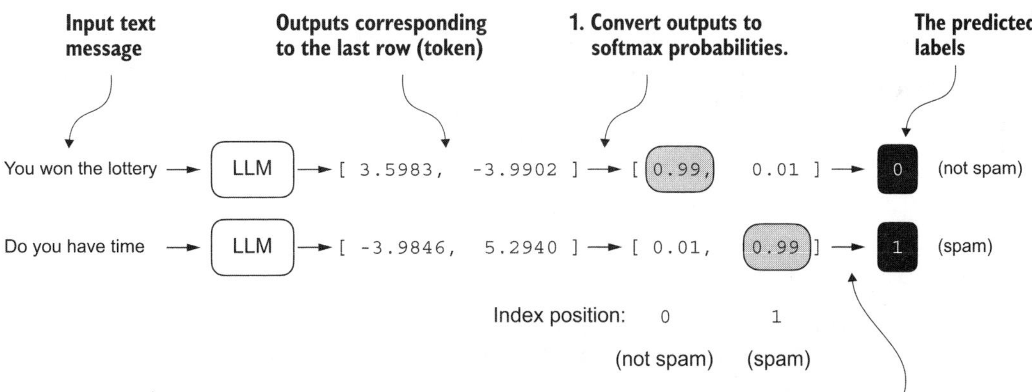

Figure 6.14 The model outputs corresponding to the last token are converted into probability scores for each input text. The class labels are obtained by looking up the index position of the highest probability score. The model predicts the spam labels incorrectly because it has not yet been trained.

Let's consider the last token output using a concrete example:

```
print("Last output token:", outputs[:, -1, :])
```

The values of the tensor corresponding to the last token are

```
Last output token: tensor([[-3.5983,  3.9902]])
```

We can obtain the class label:

```
probas = torch.softmax(outputs[:, -1, :], dim=-1)
label = torch.argmax(probas)
print("Class label:", label.item())
```

In this case, the code returns `1`, meaning the model predicts that the input text is "spam." Using the `softmax` function here is optional because the largest outputs directly correspond to the highest probability scores. Hence, we can simplify the code without using softmax:

```
logits = outputs[:, -1, :]
label = torch.argmax(logits)
print("Class label:", label.item())
```

This concept can be used to compute the classification accuracy, which measures the percentage of correct predictions across a dataset.

To determine the classification accuracy, we apply the `argmax`-based prediction code to all examples in the dataset and calculate the proportion of correct predictions by defining a `calc_accuracy_loader` function.

Listing 6.8 Calculating the classification accuracy

```
def calc_accuracy_loader(data_loader, model, device, num_batches=None):
    model.eval()
    correct_predictions, num_examples = 0, 0

    if num_batches is None:
        num_batches = len(data_loader)
    else:
        num_batches = min(num_batches, len(data_loader))
    for i, (input_batch, target_batch) in enumerate(data_loader):
        if i < num_batches:
            input_batch = input_batch.to(device)
            target_batch = target_batch.to(device)


            with torch.no_grad():
                logits = model(input_batch)[:, -1, :]     # Logits of last output token
            predicted_labels = torch.argmax(logits, dim=-1)

            num_examples += predicted_labels.shape[0]
            correct_predictions += (
```

```
                (predicted_labels == target_batch).sum().item()
            )

        else:
            break
    return correct_predictions / num_examples
```

Let's use the function to determine the classification accuracies across various datasets estimated from 10 batches for efficiency:

```
device = torch.device("cuda" if torch.cuda.is_available() else "cpu")
model.to(device)

torch.manual_seed(123)
train_accuracy = calc_accuracy_loader(
    train_loader, model, device, num_batches=10
)
val_accuracy = calc_accuracy_loader(
    val_loader, model, device, num_batches=10
)
test_accuracy = calc_accuracy_loader(
    test_loader, model, device, num_batches=10
)

print(f"Training accuracy: {train_accuracy*100:.2f}%")
print(f"Validation accuracy: {val_accuracy*100:.2f}%")
print(f"Test accuracy: {test_accuracy*100:.2f}%")
```

Via the `device` setting, the model automatically runs on a GPU if a GPU with Nvidia CUDA support is available and otherwise runs on a CPU. The output is

```
Training accuracy: 46.25%
Validation accuracy: 45.00%
Test accuracy: 48.75%
```

As we can see, the prediction accuracies are near a random prediction, which would be 50% in this case. To improve the prediction accuracies, we need to fine-tune the model.

However, before we begin fine-tuning the model, we must define the loss function we will optimize during training. Our objective is to maximize the spam classification accuracy of the model, which means that the preceding code should output the correct class labels: `0` for non-spam and `1` for spam.

Because classification accuracy is not a differentiable function, we use cross-entropy loss as a proxy to maximize accuracy. Accordingly, the `calc_loss_batch` function remains the same, with one adjustment: we focus on optimizing only the last token, `model(input_batch)[:, -1, :]`, rather than all tokens, `model(input_batch)`:

```
def calc_loss_batch(input_batch, target_batch, model, device):
    input_batch = input_batch.to(device)
    target_batch = target_batch.to(device)
    logits = model(input_batch)[:, -1, :]        # Logits of last output token
```

```
    loss = torch.nn.functional.cross_entropy(logits, target_batch)
    return loss
```

We use the `calc_loss_batch` function to compute the loss for a single batch obtained from the previously defined data loaders. To calculate the loss for all batches in a data loader, we define the `calc_loss_loader` function as before.

Listing 6.9 Calculating the classification loss

```
def calc_loss_loader(data_loader, model, device, num_batches=None):
    total_loss = 0.
    if len(data_loader) == 0:
        return float("nan")
    elif num_batches is None:
        num_batches = len(data_loader)
    else:
        num_batches = min(num_batches, len(data_loader))
    for i, (input_batch, target_batch) in enumerate(data_loader):
        if i < num_batches:
            loss = calc_loss_batch(
                input_batch, target_batch, model, device
            )
            total_loss += loss.item()
        else:
            break
    return total_loss / num_batches
```

Ensures number of batches doesn't exceed batches in data loader

Similar to calculating the training accuracy, we now compute the initial loss for each data set:

```
with torch.no_grad():
    train_loss = calc_loss_loader(
        train_loader, model, device, num_batches=5
    )
    val_loss = calc_loss_loader(val_loader, model, device, num_batches=5)
    test_loss = calc_loss_loader(test_loader, model, device, num_batches=5)
print(f"Training loss: {train_loss:.3f}")
print(f"Validation loss: {val_loss:.3f}")
print(f"Test loss: {test_loss:.3f}")
```

Disables gradient tracking for efficiency because we are not training yet

The initial loss values are

```
Training loss: 2.453
Validation loss: 2.583
Test loss: 2.322
```

Next, we will implement a training function to fine-tune the model, which means adjusting the model to minimize the training set loss. Minimizing the training set loss will help increase the classification accuracy, which is our overall goal.

6.7 Fine-tuning the model on supervised data

We must define and use the training function to fine-tune the pretrained LLM and improve its spam classification accuracy. The training loop, illustrated in figure 6.15, is the same overall training loop we used for pretraining; the only difference is that we calculate the classification accuracy instead of generating a sample text to evaluate the model.

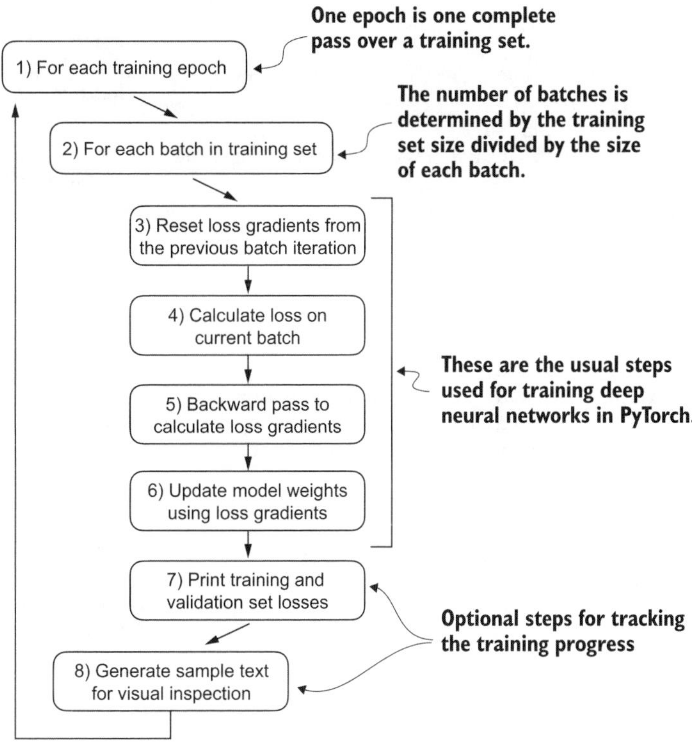

Figure 6.15 A typical training loop for training deep neural networks in PyTorch consists of several steps, iterating over the batches in the training set for several epochs. In each loop, we calculate the loss for each training set batch to determine loss gradients, which we use to update the model weights to minimize the training set loss.

The training function implementing the concepts shown in figure 6.15 also closely mirrors the `train_model_simple` function used for pretraining the model. The only two distinctions are that we now track the number of training examples seen (`examples_seen`) instead of the number of tokens, and we calculate the accuracy after each epoch instead of printing a sample text.

Listing 6.10 Fine-tuning the model to classify spam

```
def train_classifier_simple(
        model, train_loader, val_loader, optimizer, device,
        num_epochs, eval_freq, eval_iter):
    train_losses, val_losses, train_accs, val_accs = [], [], [], []   # Initialize lists to track losses and examples seen
    examples_seen, global_step = 0, -1

    for epoch in range(num_epochs):    # Main training loop
        model.train()                  # Sets model to training mode

        for input_batch, target_batch in train_loader:
            optimizer.zero_grad()      # Resets loss gradients from the previous batch iteration
            loss = calc_loss_batch(
                input_batch, target_batch, model, device
            )
            loss.backward()            # Calculates loss gradients
            optimizer.step()           # Updates model weights using loss gradients
            examples_seen += input_batch.shape[0]   # New: tracks examples instead of tokens
            global_step += 1

            # Optional evaluation step
            if global_step % eval_freq == 0:
                train_loss, val_loss = evaluate_model(
                    model, train_loader, val_loader, device, eval_iter)
                train_losses.append(train_loss)
                val_losses.append(val_loss)
                print(f"Ep {epoch+1} (Step {global_step:06d}): "
                      f"Train loss {train_loss:.3f}, "
                      f"Val loss {val_loss:.3f}"
                )

        # Calculates accuracy after each epoch
        train_accuracy = calc_accuracy_loader(
            train_loader, model, device, num_batches=eval_iter
        )
        val_accuracy = calc_accuracy_loader(
            val_loader, model, device, num_batches=eval_iter
        )

        print(f"Training accuracy: {train_accuracy*100:.2f}% | ", end="")
        print(f"Validation accuracy: {val_accuracy*100:.2f}%")
        train_accs.append(train_accuracy)
        val_accs.append(val_accuracy)

    return train_losses, val_losses, train_accs, val_accs, examples_seen
```

The `evaluate_model` function is identical to the one we used for pretraining:

```
def evaluate_model(model, train_loader, val_loader, device, eval_iter):
    model.eval()
    with torch.no_grad():
```

```
        train_loss = calc_loss_loader(
            train_loader, model, device, num_batches=eval_iter
        )
        val_loss = calc_loss_loader(
            val_loader, model, device, num_batches=eval_iter
        )
    model.train()
    return train_loss, val_loss
```

Next, we initialize the optimizer, set the number of training epochs, and initiate the training using the `train_classifier_simple` function. The training takes about 6 minutes on an M3 MacBook Air laptop computer and less than half a minute on a V100 or A100 GPU:

```
import time

start_time = time.time()
torch.manual_seed(123)
optimizer = torch.optim.AdamW(model.parameters(), lr=5e-5, weight_decay=0.1)
num_epochs = 5


train_losses, val_losses, train_accs, val_accs, examples_seen = \
    train_classifier_simple(
        model, train_loader, val_loader, optimizer, device,
        num_epochs=num_epochs, eval_freq=50,
        eval_iter=5
    )

end_time = time.time()
execution_time_minutes = (end_time - start_time) / 60
print(f"Training completed in {execution_time_minutes:.2f} minutes.")
```

The output we see during the training is as follows:

```
Ep 1 (Step 000000): Train loss 2.153, Val loss 2.392
Ep 1 (Step 000050): Train loss 0.617, Val loss 0.637
Ep 1 (Step 000100): Train loss 0.523, Val loss 0.557
Training accuracy: 70.00% | Validation accuracy: 72.50%
Ep 2 (Step 000150): Train loss 0.561, Val loss 0.489
Ep 2 (Step 000200): Train loss 0.419, Val loss 0.397
Ep 2 (Step 000250): Train loss 0.409, Val loss 0.353
Training accuracy: 82.50% | Validation accuracy: 85.00%
Ep 3 (Step 000300): Train loss 0.333, Val loss 0.320
Ep 3 (Step 000350): Train loss 0.340, Val loss 0.306
Training accuracy: 90.00% | Validation accuracy: 90.00%
Ep 4 (Step 000400): Train loss 0.136, Val loss 0.200
Ep 4 (Step 000450): Train loss 0.153, Val loss 0.132
Ep 4 (Step 000500): Train loss 0.222, Val loss 0.137
Training accuracy: 100.00% | Validation accuracy: 97.50%
Ep 5 (Step 000550): Train loss 0.207, Val loss 0.143
Ep 5 (Step 000600): Train loss 0.083, Val loss 0.074
Training accuracy: 100.00% | Validation accuracy: 97.50%
Training completed in 5.65 minutes.
```

We then use Matplotlib to plot the loss function for the training and validation set.

Listing 6.11 Plotting the classification loss

```
import matplotlib.pyplot as plt

def plot_values(
        epochs_seen, examples_seen, train_values, val_values,
        label="loss"):
    fig, ax1 = plt.subplots(figsize=(5, 3))

    ax1.plot(epochs_seen, train_values, label=f"Training {label}")
    ax1.plot(
        epochs_seen, val_values, linestyle="-.",
        label=f"Validation {label}"
    )
    ax1.set_xlabel("Epochs")
    ax1.set_ylabel(label.capitalize())
    ax1.legend()

    ax2 = ax1.twiny()
    ax2.plot(examples_seen, train_values, alpha=0)
    ax2.set_xlabel("Examples seen")

    fig.tight_layout()
    plt.savefig(f"{label}-plot.pdf")
    plt.show()

epochs_tensor = torch.linspace(0, num_epochs, len(train_losses))
examples_seen_tensor = torch.linspace(0, examples_seen, len(train_losses))

plot_values(epochs_tensor, examples_seen_tensor, train_losses, val_losses)
```

- Plots training and validation loss against epochs
- Creates a second x-axis for examples seen
- Invisible plot for aligning ticks
- Adjusts layout to make room

Figure 6.16 plots the resulting loss curves.

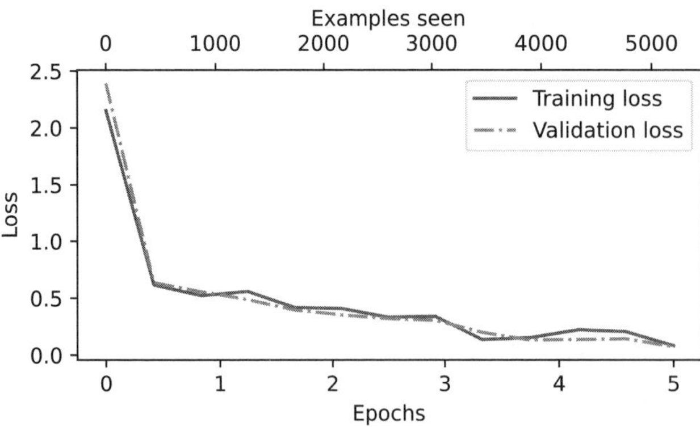

Figure 6.16 The model's training and validation loss over the five training epochs. Both the training loss, represented by the solid line, and the validation loss, represented by the dashed line, sharply decline in the first epoch and gradually stabilize toward the fifth epoch. This pattern indicates good learning progress and suggests that the model learned from the training data while generalizing well to the unseen validation data.

As we can see based on the sharp downward slope in figure 6.16, the model is learning well from the training data, and there is little to no indication of overfitting; that is, there is no noticeable gap between the training and validation set losses.

Choosing the number of epochs

Earlier, when we initiated the training, we set the number of epochs to five. The number of epochs depends on the dataset and the task's difficulty, and there is no universal solution or recommendation, although an epoch number of five is usually a good starting point. If the model overfits after the first few epochs as a loss plot (see figure 6.16), you may need to reduce the number of epochs. Conversely, if the trendline suggests that the validation loss could improve with further training, you should increase the number of epochs. In this concrete case, five epochs is a reasonable number as there are no signs of early overfitting, and the validation loss is close to 0.

Using the same `plot_values` function, let's now plot the classification accuracies:

```
epochs_tensor = torch.linspace(0, num_epochs, len(train_accs))
examples_seen_tensor = torch.linspace(0, examples_seen, len(train_accs))

plot_values(
    epochs_tensor, examples_seen_tensor, train_accs, val_accs,
    label="accuracy"
)
```

Figure 6.17 graphs the resulting accuracy. The model achieves a relatively high training and validation accuracy after epochs 4 and 5. Importantly, we previously set `eval_iter=5`

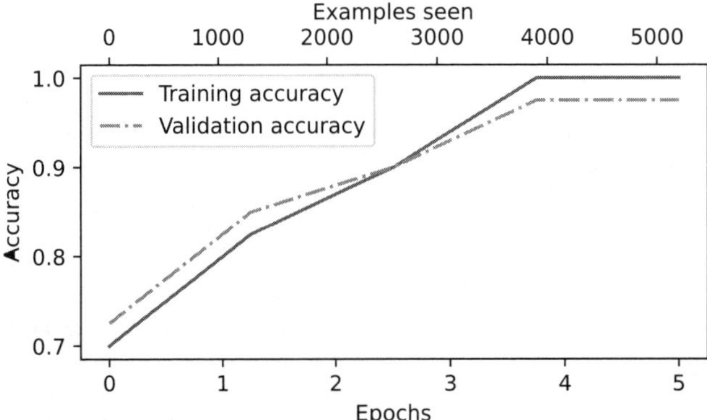

Figure 6.17 Both the training accuracy (solid line) and the validation accuracy (dashed line) increase substantially in the early epochs and then plateau, achieving almost perfect accuracy scores of 1.0. The close proximity of the two lines throughout the epochs suggests that the model does not overfit the training data very much.

when using the `train_classifier_simple` function, which means our estimations of training and validation performance are based on only five batches for efficiency during training.

Now we must calculate the performance metrics for the training, validation, and test sets across the entire dataset by running the following code, this time without defining the `eval_iter` value:

```
train_accuracy = calc_accuracy_loader(train_loader, model, device)
val_accuracy = calc_accuracy_loader(val_loader, model, device)
test_accuracy = calc_accuracy_loader(test_loader, model, device)

print(f"Training accuracy: {train_accuracy*100:.2f}%")
print(f"Validation accuracy: {val_accuracy*100:.2f}%")
print(f"Test accuracy: {test_accuracy*100:.2f}%")
```

The resulting accuracy values are

```
Training accuracy: 97.21%
Validation accuracy: 97.32%
Test accuracy: 95.67%
```

The training and test set performances are almost identical. The slight discrepancy between the training and test set accuracies suggests minimal overfitting of the training data. Typically, the validation set accuracy is somewhat higher than the test set accuracy because the model development often involves tuning hyperparameters to perform well on the validation set, which might not generalize as effectively to the test set. This situation is common, but the gap could potentially be minimized by adjusting the model's settings, such as increasing the dropout rate (`drop_rate`) or the `weight_decay` parameter in the optimizer configuration.

6.8 Using the LLM as a spam classifier

Having fine-tuned and evaluated the model, we are now ready to classify spam messages (see figure 6.18). Let's use our fine-tuned GPT-based spam classification model. The following `classify_review` function follows data preprocessing steps similar to those we used in the `SpamDataset` implemented earlier. Then, after processing text into token IDs, the function uses the model to predict an integer class label, similar to what we implemented in section 6.6, and then returns the corresponding class name.

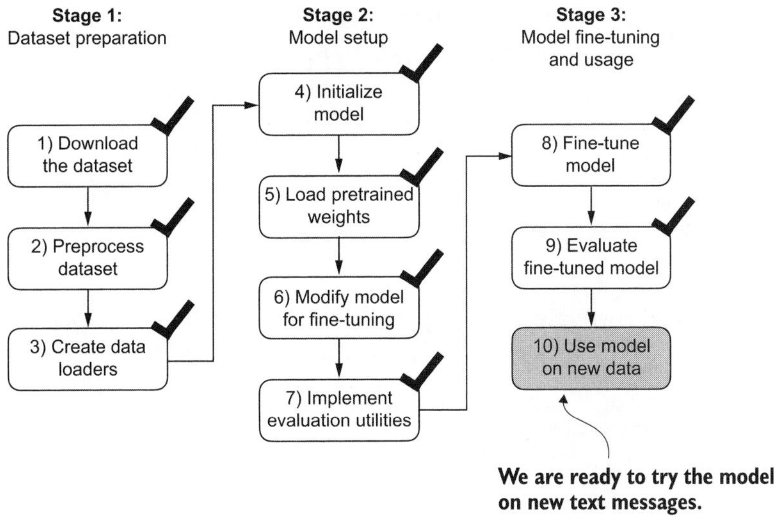

Figure 6.18 The three-stage process for classification fine-tuning our LLM. Step 10 is the final step of stage 3—using the fine-tuned model to classify new spam messages.

Listing 6.12 Using the model to classify new texts

```
def classify_review(
        text, model, tokenizer, device, max_length=None,
        pad_token_id=50256):
    model.eval()

    input_ids = tokenizer.encode(text)                    # Prepares inputs to the model
    supported_context_length = model.pos_emb.weight.shape[1]

    input_ids = input_ids[:min(                           # Truncates sequences if they are too long
        max_length, supported_context_length
    )]

    input_ids += [pad_token_id] * (max_length - len(input_ids))   # Pads sequences to the longest sequence

    input_tensor = torch.tensor(
        input_ids, device=device
    ).unsqueeze(0)                                        # Adds batch dimension

    with torch.no_grad():                                 # Models inference without gradient tracking
        logits = model(input_tensor)[:, -1, :]            # Logits of the last output token
    predicted_label = torch.argmax(logits, dim=-1).item()

    return "spam" if predicted_label == 1 else "not spam"   # Returns the classified result
```

Let's try this `classify_review` function on an example text:

```
text_1 = (
    "You are a winner you have been specially"
    " selected to receive $1000 cash or a $2000 award."
)

print(classify_review(
    text_1, model, tokenizer, device, max_length=train_dataset.max_length
))
```

The resulting model correctly predicts `"spam"`. Let's try another example:

```
text_2 = (
    "Hey, just wanted to check if we're still on"
    " for dinner tonight? Let me know!"
)

print(classify_review(
    text_2, model, tokenizer, device, max_length=train_dataset.max_length
))
```

The model again makes a correct prediction and returns a "not spam" label.

Finally, let's save the model in case we want to reuse the model later without having to train it again. We can use the `torch.save` method:

```
torch.save(model.state_dict(), "review_classifier.pth")
```

Once saved, the model can be loaded:

```
model_state_dict = torch.load("review_classifier.pth, map_location=device")
model.load_state_dict(model_state_dict)
```

Summary

- There are different strategies for fine-tuning LLMs, including classification fine-tuning and instruction fine-tuning.
- Classification fine-tuning involves replacing the output layer of an LLM via a small classification layer.
- In the case of classifying text messages as "spam" or "not spam," the new classification layer consists of only two output nodes. Previously, we used the number of output nodes equal to the number of unique tokens in the vocabulary (i.e., 50,256).
- Instead of predicting the next token in the text as in pretraining, classification fine-tuning trains the model to output a correct class label—for example, "spam" or "not spam."
- The model input for fine-tuning is text converted into token IDs, similar to pretraining.

- Before fine-tuning an LLM, we load the pretrained model as a base model.
- Evaluating a classification model involves calculating the classification accuracy (the fraction or percentage of correct predictions).
- Fine-tuning a classification model uses the same cross entropy loss function as when pretraining the LLM.

JR 965 1781

7 Fine-tuning to follow instructions

This chapter covers

- The instruction fine-tuning process of LLMs
- Preparing a dataset for supervised instruction fine-tuning
- Organizing instruction data in training batches
- Loading a pretrained LLM and fine-tuning it to follow human instructions
- Extracting LLM-generated instruction responses for evaluation
- Evaluating an instruction-fine-tuned LLM

Previously, we implemented the LLM architecture, carried out pretraining, and imported pretrained weights from external sources into our model. Then, we focused on fine-tuning our LLM for a specific classification task: distinguishing between spam and non-spam text messages. Now we'll implement the process for fine-tuning an LLM to follow human instructions, as illustrated in figure 7.1. Instruction fine-tuning is one of the main techniques behind developing LLMs for chatbot applications, personal assistants, and other conversational tasks.

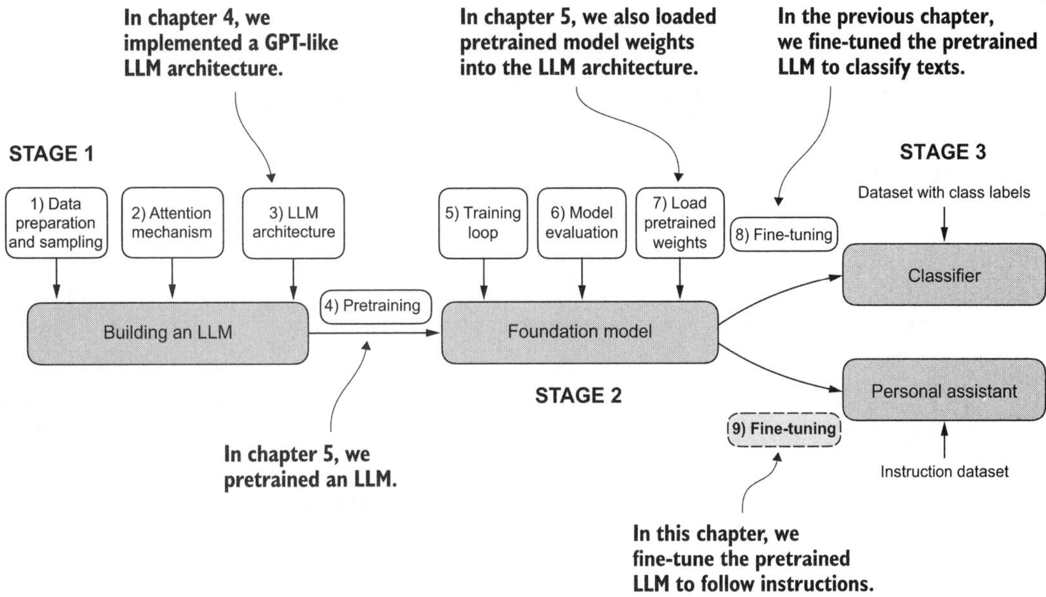

Figure 7.1 The three main stages of coding an LLM. This chapter focuses on step 9 of stage 3: fine-tuning a pretrained LLM to follow human instructions.

Figure 7.1 shows two main ways of fine-tuning an LLM: fine-tuning for classification (step 8) and fine-tuning an LLM to follow instructions (step 9). We implemented step 8 in chapter 6. Now we will fine-tune an LLM using an *instruction dataset.*

7.1 Introduction to instruction fine-tuning

We now know that pretraining an LLM involves a training procedure where it learns to generate one word at a time. The resulting pretrained LLM is capable of *text completion,* meaning it can finish sentences or write text paragraphs given a fragment as input. However, pretrained LLMs often struggle with specific instructions, such as "Fix the grammar in this text" or "Convert this text into passive voice." Later, we will examine a concrete example where we load the pretrained LLM as the basis for *instruction fine-tuning,* also known as *supervised instruction fine-tuning.*

Here, we focus on improving the LLM's ability to follow such instructions and generate a desired response, as illustrated in figure 7.2. Preparing the dataset is a key aspect of instruction fine-tuning. Then we'll complete all the steps in the three stages of the instruction fine-tuning process, beginning with the dataset preparation, as shown in figure 7.3.

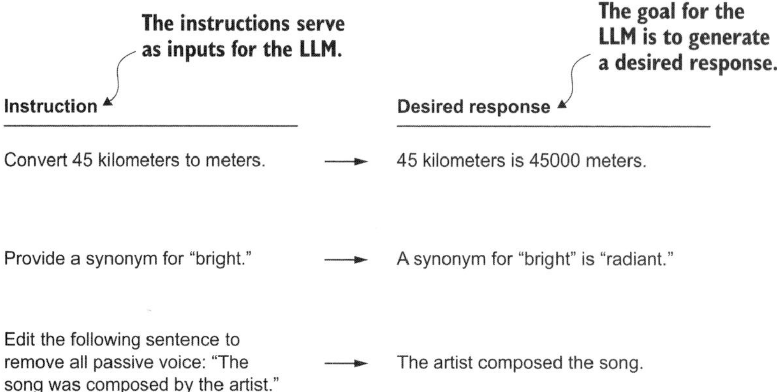

Figure 7.2 Examples of instructions that are processed by an LLM to generate desired responses

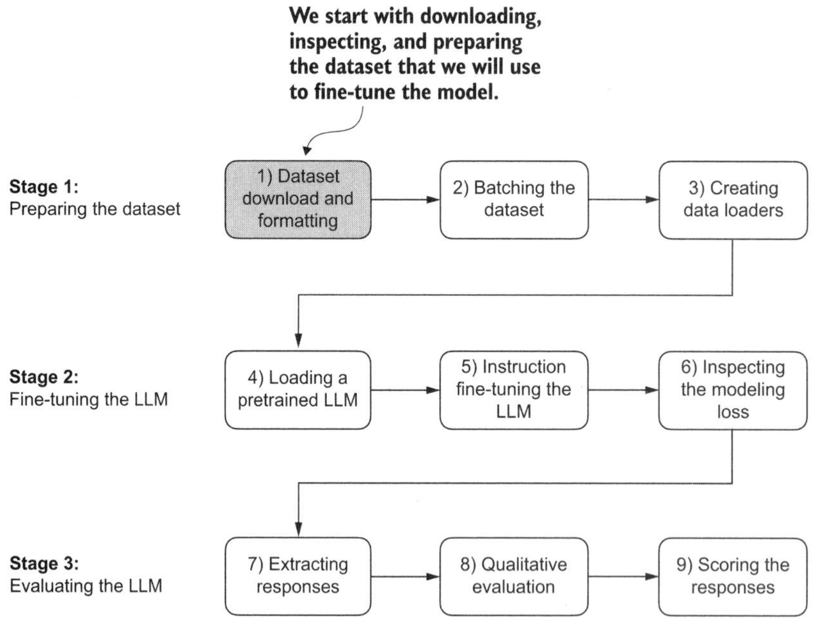

Figure 7.3 The three-stage process for instruction fine-tuning an LLM. Stage 1 involves dataset preparation, stage 2 focuses on model setup and fine-tuning, and stage 3 covers the evaluation of the model. We will begin with step 1 of stage 1: downloading and formatting the dataset.

7.2 Preparing a dataset for supervised instruction fine-tuning

Let's download and format the instruction dataset for instruction fine-tuning a pre-trained LLM. The dataset consists of 1,100 *instruction–response pairs* similar to those in figure 7.2. This dataset was created specifically for this book, but interested readers can find alternative, publicly available instruction datasets in appendix B.

The following code implements and executes a function to download this dataset, which is a relatively small file (only 204 KB) in JSON format. JSON, or JavaScript Object Notation, mirrors the structure of Python dictionaries, providing a simple structure for data interchange that is both human readable and machine friendly.

Listing 7.1 Downloading the dataset

```
import json
import os
import urllib

def download_and_load_file(file_path, url):
    if not os.path.exists(file_path):
        with urllib.request.urlopen(url) as response:
            text_data = response.read().decode("utf-8")
        with open(file_path, "w", encoding="utf-8") as file:
            file.write(text_data)
    else:                                                    # Skips download if file was already downloaded
        with open(file_path, "r", encoding="utf-8") as file:
            text_data = file.read()
    with open(file_path, "r") as file:
        data = json.load(file)
    return data

file_path = "instruction-data.json"
url = (
    "https://raw.githubusercontent.com/rasbt/LLMs-from-scratch"
    "/main/ch07/01_main-chapter-code/instruction-data.json"
)


data = download_and_load_file(file_path, url)
print("Number of entries:", len(data))
```

The output of executing the preceding code is

```
Number of entries: 1100
```

The `data` list that we loaded from the JSON file contains the 1,100 entries of the instruction dataset. Let's print one of the entries to see how each entry is structured:

```
print("Example entry:\n", data[50])
```

The content of the example entry is

```
Example entry:
 {'instruction': 'Identify the correct spelling of the following word.',
  'input': 'Ocassion', 'output': "The correct spelling is 'Occasion.'"}
```

As we can see, the example entries are Python dictionary objects containing an `'instruction'`, `'input'`, and `'output'`. Let's take a look at another example:

```
print("Another example entry:\n", data[999])
```

Based on the contents of this entry, the `'input'` field may occasionally be empty:

```
Another example entry:
 {'instruction': "What is an antonym of 'complicated'?",
  'input': '',
  'output': "An antonym of 'complicated' is 'simple'."}
```

Instruction fine-tuning involves training a model on a dataset where the input-output pairs, like those we extracted from the JSON file, are explicitly provided. There are various methods to format these entries for LLMs. Figure 7.4 illustrates two different

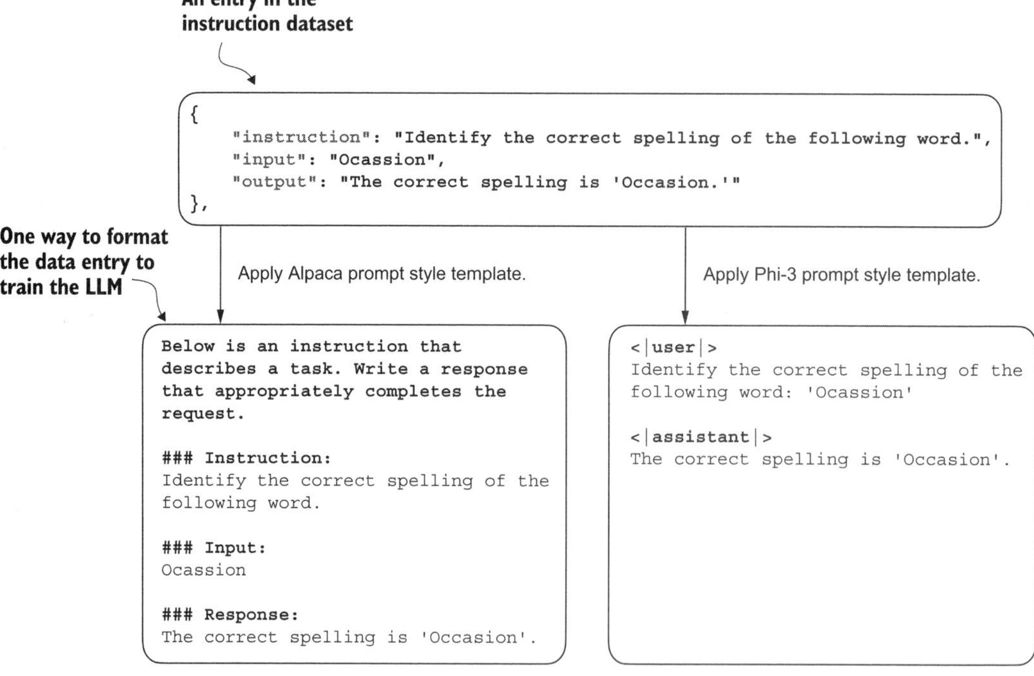

Figure 7.4 Comparison of prompt styles for instruction fine-tuning in LLMs. The Alpaca style (left) uses a structured format with defined sections for instruction, input, and response, while the Phi-3 style (right) employs a simpler format with designated `<|user|>` and `<|assistant|>` tokens.

example formats, often referred to as *prompt styles*, used in the training of notable LLMs such as Alpaca and Phi-3.

Alpaca was one of the early LLMs to publicly detail its instruction fine-tuning process. Phi-3, developed by Microsoft, is included to demonstrate the diversity in prompt styles. The rest of this chapter uses the Alpaca prompt style since it is one of the most popular ones, largely because it helped define the original approach to fine-tuning.

Exercise 7.1 Changing prompt styles

After fine-tuning the model with the Alpaca prompt style, try the Phi-3 prompt style shown in figure 7.4 and observe whether it affects the response quality of the model.

Let's define a `format_input` function that we can use to convert the entries in the `data` list into the Alpaca-style input format.

Listing 7.2 Implementing the prompt formatting function

```
def format_input(entry):
    instruction_text = (
        f"Below is an instruction that describes a task. "
        f"Write a response that appropriately completes the request."
        f"\n\n### Instruction:\n{entry['instruction']}"
    )

    input_text = (
        f"\n\n### Input:\n{entry['input']}" if entry["input"] else ""
    )
    return instruction_text + input_text
```

This `format_input` function takes a dictionary `entry` as input and constructs a formatted string. Let's test it to dataset entry `data[50]`, which we looked at earlier:

```
model_input = format_input(data[50])
desired_response = f"\n\n### Response:\n{data[50]['output']}"
print(model_input + desired_response)
```

The formatted input looks like as follows:

```
Below is an instruction that describes a task. Write a response that
appropriately completes the request.

### Instruction:
Identify the correct spelling of the following word.

### Input:
Ocassion

### Response:
The correct spelling is 'Occasion.'
```

Note that the `format_input` skips the optional `### Input:` section if the `'input'` field is empty, which we can test out by applying the `format_input` function to entry `data[999]` that we inspected earlier:

```
model_input = format_input(data[999])
desired_response = f"\n\n### Response:\n{data[999]['output']}"
print(model_input + desired_response)
```

The output shows that entries with an empty `'input'` field don't contain an `### Input:` section in the formatted input:

```
Below is an instruction that describes a task. Write a response that
appropriately completes the request.

### Instruction:
What is an antonym of 'complicated'?

### Response:
An antonym of 'complicated' is 'simple'.
```

Before we move on to setting up the PyTorch data loaders in the next section, let's divide the dataset into training, validation, and test sets analogous to what we have done with the spam classification dataset in the previous chapter. The following listing shows how we calculate the portions.

Listing 7.3 Partitioning the dataset

```
train_portion = int(len(data) * 0.85)     # Use 85% of the data for training
test_portion = int(len(data) * 0.1)       # Use 10% for testing
val_portion = len(data) - train_portion - test_portion    # Use remaining 5% for validation

train_data = data[:train_portion]
test_data = data[train_portion:train_portion + test_portion]
val_data = data[train_portion + test_portion:]

print("Training set length:", len(train_data))
print("Validation set length:", len(val_data))
print("Test set length:", len(test_data))
```

This partitioning results in the following dataset sizes:

```
Training set length: 935
Validation set length: 55
Test set length: 110
```

Having successfully downloaded and partitioned the dataset and gained a clear understanding of the dataset prompt formatting, we are now ready for the core implementation of the instruction fine-tuning process. Next, we focus on developing the method for constructing the training batches for fine-tuning the LLM.

7.3 Organizing data into training batches

As we progress into the implementation phase of our instruction fine-tuning process, the next step, illustrated in figure 7.5, focuses on constructing the training batches effectively. This involves defining a method that will ensure our model receives the formatted training data during the fine-tuning process.

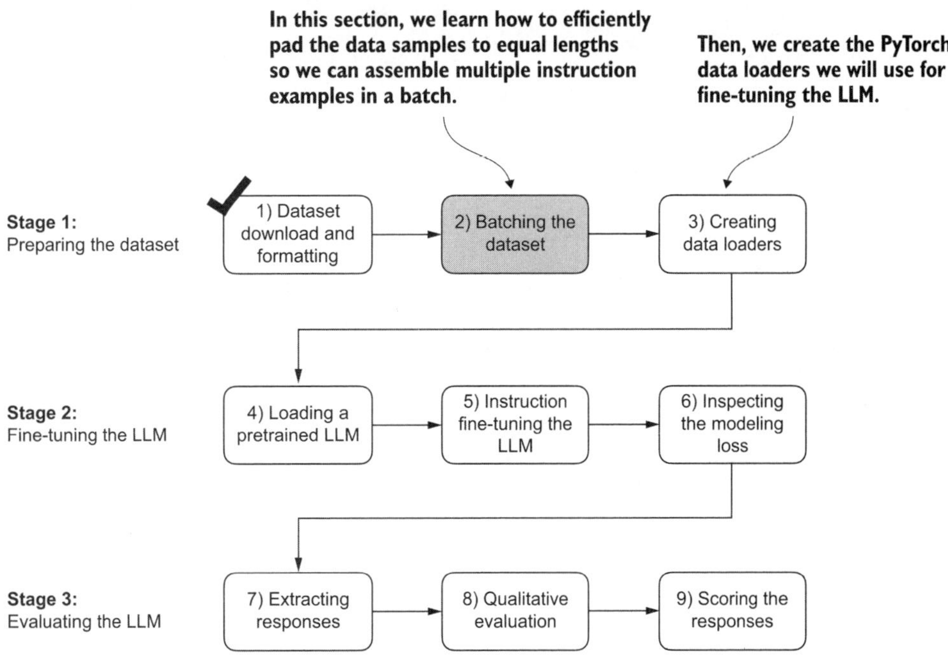

Figure 7.5 The three-stage process for instruction fine-tuning an LLM. Next, we look at step 2 of stage 1: assembling the training batches.

In the previous chapter, the training batches were created automatically by the PyTorch `DataLoader` class, which employs a default *collate* function to combine lists of samples into batches. A collate function is responsible for taking a list of individual data samples and merging them into a single batch that can be processed efficiently by the model during training.

However, the batching process for instruction fine-tuning is a bit more involved and requires us to create our own custom collate function that we will later plug into the `DataLoader`. We implement this custom collate function to handle the specific requirements and formatting of our instruction fine-tuning dataset.

Let's tackle the *batching process* in several steps, including coding the custom collate function, as illustrated in figure 7.6. First, to implement steps 2.1 and 2.2, we code an `InstructionDataset` class that applies `format_input` and *pretokenizes* all inputs in the dataset, similar to the `SpamDataset` in chapter 6. This two-step process, detailed in figure 7.7, is implemented in the `__init__` constructor method of the `InstructionDataset`.

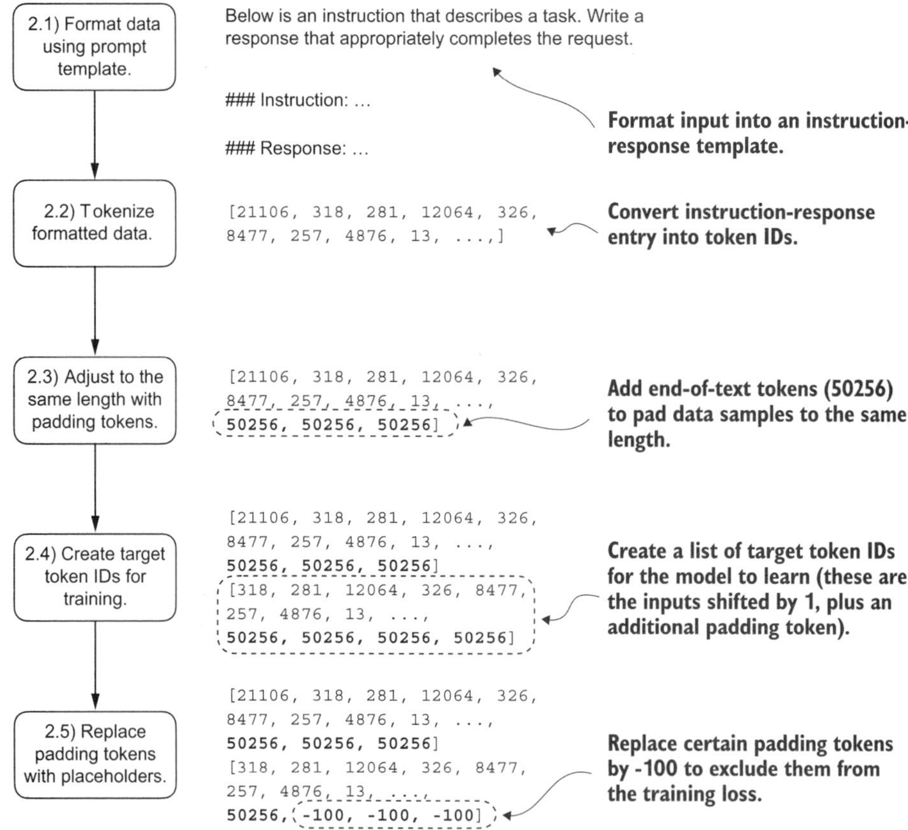

Figure 7.6 The five substeps involved in implementing the batching process: (2.1) applying the prompt template, (2.2) using tokenization from previous chapters, (2.3) adding padding tokens, (2.4) creating target token IDs, and (2.5) replacing `-100` placeholder tokens to mask padding tokens in the loss function.

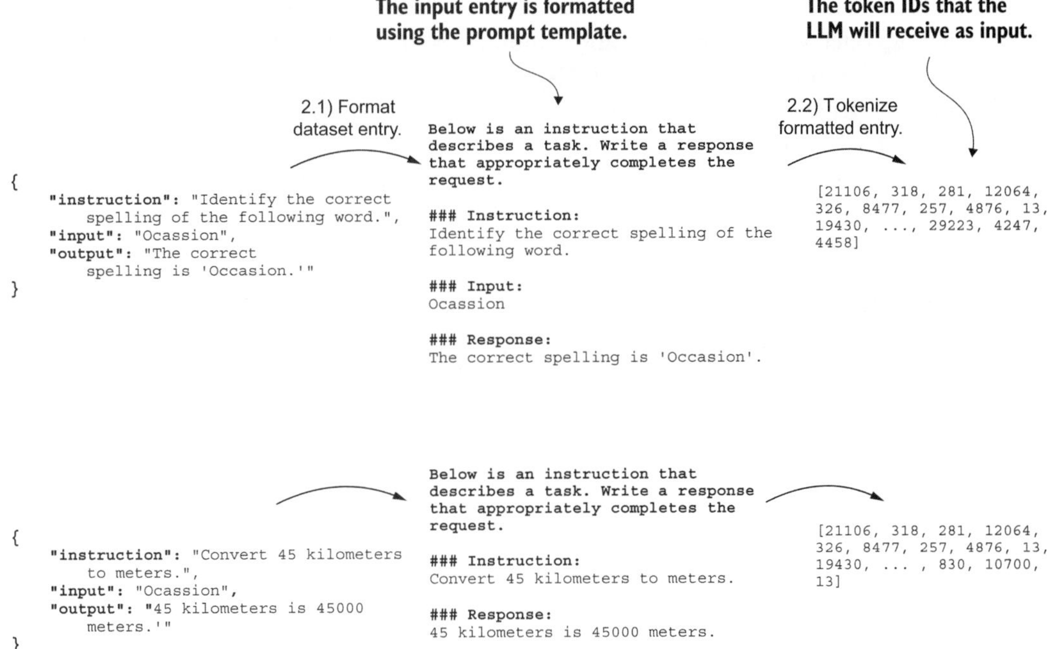

Figure 7.7 The first two steps involved in implementing the batching process. Entries are first formatted using a specific prompt template (2.1) and then tokenized (2.2), resulting in a sequence of token IDs that the model can process.

Listing 7.4 Implementing an instruction dataset class

```
import torch
from torch.utils.data import Dataset

class InstructionDataset(Dataset):
    def __init__(self, data, tokenizer):
        self.data = data
        self.encoded_texts = []
        for entry in data:                                  # Pretokenizes texts
            instruction_plus_input = format_input(entry)
            response_text = f"\n\n### Response:\n{entry['output']}"
            full_text = instruction_plus_input + response_text
            self.encoded_texts.append(
                tokenizer.encode(full_text)
            )

    def __getitem__(self, index):
        return self.encoded_texts[index]

    def __len__(self):
        return len(self.data)
```

Similar to the approach used for classification fine-tuning, we want to accelerate training by collecting multiple training examples in a batch, which necessitates padding all inputs to a similar length. As with classification fine-tuning, we use the `<|endoftext|>` token as a padding token.

Instead of appending the `<|endoftext|>` tokens to the text inputs, we can append the token ID corresponding to `<|endoftext|>` to the pretokenized inputs directly. We can use the tokenizer's `.encode` method on an `<|endoftext|>` token to remind us which token ID we should use:

```
import tiktoken
tokenizer = tiktoken.get_encoding("gpt2")
print(tokenizer.encode("<|endoftext|>", allowed_special={"<|endoftext|>"}))
```

The resulting token ID is `50256`.

Moving on to step 2.3 of the process (see figure 7.6), we adopt a more sophisticated approach by developing a custom collate function that we can pass to the data loader. This custom collate function pads the training examples in each batch to the same length while allowing different batches to have different lengths, as demonstrated in figure 7.8. This approach minimizes unnecessary padding by only extending sequences to match the longest one in each batch, not the whole dataset.

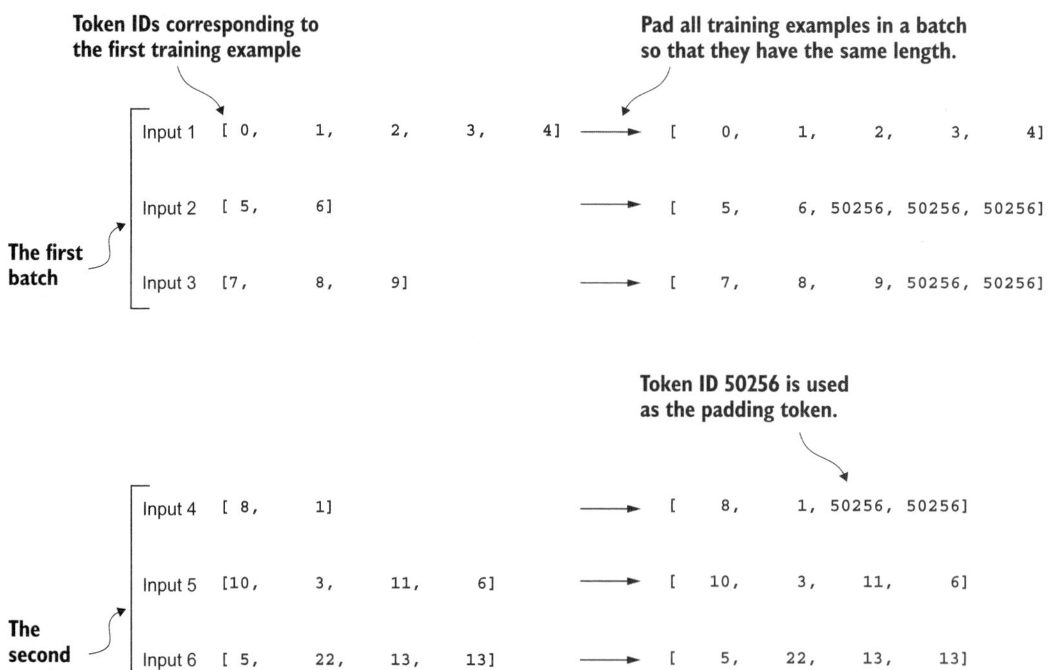

Figure 7.8 The padding of training examples in batches using token ID `50256` to ensure uniform length within each batch. Each batch may have different lengths, as shown by the first and second.

We can implement the padding process with a custom collate function:

```
def custom_collate_draft_1(
    batch,
    pad_token_id=50256,
    device="cpu"
):
    batch_max_length = max(len(item)+1 for item in batch)    <-- Finds the longest sequence in the batch
    inputs_lst = []

    for item in batch:                      <-- Pads and prepares inputs
        new_item = item.copy()
        new_item += [pad_token_id]


        padded = (
            new_item + [pad_token_id] *
            (batch_max_length - len(new_item))
        )
        inputs = torch.tensor(padded[:-1])    <-- Removes extra padded token added earlier
        inputs_lst.append(inputs)

    inputs_tensor = torch.stack(inputs_lst).to(device)    <-- Converts the list of inputs to a tensor and transfers it to the target device
    return inputs_tensor
```

The `custom_collate_draft_1` we implemented is designed to be integrated into a PyTorch `DataLoader`, but it can also function as a standalone tool. Here, we use it independently to test and verify that it operates as intended. Let's try it on three different inputs that we want to assemble into a batch, where each example gets padded to the same length:

```
inputs_1 = [0, 1, 2, 3, 4]
inputs_2 = [5, 6]
inputs_3 = [7, 8, 9]
batch = (
    inputs_1,
    inputs_2,
    inputs_3
)
print(custom_collate_draft_1(batch))
```

The resulting batch looks like the following:

```
tensor([[    0,     1,     2,     3,     4],
        [    5,     6, 50256, 50256, 50256],
        [    7,     8,     9, 50256, 50256]])
```

This output shows all inputs have been padded to the length of the longest input list, `inputs_1`, containing five token IDs.

We have just implemented our first custom collate function to create batches from lists of inputs. However, as we previously learned, we also need to create batches with the target token IDs corresponding to the batch of input IDs. These target IDs, as shown in figure 7.9, are crucial because they represent what we want the model to generate and what we need during training to calculate the loss for the weight updates. That is, we modify our custom collate function to return the target token IDs in addition to the input token IDs.

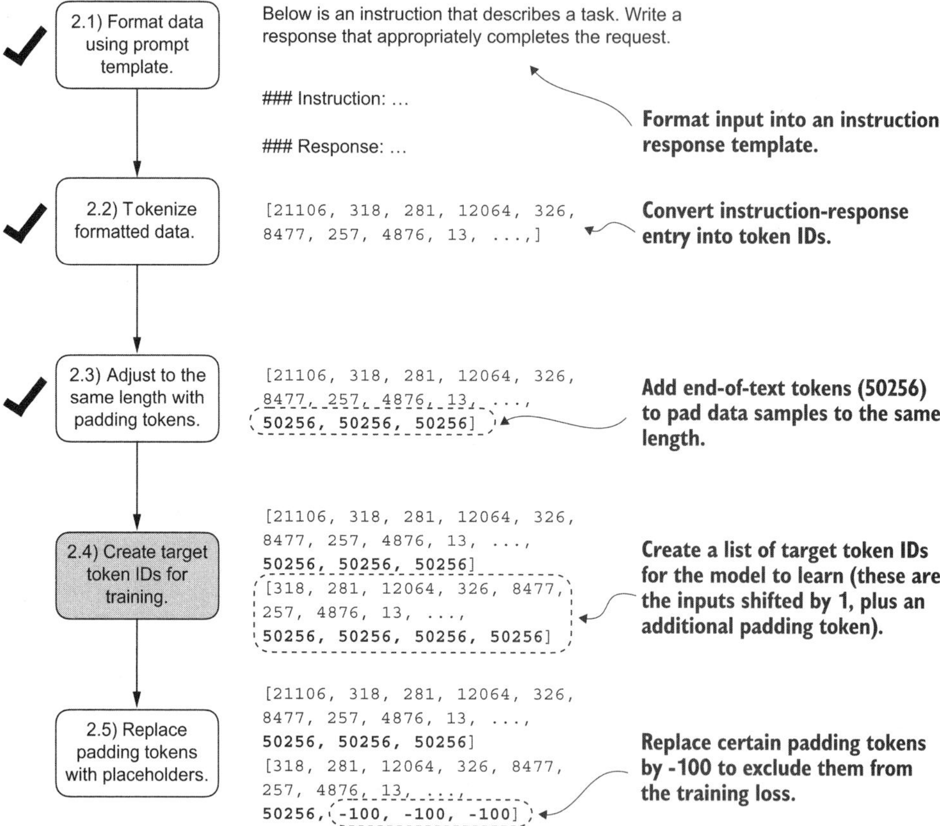

Figure 7.9 The five substeps involved in implementing the batching process. We are now focusing on step 2.4, the creation of target token IDs. This step is essential as it enables the model to learn and predict the tokens it needs to generate.

Similar to the process we used to pretrain an LLM, the target token IDs match the input token IDs but are shifted one position to the right. This setup, as shown in figure 7.10, allows the LLM to learn how to predict the next token in a sequence.

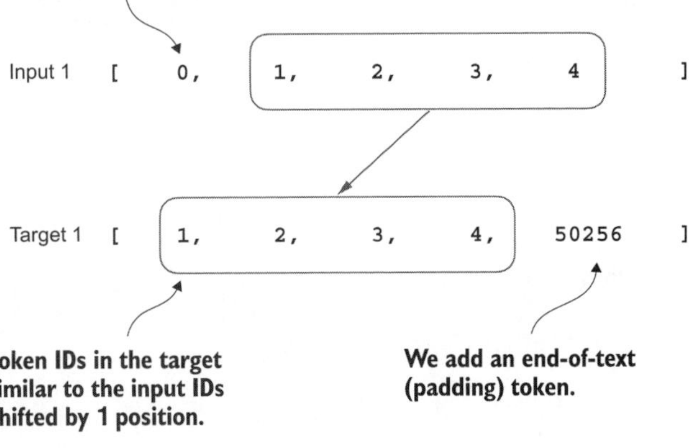
The target vector does not contain the first input ID.
Input 1 [0, 1, 2, 3, 4]
Target 1 [1, 2, 3, 4, 50256]
The token IDs in the target are similar to the input IDs but shifted by 1 position.
We add an end-of-text (padding) token.

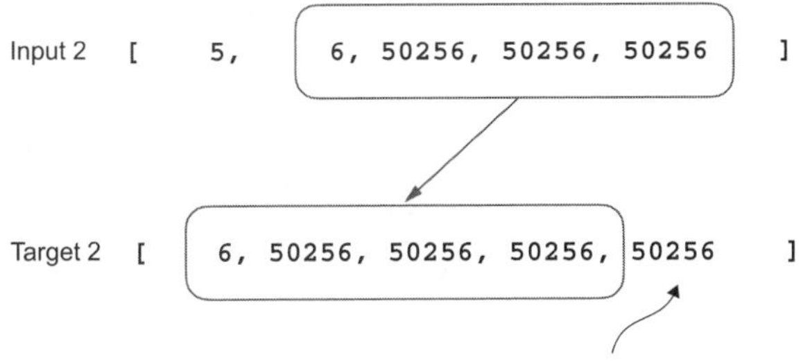
Input 2 [5, 6, 50256, 50256, 50256]
Target 2 [6, 50256, 50256, 50256, 50256]
We always add an end-of-text (padding) token to the target.

Figure 7.10 The input and target token alignment used in the instruction fine-tuning process of an LLM. For each input sequence, the corresponding target sequence is created by shifting the token IDs one position to the right, omitting the first token of the input, and appending an end-of-text token.

The following updated collate function generates the target token IDs from the input token IDs:

```
def custom_collate_draft_2(
    batch,
    pad_token_id=50256,
    device="cpu"
):
    batch_max_length = max(len(item)+1 for item in batch)
    inputs_lst, targets_lst = [], []

    for item in batch:
        new_item = item.copy()
        new_item += [pad_token_id]
```

```
        padded = (
            new_item + [pad_token_id] *
            (batch_max_length - len(new_item))
        )
        inputs = torch.tensor(padded[:-1])
        targets = torch.tensor(padded[1:])
        inputs_lst.append(inputs)
        targets_lst.append(targets)

    inputs_tensor = torch.stack(inputs_lst).to(device)
    targets_tensor = torch.stack(targets_lst).to(device)
    return inputs_tensor, targets_tensor

inputs, targets = custom_collate_draft_2(batch)
print(inputs)
print(targets)
```

Truncates the last token for inputs

Shifts +1 to the right for targets

Applied to the example `batch` consisting of three input lists we defined earlier, the new `custom_collate_draft_2` function now returns the input and the target batch:

```
tensor([[    0,     1,     2,     3,     4],
        [    5,     6, 50256, 50256, 50256],
        [    7,     8,     9, 50256, 50256]])
tensor([[    1,     2,     3,     4, 50256],
        [    6, 50256, 50256, 50256, 50256],
        [    8,     9, 50256, 50256, 50256]])
```

The first tensor represents inputs.

The second tensor represents the targets.

In the next step, we assign a `-100` placeholder value to all padding tokens, as highlighted in figure 7.11. This special value allows us to exclude these padding tokens from contributing to the training loss calculation, ensuring that only meaningful data influences model learning. We will discuss this process in more detail after we implement this modification. (When fine-tuning for classification, we did not have to worry about this since we only trained the model based on the last output token.)

However, note that we retain one end-of-text token, ID `50256`, in the target list, as depicted in figure 7.12. Retaining it allows the LLM to learn when to generate an end-of-text token in response to instructions, which we use as an indicator that the generated response is complete.

In the following listing, we modify our custom collate function to replace tokens with ID `50256` with `-100` in the target lists. Additionally, we introduce an `allowed_max_length` parameter to optionally limit the length of the samples. This adjustment will be useful if you plan to work with your own datasets that exceed the 1,024-token context size supported by the GPT-2 model.

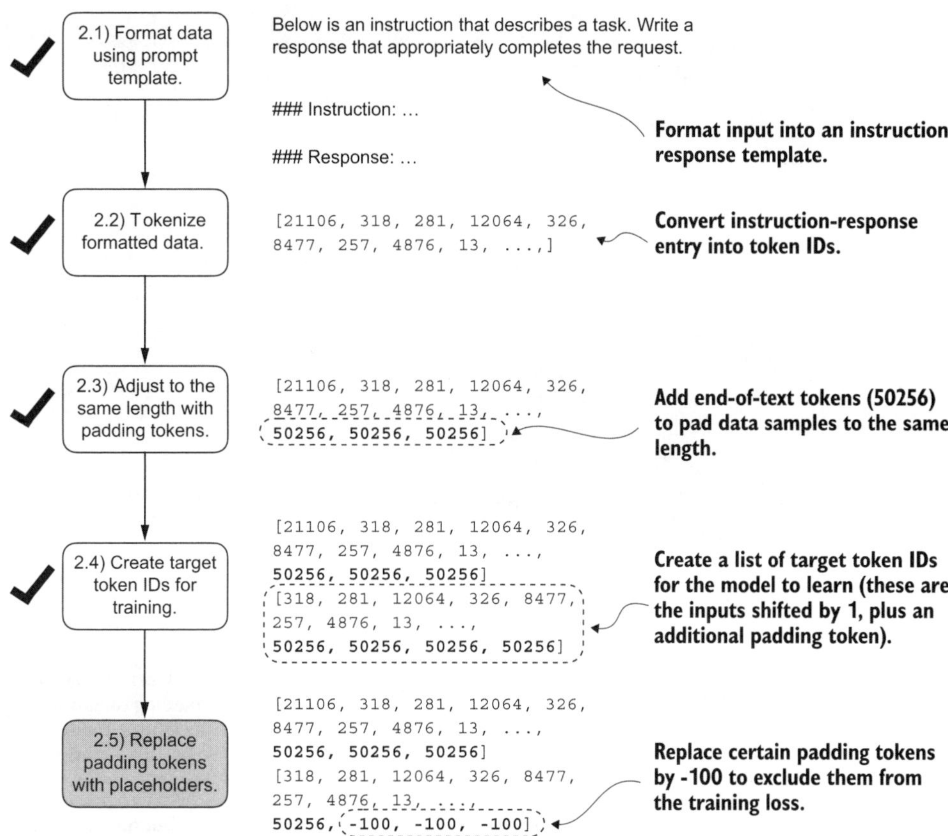

Figure 7.11 The five substeps involved in implementing the batching process. After creating the target sequence by shifting token IDs one position to the right and appending an end-of-text token, in step 2.5, we replace the end-of-text padding tokens with a placeholder value (`-100`).

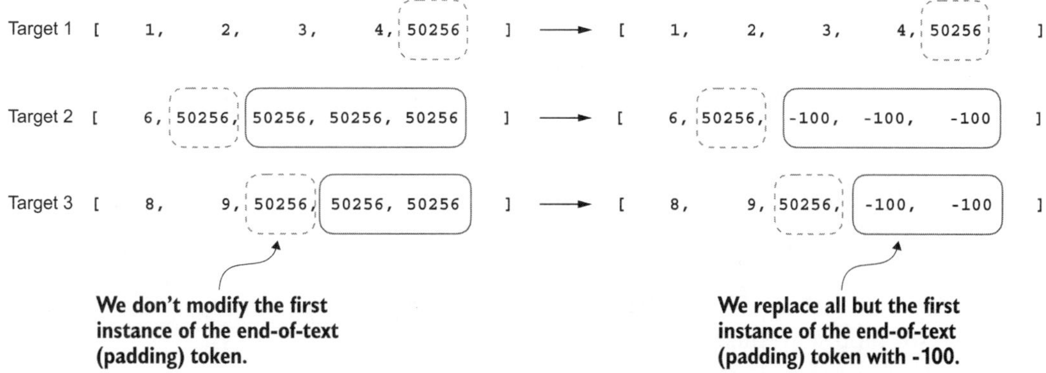

Figure 7.12 Step 2.4 in the token replacement process in the target batch for the training data preparation. We replace all but the first instance of the end-of-text token, which we use as padding, with the placeholder value `-100`, while keeping the initial end-of-text token in each target sequence.

Listing 7.5 Implementing a custom batch collate function

```
def custom_collate_fn(
    batch,
    pad_token_id=50256,
    ignore_index=-100,
    allowed_max_length=None,
    device="cpu"
):
    batch_max_length = max(len(item)+1 for item in batch)
    inputs_lst, targets_lst = [], []

    for item in batch:
        new_item = item.copy()
        new_item += [pad_token_id]


        padded = (
            new_item + [pad_token_id] *
            (batch_max_length - len(new_item))
        )
        inputs = torch.tensor(padded[:-1])
        targets = torch.tensor(padded[1:])

        mask = targets == pad_token_id
        indices = torch.nonzero(mask).squeeze()
        if indices.numel() > 1:
            targets[indices[1:]] = ignore_index

        if allowed_max_length is not None:
            inputs = inputs[:allowed_max_length]
            targets = targets[:allowed_max_length]

        inputs_lst.append(inputs)
        targets_lst.append(targets)

    inputs_tensor = torch.stack(inputs_lst).to(device)
    targets_tensor = torch.stack(targets_lst).to(device)
    return inputs_tensor, targets_tensor
```

Pads sequences to max_length

Truncates the last token for inputs

Shifts +1 to the right for targets

Replaces all but the first padding tokens in targets by ignore_index

Optionally truncates to the maximum sequence length

Again, let's try the collate function on the sample batch that we created earlier to check that it works as intended:

```
inputs, targets = custom_collate_fn(batch)
print(inputs)
print(targets)
```

The results are as follows, where the first tensor represents the inputs and the second tensor represents the targets:

```
tensor([[    0,     1,     2,     3,     4],
        [    5,     6, 50256, 50256, 50256],
        [    7,     8,     9, 50256, 50256]])
```

```
tensor([[    1,     2,     3,     4, 50256],
        [    6, 50256,  -100,  -100,  -100],
        [    8,     9, 50256,  -100,  -100]])
```

The modified collate function works as expected, altering the target list by inserting the token ID `-100`. What is the logic behind this adjustment? Let's explore the underlying purpose of this modification.

For demonstration purposes, consider the following simple and self-contained example where each output logit corresponds to a potential token from the model's vocabulary. Here's how we might calculate the cross entropy loss (introduced in chapter 5) during training when the model predicts a sequence of tokens, which is similar to what we did when we pretrained the model and fine-tuned it for classification:

```
logits_1 = torch.tensor(
    [[-1.0, 1.0],          # predictions for 1st token
     [-0.5, 1.5]]          # predictions for 2nd token
)
targets_1 = torch.tensor([0, 1]) # Correct token indices to generate
loss_1 = torch.nn.functional.cross_entropy(logits_1, targets_1)
print(loss_1)
```

The loss value calculated by the previous code is `1.1269`:

```
tensor(1.1269)
```

As we would expect, adding an additional token ID affects the loss calculation:

```
logits_2 = torch.tensor(
    [[-1.0, 1.0],
     [-0.5, 1.5],
     [-0.5, 1.5]]          # New third token ID prediction
)
targets_2 = torch.tensor([0, 1, 1])
loss_2 = torch.nn.functional.cross_entropy(logits_2, targets_2)
print(loss_2)
```

After adding the third token, the loss value is `0.7936`.

So far, we have carried out some more or less obvious example calculations using the cross entropy loss function in PyTorch, the same loss function we used in the training functions for pretraining and fine-tuning for classification. Now let's get to the interesting part and see what happens if we replace the third target token ID with `-100`:

```
targets_3 = torch.tensor([0, 1, -100])
loss_3 = torch.nn.functional.cross_entropy(logits_2, targets_3)
print(loss_3)
print("loss_1 == loss_3:", loss_1 == loss_3)
```

The resulting output is

```
tensor(1.1269)
loss_1 == loss_3: tensor(True)
```

The resulting loss on these three training examples is identical to the loss we calculated from the two training examples earlier. In other words, the cross entropy loss function ignored the third entry in the `targets_3` vector, the token ID corresponding to `-100`. (Interested readers can try to replace the `-100` value with another token ID that is not `0` or `1`; it will result in an error.)

So what's so special about `-100` that it's ignored by the cross entropy loss? The default setting of the cross entropy function in PyTorch is `cross_entropy(..., ignore_index=-100)`. This means that it ignores targets labeled with `-100`. We take advantage of this `ignore_index` to ignore the additional end-of-text (padding) tokens that we used to pad the training examples to have the same length in each batch. However, we want to keep one `50256` (end-of-text) token ID in the targets because it helps the LLM to learn to generate end-of-text tokens, which we can use as an indicator that a response is complete.

In addition to masking out padding tokens, it is also common to mask out the target token IDs that correspond to the instruction, as illustrated in figure 7.13. By masking out the LLM's target token IDs corresponding to the instruction, the cross entropy loss is only computed for the generated response target IDs. Thus, the model is trained to focus on generating accurate responses rather than memorizing instructions, which can help reduce overfitting.

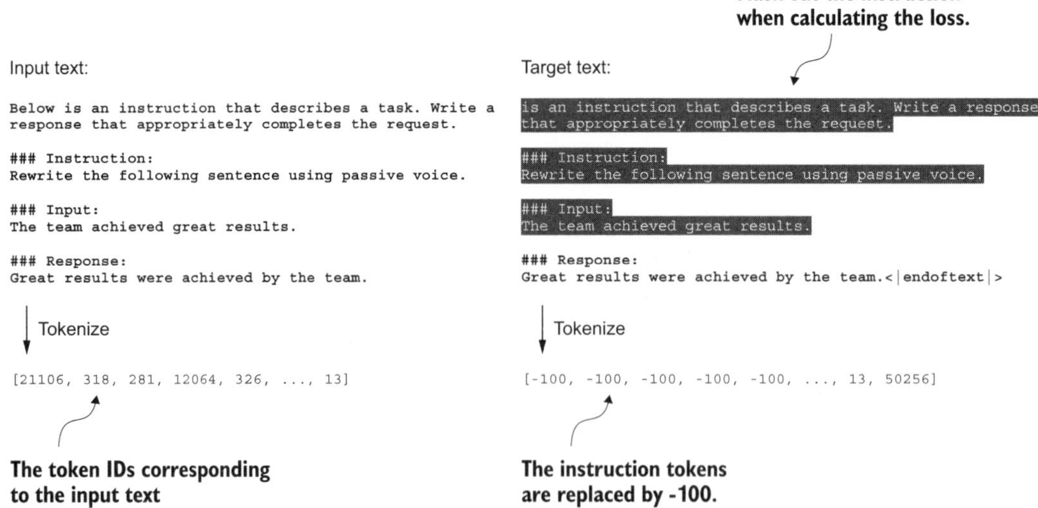

Figure 7.13 Left: The formatted input text we tokenize and then feed to the LLM during training. Right: The target text we prepare for the LLM where we can optionally mask out the instruction section, which means replacing the corresponding token IDs with the `-100` `ignore_index` value.

As of this writing, researchers are divided on whether masking the instructions is universally beneficial during instruction fine-tuning. For instance, the 2024 paper by Shi et al., "Instruction Tuning With Loss Over Instructions" (https://arxiv.org/abs/2405.14394), demonstrated that not masking the instructions benefits the LLM performance (see appendix B for more details). Here, we will not apply masking and leave it as an optional exercise for interested readers.

> **Exercise 7.2 Instruction and input masking**
>
> After completing the chapter and fine-tuning the model with `InstructionDataset`, replace the instruction and input tokens with the `-100` mask to use the instruction masking method illustrated in figure 7.13. Then evaluate whether this has a positive effect on model performance.

7.4 Creating data loaders for an instruction dataset

We have completed several stages to implement an `InstructionDataset` class and a `custom_collate_fn` function for the instruction dataset. As shown in figure 7.14, we are ready to reap the fruits of our labor by simply plugging both `InstructionDataset` objects and the `custom_collate_fn` function into PyTorch data loaders. These loaders

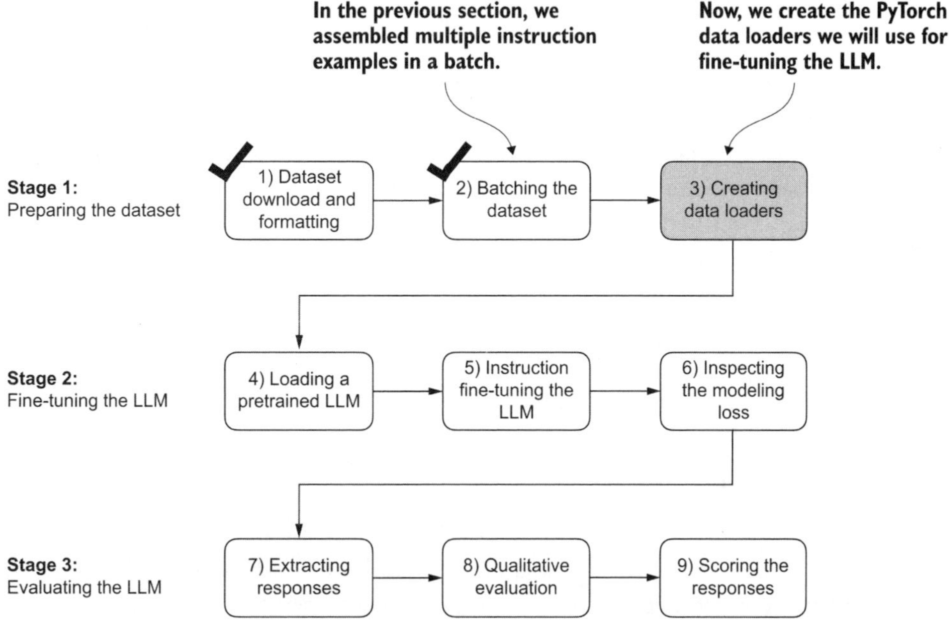

Figure 7.14 The three-stage process for instruction fine-tuning an LLM. Thus far, we have prepared the dataset and implemented a custom collate function to batch the instruction dataset. Now, we can create and apply the data loaders to the training, validation, and test sets needed for the LLM instruction fine-tuning and evaluation.

will automatically shuffle and organize the batches for the LLM instruction fine-tuning process.

Before we implement the data loader creation step, we have to briefly talk about the `device` setting of the `custom_collate_fn`. The `custom_collate_fn` includes code to move the input and target tensors (for example, `torch.stack(inputs_lst).to(device)`) to a specified device, which can be either `"cpu"` or `"cuda"` (for NVIDIA GPUs) or, optionally, `"mps"` for Macs with Apple Silicon chips.

> **NOTE** Using an `"mps"` device may result in numerical differences compared to the contents of this chapter, as Apple Silicon support in PyTorch is still experimental.

Previously, we moved the data onto the target device (for example, the GPU memory when `device="cuda"`) in the main training loop. Having this as part of the collate function offers the advantage of performing this device transfer process as a background process outside the training loop, preventing it from blocking the GPU during model training.

The following code initializes the `device` variable:

```
device = torch.device("cuda" if torch.cuda.is_available() else "cpu")
# if torch.backends.mps.is_available():
#     device = torch.device("mps")"
print("Device:", device)
```

Uncomments these two lines to use the GPU on an Apple Silicon chip

This will either print `"Device: cpu"` or `"Device: cuda"`, depending on your machine.

Next, to reuse the chosen device setting in `custom_collate_fn` when we plug it into the PyTorch `DataLoader` class, we use the `partial` function from Python's `functools` standard library to create a new version of the function with the device argument prefilled. Additionally, we set the `allowed_max_length` to `1024`, which truncates the data to the maximum context length supported by the GPT-2 model, which we will fine-tune later:

```
from functools import partial

customized_collate_fn = partial(
    custom_collate_fn,
    device=device,
    allowed_max_length=1024
)
```

Next, we can set up the data loaders as we did previously, but this time, we will use our custom collate function for the batching process.

Listing 7.6 Initializing the data loaders

```
from torch.utils.data import DataLoader

num_workers = 0      # You can try to increase this number if parallel Python processes are supported by your operating system.
batch_size = 8

torch.manual_seed(123)

train_dataset = InstructionDataset(train_data, tokenizer)
train_loader = DataLoader(
    train_dataset,
    batch_size=batch_size,
    collate_fn=customized_collate_fn,
    shuffle=True,
    drop_last=True,
    num_workers=num_workers
)

val_dataset = InstructionDataset(val_data, tokenizer)
val_loader = DataLoader(
    val_dataset,
    batch_size=batch_size,
    collate_fn=customized_collate_fn,
    shuffle=False,
    drop_last=False,
    num_workers=num_workers
)

test_dataset = InstructionDataset(test_data, tokenizer)
test_loader = DataLoader(
    test_dataset,
    batch_size=batch_size,
    collate_fn=customized_collate_fn,
    shuffle=False,
    drop_last=False,
    num_workers=num_workers
)
```

Let's examine the dimensions of the input and target batches generated by the training loader:

```
print("Train loader:")
for inputs, targets in train_loader:
    print(inputs.shape, targets.shape)
```

The output is as follows (truncated to conserve space):

```
Train loader:
torch.Size([8, 61]) torch.Size([8, 61])
torch.Size([8, 76]) torch.Size([8, 76])
torch.Size([8, 73]) torch.Size([8, 73])
...
```

```
torch.Size([8, 74]) torch.Size([8, 74])
torch.Size([8, 69]) torch.Size([8, 69])
```

This output shows that the first input and target batch have dimensions 8 × 61, where 8 represents the batch size and 61 is the number of tokens in each training example in this batch. The second input and target batch have a different number of tokens—for instance, 76. Thanks to our custom collate function, the data loader is able to create batches of different lengths. In the next section, we load a pretrained LLM that we can then fine-tune with this data loader.

7.5 Loading a pretrained LLM

We have spent a lot of time preparing the dataset for instruction fine-tuning, which is a key aspect of the supervised fine-tuning process. Many other aspects are the same as in pretraining, allowing us to reuse much of the code from earlier chapters.

Before beginning instruction fine-tuning, we must first load a pretrained GPT model that we want to fine-tune (see figure 7.15), a process we have undertaken previously. However, instead of using the smallest 124-million-parameter model as before, we load the medium-sized model with 355 million parameters. The reason for this choice is that the 124-million-parameter model is too limited in capacity to achieve

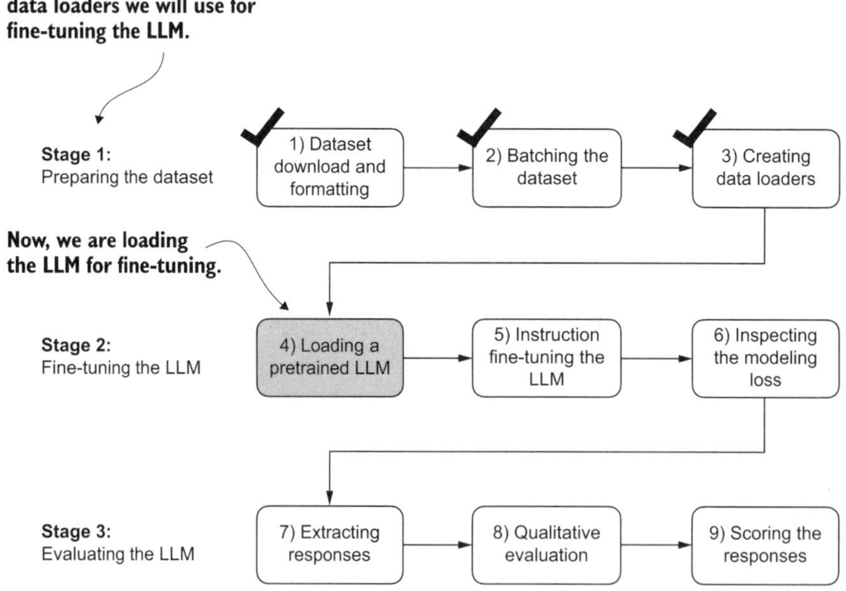

Figure 7.15 The three-stage process for instruction fine-tuning an LLM. After the dataset preparation, the process of fine-tuning an LLM for instruction-following begins with loading a pretrained LLM, which serves as the foundation for subsequent training.

satisfactory results via instruction fine-tuning. Specifically, smaller models lack the necessary capacity to learn and retain the intricate patterns and nuanced behaviors required for high-quality instruction-following tasks.

Loading our pretrained models requires the same code as when we pretrained the data (section 5.5) and fine-tuned it for classification (section 6.4), except that we now specify `"gpt2-medium (355M)"` instead of `"gpt2-small (124M)"`.

> **NOTE** Executing this code will initiate the download of the medium-sized GPT model, which has a storage requirement of approximately 1.42 gigabytes. This is roughly three times larger than the storage space needed for the small model.

Listing 7.7 Loading the pretrained model

```
from gpt_download import download_and_load_gpt2
from chapter04 import GPTModel
from chapter05 import load_weights_into_gpt

BASE_CONFIG = {
    "vocab_size": 50257,      # Vocabulary size
    "context_length": 1024,   # Context length
    "drop_rate": 0.0,         # Dropout rate
    "qkv_bias": True          # Query-key-value bias
}

model_configs = {
    "gpt2-small (124M)": {"emb_dim": 768, "n_layers": 12, "n_heads": 12},
    "gpt2-medium (355M)": {"emb_dim": 1024, "n_layers": 24, "n_heads": 16},
    "gpt2-large (774M)": {"emb_dim": 1280, "n_layers": 36, "n_heads": 20},
    "gpt2-xl (1558M)": {"emb_dim": 1600, "n_layers": 48, "n_heads": 25},
}

CHOOSE_MODEL = "gpt2-medium (355M)"
BASE_CONFIG.update(model_configs[CHOOSE_MODEL])

model_size = CHOOSE_MODEL.split(" ")[-1].lstrip("(").rstrip(")")

settings, params = download_and_load_gpt2(
    model_size=model_size,
    models_dir="gpt2"
)

model = GPTModel(BASE_CONFIG)
load_weights_into_gpt(model, params)
model.eval();
```

After executing the code, several files will be downloaded:

```
checkpoint: 100%|██████████| 77.0/77.0 [00:00<00:00, 156kiB/s]
encoder.json: 100%|██████████| 1.04M/1.04M [00:02<00:00, 467kiB/s]
hparams.json: 100%|██████████| 91.0/91.0 [00:00<00:00, 198kiB/s]
model.ckpt.data-00000-of-00001: 100%|██████████| 1.42G/1.42G
```

```
[05:50<00:00, 4.05MiB/s]
model.ckpt.index: 100%|██████████| 10.4k/10.4k [00:00<00:00, 18.1MiB/s]
model.ckpt.meta: 100%|██████████| 927k/927k [00:02<00:00, 454kiB/s]
vocab.bpe: 100%|██████████| 456k/456k [00:01<00:00, 283kiB/s]
```

Now, let's take a moment to assess the pretrained LLM's performance on one of the validation tasks by comparing its output to the expected response. This will give us a baseline understanding of how well the model performs on an instruction-following task right out of the box, prior to fine-tuning, and will help us appreciate the effect of fine-tuning later on. We will use the first example from the validation set for this assessment:

```
torch.manual_seed(123)
input_text = format_input(val_data[0])
print(input_text)
```

The content of the instruction is as follows:

```
Below is an instruction that describes a task. Write a response that
appropriately completes the request.

### Instruction:
Convert the active sentence to passive: 'The chef cooks the meal every day.'
```

Next we generate the model's response using the same `generate` function we used to pretrain the model in chapter 5:

```
from chapter05 import generate, text_to_token_ids, token_ids_to_text

token_ids = generate(
    model=model,
    idx=text_to_token_ids(input_text, tokenizer),
    max_new_tokens=35,
    context_size=BASE_CONFIG["context_length"],
    eos_id=50256,
)
generated_text = token_ids_to_text(token_ids, tokenizer)
```

The `generate` function returns the combined input and output text. This behavior was previously convenient since pretrained LLMs are primarily designed as text-completion models, where the input and output are concatenated to create coherent and legible text. However, when evaluating the model's performance on a specific task, we often want to focus solely on the model's generated response.

To isolate the model's response text, we need to subtract the length of the input instruction from the start of the `generated_text`:

```
response_text = generated_text[len(input_text):].strip()
print(response_text)
```

This code removes the input text from the beginning of the `generated_text`, leaving us with only the model's generated response. The `strip()` function is then applied to remove any leading or trailing whitespace characters. The output is

```
### Response:

The chef cooks the meal every day.

### Instruction:

Convert the active sentence to passive: 'The chef cooks the
```

This output shows that the pretrained model is not yet capable of correctly following the given instruction. While it does create a Response section, it simply repeats the original input sentence and part of the instruction, failing to convert the active sentence to passive voice as requested. So, let's now implement the fine-tuning process to improve the model's ability to comprehend and appropriately respond to such requests.

7.6 Fine-tuning the LLM on instruction data

It's time to fine-tune the LLM for instructions (figure 7.16). We will take the loaded pretrained model in the previous section and further train it using the previously prepared instruction dataset prepared earlier in this chapter. We already did all the hard work when we implemented the instruction dataset processing at the beginning of

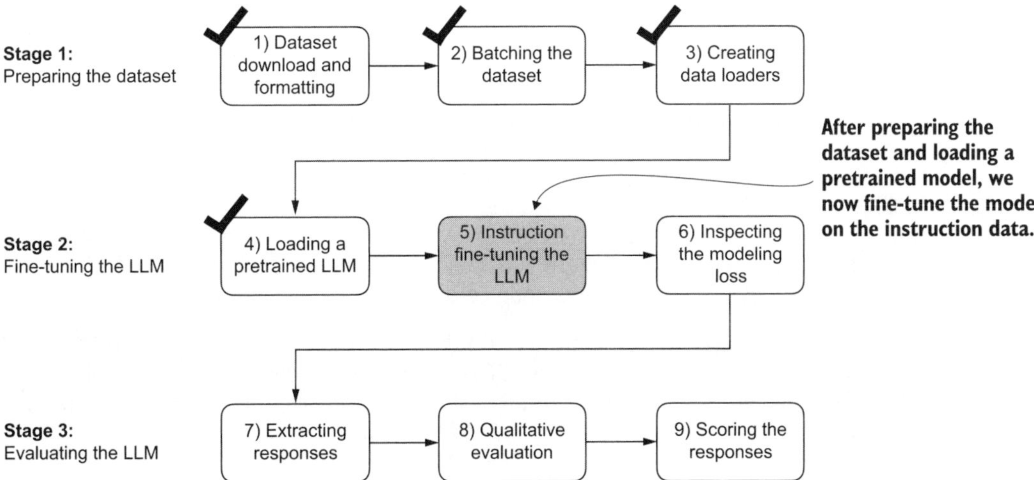

Figure 7.16 The three-stage process for instruction fine-tuning an LLM. In step 5, we train the pretrained model we previously loaded on the instruction dataset we prepared earlier.

this chapter. For the fine-tuning process itself, we can reuse the loss calculation and training functions implemented in chapter 5:

```
from chapter05 import (
    calc_loss_loader,
    train_model_simple
)
```

Before we begin training, let's calculate the initial loss for the training and validation sets:

```
model.to(device)
torch.manual_seed(123)

with torch.no_grad():
    train_loss = calc_loss_loader(
        train_loader, model, device, num_batches=5
    )
    val_loss = calc_loss_loader(
        val_loader, model, device, num_batches=5
)

print("Training loss:", train_loss)
print("Validation loss:", val_loss)
```

The initial loss values are as follows; as previously, our goal is to minimize the loss:

```
Training loss: 3.825908660888672
Validation loss: 3.7619335651397705
```

Dealing with hardware limitations

Using and training a larger model like GPT-2 medium (355 million parameters) is more computationally intensive than the smaller GPT-2 model (124 million parameters). If you encounter problems due to hardware limitations, you can switch to the smaller model by changing `CHOOSE_MODEL = "gpt2-medium (355M)"` to `CHOOSE_MODEL = "gpt2-small (124M)"` (see section 7.5). Alternatively, to speed up the model training, consider using a GPU. The following supplementary section in this book's code repository lists several options for using cloud GPUs: https://mng.bz/EOEq.

The following table provides reference run times for training each model on various devices, including CPUs and GPUs, for GPT-2. Running this code on a compatible GPU requires no code changes and can significantly speed up training. For the results shown in this chapter, I used the GPT-2 medium model and trained it on an A100 GPU.

Model name	Device	Run time for two epochs
gpt2-medium (355M)	CPU (M3 MacBook Air)	15.78 minutes
gpt2-medium (355M)	GPU (NVIDIA L4)	1.83 minutes
gpt2-medium (355M)	GPU (NVIDIA A100)	0.86 minutes
gpt2-small (124M)	CPU (M3 MacBook Air)	5.74 minutes
gpt2-small (124M)	GPU (NVIDIA L4)	0.69 minutes
gpt2-small (124M)	GPU (NVIDIA A100)	0.39 minutes

With the model and data loaders prepared, we can now proceed to train the model. The code in listing 7.8 sets up the training process, including initializing the optimizer, setting the number of epochs, and defining the evaluation frequency and starting context to evaluate generated LLM responses during training based on the first validation set instruction (`val_data[0]`) we looked at in section 7.5.

Listing 7.8 Instruction fine-tuning the pretrained LLM

```
import time

start_time = time.time()
torch.manual_seed(123)
optimizer = torch.optim.AdamW(
    model.parameters(), lr=0.00005, weight_decay=0.1
)
num_epochs = 2

train_losses, val_losses, tokens_seen = train_model_simple(
    model, train_loader, val_loader, optimizer, device,
    num_epochs=num_epochs, eval_freq=5, eval_iter=5,
    start_context=format_input(val_data[0]), tokenizer=tokenizer
)

end_time = time.time()
execution_time_minutes = (end_time - start_time) / 60
print(f"Training completed in {execution_time_minutes:.2f} minutes.")
```

The following output displays the training progress over two epochs, where a steady decrease in losses indicates improving ability to follow instructions and generate appropriate responses:

```
Ep 1 (Step 000000): Train loss 2.637, Val loss 2.626
Ep 1 (Step 000005): Train loss 1.174, Val loss 1.103
Ep 1 (Step 000010): Train loss 0.872, Val loss 0.944
Ep 1 (Step 000015): Train loss 0.857, Val loss 0.906
...
```

```
Ep 1 (Step 000115): Train loss 0.520, Val loss 0.665
Below is an instruction that describes a task. Write a response that
appropriately completes the request.  ### Instruction: Convert the
active sentence to passive: 'The chef cooks the meal every day.'
### Response: The meal is prepared every day by the chef.<|endoftext|>
The following is an instruction that describes a task.
Write a response that appropriately completes the request.
### Instruction: Convert the active sentence to passive:
Ep 2 (Step 000120): Train loss 0.438, Val loss 0.670
Ep 2 (Step 000125): Train loss 0.453, Val loss 0.685
Ep 2 (Step 000130): Train loss 0.448, Val loss 0.681
Ep 2 (Step 000135): Train loss 0.408, Val loss 0.677
...
Ep 2 (Step 000230): Train loss 0.300, Val loss 0.657
Below is an instruction that describes a task. Write a response
that appropriately completes the request.  ### Instruction:
Convert the active sentence to passive: 'The chef cooks the meal
every day.'  ### Response: The meal is cooked every day by the
chef.<|endoftext|>The following is an instruction that describes
a task. Write a response that appropriately completes the request.
### Instruction: What is the capital of the United Kingdom
Training completed in 0.87 minutes.
```

The training output shows that the model is learning effectively, as we can tell based on the consistently decreasing training and validation loss values over the two epochs. This result suggests that the model is gradually improving its ability to understand and follow the provided instructions. (Since the model demonstrated effective learning within these two epochs, extending the training to a third epoch or more is not essential and may even be counterproductive as it could lead to increased overfitting.)

Moreover, the generated responses at the end of each epoch let us inspect the model's progress in correctly executing the given task in the validation set example. In this case, the model successfully converts the active sentence `"The chef cooks the meal every day."` into its passive voice counterpart: `"The meal is cooked every day by the chef."`

We will revisit and evaluate the response quality of the model in more detail later. For now, let's examine the training and validation loss curves to gain additional insights into the model's learning process. For this, we use the same `plot_losses` function we used for pretraining:

```
from chapter05 import plot_losses
epochs_tensor = torch.linspace(0, num_epochs, len(train_losses))
plot_losses(epochs_tensor, tokens_seen, train_losses, val_losses)
```

From the loss plot shown in figure 7.17, we can see that the model's performance on both the training and validation sets improves substantially over the course of training. The rapid decrease in losses during the initial phase indicates that the model quickly learns meaningful patterns and representations from the data. Then, as training progresses to the second epoch, the losses continue to decrease but at a slower rate, suggesting that the model is fine-tuning its learned representations and converging to a stable solution.

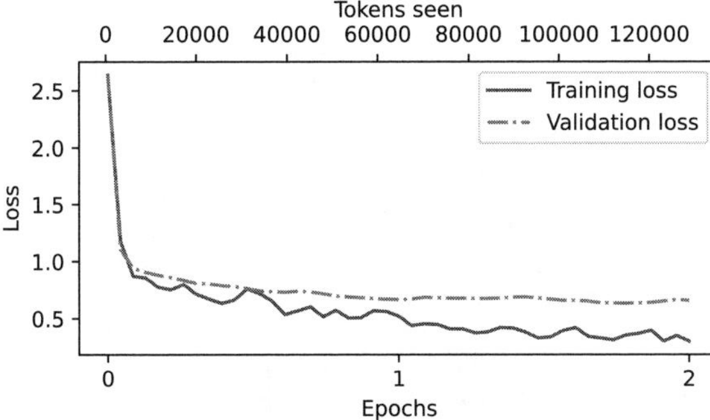

Figure 7.17 The training and validation loss trends over two epochs. The solid line represents the training loss, showing a sharp decrease before stabilizing, while the dotted line represents the validation loss, which follows a similar pattern.

While the loss plot in figure 7.17 indicates that the model is training effectively, the most crucial aspect is its performance in terms of response quality and correctness. So, next, let's extract the responses and store them in a format that allows us to evaluate and quantify the response quality.

> **Exercise 7.3 Fine-tuning on the original Alpaca dataset**
>
> The Alpaca dataset, by researchers at Stanford, is one of the earliest and most popular openly shared instruction datasets, consisting of 52,002 entries. As an alternative to the `instruction-data.json` file we use here, consider fine-tuning an LLM on this dataset. The dataset is available at https://mng.bz/NBnE.
>
> This dataset contains 52,002 entries, which is approximately 50 times more than those we used here, and most entries are longer. Thus, I highly recommend using a GPU to conduct the training, which will accelerate the fine-tuning process. If you encounter out-of-memory errors, consider reducing the `batch_size` from 8 to 4, 2, or even 1. Lowering the `allowed_max_length` from 1,024 to 512 or 256 can also help manage memory problems.

7.7 Extracting and saving responses

Having fine-tuned the LLM on the training portion of the instruction dataset, we are now ready to evaluate its performance on the held-out test set. First, we extract the model-generated responses for each input in the test dataset and collect them for manual analysis, and then we evaluate the LLM to quantify the quality of the responses, as highlighted in figure 7.18.

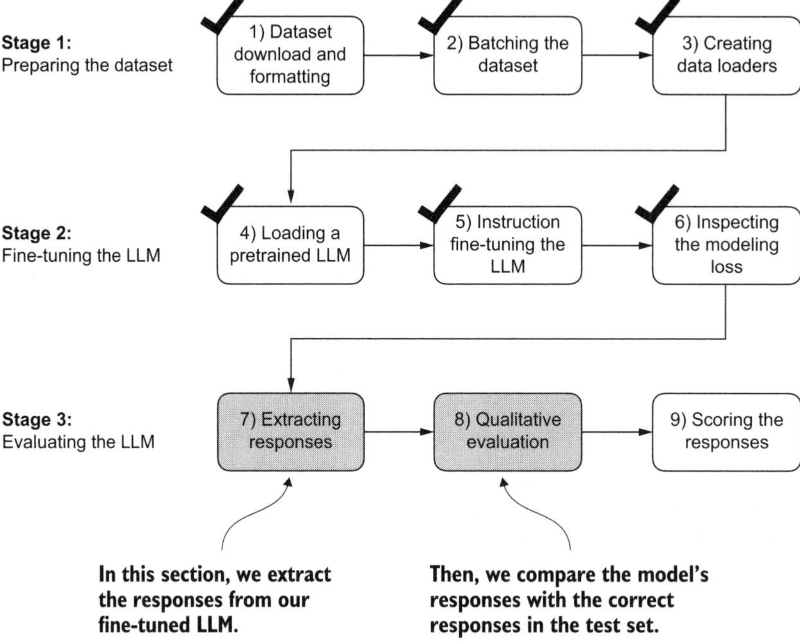

Figure 7.18 The three-stage process for instruction fine-tuning the LLM. In the first two steps of stage 3, we extract and collect the model responses on the held-out test dataset for further analysis and then evaluate the model to quantify the performance of the instruction-fine-tuned LLM.

To complete the response instruction step, we use the `generate` function. We then print the model responses alongside the expected test set answers for the first three test set entries, presenting them side by side for comparison:

```
torch.manual_seed(123)

for entry in test_data[:3]:                    # Iterates over the first three test set samples
    input_text = format_input(entry)
    token_ids = generate(                      # Uses the generate function imported in section 7.5
        model=model,
        idx=text_to_token_ids(input_text, tokenizer).to(device),
        max_new_tokens=256,
        context_size=BASE_CONFIG["context_length"],
        eos_id=50256
    )
    generated_text = token_ids_to_text(token_ids, tokenizer)

    response_text = (
        generated_text[len(input_text):]
        .replace("### Response:", "")
        .strip()
    )
```

```
    print(input_text)
    print(f"\nCorrect response:\n>> {entry['output']}")
    print(f"\nModel response:\n>> {response_text.strip()}")
    print("-------------------------------------")
```

As mentioned earlier, the `generate` function returns the combined input and output text, so we use slicing and the `.replace()` method on the `generated_text` contents to extract the model's response. The instructions, followed by the given test set response and model response, are shown next.

Below is an instruction that describes a task. Write a response that appropriately completes the request.

Instruction:

Rewrite the sentence using a simile.

Input:

The car is very fast.

Correct response:

>> The car is as fast as lightning.

Model response:

>> The car is as fast as a bullet.

Below is an instruction that describes a task. Write a response that appropriately completes the request.

Instruction:

What type of cloud is typically associated with thunderstorms?

Correct response:

>> The type of cloud typically associated with thunderstorms is cumulonimbus.

Model response:

>> The type of cloud associated with thunderstorms is a cumulus cloud.

Below is an instruction that describes a task. Write a response that appropriately completes the request.

Instruction:

Name the author of 'Pride and Prejudice.'

Correct response:

>> Jane Austen.

Model response:

>> The author of 'Pride and Prejudice' is Jane Austen.

As we can see based on the test set instructions, given responses, and the model's responses, the model performs relatively well. The answers to the first and last instructions are clearly correct, while the second answer is close but not entirely accurate. The model answers with "cumulus cloud" instead of "cumulonimbus," although it's worth noting that cumulus clouds can develop into cumulonimbus clouds, which are capable of producing thunderstorms.

Most importantly, model evaluation is not as straightforward as it is for completion fine-tuning, where we simply calculate the percentage of correct spam/non-spam class labels to obtain the classification's accuracy. In practice, instruction-fine-tuned LLMs such as chatbots are evaluated via multiple approaches:

- Short-answer and multiple-choice benchmarks, such as Measuring Massive Multitask Language Understanding (MMLU; https://arxiv.org/abs/2009.03300), which test the general knowledge of a model.
- Human preference comparison to other LLMs, such as LMSYS chatbot arena (https://arena.lmsys.org).
- Automated conversational benchmarks, where another LLM like GPT-4 is used to evaluate the responses, such as AlpacaEval (https://tatsu-lab.github.io/alpaca_eval/).

In practice, it can be useful to consider all three types of evaluation methods: multiple-choice question answering, human evaluation, and automated metrics that measure conversational performance. However, since we are primarily interested in assessing conversational performance rather than just the ability to answer multiple-choice questions, human evaluation and automated metrics may be more relevant.

Conversational performance

Conversational performance of LLMs refers to their ability to engage in human-like communication by understanding context, nuance, and intent. It encompasses skills such as providing relevant and coherent responses, maintaining consistency, and adapting to different topics and styles of interaction.

Human evaluation, while providing valuable insights, can be relatively laborious and time-consuming, especially when dealing with a large number of responses. For instance, reading and assigning ratings to all 1,100 responses would require a significant amount of effort.

So, considering the scale of the task at hand, we will implement an approach similar to automated conversational benchmarks, which involves evaluating the responses automatically using another LLM. This method will allow us to efficiently assess the quality of the generated responses without the need for extensive human involvement, thereby saving time and resources while still obtaining meaningful performance indicators.

Let's employ an approach inspired by AlpacaEval, using another LLM to evaluate our fine-tuned model's responses. However, instead of relying on a publicly available benchmark dataset, we use our own custom test set. This customization allows for a more targeted and relevant assessment of the model's performance within the context of our intended use cases, represented in our instruction dataset.

To prepare the responses for this evaluation process, we append the generated model responses to the `test_set` dictionary and save the updated data as an `"instruction-data-with-response.json"` file for record keeping. Additionally, by saving this file, we can easily load and analyze the responses in separate Python sessions later on if needed.

The following code listing uses the `generate` method in the same manner as before; however, we now iterate over the entire `test_set`. Also, instead of printing the model responses, we add them to the `test_set` dictionary.

Listing 7.9 Generating test set responses

```
from tqdm import tqdm

for i, entry in tqdm(enumerate(test_data), total=len(test_data)):
    input_text = format_input(entry)

    token_ids = generate(
        model=model,
        idx=text_to_token_ids(input_text, tokenizer).to(device),
        max_new_tokens=256,
        context_size=BASE_CONFIG["context_length"],
        eos_id=50256
    )
    generated_text = token_ids_to_text(token_ids, tokenizer)

    response_text = (
        generated_text[len(input_text):]
        .replace("### Response:", "")
        .strip()
    )
    test_data[i]["model_response"] = response_text

with open("instruction-data-with-response.json", "w") as file:
    json.dump(test_data, file, indent=4)
```

indent for pretty-printing

Processing the dataset takes about 1 minute on an A100 GPU and 6 minutes on an M3 MacBook Air:

```
100%|██████████| 110/110 [01:05<00:00,  1.68it/s]
```

Let's verify that the responses have been correctly added to the `test_set` dictionary by examining one of the entries:

```
print(test_data[0])
```

The output shows that the `model_response` has been added correctly:

```
{'instruction': 'Rewrite the sentence using a simile.',
 'input': 'The car is very fast.',
 'output': 'The car is as fast as lightning.',
 'model_response': 'The car is as fast as a bullet.'}
```

Finally, we save the model as `gpt2-medium355M-sft.pth` file to be able to reuse it in future projects:

```
import re

file_name = f"{re.sub(r'[ ()]', '', CHOOSE_MODEL) }-sft.pth"    # Removes white spaces and parentheses from file name
torch.save(model.state_dict(), file_name)
print(f"Model saved as {file_name}")
```

The saved model can then be loaded via `model.load_state_dict(torch.load("gpt2-medium355M-sft.pth"))`.

7.8 Evaluating the fine-tuned LLM

Previously, we judged the performance of an instruction-fine-tuned model by looking at its responses on three examples of the test set. While this gives us a rough idea of how well the model performs, this method does not scale well to larger amounts of responses. So, we implement a method to automate the response evaluation of the fine-tuned LLM using another, larger LLM, as highlighted in figure 7.19.

To evaluate test set responses in an automated fashion, we utilize an existing instruction-fine-tuned 8-billion-parameter Llama 3 model developed by Meta AI. This model can be run locally using the open source Ollama application (https://ollama.com).

NOTE Ollama is an efficient application for running LLMs on a laptop. It serves as a wrapper around the open source llama.cpp library (https://github.com/ggerganov/llama.cpp), which implements LLMs in pure C/C++ to maximize efficiency. However, Ollama is only a tool for generating text using LLMs (inference) and does not support training or fine-tuning LLMs.

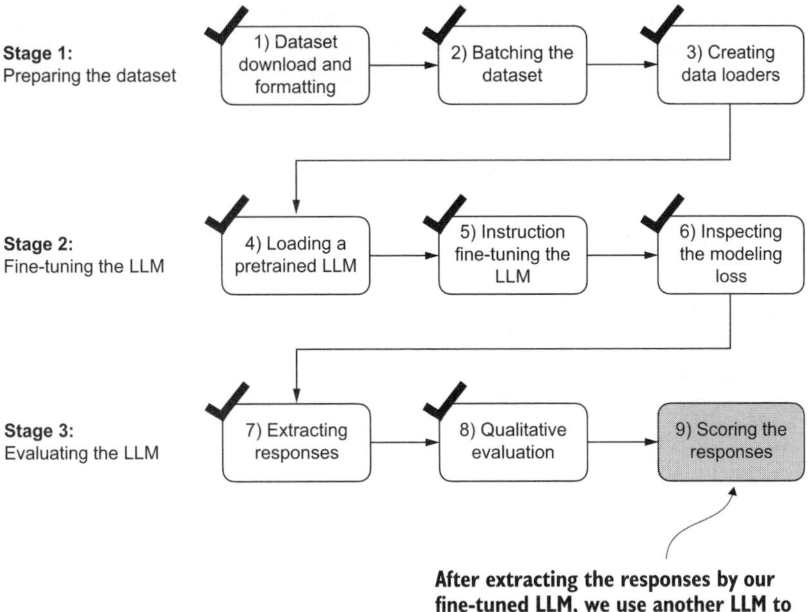

Figure 7.19 The three-stage process for instruction fine-tuning the LLM. In this last step of the instruction-fine-tuning pipeline, we implement a method to quantify the performance of the fine-tuned model by scoring the responses it generated for the test.

> **Using larger LLMs via web APIs**
>
> The 8-billion-parameter Llama 3 model is a very capable LLM that runs locally. However, it's not as capable as large proprietary LLMs such as GPT-4 offered by OpenAI. For readers interested in exploring how to utilize GPT-4 through the OpenAI API to assess generated model responses, an optional code notebook is available within the supplementary materials accompanying this book at https://mng.bz/BgEv.

To execute the following code, install Ollama by visiting https://ollama.com and follow the provided instructions for your operating system:

- *For macOS and Windows users*—Open the downloaded Ollama application. If prompted to install command-line usage, select Yes.
- *For Linux users*—Use the installation command available on the Ollama website.

Before implementing the model evaluation code, let's first download the Llama 3 model and verify that Ollama is functioning correctly by using it from the command-line terminal. To use Ollama from the command line, you must either start the Ollama application or run `ollama serve` in a separate terminal, as shown in figure 7.20.

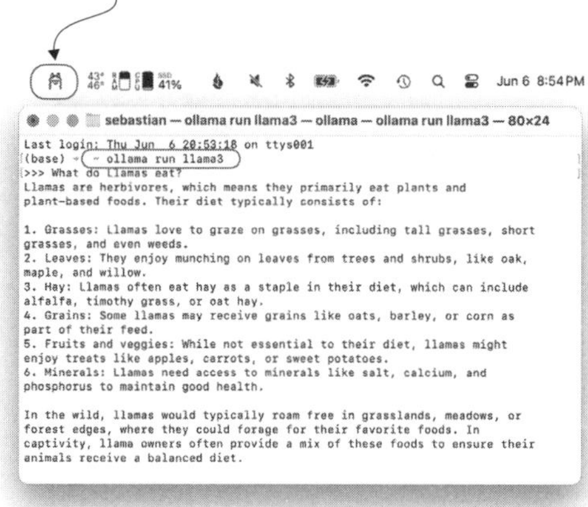

Figure 7.20 Two options for running Ollama. The left panel illustrates starting Ollama using `ollama serve`. The right panel shows a second option in macOS, running the Ollama application in the background instead of using the `ollama serve` command to start the application.

With the Ollama application or `ollama serve` running in a different terminal, execute the following command on the command line (not in a Python session) to try out the 8-billion-parameter Llama 3 model:

```
ollama run llama3
```

The first time you execute this command, this model, which takes up 4.7 GB of storage space, will be automatically downloaded. The output looks like the following:

```
pulling manifest
pulling 6a0746a1ec1a... 100% |████████████████| 4.7 GB
pulling 4fa551d4f938... 100% |████████████████|  12 KB
pulling 8ab4849b038c... 100% |████████████████|  254 B
pulling 577073ffcc6c... 100% |████████████████|  110 B
pulling 3f8eb4da87fa... 100% |████████████████|  485 B
verifying sha256 digest
writing manifest
removing any unused layers
success
```

Alternative Ollama models

The `llama3` in the `ollama run llama3` command refers to the instruction-fine-tuned 8-billion-parameter Llama 3 model. Using Ollama with the `llama3` model requires approximately 16 GB of RAM. If your machine does not have sufficient RAM, you can try using a smaller model, such as the 3.8-billion-parameter `phi3` model via `ollama run llama3`, which only requires around 8 GB of RAM.

For more powerful computers, you can also use the larger 70-billion-parameter Llama 3 model by replacing `llama3` with `llama3:70b`. However, this model requires significantly more computational resources.

Once the model download is complete, we are presented with a command-line interface that allows us to interact with the model. For example, try asking the model, "What do llamas eat?"

```
>>> What do llamas eat?
Llamas are ruminant animals, which means they have a four-chambered
stomach and eat plants that are high in fiber. In the wild,
llamas typically feed on:

1. Grasses: They love to graze on various types of grasses, including tall
grasses, wheat, oats, and barley.
```

Note that the response you see might differ since Ollama is not deterministic as of this writing.

You can end this `ollama run llama3` session using the input `/bye`. However, make sure to keep the `ollama serve` command or the Ollama application running for the remainder of this chapter.

The following code verifies that the Ollama session is running properly before we use Ollama to evaluate the test set responses:

```
import psutil

def check_if_running(process_name):
    running = False
    for proc in psutil.process_iter(["name"]):
        if process_name in proc.info["name"]:
            running = True
            break
    return running

ollama_running = check_if_running("ollama")

if not ollama_running:
    raise RuntimeError(
        "Ollama not running. Launch ollama before proceeding."
)
print("Ollama running:", check_if_running("ollama"))
```

Ensure that the output from executing the previous code displays `Ollama running: True`. If it shows `False`, verify that the `ollama serve` command or the Ollama application is actively running.

Running the code in a new Python session

If you already closed your Python session or if you prefer to execute the remaining code in a different Python session, use the following code, which loads the instruction and response data file we previously created and redefines the `format_input` function we used earlier (the `tqdm` progress bar utility is used later):

```
import json
from tqdm import tqdm

file_path = "instruction-data-with-response.json"
with open(file_path, "r") as file:
    test_data = json.load(file)

def format_input(entry):
    instruction_text = (
        f"Below is an instruction that describes a task. "
        f"Write a response that appropriately completes the request."
        f"\n\n### Instruction:\n{entry['instruction']}"
    )


    input_text = (
        f"\n\n### Input:\n{entry['input']}" if entry["input"] else ""
    )
    return instruction_text + input_text
```

An alternative to the `ollama run` command for interacting with the model is through its REST API using Python. The `query_model` function shown in the following listing demonstrates how to use the API.

Listing 7.10 Querying a local Ollama model

```
import urllib.request

def query_model(
    prompt,
    model="llama3",
    url="http://localhost:11434/api/chat"
):
    data = {                                    # Creates the data payload as a dictionary
        "model": model,
        "messages": [
            {"role": "user", "content": prompt}
        ],
        "options": {                            # Settings for deterministic responses
            "seed": 123,
```

```
            "temperature": 0,
            "num_ctx": 2048
        }
    }

    payload = json.dumps(data).encode("utf-8")          <-- Converts the dictionary to a JSON-formatted string and encodes it to bytes
    request = urllib.request.Request(
        url,
        data=payload,
        method="POST"
    )

    request.add_header("Content-Type", "application/json")    <-- Creates a request object, setting the method to POST and adding necessary headers

    response_data = ""
    with urllib.request.urlopen(request) as response:    <-- Sends the request and captures the response
        while True:
            line = response.readline().decode("utf-8")
            if not line:
                break
            response_json = json.loads(line)
            response_data += response_json["message"]["content"]

    return response_data
```

Before running the subsequent code cells in this notebook, ensure that Ollama is still running. The previous code cells should print `"Ollama running: True"` to confirm that the model is active and ready to receive requests.

The following is an example of how to use the `query_model` function we just implemented:

```
model = "llama3"
result = query_model("What do Llamas eat?", model)
print(result)
```

The resulting response is as follows:

```
Llamas are ruminant animals, which means they have a four-chambered
stomach that allows them to digest plant-based foods. Their diet
typically consists of:

1. Grasses: Llamas love to graze on grasses, including tall grasses,
short grasses, and even weeds.
...
```

Using the `query_model` function defined earlier, we can evaluate the responses generated by our fine-tuned model that prompts the Llama 3 model to rate our fine-tuned model's responses on a scale from 0 to 100 based on the given test set response as reference.

First, we apply this approach to the first three examples from the test set that we previously examined:

```
for entry in test_data[:3]:
    prompt = (
        f"Given the input `{format_input(entry)}` "
        f"and correct output `{entry['output']}`, "
        f"score the model response `{entry['model_response']}`"
        f" on a scale from 0 to 100, where 100 is the best score. "
    )
    print("\nDataset response:")
    print(">>", entry['output'])
    print("\nModel response:")
    print(">>", entry["model_response"])
    print("\nScore:")
    print(">>", query_model(prompt))
    print("\n-------------------------")
```

This code prints outputs similar to the following (as of this writing, Ollama is not fully deterministic, so the generated texts may vary):

Dataset response:

>> The car is as fast as lightning.

Model response:

>> The car is as fast as a bullet.

Score:

>> I'd rate the model response "The car is as fast as a bullet." an 85 out of 100.

Here's why:

The response uses a simile correctly, comparing the speed of the car to something else (in this case, a bullet).

The comparison is relevant and makes sense, as bullets are known for their high velocity.

The phrase "as fast as" is used correctly to introduce the simile.

The only reason I wouldn't give it a perfect score is that some people might find the comparison slightly less vivid or evocative than others. For example, comparing something to lightning (as in the original response) can be more dramatic and attention grabbing. However, "as fast as a bullet" is still a strong and effective simile that effectively conveys the idea of the car's speed.

Overall, I think the model did a great job!

Dataset response:

>> The type of cloud typically associated with thunderstorms is cumulonimbus.

Model response:

>> The type of cloud associated with thunderstorms is a cumulus cloud.

Score:

>> I'd score this model response as 40 out of 100.

Here's why:

The model correctly identifies that thunderstorms are related to clouds (correctly identifying the type of phenomenon).

However, it incorrectly specifies the type of cloud associated with thunderstorms. Cumulus clouds are not typically associated with thunderstorms; cumulonimbus clouds are.

The response lacks precision and accuracy in its description.

Overall, while the model attempts to address the instruction, it provides an incorrect answer, which is a significant error.

Dataset response:

>> Jane Austen.

Model response:

>> The author of 'Pride and Prejudice' is Jane Austen.

Score:

>> I'd rate my own response as 95 out of 100. Here's why:

The response accurately answers the question by naming the author of *Pride and Prejudice* as Jane Austen.

The response is concise and clear, making it easy to understand.

There are no grammatical errors or ambiguities that could lead to confusion.

The only reason I wouldn't give myself a perfect score is that the response is slightly redundant—it's not necessary to rephrase the question in the answer. A more concise response would be simply "Jane Austen."

The generated responses show that the Llama 3 model provides reasonable evaluations and is capable of assigning partial points when a model's answer is not entirely correct. For instance, if we consider the evaluation of the "cumulus cloud" answer, the model acknowledges the partial correctness of the response.

The previous prompt returns highly detailed evaluations in addition to the score. We can modify the prompt to just generate integer scores ranging from 0 to 100, where 100 represents the best possible score. This modification allows us to calculate an average score for our model, which serves as a more concise and quantitative assessment of its performance. The `generate_model_scores` function shown in the following listing uses a modified prompt telling the model to `"Respond with the integer number only."`

Listing 7.11 Evaluating the instruction fine-tuning LLM

```
def generate_model_scores(json_data, json_key, model="llama3"):
    scores = []
    for entry in tqdm(json_data, desc="Scoring entries"):
        prompt = (
            f"Given the input `{format_input(entry)}` "
            f"and correct output `{entry['output']}`, "
            f"score the model response `{entry[json_key]}`"
            f" on a scale from 0 to 100, where 100 is the best score. "
            f"Respond with the integer number only."      # Modified instruction line to only return the score
        )
        score = query_model(prompt, model)
        try:
            scores.append(int(score))
        except ValueError:
            print(f"Could not convert score: {score}")
            continue

    return scores
```

Let's now apply the `generate_model_scores` function to the entire `test_data` set, which takes about 1 minute on a M3 Macbook Air:

```
scores = generate_model_scores(test_data, "model_response")
print(f"Number of scores: {len(scores)} of {len(test_data)}")
print(f"Average score: {sum(scores)/len(scores):.2f}\n")
```

The results are as follows:

```
Scoring entries: 100%|████████████████████████| 110/110
[01:10<00:00,  1.56it/s]
Number of scores: 110 of 110
Average score: 50.32
```

The evaluation output shows that our fine-tuned model achieves an average score above 50, which provides a useful benchmark for comparison against other models or for experimenting with different training configurations to improve the model's performance.

It's worth noting that Ollama is not entirely deterministic across operating systems at the time of this writing, which means that the scores you obtain might vary slightly from the previous scores. To obtain more robust results, you can repeat the evaluation multiple times and average the resulting scores.

To further improve our model's performance, we can explore various strategies, such as

- Adjusting the hyperparameters during fine-tuning, such as the learning rate, batch size, or number of epochs
- Increasing the size of the training dataset or diversifying the examples to cover a broader range of topics and styles
- Experimenting with different prompts or instruction formats to guide the model's responses more effectively
- Using a larger pretrained model, which may have greater capacity to capture complex patterns and generate more accurate responses

NOTE For reference, when using the methodology described herein, the Llama 3 8B base model, without any fine-tuning, achieves an average score of 58.51 on the test set. The Llama 3 8B instruct model, which has been fine-tuned on a general instruction-following dataset, achieves an impressive average score of 82.6.

Exercise 7.4 Parameter-efficient fine-tuning with LoRA

To instruction fine-tune an LLM more efficiently, modify the code in this chapter to use the low-rank adaptation method (LoRA) from appendix E. Compare the training run time and model performance before and after the modification.

7.9 Conclusions

This chapter marks the conclusion of our journey through the LLM development cycle. We have covered all the essential steps, including implementing an LLM architecture, pretraining an LLM, and fine-tuning it for specific tasks, as summarized in figure 7.21. Let's discuss some ideas for what to look into next.

7.9.1 What's next?

While we covered the most essential steps, there is an optional step that can be performed after instruction fine-tuning: preference fine-tuning. Preference fine-tuning is particularly useful for customizing a model to better align with specific user preferences. If you are interested in exploring this further, see the `04_preference-tuning-with-dpo` folder in this book's supplementary GitHub repository at https://mng.bz/dZwD.

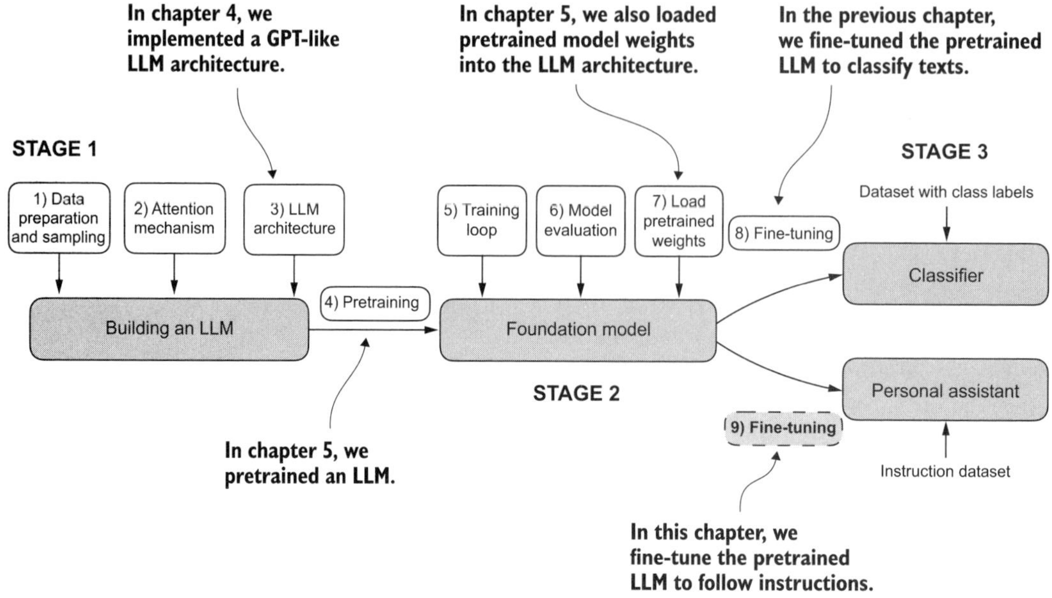

Figure 7.21 The three main stages of coding an LLM.

In addition to the main content covered in this book, the GitHub repository also contains a large selection of bonus material that you may find valuable. To learn more about these additional resources, visit the Bonus Material section on the repository's README page: https://mng.bz/r12g.

7.9.2 Staying up to date in a fast-moving field

The fields of AI and LLM research are evolving at a rapid (and, depending on who you ask, exciting) pace. One way to keep up with the latest advancements is to explore recent research papers on arXiv at https://arxiv.org/list/cs.LG/recent. Additionally, many researchers and practitioners are very active in sharing and discussing the latest developments on social media platforms like X (formerly Twitter) and Reddit. The subreddit r/LocalLLaMA, in particular, is a good resource for connecting with the community and staying informed about the latest tools and trends. I also regularly share insights and write about the latest in LLM research on my blog, available at https://magazine.sebastianraschka.com and https://sebastianraschka.com/blog/.

7.9.3 Final words

I hope you have enjoyed this journey of implementing an LLM from the ground up and coding the pretraining and fine-tuning functions from scratch. In my opinion, building an LLM from scratch is the most effective way to gain a deep understanding of how LLMs work. I hope that this hands-on approach has provided you with valuable insights and a solid foundation in LLM development.

While the primary purpose of this book is educational, you may be interested in utilizing different and more powerful LLMs for real-world applications. For this, I recommend exploring popular tools such as Axolotl (https://github.com/OpenAccess-AI-Collective/axolotl) or LitGPT (https://github.com/Lightning-AI/litgpt), which I am actively involved in developing.

Thank you for joining me on this learning journey, and I wish you all the best in your future endeavors in the exciting field of LLMs and AI!

Summary

- The instruction-fine-tuning process adapts a pretrained LLM to follow human instructions and generate desired responses.
- Preparing the dataset involves downloading an instruction-response dataset, formatting the entries, and splitting it into train, validation, and test sets.
- Training batches are constructed using a custom collate function that pads sequences, creates target token IDs, and masks padding tokens.
- We load a pretrained GPT-2 medium model with 355 million parameters to serve as the starting point for instruction fine-tuning.
- The pretrained model is fine-tuned on the instruction dataset using a training loop similar to pretraining.
- Evaluation involves extracting model responses on a test set and scoring them (for example, using another LLM).
- The Ollama application with an 8-billion-parameter Llama model can be used to automatically score the fine-tuned model's responses on the test set, providing an average score to quantify performance.

appendix A
Introduction to PyTorch

This appendix is designed to equip you with the necessary skills and knowledge to put deep learning into practice and implement large language models (LLMs) from scratch. PyTorch, a popular Python-based deep learning library, will be our primary tool for this book. I will guide you through setting up a deep learning workspace armed with PyTorch and GPU support.

Then you'll learn about the essential concept of tensors and their usage in PyTorch. We will also delve into PyTorch's automatic differentiation engine, a feature that enables us to conveniently and efficiently use backpropagation, which is a crucial aspect of neural network training.

This appendix is meant as a primer for those new to deep learning in PyTorch. While it explains PyTorch from the ground up, it's not meant to be an exhaustive coverage of the PyTorch library. Instead, we'll focus on the PyTorch fundamentals we will use to implement LLMs. If you are already familiar with deep learning, you may skip this appendix and directly move on to chapter 2.

A.1 What is PyTorch?

PyTorch (https://pytorch.org/) is an open source Python-based deep learning library. According to *Papers With Code* (https://paperswithcode.com/trends), a platform that tracks and analyzes research papers, PyTorch has been the most widely used deep learning library for research since 2019 by a wide margin. And, according to the *Kaggle Data Science and Machine Learning Survey 2022* (https://www.kaggle.com/c/kaggle-survey-2022), the number of respondents using PyTorch is approximately 40%, which grows every year.

One of the reasons PyTorch is so popular is its user-friendly interface and efficiency. Despite its accessibility, it doesn't compromise on flexibility, allowing advanced users to tweak lower-level aspects of their models for customization and optimization. In short, for many practitioners and researchers, PyTorch offers just the right balance between usability and features.

A.1.1 The three core components of PyTorch

PyTorch is a relatively comprehensive library, and one way to approach it is to focus on its three broad components, summarized in figure A.1.

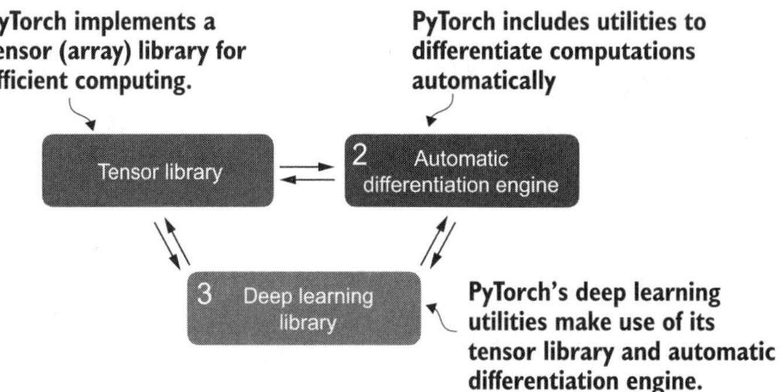

Figure A.1 PyTorch's three main components include a tensor library as a fundamental building block for computing, automatic differentiation for model optimization, and deep learning utility functions, making it easier to implement and train deep neural network models.

First, PyTorch is a *tensor library* that extends the concept of the array-oriented programming library NumPy with the additional feature that accelerates computation on GPUs, thus providing a seamless switch between CPUs and GPUs. Second, PyTorch is an *automatic differentiation engine*, also known as autograd, that enables the automatic computation of gradients for tensor operations, simplifying backpropagation and model optimization. Finally, PyTorch is a *deep learning library*. It offers modular, flexible, and efficient building blocks, including pretrained models, loss functions, and optimizers, for designing and training a wide range of deep learning models, catering to both researchers and developers.

A.1.2 Defining deep learning

In the news, LLMs are often referred to as AI models. However, LLMs are also a type of deep neural network, and PyTorch is a deep learning library. Sound confusing? Let's take a brief moment and summarize the relationship between these terms before we proceed.

AI is fundamentally about creating computer systems capable of performing tasks that usually require human intelligence. These tasks include understanding natural language, recognizing patterns, and making decisions. (Despite significant progress, AI is still far from achieving this level of general intelligence.)

Machine learning represents a subfield of AI, as illustrated in figure A.2, that focuses on developing and improving learning algorithms. The key idea behind machine learning is to enable computers to learn from data and make predictions or decisions without being explicitly programmed to perform the task. This involves developing algorithms that can identify patterns, learn from historical data, and improve their performance over time with more data and feedback.

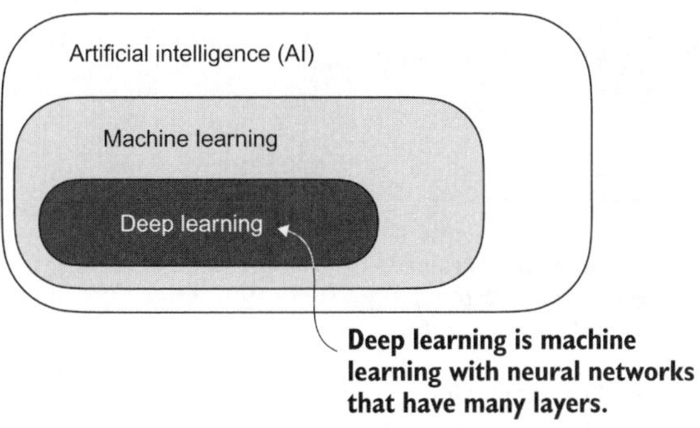
Artificial intelligence (AI)
Machine learning
Deep learning
Deep learning is machine learning with neural networks that have many layers.

Figure A.2 Deep learning is a subcategory of machine learning focused on implementing deep neural networks. Machine learning is a subcategory of AI that is concerned with algorithms that learn from data. AI is the broader concept of machines being able to perform tasks that typically require human intelligence.

Machine learning has been integral in the evolution of AI, powering many of the advancements we see today, including LLMs. Machine learning is also behind technologies like recommendation systems used by online retailers and streaming services, email spam filtering, voice recognition in virtual assistants, and even self-driving cars. The introduction and advancement of machine learning have significantly enhanced AI's capabilities, enabling it to move beyond strict rule-based systems and adapt to new inputs or changing environments.

Deep learning is a subcategory of machine learning that focuses on the training and application of deep neural networks. These deep neural networks were originally inspired by how the human brain works, particularly the interconnection between many neurons. The "deep" in deep learning refers to the multiple hidden layers of artificial neurons or nodes that allow them to model complex, nonlinear relationships in the data. Unlike traditional machine learning techniques that excel at simple pattern recognition, deep learning is particularly good at handling unstructured data like images, audio, or text, so it is particularly well suited for LLMs.

The typical predictive modeling workflow (also referred to as *supervised learning*) in machine learning and deep learning is summarized in figure A.3.

Using a learning algorithm, a model is trained on a training dataset consisting of examples and corresponding labels. In the case of an email spam classifier, for example, the training dataset consists of emails and their "spam" and "not spam" labels that a human identified. Then the trained model can be used on new observations (i.e., new emails) to predict their unknown label ("spam" or "not spam"). Of course, we also want to add a model evaluation between the training and inference stages to

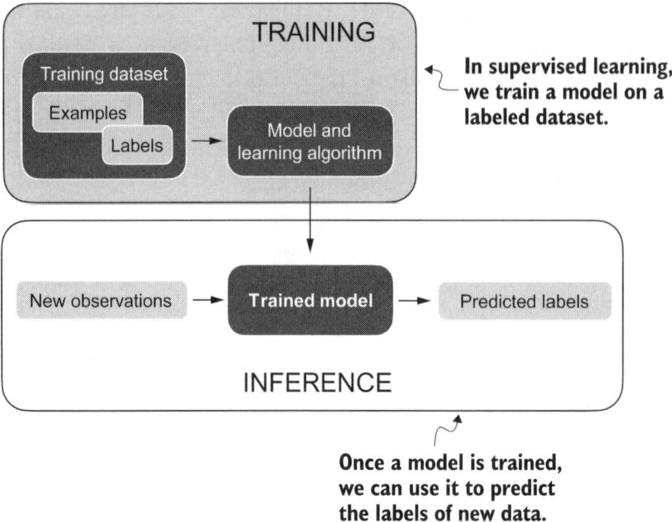

Figure A.3 The supervised learning workflow for predictive modeling consists of a training stage where a model is trained on labeled examples in a training dataset. The trained model can then be used to predict the labels of new observations.

ensure that the model satisfies our performance criteria before using it in a real-world application.

If we train LLMs to classify texts, the workflow for training and using LLMs is similar to that depicted in figure A.3. If we are interested in training LLMs to generate texts, which is our main focus, figure A.3 still applies. In this case, the labels during pretraining can be derived from the text itself (the next-word prediction task introduced in chapter 1). The LLM will generate entirely new text (instead of predicting labels), given an input prompt during inference.

A.1.3 Installing PyTorch

PyTorch can be installed just like any other Python library or package. However, since PyTorch is a comprehensive library featuring CPU- and GPU-compatible codes, the installation may require additional explanation.

> **Python version**
>
> Many scientific computing libraries do not immediately support the newest version of Python. Therefore, when installing PyTorch, it's advisable to use a version of Python that is one or two releases older. For instance, if the latest version of Python is 3.13, using Python 3.11 or 3.12 is recommended.

For instance, there are two versions of PyTorch: a leaner version that only supports CPU computing and a full version that supports both CPU and GPU computing. If your machine has a CUDA-compatible GPU that can be used for deep learning (ideally, an NVIDIA T4, RTX 2080 Ti, or newer), I recommend installing the GPU version. Regardless, the default command for installing PyTorch in a code terminal is:

```
pip install torch
```

Suppose your computer supports a CUDA-compatible GPU. In that case, it will automatically install the PyTorch version that supports GPU acceleration via CUDA, assuming the Python environment you're working on has the necessary dependencies (like `pip`) installed.

> **NOTE** As of this writing, PyTorch has also added experimental support for AMD GPUs via ROCm. See https://pytorch.org for additional instructions.

To explicitly install the CUDA-compatible version of PyTorch, it's often better to specify the CUDA you want PyTorch to be compatible with. PyTorch's official website (https://pytorch.org) provides the commands to install PyTorch with CUDA support for different operating systems. Figure A.4 shows a command that will also install PyTorch, as well as the `torchvision` and `torchaudio` libraries, which are optional for this book.

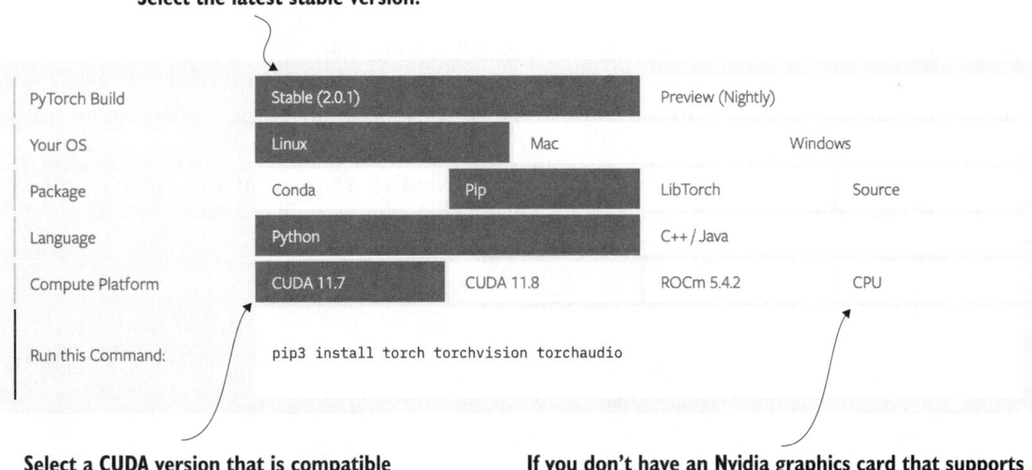

Figure A.4 Access the PyTorch installation recommendation on https://pytorch.org to customize and select the installation command for your system.

I use PyTorch 2.4.0 for the examples, so I recommend that you use the following command to install the exact version to guarantee compatibility with this book:

```
pip install torch==2.4.0
```

However, as mentioned earlier, given your operating system, the installation command might differ slightly from the one shown here. Thus, I recommend that you visit https://pytorch.org and use the installation menu (see figure A.4) to select the installation command for your operating system. Remember to replace `torch` with `torch==2.4.0` in the command.

To check the version of PyTorch, execute the following code in PyTorch:

```
import torch
torch.__version__
```

This prints

```
'2.4.0'
```

PyTorch and Torch

The Python library is named PyTorch primarily because it's a continuation of the Torch library but adapted for Python (hence, "PyTorch"). "Torch" acknowledges the library's roots in Torch, a scientific computing framework with wide support for machine learning algorithms, which was initially created using the Lua programming language.

If you are looking for additional recommendations and instructions for setting up your Python environment or installing the other libraries used in this book, visit the supplementary GitHub repository of this book at https://github.com/rasbt/LLMs-from-scratch.

After installing PyTorch, you can check whether your installation recognizes your built-in NVIDIA GPU by running the following code in Python:

```
import torch
torch.cuda.is_available()
```

This returns

```
True
```

If the command returns `True`, you are all set. If the command returns `False`, your computer may not have a compatible GPU, or PyTorch does not recognize it. While GPUs are not required for the initial chapters in this book, which are focused on implementing LLMs for educational purposes, they can significantly speed up deep learning–related computations.

If you don't have access to a GPU, there are several cloud computing providers where users can run GPU computations against an hourly cost. A popular Jupyter notebook–like environment is Google Colab (https://colab.research.google.com), which provides time-limited access to GPUs as of this writing. Using the Runtime menu, it is possible to select a GPU, as shown in the screenshot in figure A.5.

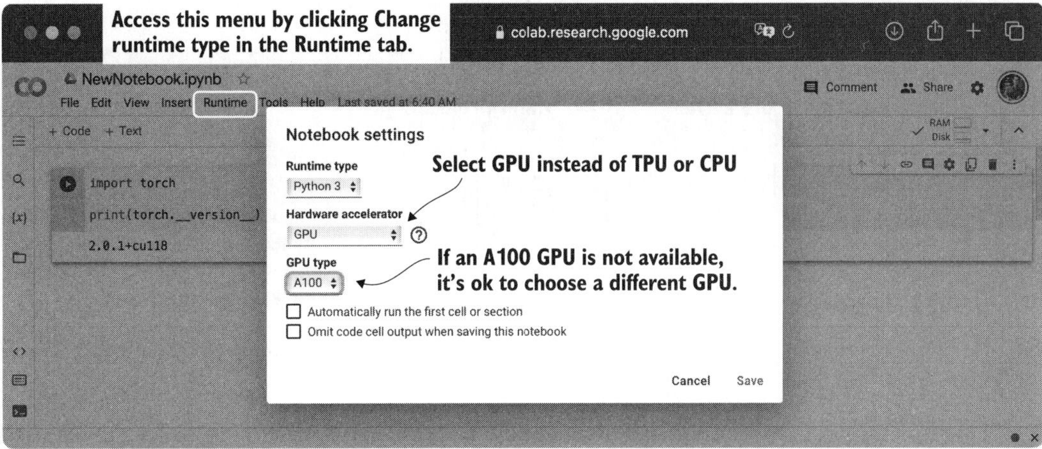

Figure A.5 **Select a GPU device for Google Colab under the Runtime/Change Runtime Type menu.**

PyTorch on Apple Silicon

If you have an Apple Mac with an Apple Silicon chip (like the M1, M2, M3, or newer models), you can use its capabilities to accelerate PyTorch code execution. To use your Apple Silicon chip for PyTorch, you first need to install PyTorch as you normally would. Then, to check whether your Mac supports PyTorch acceleration with its Apple Silicon chip, you can run a simple code snippet in Python:

```
print(torch.backends.mps.is_available())
```

If it returns `True`, it means that your Mac has an Apple Silicon chip that can be used to accelerate PyTorch code.

Exercise A.1

Install and set up PyTorch on your computer

Exercise A.2

Run the supplementary code at https://mng.bz/o05v that checks whether your environment is set up correctly.

A.2 Understanding tensors

Tensors represent a mathematical concept that generalizes vectors and matrices to potentially higher dimensions. In other words, tensors are mathematical objects that can be characterized by their order (or rank), which provides the number of dimensions. For example, a scalar (just a number) is a tensor of rank 0, a vector is a tensor of rank 1, and a matrix is a tensor of rank 2, as illustrated in figure A.6.

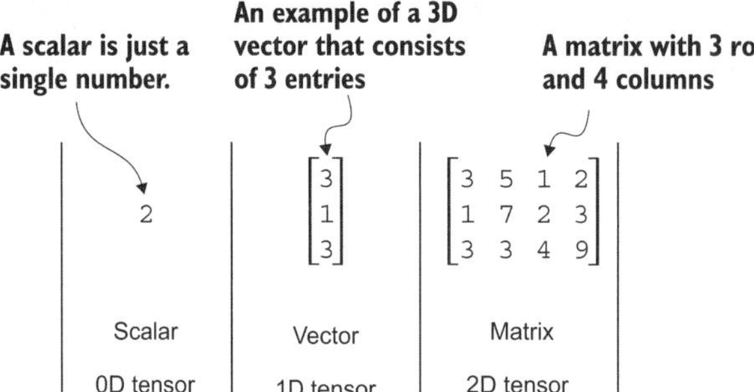

Figure A.6 Tensors with different ranks. Here 0D corresponds to rank 0, 1D to rank 1, and 2D to rank 2. A three-dimensional vector, which consists of three elements, is still a rank 1 tensor.

From a computational perspective, tensors serve as data containers. For instance, they hold multidimensional data, where each dimension represents a different feature. Tensor libraries like PyTorch can create, manipulate, and compute with these arrays efficiently. In this context, a tensor library functions as an array library.

PyTorch tensors are similar to NumPy arrays but have several additional features that are important for deep learning. For example, PyTorch adds an automatic differentiation engine, simplifying *computing gradients* (see section A.4). PyTorch tensors also support GPU computations to speed up deep neural network training (see section A.8).

> **PyTorch with a NumPy-like API**
>
> PyTorch adopts most of the NumPy array API and syntax for its tensor operations. If you are new to NumPy, you can get a brief overview of the most relevant concepts via my article "Scientific Computing in Python: Introduction to NumPy and Matplotlib" at https://sebastianraschka.com/blog/2020/numpy-intro.html.

A.2.1 Scalars, vectors, matrices, and tensors

As mentioned earlier, PyTorch tensors are data containers for array-like structures. A scalar is a zero-dimensional tensor (for instance, just a number), a vector is a one-dimensional tensor, and a matrix is a two-dimensional tensor. There is no specific term for higher-dimensional tensors, so we typically refer to a three-dimensional tensor as just a 3D tensor, and so forth. We can create objects of PyTorch's `Tensor` class using the `torch.tensor` function as shown in the following listing.

Listing A.1 Creating PyTorch tensors

```
import torch

tensor0d = torch.tensor(1)

tensor1d = torch.tensor([1, 2, 3])

tensor2d = torch.tensor([[1, 2],
                         [3, 4]])

tensor3d = torch.tensor([[[1, 2], [3, 4]],
                         [[5, 6], [7, 8]]])
```

Creates a zero-dimensional tensor (scalar) from a Python integer

Creates a one-dimensional tensor (vector) from a Python list

Creates a two-dimensional tensor from a nested Python list

Creates a three-dimensional tensor from a nested Python list

A.2.2 Tensor data types

PyTorch adopts the default 64-bit integer data type from Python. We can access the data type of a tensor via the `.dtype` attribute of a tensor:

```
tensor1d = torch.tensor([1, 2, 3])
print(tensor1d.dtype)
```

This prints

```
torch.int64
```

If we create tensors from Python floats, PyTorch creates tensors with a 32-bit precision by default:

```
floatvec = torch.tensor([1.0, 2.0, 3.0])
print(floatvec.dtype)
```

The output is

```
torch.float32
```

This choice is primarily due to the balance between precision and computational efficiency. A 32-bit floating-point number offers sufficient precision for most deep learning tasks while consuming less memory and computational resources than a 64-bit floating-point number. Moreover, GPU architectures are optimized for 32-bit computations, and using this data type can significantly speed up model training and inference.

Moreover, it is possible to change the precision using a tensor's `.to` method. The following code demonstrates this by changing a 64-bit integer tensor into a 32-bit float tensor:

```
floatvec = tensor1d.to(torch.float32)
print(floatvec.dtype)
```

This returns

```
torch.float32
```

For more information about different tensor data types available in PyTorch, check the official documentation at https://pytorch.org/docs/stable/tensors.html.

A.2.3 Common PyTorch tensor operations

Comprehensive coverage of all the different PyTorch tensor operations and commands is outside the scope of this book. However, I will briefly describe relevant operations as we introduce them throughout the book.

We have already introduced the `torch.tensor()` function to create new tensors:

```
tensor2d = torch.tensor([[1, 2, 3],
                         [4, 5, 6]])
print(tensor2d)
```

This prints

```
tensor([[1, 2, 3],
        [4, 5, 6]])
```

In addition, the `.shape` attribute allows us to access the shape of a tensor:

```
print(tensor2d.shape)
```

The output is

```
torch.Size([2, 3])
```

As you can see, `.shape` returns `[2, 3]`, meaning the tensor has two rows and three columns. To reshape the tensor into a 3×2 tensor, we can use the `.reshape` method:

```
print(tensor2d.reshape(3, 2))
```

This prints

```
tensor([[1, 2],
        [3, 4],
        [5, 6]])
```

However, note that the more common command for reshaping tensors in PyTorch is `.view()`:

```
print(tensor2d.view(3, 2))
```

The output is

```
tensor([[1, 2],
        [3, 4],
        [5, 6]])
```

Similar to `.reshape` and `.view`, in several cases, PyTorch offers multiple syntax options for executing the same computation. PyTorch initially followed the original Lua

Torch syntax convention but then, by popular request, added syntax to make it similar to NumPy. (The subtle difference between `.view()` and `.reshape()` in PyTorch lies in their handling of memory layout: `.view()` requires the original data to be contiguous and will fail if it isn't, whereas `.reshape()` will work regardless, copying the data if necessary to ensure the desired shape.)

Next, we can use `.T` to transpose a tensor, which means flipping it across its diagonal. Note that this is similar to reshaping a tensor, as you can see based on the following result:

```
print(tensor2d.T)
```

The output is

```
tensor([[1, 4],
        [2, 5],
        [3, 6]])
```

Lastly, the common way to multiply two matrices in PyTorch is the `.matmul` method:

```
print(tensor2d.matmul(tensor2d.T))
```

The output is

```
tensor([[14, 32],
        [32, 77]])
```

However, we can also adopt the `@` operator, which accomplishes the same thing more compactly:

```
print(tensor2d @ tensor2d.T)
```

This prints

```
tensor([[14, 32],
        [32, 77]])
```

As mentioned earlier, I introduce additional operations when needed. For readers who'd like to browse through all the different tensor operations available in PyTorch (we won't need most of these), I recommend checking out the official documentation at https://pytorch.org/docs/stable/tensors.html.

A.3 Seeing models as computation graphs

Now let's look at PyTorch's automatic differentiation engine, also known as autograd. PyTorch's autograd system provides functions to compute gradients in dynamic computational graphs automatically.

A computational graph is a directed graph that allows us to express and visualize mathematical expressions. In the context of deep learning, a computation graph lays out the sequence of calculations needed to compute the output of a neural network—we will need this to compute the required gradients for backpropagation, the main training algorithm for neural networks.

Let's look at a concrete example to illustrate the concept of a computation graph. The code in the following listing implements the forward pass (prediction step) of a simple logistic regression classifier, which can be seen as a single-layer neural network. It returns a score between 0 and 1, which is compared to the true class label (0 or 1) when computing the loss.

Listing A.2 A logistic regression forward pass

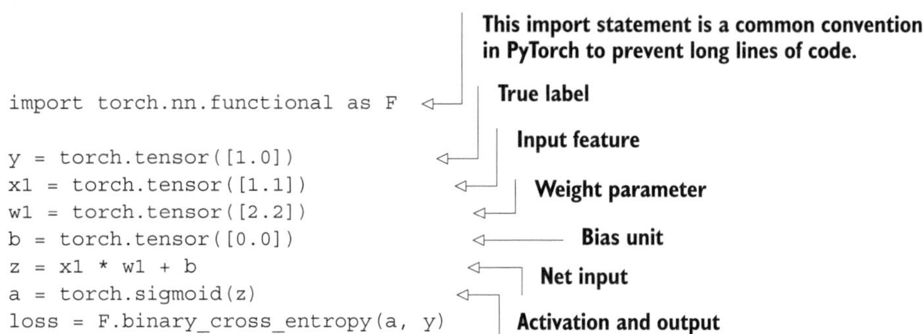

```
import torch.nn.functional as F

y = torch.tensor([1.0])
x1 = torch.tensor([1.1])
w1 = torch.tensor([2.2])
b = torch.tensor([0.0])
z = x1 * w1 + b
a = torch.sigmoid(z)
loss = F.binary_cross_entropy(a, y)
```


If not all components in the preceding code make sense to you, don't worry. The point of this example is not to implement a logistic regression classifier but rather to illustrate how we can think of a sequence of computations as a computation graph, as shown in figure A.7.

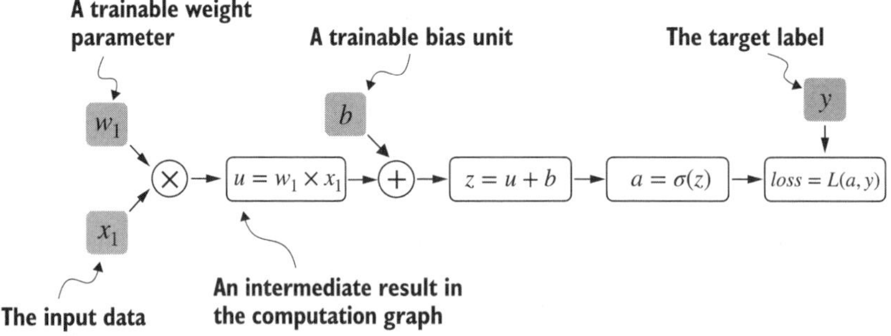

Figure A.7 A logistic regression forward pass as a computation graph. The input feature x_1 is multiplied by a model weight w_1 and passed through an activation function σ after adding the bias. The loss is computed by comparing the model output *a* with a given label *y*.

In fact, PyTorch builds such a computation graph in the background, and we can use this to calculate gradients of a loss function with respect to the model parameters (here w_1 and b) to train the model.

A.4 Automatic differentiation made easy

If we carry out computations in PyTorch, it will build a computational graph internally by default if one of its terminal nodes has the `requires_grad` attribute set to `True`. This is useful if we want to compute gradients. Gradients are required when training neural networks via the popular backpropagation algorithm, which can be considered an implementation of the *chain rule* from calculus for neural networks, illustrated in figure A.8.

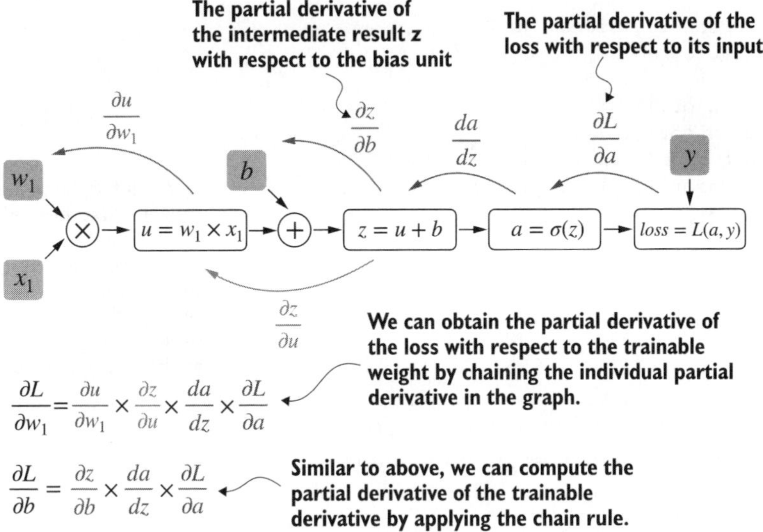

Figure A.8 The most common way of computing the loss gradients in a computation graph involves applying the chain rule from right to left, also called reverse-model automatic differentiation or backpropagation. We start from the output layer (or the loss itself) and work backward through the network to the input layer. We do this to compute the gradient of the loss with respect to each parameter (weights and biases) in the network, which informs how we update these parameters during training.

PARTIAL DERIVATIVES AND GRADIENTS

Figure A.8 shows partial derivatives, which measure the rate at which a function changes with respect to one of its variables. A *gradient* is a vector containing all of the partial derivatives of a multivariate function, a function with more than one variable as input.

If you are not familiar with or don't remember the partial derivatives, gradients, or chain rule from calculus, don't worry. On a high level, all you need to know for this book is that the chain rule is a way to compute gradients of a loss function given the model's parameters in a computation graph. This provides the information needed to update each parameter to minimize the loss function, which serves as a proxy for measuring the model's performance using a method such as gradient descent. We will revisit the computational implementation of this training loop in PyTorch in section A.7.

How is this all related to the automatic differentiation (autograd) engine, the second component of the PyTorch library mentioned earlier? PyTorch's autograd engine constructs a computational graph in the background by tracking every operation performed on tensors. Then, calling the `grad` function, we can compute the gradient of the loss concerning the model parameter `w1`, as shown in the following listing.

Listing A.3 Computing gradients via autograd

```
import torch.nn.functional as F
from torch.autograd import grad

y = torch.tensor([1.0])
x1 = torch.tensor([1.1])
w1 = torch.tensor([2.2], requires_grad=True)
b = torch.tensor([0.0], requires_grad=True)

z = x1 * w1 + b
a = torch.sigmoid(z)

loss = F.binary_cross_entropy(a, y)

grad_L_w1 = grad(loss, w1, retain_graph=True)
grad_L_b = grad(loss, b, retain_graph=True)
```

By default, PyTorch destroys the computation graph after calculating the gradients to free memory. However, since we will reuse this computation graph shortly, we set retain_graph=True so that it stays in memory.

The resulting values of the loss given the model's parameters are

```
print(grad_L_w1)
print(grad_L_b)
```

This prints

```
(tensor([-0.0898]),)
(tensor([-0.0817]),)
```

Here, we have been using the grad function manually, which can be useful for experimentation, debugging, and demonstrating concepts. But, in practice, PyTorch provides even more high-level tools to automate this process. For instance, we can call `.backward` on the loss, and PyTorch will compute the gradients of all the leaf nodes in the graph, which will be stored via the tensors' `.grad` attributes:

```
loss.backward()
print(w1.grad)
print(b.grad)
```

The outputs are

```
(tensor([-0.0898]),)
(tensor([-0.0817]),)
```

I've provided you with a lot of information, and you may be overwhelmed by the calculus concepts, but don't worry. While this calculus jargon is a means to explain PyTorch's autograd component, all you need to take away is that PyTorch takes care of the calculus for us via the `.backward` method—we won't need to compute any derivatives or gradients by hand.

A.5 Implementing multilayer neural networks

Next, we focus on PyTorch as a library for implementing deep neural networks. To provide a concrete example, let's look at a multilayer perceptron, a fully connected neural network, as illustrated in figure A.9.

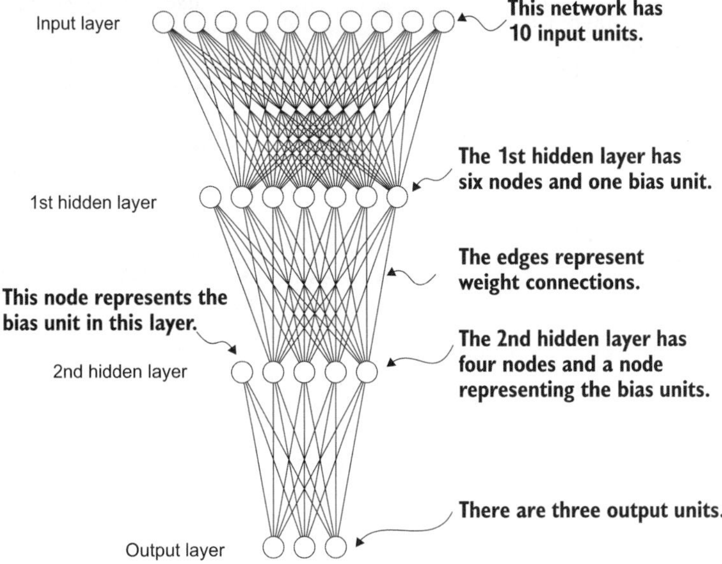

Figure A.9 A multilayer perceptron with two hidden layers. Each node represents a unit in the respective layer. For illustration purposes, each layer has a very small number of nodes.

When implementing a neural network in PyTorch, we can subclass the `torch.nn.Module` class to define our own custom network architecture. This `Module` base class provides a lot of functionality, making it easier to build and train models. For instance, it allows us to encapsulate layers and operations and keep track of the model's parameters.

Within this subclass, we define the network layers in the `__init__` constructor and specify how the layers interact in the forward method. The forward method describes how the input data passes through the network and comes together as a computation graph. In contrast, the backward method, which we typically do not need to implement ourselves, is used during training to compute gradients of the loss function given the model parameters (see section A.7). The code in the following listing implements a classic multilayer perceptron with two hidden layers to illustrate a typical usage of the `Module` class.

Listing A.4 A multilayer perceptron with two hidden layers

```
class NeuralNetwork(torch.nn.Module):
    def __init__(self, num_inputs, num_outputs):
        super().__init__()

        self.layers = torch.nn.Sequential(

            # 1st hidden layer
            torch.nn.Linear(num_inputs, 30),
            torch.nn.ReLU(),

            # 2nd hidden layer
            torch.nn.Linear(30, 20),
            torch.nn.ReLU(),

            # output layer
            torch.nn.Linear(20, num_outputs),
        )

    def forward(self, x):
        logits = self.layers(x)
        return logits
```

Coding the number of inputs and outputs as variables allows us to reuse the same code for datasets with different numbers of features and classes

The Linear layer takes the number of input and output nodes as arguments.

Nonlinear activation functions are placed between the hidden layers.

The number of output nodes of one hidden layer has to match the number of inputs of the next layer.

The outputs of the last layer are called logits.

We can then instantiate a new neural network object as follows:

```
model = NeuralNetwork(50, 3)
```

Before using this new `model` object, we can call `print` on the model to see a summary of its structure:

```
print(model)
```

This prints

```
NeuralNetwork(
  (layers): Sequential(
    (0): Linear(in_features=50, out_features=30, bias=True)
    (1): ReLU()
    (2): Linear(in_features=30, out_features=20, bias=True)
    (3): ReLU()
    (4): Linear(in_features=20, out_features=3, bias=True)
  )
)
```

Note that we use the `Sequential` class when we implement the `NeuralNetwork` class. `Sequential` is not required, but it can make our life easier if we have a series of layers we want to execute in a specific order, as is the case here. This way, after instantiating `self.layers = Sequential(...)` in the `__init__` constructor, we just have to call the `self.layers` instead of calling each layer individually in the `NeuralNetwork`'s `forward` method.

Next, let's check the total number of trainable parameters of this model:

```
num_params = sum(p.numel() for p in model.parameters() if p.requires_grad)
print("Total number of trainable model parameters:", num_params)
```

This prints

```
Total number of trainable model parameters: 2213
```

Each parameter for which `requires_grad=True` counts as a trainable parameter and will be updated during training (see section A.7).

In the case of our neural network model with the preceding two hidden layers, these trainable parameters are contained in the `torch.nn.Linear` layers. A `Linear` layer multiplies the inputs with a weight matrix and adds a bias vector. This is sometimes referred to as a *feedforward* or *fully connected* layer.

Based on the `print(model)` call we executed here, we can see that the first `Linear` layer is at index position 0 in the layers attribute. We can access the corresponding weight parameter matrix as follows:

```
print(model.layers[0].weight)
```

This prints

```
Parameter containing:
tensor([[ 0.1174, -0.1350, -0.1227,  ...,  0.0275, -0.0520, -0.0192],
        [-0.0169,  0.1265,  0.0255,  ..., -0.1247,  0.1191, -0.0698],
        [-0.0973, -0.0974, -0.0739,  ..., -0.0068, -0.0892,  0.1070],
        ...,
        [-0.0681,  0.1058, -0.0315,  ..., -0.1081, -0.0290, -0.1374],
        [-0.0159,  0.0587, -0.0916,  ..., -0.1153,  0.0700,  0.0770],
        [-0.1019,  0.1345, -0.0176,  ...,  0.0114, -0.0559, -0.0088]],
       requires_grad=True)
```

Since this large matrix is not shown in its entirety, let's use the `.shape` attribute to show its dimensions:

```
print(model.layers[0].weight.shape)
```

The result is

```
torch.Size([30, 50])
```

(Similarly, you could access the bias vector via `model.layers[0].bias`.)

The weight matrix here is a 30 × 50 matrix, and we can see that `requires_grad` is set to `True`, which means its entries are trainable—this is the default setting for weights and biases in `torch.nn.Linear`.

If you execute the preceding code on your computer, the numbers in the weight matrix will likely differ from those shown. The model weights are initialized with small random numbers, which differ each time we instantiate the network. In deep learning, initializing model weights with small random numbers is desired to break symmetry during training. Otherwise, the nodes would be performing the same operations and updates during backpropagation, which would not allow the network to learn complex mappings from inputs to outputs.

However, while we want to keep using small random numbers as initial values for our layer weights, we can make the random number initialization reproducible by seeding PyTorch's random number generator via `manual_seed`:

```
torch.manual_seed(123)
model = NeuralNetwork(50, 3)
print(model.layers[0].weight)
```

The result is

```
Parameter containing:
tensor([[-0.0577,  0.0047, -0.0702,  ...,  0.0222,  0.1260,  0.0865],
        [ 0.0502,  0.0307,  0.0333,  ...,  0.0951,  0.1134, -0.0297],
        [ 0.1077, -0.1108,  0.0122,  ...,  0.0108, -0.1049, -0.1063],
        ...,
        [-0.0787,  0.1259,  0.0803,  ...,  0.1218,  0.1303, -0.1351],
        [ 0.1359,  0.0175, -0.0673,  ...,  0.0674,  0.0676,  0.1058],
        [ 0.0790,  0.1343, -0.0293,  ...,  0.0344, -0.0971, -0.0509]],
       requires_grad=True)
```

Now that we have spent some time inspecting the `NeuralNetwork` instance, let's briefly see how it's used via the forward pass:

```
torch.manual_seed(123)
X = torch.rand((1, 50))
out = model(X)
print(out)
```

The result is

```
tensor([[-0.1262,  0.1080, -0.1792]], grad_fn=<AddmmBackward0>)
```

In the preceding code, we generated a single random training example `X` as a toy input (note that our network expects 50-dimensional feature vectors) and fed it to the model, returning three scores. When we call `model(x)`, it will automatically execute the forward pass of the model.

The forward pass refers to calculating output tensors from input tensors. This involves passing the input data through all the neural network layers, starting from the input layer, through hidden layers, and finally to the output layer.

These three numbers returned here correspond to a score assigned to each of the three output nodes. Notice that the output tensor also includes a `grad_fn` value.

Here, grad_fn=<AddmmBackward0> represents the last-used function to compute a variable in the computational graph. In particular, grad_fn=<AddmmBackward0> means that the tensor we are inspecting was created via a matrix multiplication and addition operation. PyTorch will use this information when it computes gradients during backpropagation. The <AddmmBackward0> part of grad_fn=<AddmmBackward0> specifies the operation performed. In this case, it is an Addmm operation. Addmm stands for matrix multiplication (mm) followed by an addition (Add).

If we just want to use a network without training or backpropagation—for example, if we use it for prediction after training—constructing this computational graph for backpropagation can be wasteful as it performs unnecessary computations and consumes additional memory. So, when we use a model for inference (for instance, making predictions) rather than training, the best practice is to use the torch.no_grad() context manager. This tells PyTorch that it doesn't need to keep track of the gradients, which can result in significant savings in memory and computation:

```
with torch.no_grad():
    out = model(X)
print(out)
```

The result is

```
tensor([[-0.1262,  0.1080, -0.1792]])
```

In PyTorch, it's common practice to code models such that they return the outputs of the last layer (logits) without passing them to a nonlinear activation function. That's because PyTorch's commonly used loss functions combine the softmax (or sigmoid for binary classification) operation with the negative log-likelihood loss in a single class. The reason for this is numerical efficiency and stability. So, if we want to compute class-membership probabilities for our predictions, we have to call the softmax function explicitly:

```
with torch.no_grad():
    out = torch.softmax(model(X), dim=1)
print(out)
```

This prints

```
tensor([[0.3113, 0.3934, 0.2952]]))
```

The values can now be interpreted as class-membership probabilities that sum up to 1. The values are roughly equal for this random input, which is expected for a randomly initialized model without training.

A.6 Setting up efficient data loaders

Before we can train our model, we have to briefly discuss creating efficient data loaders in PyTorch, which we will iterate over during training. The overall idea behind data loading in PyTorch is illustrated in figure A.10.

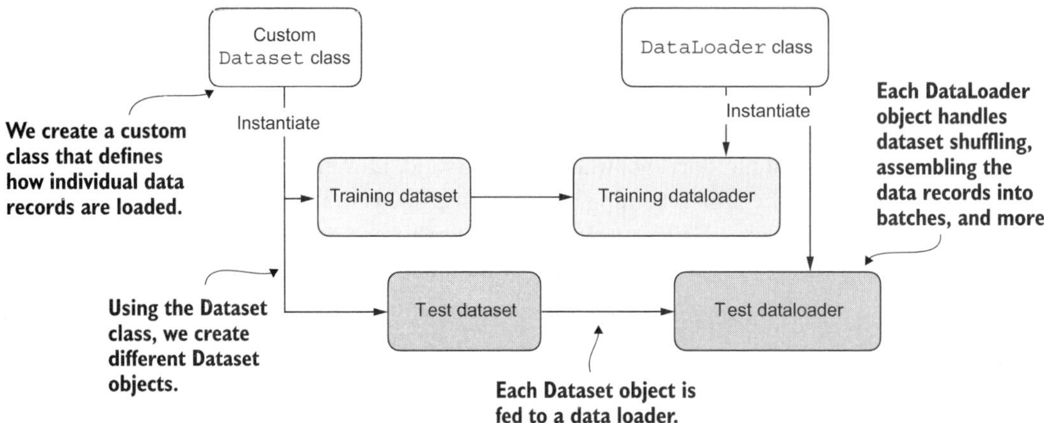

Figure A.10 PyTorch implements a `Dataset` and a `DataLoader` class. The `Dataset` class is used to instantiate objects that define how each data record is loaded. The `DataLoader` handles how the data is shuffled and assembled into batches.

Following figure A.10, we will implement a custom `Dataset` class, which we will use to create a training and a test dataset that we'll then use to create the data loaders. Let's start by creating a simple toy dataset of five training examples with two features each. Accompanying the training examples, we also create a tensor containing the corresponding class labels: three examples belong to class 0, and two examples belong to class 1. In addition, we make a test set consisting of two entries. The code to create this dataset is shown in the following listing.

Listing A.5 Creating a small toy dataset

```
X_train = torch.tensor([
    [-1.2, 3.1],
    [-0.9, 2.9],
    [-0.5, 2.6],
    [2.3, -1.1],
    [2.7, -1.5]
])
y_train = torch.tensor([0, 0, 0, 1, 1])

X_test = torch.tensor([
    [-0.8, 2.8],
    [2.6, -1.6],
])
y_test = torch.tensor([0, 1])
```

NOTE PyTorch requires that class labels start with label 0, and the largest class label value should not exceed the number of output nodes minus 1 (since Python index counting starts at zero). So, if we have class labels 0, 1, 2, 3, and 4, the neural network output layer should consist of five nodes.

Next, we create a custom dataset class, `ToyDataset`, by subclassing from PyTorch's `Dataset` parent class, as shown in the following listing.

Listing A.6 Defining a custom `Dataset` class

```
from torch.utils.data import Dataset

class ToyDataset(Dataset):
    def __init__(self, X, y):
        self.features = X
        self.labels = y

    def __getitem__(self, index):
        one_x = self.features[index]
        one_y = self.labels[index]
        return one_x, one_y

    def __len__(self):
        return self.labels.shape[0]

train_ds = ToyDataset(X_train, y_train)
test_ds = ToyDataset(X_test, y_test)
```

Instructions for retrieving exactly one data record and the corresponding label

Instructions for returning the total length of the dataset

The purpose of this custom `ToyDataset` class is to instantiate a PyTorch `DataLoader`. But before we get to this step, let's briefly go over the general structure of the `ToyDataset` code.

In PyTorch, the three main components of a custom `Dataset` class are the `__init__` constructor, the `__getitem__` method, and the `__len__` method (see listing A.6). In the `__init__` method, we set up attributes that we can access later in the `__getitem__` and `__len__` methods. These could be file paths, file objects, database connectors, and so on. Since we created a tensor dataset that sits in memory, we simply assign `X` and `y` to these attributes, which are placeholders for our tensor objects.

In the `__getitem__` method, we define instructions for returning exactly one item from the dataset via an `index`. This refers to the features and the class label corresponding to a single training example or test instance. (The data loader will provide this `index`, which we will cover shortly.)

Finally, the `__len__` method contains instructions for retrieving the length of the dataset. Here, we use the `.shape` attribute of a tensor to return the number of rows in the feature array. In the case of the training dataset, we have five rows, which we can double-check:

```
print(len(train_ds))
```

The result is

```
5
```

Now that we've defined a PyTorch `Dataset` class we can use for our toy dataset, we can use PyTorch's `DataLoader` class to sample from it, as shown in the following listing.

Listing A.7 Instantiating data loaders

```
from torch.utils.data import DataLoader


torch.manual_seed(123)

train_loader = DataLoader(
    dataset=train_ds,        # The ToyDataset instance created earlier serves as input to the data loader.
    batch_size=2,
    shuffle=True,            # Whether or not to shuffle the data
    num_workers=0            # The number of background processes
)

test_loader = DataLoader(
    dataset=test_ds,
    batch_size=2,
    shuffle=False,           # It is not necessary to shuffle a test dataset.
    num_workers=0
)
```

After instantiating the training data loader, we can iterate over it. The iteration over the `test_loader` works similarly but is omitted for brevity:

```
for idx, (x, y) in enumerate(train_loader):
    print(f"Batch {idx+1}:", x, y)
```

The result is

```
Batch 1: tensor([[-1.2000,  3.1000],
                 [-0.5000,  2.6000]]) tensor([0, 0])
Batch 2: tensor([[ 2.3000, -1.1000],
                 [-0.9000,  2.9000]]) tensor([1, 0])
Batch 3: tensor([[ 2.7000, -1.5000]]) tensor([1])
```

As we can see based on the preceding output, the `train_loader` iterates over the training dataset, visiting each training example exactly once. This is known as a training epoch. Since we seeded the random number generator using `torch.manual_seed(123)` here, you should get the exact same shuffling order of training examples. However, if you iterate over the dataset a second time, you will see that the shuffling order will change. This is desired to prevent deep neural networks from getting caught in repetitive update cycles during training.

We specified a batch size of 2 here, but the third batch only contains a single example. That's because we have five training examples, and 5 is not evenly divisible by 2.

In practice, having a substantially smaller batch as the last batch in a training epoch can disturb the convergence during training. To prevent this, set `drop_last=True`, which will drop the last batch in each epoch, as shown in the following listing.

Listing A.8 A training loader that drops the last batch

```
train_loader = DataLoader(
    dataset=train_ds,
    batch_size=2,
    shuffle=True,
    num_workers=0,
    drop_last=True
)
```

Now, iterating over the training loader, we can see that the last batch is omitted:

```
for idx, (x, y) in enumerate(train_loader):
    print(f"Batch {idx+1}:", x, y)
```

The result is

```
Batch 1: tensor([[-0.9000,  2.9000],
        [ 2.3000, -1.1000]]) tensor([0, 1])
Batch 2: tensor([[ 2.7000, -1.5000],
        [-0.5000,  2.6000]]) tensor([1, 0])
```

Lastly, let's discuss the setting `num_workers=0` in the `DataLoader`. This parameter in PyTorch's `DataLoader` function is crucial for parallelizing data loading and preprocessing. When `num_workers` is set to 0, the data loading will be done in the main process and not in separate worker processes. This might seem unproblematic, but it can lead to significant slowdowns during model training when we train larger networks on a GPU. Instead of focusing solely on the processing of the deep learning model, the CPU must also take time to load and preprocess the data. As a result, the GPU can sit idle while waiting for the CPU to finish these tasks. In contrast, when `num_workers` is set to a number greater than 0, multiple worker processes are launched to load data in parallel, freeing the main process to focus on training your model and better utilizing your system's resources (figure A.11).

However, if we are working with very small datasets, setting `num_workers` to 1 or larger may not be necessary since the total training time takes only fractions of a second anyway. So, if you are working with tiny datasets or interactive environments such as Jupyter notebooks, increasing `num_workers` may not provide any noticeable speedup. It may, in fact, lead to some problems. One potential problem is the overhead of spinning up multiple worker processes, which could take longer than the actual data loading when your dataset is small.

Furthermore, for Jupyter notebooks, setting `num_workers` to greater than 0 can sometimes lead to problems related to the sharing of resources between different processes, resulting in errors or notebook crashes. Therefore, it's essential to understand

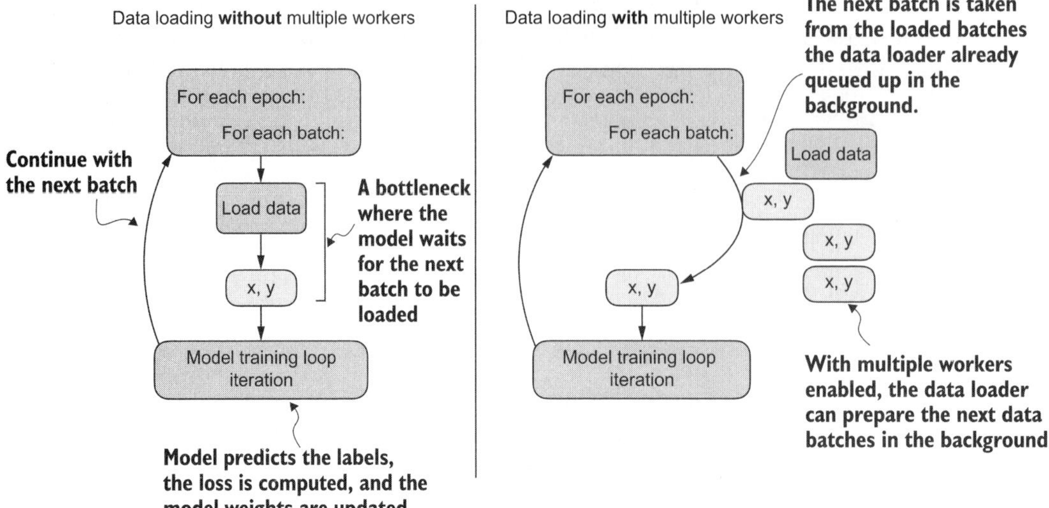
Data loading **without** multiple workers
For each epoch:
For each batch:
Load data
x, y
Model training loop iteration
Continue with the next batch
A bottleneck where the model waits for the next batch to be loaded
Model predicts the labels, the loss is computed, and the model weights are updated.
Data loading **with** multiple workers
The next batch is taken from the loaded batches the data loader already queued up in the background.
For each epoch:
For each batch:
Load data
x, y
x, y
x, y
x, y
Model training loop iteration
With multiple workers enabled, the data loader can prepare the next data batches in the background.

Figure A.11 Loading data without multiple workers (setting `num_workers=0`) will create a data loading bottleneck where the model sits idle until the next batch is loaded (left). If multiple workers are enabled, the data loader can queue up the next batch in the background (right).

the tradeoff and make a calculated decision on setting the `num_workers` parameter. When used correctly, it can be a beneficial tool but should be adapted to your specific dataset size and computational environment for optimal results.

In my experience, setting `num_workers=4` usually leads to optimal performance on many real-world datasets, but optimal settings depend on your hardware and the code used for loading a training example defined in the `Dataset` class.

A.7 A typical training loop

Let's now train a neural network on the toy dataset. The following listing shows the training code.

Listing A.9 Neural network training in PyTorch

```
import torch.nn.functional as F

torch.manual_seed(123)
model = NeuralNetwork(num_inputs=2, num_outputs=2)      <- The dataset has two features and two classes.
optimizer = torch.optim.SGD(
    model.parameters(), lr=0.5
)                                                       <- The optimizer needs to know which parameters to optimize.

num_epochs = 3
for epoch in range(num_epochs):

    model.train()
```

```
    for batch_idx, (features, labels) in enumerate(train_loader):
        logits = model(features)

        loss = F.cross_entropy(logits, labels)

        optimizer.zero_grad()
        loss.backward()
        optimizer.step()

        ### LOGGING
        print(f"Epoch: {epoch+1:03d}/{num_epochs:03d}"
              f" | Batch {batch_idx:03d}/{len(train_loader):03d}"
              f" | Train Loss: {loss:.2f}")

model.eval()
# Insert optional model evaluation code
```

Sets the gradients from the previous round to 0 to prevent unintended gradient accumulation

Computes the gradients of the loss given the model parameters

The optimizer uses the gradients to update the model parameters.

Running this code yields the following outputs:

```
Epoch: 001/003 | Batch 000/002 | Train Loss: 0.75
Epoch: 001/003 | Batch 001/002 | Train Loss: 0.65
Epoch: 002/003 | Batch 000/002 | Train Loss: 0.44
Epoch: 002/003 | Batch 001/002 | Trainl Loss: 0.13
Epoch: 003/003 | Batch 000/002 | Train Loss: 0.03
Epoch: 003/003 | Batch 001/002 | Train Loss: 0.00
```

As we can see, the loss reaches 0 after three epochs, a sign that the model converged on the training set. Here, we initialize a model with two inputs and two outputs because our toy dataset has two input features and two class labels to predict. We used a stochastic gradient descent (`SGD`) optimizer with a learning rate (`lr`) of 0.5. The learning rate is a hyperparameter, meaning it's a tunable setting that we must experiment with based on observing the loss. Ideally, we want to choose a learning rate such that the loss converges after a certain number of epochs—the number of epochs is another hyperparameter to choose.

Exercise A.3

How many parameters does the neural network introduced in listing A.9 have?

In practice, we often use a third dataset, a so-called validation dataset, to find the optimal hyperparameter settings. A validation dataset is similar to a test set. However, while we only want to use a test set precisely once to avoid biasing the evaluation, we usually use the validation set multiple times to tweak the model settings.

We also introduced new settings called `model.train()` and `model.eval()`. As these names imply, these settings are used to put the model into a training and an evaluation mode. This is necessary for components that behave differently during training and inference, such as *dropout* or *batch normalization* layers. Since we don't have dropout or other components in our `NeuralNetwork` class that are affected by these settings, using `model.train()` and `model.eval()` is redundant in our preceding code. However, it's best practice to include them anyway to avoid unexpected behaviors when we change the model architecture or reuse the code to train a different model.

As discussed earlier, we pass the logits directly into the `cross_entropy` loss function, which will apply the `softmax` function internally for efficiency and numerical stability reasons. Then, calling `loss.backward()` will calculate the gradients in the computation graph that PyTorch constructed in the background. The `optimizer.step()` method will use the gradients to update the model parameters to minimize the loss. In the case of the SGD optimizer, this means multiplying the gradients with the learning rate and adding the scaled negative gradient to the parameters.

> **NOTE** To prevent undesired gradient accumulation, it is important to include an `optimizer.zero_grad()` call in each update round to reset the gradients to 0. Otherwise, the gradients will accumulate, which may be undesired.

After we have trained the model, we can use it to make predictions:

```
model.eval()
with torch.no_grad():
    outputs = model(X_train)
print(outputs)
```

The results are

```
tensor([[ 2.8569, -4.1618],
        [ 2.5382, -3.7548],
        [ 2.0944, -3.1820],
        [-1.4814,  1.4816],
        [-1.7176,  1.7342]])
```

To obtain the class membership probabilities, we can then use PyTorch's `softmax` function:

```
torch.set_printoptions(sci_mode=False)
probas = torch.softmax(outputs, dim=1)
print(probas)
```

This outputs

```
tensor([[    0.9991,     0.0009],
        [    0.9982,     0.0018],
        [    0.9949,     0.0051],
        [    0.0491,     0.9509],
        [    0.0307,     0.9693]])
```

Let's consider the first row in the preceding code output. Here, the first value (column) means that the training example has a 99.91% probability of belonging to class

0 and a 0.09% probability of belonging to class 1. (The `set_printoptions` call is used here to make the outputs more legible.)

We can convert these values into class label predictions using PyTorch's `argmax` function, which returns the index position of the highest value in each row if we set `dim=1` (setting `dim=0` would return the highest value in each column instead):

```
predictions = torch.argmax(probas, dim=1)
print(predictions)
```

This prints

```
tensor([0, 0, 0, 1, 1])
```

Note that it is unnecessary to compute `softmax` probabilities to obtain the class labels. We could also apply the `argmax` function to the logits (outputs) directly:

```
predictions = torch.argmax(outputs, dim=1)
print(predictions)
```

The output is

```
tensor([0, 0, 0, 1, 1])
```

Here, we computed the predicted labels for the training dataset. Since the training dataset is relatively small, we could compare it to the true training labels by eye and see that the model is 100% correct. We can double-check this using the `==` comparison operator:

```
predictions == y_train
```

The results are

```
tensor([True, True, True, True, True])
```

Using `torch.sum`, we can count the number of correct predictions:

```
torch.sum(predictions == y_train)
```

The output is

```
5
```

Since the dataset consists of five training examples, we have five out of five predictions that are correct, which has 5/5 × 100% = 100% prediction accuracy.

To generalize the computation of the prediction accuracy, let's implement a `compute_accuracy` function, as shown in the following listing.

Listing A.10 A function to compute the prediction accuracy

```
def compute_accuracy(model, dataloader):

    model = model.eval()
    correct = 0.0
    total_examples = 0

    for idx, (features, labels) in enumerate(dataloader):

        with torch.no_grad():
            logits = model(features)

        predictions = torch.argmax(logits, dim=1)
        compare = labels == predictions          # A
        correct += torch.sum(compare)            # B
        total_examples += len(compare)

    return (correct / total_examples).item()     # C
```

A: Returns a tensor of True/False values depending on whether the labels match

B: The sum operation counts the number of True values.

C: The fraction of correct prediction, a value between 0 and 1. .item() returns the value of the tensor as a Python float.

The code iterates over a data loader to compute the number and fraction of the correct predictions. When we work with large datasets, we typically can only call the model on a small part of the dataset due to memory limitations. The `compute_accuracy` function here is a general method that scales to datasets of arbitrary size since, in each iteration, the dataset chunk that the model receives is the same size as the batch size seen during training. The internals of the `compute_accuracy` function are similar to what we used before when we converted the logits to the class labels.

We can then apply the function to the training:

```
print(compute_accuracy(model, train_loader))
```

The result is

```
1.0
```

Similarly, we can apply the function to the test set:

```
print(compute_accuracy(model, test_loader))
```

This prints

```
1.0
```

A.8 Saving and loading models

Now that we've trained our model, let's see how to save it so we can reuse it later. Here's the recommended way how we can save and load models in PyTorch:

```
torch.save(model.state_dict(), "model.pth")
```

The model's `state_dict` is a Python dictionary object that maps each layer in the model to its trainable parameters (weights and biases). `"model.pth"` is an arbitrary filename for the model file saved to disk. We can give it any name and file ending we like; however, `.pth` and `.pt` are the most common conventions.

Once we saved the model, we can restore it from disk:

```
model = NeuralNetwork(2, 2)
model.load_state_dict(torch.load("model.pth"))
```

The `torch.load("model.pth")` function reads the file `"model.pth"` and reconstructs the Python dictionary object containing the model's parameters while `model.load_state_dict()` applies these parameters to the model, effectively restoring its learned state from when we saved it.

The line `model = NeuralNetwork(2, 2)` is not strictly necessary if you execute this code in the same session where you saved a model. However, I included it here to illustrate that we need an instance of the model in memory to apply the saved parameters. Here, the `NeuralNetwork(2, 2)` architecture needs to match the original saved model exactly.

A.9 Optimizing training performance with GPUs

Next, let's examine how to utilize GPUs, which accelerate deep neural network training compared to regular CPUs. First, we'll look at the main concepts behind GPU computing in PyTorch. Then we will train a model on a single GPU. Finally, we'll look at distributed training using multiple GPUs.

A.9.1 PyTorch computations on GPU devices

Modifying the training loop to run optionally on a GPU is relatively simple and only requires changing three lines of code (see section A.7). Before we make the modifications, it's crucial to understand the main concept behind GPU computations within PyTorch. In PyTorch, a device is where computations occur and data resides. The CPU and the GPU are examples of devices. A PyTorch tensor resides in a device, and its operations are executed on the same device.

Let's see how this works in action. Assuming that you installed a GPU-compatible version of PyTorch (see section A.1.3), we can double-check that our runtime indeed supports GPU computing via the following code:

```
print(torch.cuda.is_available())
```

The result is

```
True
```

Now, suppose we have two tensors that we can add; this computation will be carried out on the CPU by default:

```
tensor_1 = torch.tensor([1., 2., 3.])
tensor_2 = torch.tensor([4., 5., 6.])
print(tensor_1 + tensor_2)
```

This outputs

```
tensor([5., 7., 9.])
```

We can now use the `.to()` method. This method is the same as the one we use to change a tensor's datatype (see 2.2.2) to transfer these tensors onto a GPU and perform the addition there:

```
tensor_1 = tensor_1.to("cuda")
tensor_2 = tensor_2.to("cuda")
print(tensor_1 + tensor_2)
```

The output is

```
tensor([5., 7., 9.], device='cuda:0')
```

The resulting tensor now includes the device information, `device='cuda:0'`, which means that the tensors reside on the first GPU. If your machine hosts multiple GPUs, you can specify which GPU you'd like to transfer the tensors to. You do so by indicating the device ID in the transfer command. For instance, you can use `.to("cuda:0")`, `.to("cuda:1")`, and so on.

However, all tensors must be on the same device. Otherwise, the computation will fail, where one tensor resides on the CPU and the other on the GPU:

```
tensor_1 = tensor_1.to("cpu")
print(tensor_1 + tensor_2)
```

The results are

```
RuntimeError      Traceback (most recent call last)
<ipython-input-7-4ff3c4d20fc3> in <cell line: 2>()
      1 tensor_1 = tensor_1.to("cpu")
----> 2 print(tensor_1 + tensor_2)
RuntimeError: Expected all tensors to be on the same device, but found at
least two devices, cuda:0 and cpu!
```

In sum, we only need to transfer the tensors onto the same GPU device, and PyTorch will handle the rest.

A.9.2 Single-GPU training

Now that we are familiar with transferring tensors to the GPU, we can modify the training loop to run on a GPU. This step requires only changing three lines of code, as shown in the following listing.

Listing A.11 A training loop on a GPU

```
torch.manual_seed(123)
model = NeuralNetwork(num_inputs=2, num_outputs=2)

device = torch.device("cuda")          # Defines a device variable that defaults to a GPU
model = model.to(device)               # Transfers the model onto the GPU

optimizer = torch.optim.SGD(model.parameters(), lr=0.5)

num_epochs = 3

for epoch in range(num_epochs):

    model.train()
    for batch_idx, (features, labels) in enumerate(train_loader):
        features, labels = features.to(device), labels.to(device)    # Transfers the data onto the GPU
        logits = model(features)
        loss = F.cross_entropy(logits, labels) # Loss function

        optimizer.zero_grad()
        loss.backward()
        optimizer.step()

        ### LOGGING
        print(f"Epoch: {epoch+1:03d}/{num_epochs:03d}"
              f" | Batch {batch_idx:03d}/{len(train_loader):03d}"
              f" | Train/Val Loss: {loss:.2f}")

    model.eval()
    # Insert optional model evaluation code
```

Running the preceding code will output the following, similar to the results obtained on the CPU (section A.7):

```
Epoch: 001/003 | Batch 000/002 | Train/Val Loss: 0.75
Epoch: 001/003 | Batch 001/002 | Train/Val Loss: 0.65
Epoch: 002/003 | Batch 000/002 | Train/Val Loss: 0.44
Epoch: 002/003 | Batch 001/002 | Train/Val Loss: 0.13
Epoch: 003/003 | Batch 000/002 | Train/Val Loss: 0.03
Epoch: 003/003 | Batch 001/002 | Train/Val Loss: 0.00
```

We can use `.to("cuda")` instead of `device = torch.device("cuda")`. Transferring a tensor to `"cuda"` instead of `torch.device("cuda")` works as well and is shorter (see section A.9.1). We can also modify the statement, which will make the same code executable on a CPU if a GPU is not available. This is considered best practice when sharing PyTorch code:

```
device = torch.device("cuda" if torch.cuda.is_available() else "cpu")
```

In the case of the modified training loop here, we probably won't see a speedup due to the memory transfer cost from CPU to GPU. However, we can expect a significant speedup when training deep neural networks, especially LLMs.

PyTorch on macOS

On an Apple Mac with an Apple Silicon chip (like the M1, M2, M3, or newer models) instead of a computer with an Nvidia GPU, you can change

```
device = torch.device("cuda" if torch.cuda.is_available() else "cpu")
```

to

```
device = torch.device(
    "mps" if torch.backends.mps.is_available() else "cpu"
)
```

to take advantage of this chip.

Exercise A.4

Compare the run time of matrix multiplication on a CPU to a GPU. At what matrix size do you begin to see the matrix multiplication on the GPU being faster than on the CPU? Hint: use the `%timeit` command in Jupyter to compare the run time. For example, given matrices `a` and `b`, run the command `%timeit a @ b` in a new notebook cell.

A.9.3 Training with multiple GPUs

Distributed training is the concept of dividing the model training across multiple GPUs and machines. Why do we need this? Even when it is possible to train a model on a single GPU or machine, the process could be exceedingly time-consuming. The training time can be significantly reduced by distributing the training process across multiple machines, each with potentially multiple GPUs. This is particularly crucial in the experimental stages of model development, where numerous training iterations might be necessary to fine-tune the model parameters and architecture.

> **NOTE** For this book, access to or use of multiple GPUs is not required. This section is included for those interested in how multi-GPU computing works in PyTorch.

Let's begin with the most basic case of distributed training: PyTorch's `DistributedDataParallel` (DDP) strategy. DDP enables parallelism by splitting the input data across the available devices and processing these data subsets simultaneously.

How does this work? PyTorch launches a separate process on each GPU, and each process receives and keeps a copy of the model; these copies will be synchronized during training. To illustrate this, suppose we have two GPUs that we want to use to train a neural network, as shown in figure A.12.

Each of the two GPUs will receive a copy of the model. Then, in every training iteration, each model will receive a minibatch (or just "batch") from the data loader. We

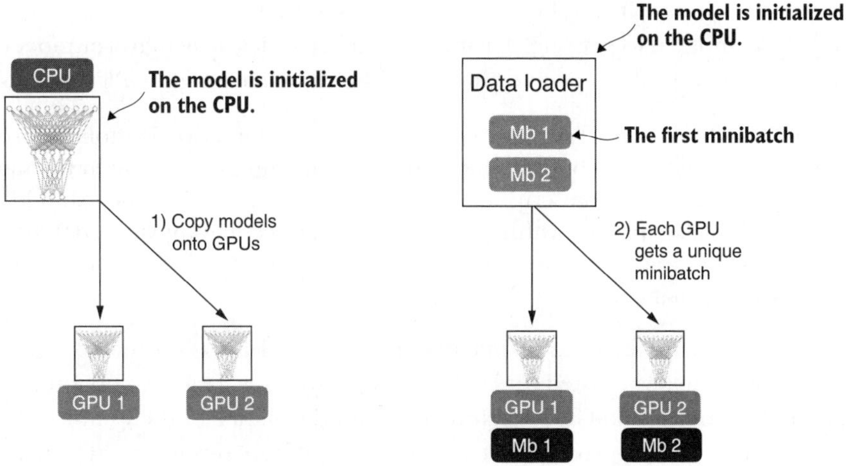

Figure A.12 The model and data transfer in DDP involves two key steps. First, we create a copy of the model on each of the GPUs. Then we divide the input data into unique minibatches that we pass on to each model copy.

can use a `DistributedSampler` to ensure that each GPU will receive a different, non-overlapping batch when using DDP.

Since each model copy will see a different sample of the training data, the model copies will return different logits as outputs and compute different gradients during the backward pass. These gradients are then averaged and synchronized during training to update the models. This way, we ensure that the models don't diverge, as illustrated in figure A.13.

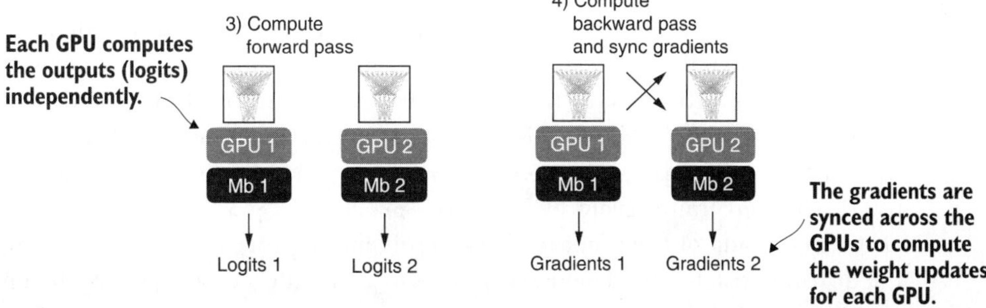

Figure A.13 The forward and backward passes in DDP are executed independently on each GPU with its corresponding data subset. Once the forward and backward passes are completed, gradients from each model replica (on each GPU) are synchronized across all GPUs. This ensures that every model replica has the same updated weights.

The benefit of using DDP is the enhanced speed it offers for processing the dataset compared to a single GPU. Barring a minor communication overhead between devices that comes with DDP use, it can theoretically process a training epoch in half the time with two GPUs compared to just one. The time efficiency scales up with the number of GPUs, allowing us to process an epoch eight times faster if we have eight GPUs, and so on.

NOTE DDP does not function properly within interactive Python environments like Jupyter notebooks, which don't handle multiprocessing in the same way a standalone Python script does. Therefore, the following code should be executed as a script, not within a notebook interface like Jupyter. DDP needs to spawn multiple processes, and each process should have its own Python interpreter instance.

Let's now see how this works in practice. For brevity, I focus on the core parts of the code that need to be adjusted for DDP training. However, readers who want to run the code on their own multi-GPU machine or a cloud instance of their choice should use the standalone script provided in this book's GitHub repository at https://github.com/rasbt/LLMs-from-scratch.

First, we import a few additional submodules, classes, and functions for distributed training PyTorch, as shown in the following listing.

Listing A.12 PyTorch utilities for distributed training

```
import torch.multiprocessing as mp
from torch.utils.data.distributed import DistributedSampler
from torch.nn.parallel import DistributedDataParallel as DDP
from torch.distributed import init_process_group, destroy_process_group
```

Before we dive deeper into the changes to make the training compatible with DDP, let's briefly go over the rationale and usage for these newly imported utilities that we need alongside the `DistributedDataParallel` class.

PyTorch's `multiprocessing` submodule contains functions such as `multiprocessing.spawn`, which we will use to spawn multiple processes and apply a function to multiple inputs in parallel. We will use it to spawn one training process per GPU. If we spawn multiple processes for training, we will need a way to divide the dataset among these different processes. For this, we will use the `DistributedSampler`.

`init_process_group` and `destroy_process_group` are used to initialize and quit the distributed training mods. The `init_process_group` function should be called at the beginning of the training script to initialize a process group for each process in the distributed setup, and `destroy_process_group` should be called at the end of the training script to destroy a given process group and release its resources. The code in the following listing illustrates how these new components are used to implement DDP training for the `NeuralNetwork` model we implemented earlier.

Listing A.13 Model training with the `DistributedDataParallel` strategy

```
def ddp_setup(rank, world_size):
    os.environ["MASTER_ADDR"] = "localhost"    # Address of the main node
```

```
    os.environ["MASTER_PORT"] = "12345"
    init_process_group(
        backend="nccl",
        rank=rank,
        world_size=world_size
    )
    torch.cuda.set_device(rank)

def prepare_dataset():
    # insert dataset preparation code
    train_loader = DataLoader(
        dataset=train_ds,
        batch_size=2,
        shuffle=False,
        pin_memory=True,
        drop_last=True,
        sampler=DistributedSampler(train_ds)
    )
    return train_loader, test_loader

def main(rank, world_size, num_epochs):
    ddp_setup(rank, world_size)
    train_loader, test_loader = prepare_dataset()
    model = NeuralNetwork(num_inputs=2, num_outputs=2)
    model.to(rank)
    optimizer = torch.optim.SGD(model.parameters(), lr=0.5)
    model = DDP(model, device_ids=[rank])
    for epoch in range(num_epochs):
    for features, labels in train_loader:
            features, labels = features.to(rank), labels.to(rank)
            # insert model prediction and backpropagation code
            print(f"[GPU{rank}] Epoch: {epoch+1:03d}/{num_epochs:03d}"
                  f" | Batchsize {labels.shape[0]:03d}"
                  f" | Train/Val Loss: {loss:.2f}")

    model.eval()
    train_acc = compute_accuracy(model, train_loader, device=rank)
    print(f"[GPU{rank}] Training accuracy", train_acc)
    test_acc = compute_accuracy(model, test_loader, device=rank)
    print(f"[GPU{rank}] Test accuracy", test_acc)
    destroy_process_group()

if __name__ == "__main__":
    print("Number of GPUs available:", torch.cuda.device_count())
    torch.manual_seed(123)
    num_epochs = 3
    world_size = torch.cuda.device_count()
    mp.spawn(main, args=(world_size, num_epochs), nprocs=world_size)
```

Any free port on the machine

world_size is the number of GPUs to use.

nccl stands for NVIDIA Collective Communication Library.

rank refers to the index of the GPU we want to use.

Sets the current GPU device on which tensors will be allocated and operations will be performed

Distibuted-Sampler takes care of the shuffling now.

Enables faster memory transfer when training on GPU

Splits the dataset into distinct, non-overlapping subsets for each process (GPU)

The main function running the model training

rank is the GPU ID

Cleans up resource allocation

Launches the main function using multiple processes, where nprocs=world_size means one process per GPU.

Before we run this code, let's summarize how it works in addition to the preceding annotations. We have a `__name__ == "__main__"` clause at the bottom containing code executed when we run the code as a Python script instead of importing it as a module.

QG 986 9022

This code first prints the number of available GPUs using `torch.cuda.device_count()`, sets a random seed for reproducibility, and then spawns new processes using PyTorch's `multiprocessesing.spawn` function. Here, the `spawn` function launches one process per GPU setting `nproces=world_size`, where the world size is the number of available GPUs. This `spawn` function launches the code in the `main` function we define in the same script with some additional arguments provided via `args`. Note that the `main` function has a `rank` argument that we don't include in the `mp.spawn()` call. That's because the `rank`, which refers to the process ID we use as the GPU ID, is already passed automatically.

The `main` function sets up the distributed environment via `ddp_setup`—another function we defined—loads the training and test sets, sets up the model, and carries out the training. Compared to the single-GPU training (section A.9.2), we now transfer the model and data to the target device via `.to(rank)`, which we use to refer to the GPU device ID. Also, we wrap the model via `DDP`, which enables the synchronization of the gradients between the different GPUs during training. After the training finishes and we evaluate the models, we use `destroy_process_group()` to cleanly exit the distributed training and free up the allocated resources.

Earlier I mentioned that each GPU will receive a different subsample of the training data. To ensure this, we set `sampler=DistributedSampler(train_ds)` in the training loader.

The last function to discuss is `ddp_setup`. It sets the main node's address and port to allow for communication between the different processes, initializes the process group with the NCCL backend (designed for GPU-to-GPU communication), and sets the `rank` (process identifier) and world size (total number of processes). Finally, it specifies the GPU device corresponding to the current model training process rank.

SELECTING AVAILABLE GPUS ON A MULTI-GPU MACHINE

If you wish to restrict the number of GPUs used for training on a multi-GPU machine, the simplest way is to use the `CUDA_VISIBLE_DEVICES` environment variable. To illustrate this, suppose your machine has multiple GPUs, and you only want to use one GPU—for example, the GPU with index 0. Instead of `python some_script.py`, you can run the following code from the terminal:

```
CUDA_VISIBLE_DEVICES=0 python some_script.py
```

Or, if your machine has four GPUs and you only want to use the first and third GPU, you can use

```
CUDA_VISIBLE_DEVICES=0,2 python some_script.py
```

Setting `CUDA_VISIBLE_DEVICES` in this way is a simple and effective way to manage GPU allocation without modifying your PyTorch scripts.

Let's now run this code and see how it works in practice by launching the code as a script from the terminal:

```
python ch02-DDP-script.py
```

Note that it should work on both single and multi-GPU machines. If we run this code on a single GPU, we should see the following output:

```
PyTorch version: 2.2.1+cu117
CUDA available: True
Number of GPUs available: 1
[GPU0] Epoch: 001/003 | Batchsize 002 | Train/Val Loss: 0.62
[GPU0] Epoch: 001/003 | Batchsize 002 | Train/Val Loss: 0.32
[GPU0] Epoch: 002/003 | Batchsize 002 | Train/Val Loss: 0.11
[GPU0] Epoch: 002/003 | Batchsize 002 | Train/Val Loss: 0.07
[GPU0] Epoch: 003/003 | Batchsize 002 | Train/Val Loss: 0.02
[GPU0] Epoch: 003/003 | Batchsize 002 | Train/Val Loss: 0.03
[GPU0] Training accuracy 1.0
[GPU0] Test accuracy 1.0
```

The code output looks similar to that using a single GPU (section A.9.2), which is a good sanity check.

Now, if we run the same command and code on a machine with two GPUs, we should see the following:

```
PyTorch version: 2.2.1+cu117
CUDA available: True
Number of GPUs available: 2
[GPU1] Epoch: 001/003 | Batchsize 002 | Train/Val Loss: 0.60
[GPU0] Epoch: 001/003 | Batchsize 002 | Train/Val Loss: 0.59
[GPU0] Epoch: 002/003 | Batchsize 002 | Train/Val Loss: 0.16
[GPU1] Epoch: 002/003 | Batchsize 002 | Train/Val Loss: 0.17
[GPU0] Epoch: 003/003 | Batchsize 002 | Train/Val Loss: 0.05
[GPU1] Epoch: 003/003 | Batchsize 002 | Train/Val Loss: 0.05
[GPU1] Training accuracy 1.0
[GPU0] Training accuracy 1.0
[GPU1] Test accuracy 1.0
[GPU0] Test accuracy 1.0
```

As expected, we can see that some batches are processed on the first GPU (`GPU0`) and others on the second (`GPU1`). However, we see duplicated output lines when printing the training and test accuracies. Each process (in other words, each GPU) prints the test accuracy independently. Since DDP replicates the model onto each GPU and each process runs independently, if you have a print statement inside your testing loop, each process will execute it, leading to repeated output lines. If this bothers you, you can fix it using the rank of each process to control your print statements:

```
if rank == 0:                                  # Only print in the first process
    print("Test accuracy: ", accuracy)
```

This is, in a nutshell, how distributed training via DDP works. If you are interested in additional details, I recommend checking the official API documentation at https://mng.bz/9dPr.

Alternative PyTorch APIs for multi-GPU training

If you prefer a more straightforward way to use multiple GPUs in PyTorch, you can consider add-on APIs like the open-source Fabric library. I wrote about it in "Accelerating PyTorch Model Training: Using Mixed-Precision and Fully Sharded Data Parallelism" (https://mng.bz/jXle).

Summary

- PyTorch is an open source library with three core components: a tensor library, automatic differentiation functions, and deep learning utilities.
- PyTorch's tensor library is similar to array libraries like NumPy.
- In the context of PyTorch, tensors are array-like data structures representing scalars, vectors, matrices, and higher-dimensional arrays.
- PyTorch tensors can be executed on the CPU, but one major advantage of PyTorch's tensor format is its GPU support to accelerate computations.
- The automatic differentiation (autograd) capabilities in PyTorch allow us to conveniently train neural networks using backpropagation without manually deriving gradients.
- The deep learning utilities in PyTorch provide building blocks for creating custom deep neural networks.
- PyTorch includes `Dataset` and `DataLoader` classes to set up efficient data-loading pipelines.
- It's easiest to train models on a CPU or single GPU.
- Using `DistributedDataParallel` is the simplest way in PyTorch to accelerate the training if multiple GPUs are available.

appendix B References and further reading

Chapter 1

Custom-built LLMs are able to outperform general-purpose LLMs as a team at Bloomberg showed via a version of GPT pretrained on finance data from scratch. The custom LLM outperformed ChatGPT on financial tasks while maintaining good performance on general LLM benchmarks:

- "BloombergGPT: A Large Language Model for Finance" (2023) by Wu et al., https://arxiv.org/abs/2303.17564

Existing LLMs can be adapted and fine-tuned to outperform general LLMs as well, which teams from Google Research and Google DeepMind showed in a medical context:

- "Towards Expert-Level Medical Question Answering with Large Language Models" (2023) by Singhal et al., https://arxiv.org/abs/2305.09617

The following paper proposed the original transformer architecture:

- "Attention Is All You Need" (2017) by Vaswani et al., https://arxiv.org/abs/1706.03762

On the original encoder-style transformer, called BERT, see

- "BERT: Pre-training of Deep Bidirectional Transformers for Language Understanding" (2018) by Devlin et al., https://arxiv.org/abs/1810.04805

The paper describing the decoder-style GPT-3 model, which inspired modern LLMs and will be used as a template for implementing an LLM from scratch in this book, is

- "Language Models are Few-Shot Learners" (2020) by Brown et al., https://arxiv.org/abs/2005.14165

The following covers the original vision transformer for classifying images, which illustrates that transformer architectures are not only restricted to text inputs:

- "An Image is Worth 16x16 Words: Transformers for Image Recognition at Scale" (2020) by Dosovitskiy et al., https://arxiv.org/abs/2010.11929

The following experimental (but less popular) LLM architectures serve as examples that not all LLMs need to be based on the transformer architecture:

- "RWKV: Reinventing RNNs for the Transformer Era" (2023) by Peng et al., https://arxiv.org/abs/2305.13048
- "Hyena Hierarchy: Towards Larger Convolutional Language Models" (2023) by Poli et al., https://arxiv.org/abs/2302.10866
- "Mamba: Linear-Time Sequence Modeling with Selective State Spaces" (2023) by Gu and Dao, https://arxiv.org/abs/2312.00752

Meta AI's model is a popular implementation of a GPT-like model that is openly available in contrast to GPT-3 and ChatGPT:

- "Llama 2: Open Foundation and Fine-Tuned Chat Models" (2023) by Touvron et al., https://arxiv.org/abs/2307.092881

For readers interested in additional details about the dataset references in section 1.5, this paper describes the publicly available *The Pile* dataset curated by Eleuther AI:

- "The Pile: An 800GB Dataset of Diverse Text for Language Modeling" (2020) by Gao et al., https://arxiv.org/abs/2101.00027

The following paper provides the reference for InstructGPT for fine-tuning GPT-3, which was mentioned in section 1.6 and will be discussed in more detail in chapter 7:

- "Training Language Models to Follow Instructions with Human Feedback" (2022) by Ouyang et al., https://arxiv.org/abs/2203.02155

Chapter 2

Readers who are interested in discussion and comparison of embedding spaces with latent spaces and the general notion of vector representations can find more information in the first chapter of my book:

- *Machine Learning Q and AI* (2023) by Sebastian Raschka, https://leanpub.com/machine-learning-q-and-ai

The following paper provides more in-depth discussions of how byte pair encoding is used as a tokenization method:

- "Neural Machine Translation of Rare Words with Subword Units" (2015) by Sennrich et al., https://arxiv.org/abs/1508.07909

The code for the byte pair encoding tokenizer used to train GPT-2 was open-sourced by OpenAI:

- https://github.com/openai/gpt-2/blob/master/src/encoder.py

OpenAI provides an interactive web UI to illustrate how the byte pair tokenizer in GPT models works:

- https://platform.openai.com/tokenizer

For readers interested in coding and training a BPE tokenizer from the ground up, Andrej Karpathy's GitHub repository `minbpe` offers a minimal and readable implementation:

- "A Minimal Implementation of a BPE Tokenizer," https://github.com/karpathy/minbpe

Readers who are interested in studying alternative tokenization schemes that are used by some other popular LLMs can find more information in the SentencePiece and WordPiece papers:

- "SentencePiece: A Simple and Language Independent Subword Tokenizer and Detokenizer for Neural Text Processing" (2018) by Kudo and Richardson, https://aclanthology.org/D18-2012/
- "Fast WordPiece Tokenization" (2020) by Song et al., https://arxiv.org/abs/2012.15524

Chapter 3

Readers interested in learning more about Bahdanau attention for RNN and language translation can find detailed insights in the following paper:

- "Neural Machine Translation by Jointly Learning to Align and Translate" (2014) by Bahdanau, Cho, and Bengio, https://arxiv.org/abs/1409.0473

The concept of self-attention as scaled dot-product attention was introduced in the original transformer paper:

- "Attention Is All You Need" (2017) by Vaswani et al., https://arxiv.org/abs/1706.03762

FlashAttention is a highly efficient implementation of a self-attention mechanism, which accelerates the computation process by optimizing memory access patterns. FlashAttention is mathematically the same as the standard self-attention mechanism but optimizes the computational process for efficiency:

- "FlashAttention: Fast and Memory-Efficient Exact Attention with IO-Awareness" (2022) by Dao et al., https://arxiv.org/abs/2205.14135
- "FlashAttention-2: Faster Attention with Better Parallelism and Work Partitioning" (2023) by Dao, https://arxiv.org/abs/2307.08691

PyTorch implements a function for self-attention and causal attention that supports FlashAttention for efficiency. This function is beta and subject to change:

- `scaled_dot_product_attention` documentation: https://mng.bz/NRJd

PyTorch also implements an efficient `MultiHeadAttention` class based on the `scaled_dot_product` function:

- `MultiHeadAttention` documentation: https://mng.bz/DdJV

Dropout is a regularization technique used in neural networks to prevent overfitting by randomly dropping units (along with their connections) from the neural network during training:

- "Dropout: A Simple Way to Prevent Neural Networks from Overfitting" (2014) by Srivastava et al., https://jmlr.org/papers/v15/srivastava14a.html

While using the multi-head attention based on scaled-dot product attention remains the most common variant of self-attention in practice, authors have found that it's possible to also achieve good performance without the value weight matrix and projection layer:

- "Simplifying Transformer Blocks" (2023) by He and Hofmann, https://arxiv.org/abs/2311.01906

Chapter 4

The following paper introduces a technique that stabilizes the hidden state dynamics neural networks by normalizing the summed inputs to the neurons within a hidden layer, significantly reducing training time compared to previously published methods:

- "Layer Normalization" (2016) by Ba, Kiros, and Hinton, https://arxiv.org/abs/1607.06450

Post-LayerNorm, used in the original transformer model, applies layer normalization after the self-attention and feed forward networks. In contrast, Pre-LayerNorm, as adopted in models like GPT-2 and newer LLMs, applies layer normalization before these components, which can lead to more stable training dynamics and has been shown to improve performance in some cases, as discussed in the following papers:

- "On Layer Normalization in the Transformer Architecture" (2020) by Xiong et al., https://arxiv.org/abs/2002.04745
- "ResiDual: Transformer with Dual Residual Connections" (2023) by Tie et al., https://arxiv.org/abs/2304.14802

A popular variant of LayerNorm used in modern LLMs is RMSNorm due to its improved computing efficiency. This variant simplifies the normalization process by normalizing the inputs using only the root mean square of the inputs, without subtracting the mean before squaring. This means it does not center the data before computing the scale. RMSNorm is described in more detail in

- "Root Mean Square Layer Normalization" (2019) by Zhang and Sennrich, https://arxiv.org/abs/1910.07467

The Gaussian Error Linear Unit (GELU) activation function combines the properties of both the classic ReLU activation function and the normal distribution's cumulative distribution function to model layer outputs, allowing for stochastic regularization and nonlinearities in deep learning models:

- "Gaussian Error Linear Units (GELUs)" (2016) by Hendricks and Gimpel, https://arxiv.org/abs/1606.08415

The GPT-2 paper introduced a series of transformer-based LLMs with varying sizes—124 million, 355 million, 774 million, and 1.5 billion parameters:

- "Language Models Are Unsupervised Multitask Learners" (2019) by Radford et al., https://mng.bz/lMgo

OpenAI's GPT-3 uses fundamentally the same architecture as GPT-2, except that the largest version (175 billion) is 100x larger than the largest GPT-2 model and has been trained on much more data. Interested readers can refer to the official GPT-3 paper by OpenAI and the technical overview by Lambda Labs, which calculates that training GPT-3 on a single RTX 8000 consumer GPU would take 665 years:

- "Language Models are Few-Shot Learners" (2023) by Brown et al., https://arxiv.org/abs/2005.14165
- "OpenAI's GPT-3 Language Model: A Technical Overview," https://lambdalabs.com/blog/demystifying-gpt-3

NanoGPT is a code repository with a minimalist yet efficient implementation of a GPT-2 model, similar to the model implemented in this book. While the code in this book is different from nanoGPT, this repository inspired the reorganization of a large GPT Python parent class implementation into smaller submodules:

- "NanoGPT, a Repository for Training Medium-Sized GPTs, https://github.com/karpathy/nanoGPT

An informative blog post showing that most of the computation in LLMs is spent in the feed forward layers rather than attention layers when the context size is smaller than 32,000 tokens is:

- "In the Long (Context) Run" by Harm de Vries, https://www.harmdevries.com/post/context-length/

Chapter 5

For information on detailing the loss function and applying a log transformation to make it easier to handle for mathematical optimization, see my lecture video:

- L8.2 Logistic Regression Loss Function, https://www.youtube.com/watch?v=GxJe0DZvydM

The following lecture and code example by the author explain how PyTorch's cross-entropy functions works under the hood:

- L8.7.1 OneHot Encoding and Multi-category Cross Entropy, https://www.youtube.com/watch?v=4n71-tZ94yk
- Understanding Onehot Encoding and Cross Entropy in PyTorch, https://mng.bz/o05v

The following two papers detail the dataset, hyperparameter, and architecture details used for pretraining LLMs:

- "Pythia: A Suite for Analyzing Large Language Models Across Training and Scaling" (2023) by Biderman et al., https://arxiv.org/abs/2304.01373
- "OLMo: Accelerating the Science of Language Models" (2024) by Groeneveld et al., https://arxiv.org/abs/2402.00838

The following supplementary code available for this book contains instructions for preparing 60,000 public domain books from Project Gutenberg for LLM training:

- Pretraining GPT on the Project Gutenberg Dataset, https://mng.bz/Bdw2

Chapter 5 discusses the pretraining of LLMs, and appendix D covers more advanced training functions, such as linear warmup and cosine annealing. The following paper finds that similar techniques can be successfully applied to continue pretraining already pretrained LLMs, along with additional tips and insights:

- "Simple and Scalable Strategies to Continually Pre-train Large Language Models" (2024) by Ibrahim et al., https://arxiv.org/abs/2403.08763

BloombergGPT is an example of a domain-specific LLM created by training on both general and domain-specific text corpora, specifically in the field of finance:

- "BloombergGPT: A Large Language Model for Finance" (2023) by Wu et al., https://arxiv.org/abs/2303.17564

GaLore is a recent research project that aims to make LLM pretraining more efficient. The required code change boils down to just replacing PyTorch's `AdamW` optimizer in the training function with the `GaLoreAdamW` optimizer provided by the `galore-torch` Python package:

- "GaLore: Memory-Efficient LLM Training by Gradient Low-Rank Projection" (2024) by Zhao et al., https://arxiv.org/abs/2403.03507
- GaLore code repository, https://github.com/jiaweizzhao/GaLore

The following papers and resources share openly available, large-scale pretraining datasets for LLMs that consist of hundreds of gigabytes to terabytes of text data:

- "Dolma: An Open Corpus of Three Trillion Tokens for LLM Pretraining Research" (2024) by Soldaini et al., https://arxiv.org/abs/2402.00159

- "The Pile: An 800GB Dataset of Diverse Text for Language Modeling" (2020) by Gao et al., https://arxiv.org/abs/2101.00027
- "The RefinedWeb Dataset for Falcon LLM: Outperforming Curated Corpora with Web Data, and Web Data Only," (2023) by Penedo et al., https://arxiv.org/abs/2306.01116
- "RedPajama," by Together AI, https://mng.bz/d6nw
- The FineWeb Dataset, which includes more than 15 trillion tokens of cleaned and deduplicated English web data sourced from CommonCrawl, https://mng.bz/rVzy

The paper that originally introduced top-k sampling is

- "Hierarchical Neural Story Generation" (2018) by Fan et al., https://arxiv.org/abs/1805.04833

An alternative to top-k sampling is top-p sampling (not covered in chapter 5), which selects from the smallest set of top tokens whose cumulative probability exceeds a threshold *p*, while top-k sampling picks from the top *k* tokens by probability:

- Top-p sampling, https://en.wikipedia.org/wiki/Top-p_sampling

Beam search (not covered in chapter 5) is an alternative decoding algorithm that generates output sequences by keeping only the top-scoring partial sequences at each step to balance efficiency and quality:

- "Diverse Beam Search: Decoding Diverse Solutions from Neural Sequence Models" (2016) by Vijayakumar et al., https://arxiv.org/abs/1610.02424

Chapter 6

Additional resources that discuss the different types of fine-tuning are

- "Using and Finetuning Pretrained Transformers," https://mng.bz/VxJG
- "Finetuning Large Language Models," https://mng.bz/x28X

Additional experiments, including a comparison of fine-tuning the first output token versus the last output token, can be found in the supplementary code material on GitHub:

- Additional spam classification experiments, https://mng.bz/AdJx

For a binary classification task, such as spam classification, it is technically possible to use only a single output node instead of two output nodes, as I discuss in the following article:

- "Losses Learned—Optimizing Negative Log-Likelihood and Cross-Entropy in PyTorch," https://mng.bz/ZEJA

You can find additional experiments on fine-tuning different layers of an LLM in the following article, which shows that fine-tuning the last transformer block, in addition to the output layer, improves the predictive performance substantially:

- "Finetuning Large Language Models," https://mng.bz/RZJv

Readers can find additional resources and information for dealing with imbalanced classification datasets in the imbalanced-learn documentation:

- "Imbalanced-Learn User Guide," https://mng.bz/2KNa

For readers interested in classifying spam emails rather than spam text messages, the following resource provides a large email spam classification dataset in a convenient CSV format similar to the dataset format used in chapter 6:

- Email Spam Classification Dataset, https://mng.bz/1GEq

GPT-2 is a model based on the decoder module of the transformer architecture, and its primary purpose is to generate new text. As an alternative, encoder-based models such as BERT and RoBERTa can be effective for classification tasks:

- "BERT: Pre-training of Deep Bidirectional Transformers for Language Understanding" (2018) by Devlin et al., https://arxiv.org/abs/1810.04805
- "RoBERTa: A Robustly Optimized BERT Pretraining Approach" (2019) by Liu et al., https://arxiv.org/abs/1907.11692
- "Additional Experiments Classifying the Sentiment of 50k IMDB Movie Reviews," https://mng.bz/PZJR

Recent papers are showing that the classification performance can be further improved by removing the causal mask during classification fine-tuning alongside other modifications:

- "Label Supervised LLaMA Finetuning" (2023) by Li et al., https://arxiv.org/abs/2310.01208
- "LLM2Vec: Large Language Models Are Secretly Powerful Text Encoders" (2024) by BehnamGhader et al., https://arxiv.org/abs/2404.05961

Chapter 7

The Alpaca dataset for instruction fine-tuning contains 52,000 instruction–response pairs and is one of the first and most popular publicly available datasets for instruction fine-tuning:

- "Stanford Alpaca: An Instruction-Following Llama Model," https://github.com/tatsu-lab/stanford_alpaca

Additional publicly accessible datasets suitable for instruction fine-tuning include

- LIMA, https://huggingface.co/datasets/GAIR/lima
  - For more information, see "LIMA: Less Is More for Alignment," Zhou et al., https://arxiv.org/abs/2305.11206

- UltraChat, https://huggingface.co/datasets/openchat/ultrachat-sharegpt
  - A large-scale dataset consisting of 805,000 instruction–response pairs; for more information, see "Enhancing Chat Language Models by Scaling High-quality Instructional Conversations," by Ding et al., https://arxiv.org/abs/2305.14233
- Alpaca GPT4, https://mng.bz/Aa0p
  - An Alpaca-like dataset with 52,000 instruction–response pairs generated with GPT-4 instead of GPT-3.5

Phi-3 is a 3.8-billion-parameter model with an instruction-fine-tuned variant that is reported to be comparable to much larger proprietary models, such as GPT-3.5:

- "Phi-3 Technical Report: A Highly Capable Language Model Locally on Your Phone" (2024) by Abdin et al., https://arxiv.org/abs/2404.14219

Researchers propose a synthetic instruction data generation method that generates 300,000 high-quality instruction-response pairs from an instruction fine-tuned Llama-3 model. A pretrained Llama 3 base model fine-tuned on these instruction examples performs comparably to the original instruction fine-tuned Llama-3 model:

- "Magpie: Alignment Data Synthesis from Scratch by Prompting Aligned LLMs with Nothing" (2024) by Xu et al., https://arxiv.org/abs/2406.08464

Research has shown that not masking the instructions and inputs in instruction fine-tuning effectively improves performance on various NLP tasks and open-ended generation benchmarks, particularly when trained on datasets with lengthy instructions and brief outputs or when using a small number of training examples:

- "Instruction Tuning with Loss Over Instructions" (2024) by Shi, https://arxiv.org/abs/2405.14394

Prometheus and PHUDGE are openly available LLMs that match GPT-4 in evaluating long-form responses with customizable criteria. We don't use these because at the time of this writing, they are not supported by Ollama and thus cannot be executed efficiently on a laptop:

- "Prometheus: Inducing Finegrained Evaluation Capability in Language Models" (2023) by Kim et al., https://arxiv.org/abs/2310.08491
- "PHUDGE: Phi-3 as Scalable Judge" (2024) by Deshwal and Chawla, "https://arxiv.org/abs/2405.08029
- "Prometheus 2: An Open Source Language Model Specialized in Evaluating Other Language Models" (2024), by Kim et al., https://arxiv.org/abs/2405.01535

The results in the following report support the view that large language models primarily acquire factual knowledge during pretraining and that fine-tuning mainly enhances their efficiency in using this knowledge. Furthermore, this study explores how fine-tuning large language models with new factual information affects their ability to use preexisting knowledge, revealing that models learn new facts more slowly and their introduction during fine-tuning increases the model's tendency to generate incorrect information:

- "Does Fine-Tuning LLMs on New Knowledge Encourage Hallucinations?" (2024) by Gekhman, https://arxiv.org/abs/2405.05904

Preference fine-tuning is an optional step after instruction fine-tuning to align the LLM more closely with human preferences. The following articles by the author provide more information about this process:

- "LLM Training: RLHF and Its Alternatives," https://mng.bz/ZVPm
- "Tips for LLM Pretraining and Evaluating Reward Models," https://mng.bz/RNXj

Appendix A

While appendix A should be sufficient to get you up to speed, if you are looking for more comprehensive introductions to deep learning, I recommend the following books:

- *Machine Learning with PyTorch and Scikit-Learn* (2022) by Sebastian Raschka, Hayden Liu, and Vahid Mirjalili. ISBN 978-1801819312
- *Deep Learning with PyTorch* (2021) by Eli Stevens, Luca Antiga, and Thomas Viehmann. ISBN 978-1617295263

For a more thorough introduction to the concepts of tensors, readers can find a 15-minute video tutorial that I recorded:

- "Lecture 4.1: Tensors in Deep Learning," https://www.youtube.com/watch?v=JXfDlgrfOBY

If you want to learn more about model evaluation in machine learning, I recommend my article

- "Model Evaluation, Model Selection, and Algorithm Selection in Machine Learning" (2018) by Sebastian Raschka, https://arxiv.org/abs/1811.12808

For readers who are interested in a refresher or gentle introduction to calculus, I've written a chapter on calculus that is freely available on my website:

- "Introduction to Calculus," by Sebastian Raschka, https://mng.bz/WEyW

Why does PyTorch not call `optimizer.zero_grad()` automatically for us in the background? In some instances, it may be desirable to accumulate the gradients, and PyTorch will leave this as an option for us. If you want to learn more about gradient accumulation, please see the following article:

- "Finetuning Large Language Models on a Single GPU Using Gradient Accumulation" by Sebastian Raschka, https://mng.bz/8wPD

This appendix covers DDP, which is a popular approach for training deep learning models across multiple GPUs. For more advanced use cases where a single model doesn't fit onto the GPU, you may also consider PyTorch's Fully Sharded Data Parallel (FSDP) method, which performs distributed data parallelism and distributes large layers across different GPUs. For more information, see this overview with further links to the API documentation:

- "Introducing PyTorch Fully Sharded Data Parallel (FSDP) API," https://mng.bz/EZJR

appendix C Exercise solutions

The complete code examples for the exercises' answers can be found in the supplementary GitHub repository at https://github.com/rasbt/LLMs-from-scratch.

Chapter 2

Exercise 2.1

You can obtain the individual token IDs by prompting the encoder with one string at a time:

```
print(tokenizer.encode("Ak"))
print(tokenizer.encode("w"))
# ...
```

This prints

```
[33901]
[86]
# ...
```

You can then use the following code to assemble the original string:

```
print(tokenizer.decode([33901, 86, 343, 86, 220, 959]))
```

This returns

```
'Akwirw ier'
```

Exercise 2.2

The code for the data loader with `max_length=2` and `stride=2`:

```
dataloader = create_dataloader(
    raw_text, batch_size=4, max_length=2, stride=2
)
```

It produces batches of the following format:

```
tensor([[  40,  367],
        [2885, 1464],
        [1807, 3619],
        [ 402,  271]])
```

The code of the second data loader with `max_length=8` and `stride=2`:

```
dataloader = create_dataloader(
    raw_text, batch_size=4, max_length=8, stride=2
)
```

An example batch looks like

```
tensor([[   40,   367,  2885,  1464,  1807,  3619,   402,   271],
        [ 2885,  1464,  1807,  3619,   402,   271, 10899,  2138],
        [ 1807,  3619,   402,   271, 10899,  2138,   257,  7026],
        [  402,   271, 10899,  2138,   257,  7026, 15632,   438]])
```

Chapter 3

Exercise 3.1

The correct weight assignment is

```
sa_v1.W_query = torch.nn.Parameter(sa_v2.W_query.weight.T)
sa_v1.W_key = torch.nn.Parameter(sa_v2.W_key.weight.T)
sa_v1.W_value = torch.nn.Parameter(sa_v2.W_value.weight.T)
```

Exercise 3.2

To achieve an output dimension of 2, similar to what we had in single-head attention, we need to change the projection dimension `d_out` to 1.

```
d_out = 1
mha = MultiHeadAttentionWrapper(d_in, d_out, block_size, 0.0, num_heads=2)
```

Exercise 3.3

The initialization for the smallest GPT-2 model is

```
block_size = 1024
d_in, d_out = 768, 768
num_heads = 12
mha = MultiHeadAttention(d_in, d_out, block_size, 0.0, num_heads)
```

Chapter 4

Exercise 4.1

We can calculate the number of parameters in the feed forward and attention modules as follows:

```
block = TransformerBlock(GPT_CONFIG_124M)

total_params = sum(p.numel() for p in block.ff.parameters())
print(f"Total number of parameters in feed forward module: {total_params:,}")

total_params = sum(p.numel() for p in block.att.parameters())
print(f"Total number of parameters in attention module: {total_params:,}")
```

As we can see, the feed forward module contains approximately twice as many parameters as the attention module:

```
Total number of parameters in feed forward module: 4,722,432
Total number of parameters in attention module: 2,360,064
```

Exercise 4.2

To instantiate the other GPT model sizes, we can modify the configuration dictionary as follows (here shown for GPT-2 XL):

```
GPT_CONFIG = GPT_CONFIG_124M.copy()
GPT_CONFIG["emb_dim"] = 1600
GPT_CONFIG["n_layers"] = 48
GPT_CONFIG["n_heads"] = 25
model = GPTModel(GPT_CONFIG)
```

Then, reusing the code from section 4.6 to calculate the number of parameters and RAM requirements, we find

```
gpt2-xl:
Total number of parameters: 1,637,792,000
Number of trainable parameters considering weight tying: 1,557,380,800
Total size of the model: 6247.68 MB
```

Exercise 4.3

There are three distinct places in chapter 4 where we used dropout layers: the embedding layer, shortcut layer, and multi-head attention module. We can control the dropout rates for each of the layers by coding them separately in the config file and then modifying the code implementation accordingly.

The modified configuration is as follows:

```
GPT_CONFIG_124M = {
    "vocab_size": 50257,
    "context_length": 1024,
    "emb_dim": 768,
```

```
    "n_heads": 12,
    "n_layers": 12,
    "drop_rate_attn": 0.1,                  # Dropout for multi-head attention
    "drop_rate_shortcut": 0.1,              # Dropout for shortcut connections
    "drop_rate_emb": 0.1,                   # Dropout for embedding layer
    "qkv_bias": False
}
```

The modified `TransformerBlock` and `GPTModel` look like

```
class TransformerBlock(nn.Module):
    def __init__(self, cfg):
        super().__init__()
        self.att = MultiHeadAttention(
            d_in=cfg["emb_dim"],
            d_out=cfg["emb_dim"],
            context_length=cfg["context_length"],
            num_heads=cfg["n_heads"],
            dropout=cfg["drop_rate_attn"],        # Dropout for multi-head attention
            qkv_bias=cfg["qkv_bias"])
        self.ff = FeedForward(cfg)
        self.norm1 = LayerNorm(cfg["emb_dim"])
        self.norm2 = LayerNorm(cfg["emb_dim"])
        self.drop_shortcut = nn.Dropout(          # Dropout for shortcut connections
            cfg["drop_rate_shortcut"]
        )

    def forward(self, x):
        shortcut = x
        x = self.norm1(x)
        x = self.att(x)
        x = self.drop_shortcut(x)
        x = x + shortcut

        shortcut = x
        x = self.norm2(x)
        x = self.ff(x)
        x = self.drop_shortcut(x)
        x = x + shortcut
        return x


class GPTModel(nn.Module):
    def __init__(self, cfg):
        super().__init__()
        self.tok_emb = nn.Embedding(
            cfg["vocab_size"], cfg["emb_dim"]
        )
        self.pos_emb = nn.Embedding(
            cfg["context_length"], cfg["emb_dim"]
        )
        self.drop_emb = nn.Dropout(cfg["drop_rate_emb"])    # Dropout for embedding layer
```

```
        self.trf_blocks = nn.Sequential(
            *[TransformerBlock(cfg) for _ in range(cfg["n_layers"])])

        self.final_norm = LayerNorm(cfg["emb_dim"])
        self.out_head = nn.Linear(
            cfg["emb_dim"], cfg["vocab_size"], bias=False
        )

    def forward(self, in_idx):
        batch_size, seq_len = in_idx.shape
        tok_embeds = self.tok_emb(in_idx)
        pos_embeds = self.pos_emb(
            torch.arange(seq_len, device=in_idx.device)
        )
        x = tok_embeds + pos_embeds
        x = self.drop_emb(x)
        x = self.trf_blocks(x)
        x = self.final_norm(x)
        logits = self.out_head(x)
        return logitss
```

Chapter 5

Exercise 5.1

We can print the number of times the token (or word) "pizza" is sampled using the `print_sampled_tokens` function we defined in this section. Let's start with the code we defined in section 5.3.1.

The "pizza" token is sampled 0x if the temperature is 0 or 0.1, and it is sampled 32× if the temperature is scaled up to 5. The estimated probability is 32/1000 × 100% = 3.2%.

The actual probability is 4.3% and is contained in the rescaled softmax probability tensor (`scaled_probas[2][6]`).

Exercise 5.2

Top-k sampling and temperature scaling are settings that have to be adjusted based on the LLM and the desired degree of diversity and randomness in the output.

When using relatively small top-k values (e.g., smaller than 10) and when the temperature is set below 1, the model's output becomes less random and more deterministic. This setting is useful when we need the generated text to be more predictable, coherent, and closer to the most likely outcomes based on the training data.

Applications for such low k and temperature settings include generating formal documents or reports where clarity and accuracy are most important. Other examples of applications include technical analysis or code-generation tasks, where precision is crucial. Also, question answering and educational content require accurate answers where a temperature below 1 is helpful.

On the other hand, larger top-k values (e.g., values in the range of 20 to 40) and temperature values above 1 are useful when using LLMs for brainstorming or generating creative content, such as fiction.

Exercise 5.3

There are multiple ways to force deterministic behavior with the `generate` function:

1 Setting to `top_k=None` and applying no temperature scaling
2 Setting `top_k=1`

Exercise 5.4

In essence, we have to load the model and optimizer that we saved in the main chapter:

```
checkpoint = torch.load("model_and_optimizer.pth")
model = GPTModel(GPT_CONFIG_124M)
model.load_state_dict(checkpoint["model_state_dict"])
optimizer = torch.optim.AdamW(model.parameters(), lr=5e-4, weight_decay=0.1)
optimizer.load_state_dict(checkpoint["optimizer_state_dict"])
```

Then, call the `train_simple_function` with `num_epochs=1` to train the model for another epoch.

Exercise 5.5

We can use the following code to calculate the training and validation set losses of the GPT model:

```
train_loss = calc_loss_loader(train_loader, gpt, device)
val_loss = calc_loss_loader(val_loader, gpt, device)
```

The resulting losses for the 124-million parameter are as follows:

```
Training loss: 3.754748503367106
Validation loss: 3.559617757797241
```

The main observation is that the training and validation set performances are in the same ballpark. This can have multiple explanations:

1 "The Verdict" was not part of the pretraining dataset when OpenAI trained GPT-2. Hence, the model is not explicitly overfitting to the training set and performs similarly well on the training and validation set portions of "The Verdict." (The validation set loss is slightly lower than the training set loss, which is unusual in deep learning. However, it's likely due to random noise since the dataset is relatively small. In practice, if there is no overfitting, the training and validation set performances are expected to be roughly identical).
2 "The Verdict" was part of GPT-2's training dataset. In this case, we can't tell whether the model is overfitting the training data because the validation set would have been used for training as well. To evaluate the degree of overfitting, we'd need a new dataset generated after OpenAI finished training GPT-2 to make sure that it couldn't have been part of the pretraining.

Exercise 5.6

In the main chapter, we experimented with the smallest GPT-2 model, which has only 124-million parameters. The reason was to keep the resource requirements as low as possible. However, you can easily experiment with larger models with minimal code changes. For example, instead of loading the 1,558 million instead of 124 million model weights in chapter 5, the only two lines of code that we have to change are the following:

```
hparams, params = download_and_load_gpt2(model_size="124M", models_dir="gpt2")
model_name = "gpt2-small (124M)"
```

The updated code is

```
hparams, params = download_and_load_gpt2(model_size="1558M", models_dir="gpt2")
model_name = "gpt2-xl (1558M)"
```

Chapter 6

Exercise 6.1

We can pad the inputs to the maximum number of tokens the model supports by setting the max length to `max_length = 1024` when initializing the datasets:

```
train_dataset = SpamDataset(..., max_length=1024, ...)
val_dataset = SpamDataset(..., max_length=1024, ...)
test_dataset = SpamDataset(..., max_length=1024, ...)
```

However, the additional padding results in a substantially worse test accuracy of 78.33% (vs. the 95.67% in the main chapter).

Exercise 6.2

Instead of fine-tuning just the final transformer block, we can fine-tune the entire model by removing the following lines from the code:

```
for param in model.parameters():
    param.requires_grad = False
```

This modification results in a 1% improved test accuracy of 96.67% (vs. the 95.67% in the main chapter).

Exercise 6.3

Rather than fine-tuning the last output token, we can fine-tune the first output token by changing `model(input_batch)[:, -1, :]` to `model(input_batch)[:, 0, :]` everywhere in the code.

As expected, since the first token contains less information than the last token, this change results in a substantially worse test accuracy of 75.00% (vs. the 95.67% in the main chapter).

Chapter 7

Exercise 7.1

The Phi-3 prompt format, which is shown in figure 7.4, looks like the following for a given example input:

```
<user>
Identify the correct spelling of the following word: 'Occasion'

<assistant>
The correct spelling is 'Occasion'.
```

To use this template, we can modify the `format_input` function as follows:

```
def format_input(entry):
    instruction_text = (
        f"<|user|>\n{entry['instruction']}"
    )
    input_text = f"\n{entry['input']}" if entry["input"] else ""
    return instruction_text + input_text
```

Lastly, we also have to update the way we extract the generated response when we collect the test set responses:

```
for i, entry in tqdm(enumerate(test_data), total=len(test_data)):
    input_text = format_input(entry)
    tokenizer=tokenizer
    token_ids = generate(
        model=model,
        idx=text_to_token_ids(input_text, tokenizer).to(device),
        max_new_tokens=256,
        context_size=BASE_CONFIG["context_length"],
        eos_id=50256
    )
    generated_text = token_ids_to_text(token_ids, tokenizer)
    response_text = (
        generated_text[len(input_text):]
        .replace("<|assistant|>:", "")
        .strip()
    )
    test_data[i]["model_response"] = response_text
```

New: Adjust ###Response to <|assistant|>

Fine-tuning the model with the Phi-3 template is approximately 17% faster since it results in shorter model inputs. The score is close to 50, which is in the same ballpark as the score we previously achieved with the Alpaca-style prompts.

Exercise 7.2

To mask out the instructions as shown in figure 7.13, we need to make slight modifications to the `InstructionDataset` class and `custom_collate_fn` function. We can modify the `InstructionDataset` class to collect the lengths of the instructions, which we will use in the collate function to locate the instruction content positions in the targets when we code the collate function, as follows:

```
class InstructionDataset(Dataset):
    def __init__(self, data, tokenizer):
        self.data = data
        self.instruction_lengths = []          # Separate list for instruction lengths
        self.encoded_texts = []

        for entry in data:
            instruction_plus_input = format_input(entry)
            response_text = f"\n\n### Response:\n{entry['output']}"
            full_text = instruction_plus_input + response_text

            self.encoded_texts.append(
                tokenizer.encode(full_text)
            )
            instruction_length = (
                len(tokenizer.encode(instruction_plus_input)
            )
            self.instruction_lengths.append(instruction_length)   # Collects instruction lengths

    def __getitem__(self, index):     # Returns both instruction lengths and texts separately
        return self.instruction_lengths[index], self.encoded_texts[index]

    def __len__(self):
        return len(self.data)
```

Next, we update the `custom_collate_fn` where each `batch` is now a tuple containing `(instruction_length, item)` instead of just `item` due to the changes in the `InstructionDataset` dataset. In addition, we now mask the corresponding instruction tokens in the target ID list:

```
def custom_collate_fn(
    batch,
    pad_token_id=50256,
    ignore_index=-100,
    allowed_max_length=None,
    device="cpu"
):

    batch_max_length = max(len(item)+1 for instruction_length, item in batch)
    inputs_lst, targets_lst = [], []            # batch is now a tuple.

    for instruction_length, item in batch:      # batch is now a tuple.
        new_item = item.copy()
        new_item += [pad_token_id]
        padded = (
            new_item + [pad_token_id] * (batch_max_length - len(new_item))
        )
        inputs = torch.tensor(padded[:-1])
        targets = torch.tensor(padded[1:])
        mask = targets == pad_token_id
```

```
        indices = torch.nonzero(mask).squeeze()
        if indices.numel() > 1:
            targets[indices[1:]] = ignore_index

        targets[:instruction_length-1] = -100         # Masks all input and instruction tokens in the targets

        if allowed_max_length is not None:
            inputs = inputs[:allowed_max_length]
            targets = targets[:allowed_max_length]

        inputs_lst.append(inputs)
        targets_lst.append(targets)

    inputs_tensor = torch.stack(inputs_lst).to(device)
    targets_tensor = torch.stack(targets_lst).to(device)

    return inputs_tensor, targets_tensor
```

When evaluating a model fine-tuned with this instruction masking method, it performs slightly worse (approximately 4 points using the Ollama Llama 3 method from chapter 7). This is consistent with observations in the "Instruction Tuning With Loss Over Instructions" paper (https://arxiv.org/abs/2405.14394).

Exercise 7.3

To fine-tune the model on the original Stanford Alpaca dataset (https://github.com/tatsu-lab/stanford_alpaca), we just have to change the file URL from

```
url = "https://raw.githubusercontent.com/rasbt/LLMs-from-scratch/main/ch07/
01_main-chapter-code/instruction-data.json"
```

to

```
url = "https://raw.githubusercontent.com/tatsu-lab/stanford_alpaca/main/
alpaca_data.json"
```

Note that the dataset contains 52,000 entries (50x more than in chapter 7), and the entries are longer than the ones we worked with in chapter 7.

Thus, it's highly recommended that the training be run on a GPU.

If you encounter out-of-memory errors, consider reducing the batch size from 8 to 4, 2, or 1. In addition to lowering the batch size, you may also want to consider lowering the `allowed_max_length` from 1024 to 512 or 256.

Below are a few examples from the Alpaca dataset, including the generated model responses:

Exercise 7.4

To instruction fine-tune the model using LoRA, use the relevant classes and functions from appendix E:

```
from appendix_E import LoRALayer, LinearWithLoRA, replace_linear_with_lora
```

Next, add the following lines of code below the model loading code in section 7.5:

```
total_params = sum(p.numel() for p in model.parameters() if p.requires_grad)
print(f"Total trainable parameters before: {total_params:,}")

for param in model.parameters():
    param.requires_grad = False

total_params = sum(p.numel() for p in model.parameters() if p.requires_grad)
print(f"Total trainable parameters after: {total_params:,}")
replace_linear_with_lora(model, rank=16, alpha=16)

total_params = sum(p.numel() for p in model.parameters() if p.requires_grad)
print(f"Total trainable LoRA parameters: {total_params:,}")
model.to(device)
```

Note that, on an Nvidia L4 GPU, the fine-tuning with LoRA takes 1.30 min to run on an L4. On the same GPU, the original code takes 1.80 minutes to run. So, LoRA is approximately 28% faster in this case. The score, evaluated with the Ollama Llama 3 method from chapter 7, is around 50, which is in the same ballpark as the original model.

Appendix A

Exercise A.1

The network has two inputs and two outputs. In addition, there are two hidden layers with 30 and 20 nodes, respectively. Programmatically, we can calculate the number of parameters as follows:

```
model = NeuralNetwork(2, 2)
num_params = sum(p.numel() for p in model.parameters() if p.requires_grad)
print("Total number of trainable model parameters:", num_params)
```

This returns

```
752
```

We can also calculate this manually:

- *First hidden layer*—2 inputs times 30 hidden units plus 30 bias units
- *Second hidden layer*—30 incoming units times 20 nodes plus 20 bias units
- *Output layer*—20 incoming nodes times 2 output nodes plus 2 bias units

Then, adding all the parameters in each layer results in $2 \times 30 + 30 + 30 \times 20 + 20 + 20 \times 2 + 2 = 752$.

Exercise A.2

The exact run-time results will be specific to the hardware used for this experiment. In my experiments, I observed significant speedups even for small matrix multiplications as the following one when using a Google Colab instance connected to a V100 GPU:

```
a = torch.rand(100, 200)
b = torch.rand(200, 300)
%timeit a@b
```

On the CPU, this resulted in

```
63.8 µs ± 8.7 µs per loop
```

When executed on a GPU,

```
a, b = a.to("cuda"), b.to("cuda")
%timeit a @ b
```

the result was

```
13.8 µs ± 425 ns per loop
```

In this case, on a V100, the computation was approximately four times faster.

Exercise A.3

The network has two inputs and two outputs. In addition, there are 2 hidden layers with 30 and 20 nodes, respectively. Programmatically, we can calculate the number of parameters as follows:

```
model = NeuralNetwork(2, 2)
num_params = sum(p.numel() for p in model.parameters() if p.requires_grad)
print("Total number of trainable model parameters:", num_params)
```

This returns

```
752
```

We can also calculate this manually as follows:

- *First hidden layer:* 2 inputs times 30 hidden units plus 30 bias units
- *Second hidden layer:* 30 incoming units times 20 nodes plus 20 bias units
- *Output layer:* 20 incoming nodes times 2 output nodes plus 2 bias units

Then, adding all the parameters in each layer results in 2×30+30 + 30×20+20 + 20×2+2 = 752.

Exercise A.4

The exact run-time results will be specific to the hardware used for this experiment. In my experiments, I observed significant speed-ups even for small matrix multiplications when using a Google Colab instance connected to a V100 GPU:

```
a = torch.rand(100, 200)
b = torch.rand(200, 300)
%timeit a@b
```

On the CPU this resulted in

```
63.8 µs ± 8.7 µs per loop
```

When executed on a GPU

```
a, b = a.to("cuda"), b.to("cuda")
%timeit a @ b
```

The result was

```
13.8 µs ± 425 ns per loop
```

In this case, on a V100, the computation was approximately four times faster.

appendix D Adding bells and whistles to the training loop

In this appendix, we enhance the training function for the pretraining and fine-tuning processes covered in chapters 5 to 7. In particular, it covers *learning rate warmup*, *cosine decay*, and *gradient clipping*. We then incorporate these techniques into the training function and pretrain an LLM.

To make the code self-contained, we reinitialize the model we trained in chapter 5:

```
import torch
from chapter04 import GPTModel

GPT_CONFIG_124M = {
    "vocab_size": 50257,          # Vocabulary size

    "context_length": 256,        # Shortened context length (orig: 1024)
    "emb_dim": 768,               # Embedding dimension
    "n_heads": 12,                # Number of attention heads
    "n_layers": 12,               # Number of layers
    "drop_rate": 0.1,             # Dropout rate
    "qkv_bias": False             # Query-key-value bias
}
device = torch.device("cuda" if torch.cuda.is_available() else "cpu")
torch.manual_seed(123)
model = GPTModel(GPT_CONFIG_124M)
model.to(device)
model.eval()
```

After initializing the model, we need to initialize the data loaders. First, we load the "The Verdict" short story:

```
import os
import urllib.request

file_path = "the-verdict.txt"

url = (
    "https://raw.githubusercontent.com/rasbt/LLMs-from-scratch/"
    "main/ch02/01_main-chapter-code/the-verdict.txt"
)

if not os.path.exists(file_path):
    with urllib.request.urlopen(url) as response:
        text_data = response.read().decode('utf-8')
    with open(file_path, "w", encoding="utf-8") as file:
        file.write(text_data)
else:
    with open(file_path, "r", encoding="utf-8") as file:
        text_data = file.read()
```

Next, we load the `text_data` into the data loaders:

```
from previous_chapters import create_dataloader_v1

train_ratio = 0.90
split_idx = int(train_ratio * len(text_data))
torch.manual_seed(123)
train_loader = create_dataloader_v1(
    text_data[:split_idx],
    batch_size=2,
    max_length=GPT_CONFIG_124M["context_length"],
    stride=GPT_CONFIG_124M["context_length"],
    drop_last=True,
    shuffle=True,
    num_workers=0
)
val_loader = create_dataloader_v1(
    text_data[split_idx:],
    batch_size=2,
    max_length=GPT_CONFIG_124M["context_length"],
    stride=GPT_CONFIG_124M["context_length"],
    drop_last=False,
    shuffle=False,
    num_workers=0
)
```

D.1 Learning rate warmup

Implementing a learning rate warmup can stabilize the training of complex models such as LLMs. This process involves gradually increasing the learning rate from a very low initial value (`initial_lr`) to a maximum value specified by the user (`peak_lr`). Starting the training with smaller weight updates decreases the risk of the model encountering large, destabilizing updates during its training phase.

Suppose we plan to train an LLM for 15 epochs, starting with an initial learning rate of 0.0001 and increasing it to a maximum learning rate of 0.01:

```
n_epochs = 15
initial_lr = 0.0001
peak_lr = 0.01
warmup_steps = 20
```

The number of warmup steps is usually set between 0.1% and 20% of the total number of steps, which we can calculate as follows:

```
total_steps = len(train_loader) * n_epochs
warmup_steps = int(0.2 * total_steps)          # 20% warmup
print(warmup_steps)
```

This prints `27`, meaning that we have 20 warmup steps to increase the initial learning rate from 0.0001 to 0.01 in the first 27 training steps.

Next, we implement a simple training loop template to illustrate this warmup process:

```
optimizer = torch.optim.AdamW(model.parameters(), weight_decay=0.1)
lr_increment = (peak_lr - initial_lr) / warmup_steps

global_step = -1
track_lrs = []

for epoch in range(n_epochs):
    for input_batch, target_batch in train_loader:
        optimizer.zero_grad()
        global_step += 1

        if global_step < warmup_steps:
            lr = initial_lr + global_step * lr_increment
        else:
            lr = peak_lr

        for param_group in optimizer.param_groups:
            param_group["lr"] = lr
        track_lrs.append(optimizer.param_groups[0]["lr"])
```

This increment is determined by how much we increase the inital_lr in each of the 20 warmup steps.

Executes a typical training loop iterating over the batches in the training loader in each epoch

Updates the learning rate if we are still in the warmup phase

Applies the calculated learning rate to the optimizer

In a complete training loop, the loss and the model updates would be calculated, which are omitted here for simplicity.

After running the preceding code, we visualize how the learning rate was changed by the training loop to verify that the learning rate warmup works as intended:

```
import matplotlib.pyplot as plt

plt.ylabel("Learning rate")
plt.xlabel("Step")
total_training_steps = len(train_loader) * n_epochs
plt.plot(range(total_training_steps), track_lrs);
plt.show()
```

The resulting plot shows that the learning rate starts with a low value and increases for 20 steps until it reaches the maximum value after 20 steps (figure D.1).

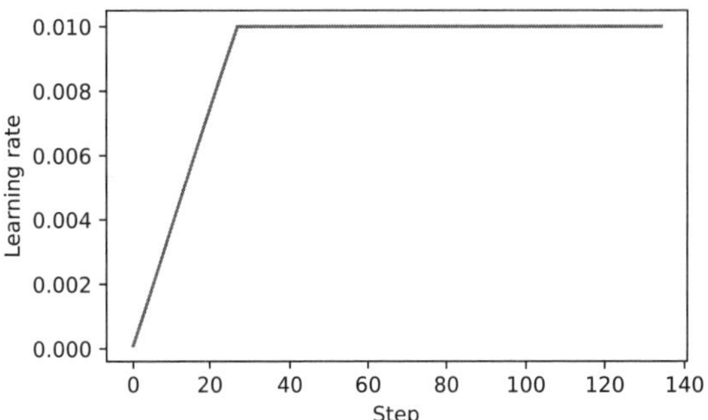

Figure D.1 The learning rate warmup increases the learning rate for the first 20 training steps. After 20 steps, the learning rate reaches the peak of 0.01 and remains constant for the rest of the training.

Next, we will modify the learning rate further so that it decreases after reaching the maximum learning rate, which further helps improve the model training.

D.2 Cosine decay

Another widely adopted technique for training complex deep neural networks and LLMs is *cosine decay*. This method modulates the learning rate throughout the training epochs, making it follow a cosine curve after the warmup stage.

In its popular variant, cosine decay reduces (or decays) the learning rate to nearly zero, mimicking the trajectory of a half-cosine cycle. The gradual learning decrease in cosine decay aims to decelerate the pace at which the model updates its weights. This is particularly important because it helps minimize the risk of overshooting the loss minima during the training process, which is essential for ensuring the stability of the training during its later phases.

We can modify the training loop template by adding cosine decay:

```
import math

min_lr = 0.1 * initial_lr
track_lrs = []
lr_increment = (peak_lr - initial_lr) / warmup_steps
global_step = -1

for epoch in range(n_epochs):
    for input_batch, target_batch in train_loader:
        optimizer.zero_grad()
        global_step += 1

        if global_step < warmup_steps:                          # Applies linear warmup
            lr = initial_lr + global_step * lr_increment
        else:                                                   # Uses cosine annealing after warmup
            progress = ((global_step - warmup_steps) /
                        (total_training_steps - warmup_steps))
```

```
        lr = min_lr + (peak_lr - min_lr) * 0.5 * (
            1 + math.cos(math.pi * progress)
        )

    for param_group in optimizer.param_groups:
        param_group["lr"] = lr
    track_lrs.append(optimizer.param_groups[0]["lr"])
```

Again, to verify that the learning rate has changed as intended, we plot the learning rate:

```
plt.ylabel("Learning rate")
plt.xlabel("Step")
plt.plot(range(total_training_steps), track_lrs)
plt.show()
```

The resulting learning rate plot shows that the learning rate starts with a linear warmup phase, which increases for 20 steps until it reaches the maximum value after 20 steps. After the 20 steps of linear warmup, cosine decay kicks in, reducing the learning rate gradually until it reaches its minimum (figure D.2).

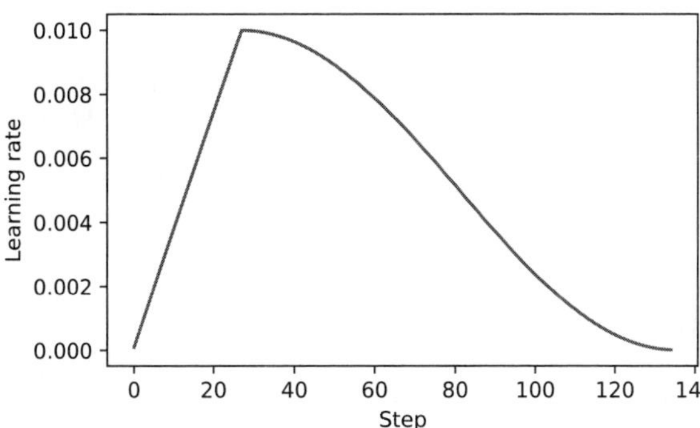

Figure D.2 The first 20 steps of linear learning rate warmup are followed by a cosine decay, which reduces the learning rate in a half-cosine cycle until it reaches its minimum point at the end of training.

D.3 Gradient clipping

Gradient clipping is another important technique for enhancing stability during LLM training. This method involves setting a threshold above which gradients are downscaled to a predetermined maximum magnitude. This process ensures that the updates to the model's parameters during backpropagation stay within a manageable range.

For example, applying the `max_norm=1.0` setting within PyTorch's `clip_grad_norm_` function ensures that the norm of the gradients does not surpass 1.0. Here, the term "norm" signifies the measure of the gradient vector's length, or magnitude, within the model's parameter space, specifically referring to the L2 norm, also known as the Euclidean norm.

In mathematical terms, for a vector $\boldsymbol{v}$ composed of components $\boldsymbol{v} = [v_1, v_2, ..., v_n]$, the L2 norm is

$$|\boldsymbol{v}|_2 = \sqrt{v_1^2 + v_2^2 + \cdots + v_n^2}$$

This calculation method is also applied to matrices. For instance, consider a gradient matrix given by

$$\mathbf{G} = \begin{bmatrix} 1 & 2 \\ 3 & 4 \end{bmatrix}$$

If we want to clip these gradients to a `max_norm` of 1, we first compute the L2 norm of these gradients, which is

$$|\mathbf{G}|_2 = \sqrt{1^2 + 2^2 + 2^2 + 4^2} = \sqrt{25} = 5$$

Given that $|\mathbf{G}|_2 = 5$ exceeds our `max_norm` of 1, we scale down the gradients to ensure their norm equals exactly 1. This is achieved through a scaling factor, calculated as `max_norm`$/|\mathbf{G}|_2 = 1/5$. Consequently, the adjusted gradient matrix **G'** becomes

$$\mathbf{G}' = \frac{1}{5} \times G = \begin{bmatrix} \frac{1}{5} & \frac{2}{5} \\ \frac{2}{5} & \frac{4}{5} \end{bmatrix}$$

To illustrate this gradient clipping process, we begin by initializing a new model and calculating the loss for a training batch, similar to the procedure in a standard training loop:

```
from chapter05 import calc_loss_batch

torch.manual_seed(123)
model = GPTModel(GPT_CONFIG_124M)
model.to(device)
loss = calc_loss_batch(input_batch, target_batch, model, device)
loss.backward()
```

Upon calling the `.backward()` method, PyTorch calculates the loss gradients and stores them in a `.grad` attribute for each model weight (parameter) tensor.

To clarify the point, we can define the following `find_highest_gradient` utility function to identify the highest gradient value by scanning all the `.grad` attributes of the model's weight tensors after calling `.backward()`:

```
def find_highest_gradient(model):
    max_grad = None
    for param in model.parameters():
        if param.grad is not None:
            grad_values = param.grad.data.flatten()
            max_grad_param = grad_values.max()
            if max_grad is None or max_grad_param > max_grad:
                max_grad = max_grad_param
    return max_grad
print(find_highest_gradient(model))
```

The largest gradient value identified by the preceding code is

```
tensor(0.0411)
```

Let's now apply gradient clipping and see how this affects the largest gradient value:

```
torch.nn.utils.clip_grad_norm_(model.parameters(), max_norm=1.0)
print(find_highest_gradient(model))
```

The largest gradient value after applying the gradient clipping with the max norm of 1 is substantially smaller than before:

```
tensor(0.0185)
```

D.4 The modified training function

Finally, we improve the `train_model_simple` training function (see chapter 5) by adding the three concepts introduced herein: linear warmup, cosine decay, and gradient clipping. Together, these methods help stabilize LLM training.

The code, with the changes compared to the `train_model_simple` annotated, is as follows:

```
from chapter05 import evaluate_model, generate_and_print_sample


def train_model(model, train_loader, val_loader, optimizer, device,
                n_epochs, eval_freq, eval_iter, start_context, tokenizer,
                warmup_steps, initial_lr=3e-05, min_lr=1e-6):

    train_losses, val_losses, track_tokens_seen, track_lrs = [], [], [], []
    tokens_seen, global_step = 0, -1

    peak_lr = optimizer.param_groups[0]["lr"]
    total_training_steps = len(train_loader) * n_epochs
    lr_increment = (peak_lr - initial_lr) / warmup_steps

    for epoch in range(n_epochs):
        model.train()
        for input_batch, target_batch in train_loader:
            optimizer.zero_grad()
            global_step += 1

            if global_step < warmup_steps:
                lr = initial_lr + global_step * lr_increment
            else:
                progress = ((global_step - warmup_steps) /
                            (total_training_steps - warmup_steps))
                lr = min_lr + (peak_lr - min_lr) * 0.5 * (
                    1 + math.cos(math.pi * progress))
```

Retrieves the initial learning rate from the optimizer, assuming we use it as the peak learning rate

Calculates the total number of iterations in the training process

Calculates the learning rate increment during the warmup phase

Adjusts the learning rate based on the current phase (warmup or cosine annealing)

```
            for param_group in optimizer.param_groups:
                param_group["lr"] = lr
            track_lrs.append(lr)
            loss = calc_loss_batch(input_batch, target_batch, model, device)
            loss.backward()

            if global_step > warmup_steps:
                torch.nn.utils.clip_grad_norm_(
                    model.parameters(), max_norm=1.0
                )

            optimizer.step()
            tokens_seen += input_batch.numel()

            if global_step % eval_freq == 0:
                train_loss, val_loss = evaluate_model(
                    model, train_loader, val_loader,
                    device, eval_iter
                )
                train_losses.append(train_loss)
                val_losses.append(val_loss)
                track_tokens_seen.append(tokens_seen)
                print(f"Ep {epoch+1} (Iter {global_step:06d}): "
                      f"Train loss {train_loss:.3f}, "
                      f"Val loss {val_loss:.3f}"
                )


        generate_and_print_sample(
            model, tokenizer, device, start_context
        )

    return train_losses, val_losses, track_tokens_seen, track_lrs
```

Applies the calculated learning rate to the optimizer

Applies gradient clipping after the warmup phase to avoid exploding gradients

Everything below here remains unchanged compared to the train_model_simple function used in chapter 5.

After defining the `train_model` function, we can use it in a similar fashion to train the model compared to the `train_model_simple` method we used for pretraining:

```
import tiktoken

torch.manual_seed(123)
model = GPTModel(GPT_CONFIG_124M)
model.to(device)
peak_lr = 5e-4
optimizer = torch.optim.AdamW(model.parameters(), weight_decay=0.1)
tokenizer = tiktoken.get_encoding("gpt2")

n_epochs = 15
train_losses, val_losses, tokens_seen, lrs = train_model(
    model, train_loader, val_loader, optimizer, device, n_epochs=n_epochs,
    eval_freq=5, eval_iter=1, start_context="Every effort moves you",
    tokenizer=tokenizer, warmup_steps=warmup_steps,
    initial_lr=1e-5, min_lr=1e-5
)
```

The training will take about 5 minutes to complete on a MacBook Air or similar laptop and prints the following outputs:

```
Ep 1 (Iter 000000): Train loss 10.934, Val loss 10.939
Ep 1 (Iter 000005): Train loss 9.151, Val loss 9.461
Every effort moves you,,,,,,,,,,,,,,,,,,,,,,,,,,,,,,,,,,,,,,,,,,,,,,,,,,
Ep 2 (Iter 000010): Train loss 7.949, Val loss 8.184
Ep 2 (Iter 000015): Train loss 6.362, Val loss 6.876
Every effort moves you,,,,,,,,,,,,,,,,,,, the,,,,,,,,, the,,,,,,,,,,,
the,,,,,,,,
...
Ep 15 (Iter 000130): Train loss 0.041, Val loss 6.915
Every effort moves you?"  "Yes--quite insensible to the irony. She wanted him
vindicated--and by me!"  He laughed again, and threw back his head to look up
at the sketch of the donkey. "There were days when I
```

Like pretraining, the model begins to overfit after a few epochs since it is a very small dataset, and we iterate over it multiple times. Nonetheless, we can see that the function is working since it minimizes the training set loss.

Readers are encouraged to train the model on a larger text dataset and compare the results obtained with this more sophisticated training function to the results that can be obtained with the `train_model_simple` function.

appendix E *Parameter-efficient fine-tuning with LoRA*

Low-rank adaptation (*LoRA*) is one of the most widely used techniques for *parameter-efficient fine-tuning*. The following discussion is based on the spam classification fine-tuning example given in chapter 6. However, LoRA fine-tuning is also applicable to the supervised *instruction fine-tuning* discussed in chapter 7.

E.1 Introduction to LoRA

LoRA is a technique that adapts a pretrained model to better suit a specific, often smaller dataset by adjusting only a small subset of the model's weight parameters. The "low-rank" aspect refers to the mathematical concept of limiting model adjustments to a smaller dimensional subspace of the total weight parameter space. This effectively captures the most influential directions of the weight parameter changes during training. The LoRA method is useful and popular because it enables efficient fine-tuning of large models on task-specific data, significantly cutting down on the computational costs and resources usually required for fine-tuning.

Suppose a large weight matrix W is associated with a specific layer. LoRA can be applied to all linear layers in an LLM. However, we focus on a single layer for illustration purposes.

When training deep neural networks, during backpropagation, we learn a ΔW matrix, which contains information on how much we want to update the original weight parameters to minimize the loss function during training. Hereafter, I use the term "weight" as shorthand for the model's weight parameters.

In regular training and fine-tuning, the weight update is defined as follows:

$$W_{updated} = W + \Delta W$$

The LoRA method, proposed by Hu et al. (https://arxiv.org/abs/2106.09685), offers a more efficient alternative to computing the weight updates ΔW by learning an approximation of it:

$$\Delta W \approx AB$$

where A and B are two matrices much smaller than W, and AB represents the matrix multiplication product between A and B.

Using LoRA, we can then reformulate the weight update we defined earlier:

$$W_{updated} = W + AB$$

Figure E.1 illustrates the weight update formulas for full fine-tuning and LoRA side by side.

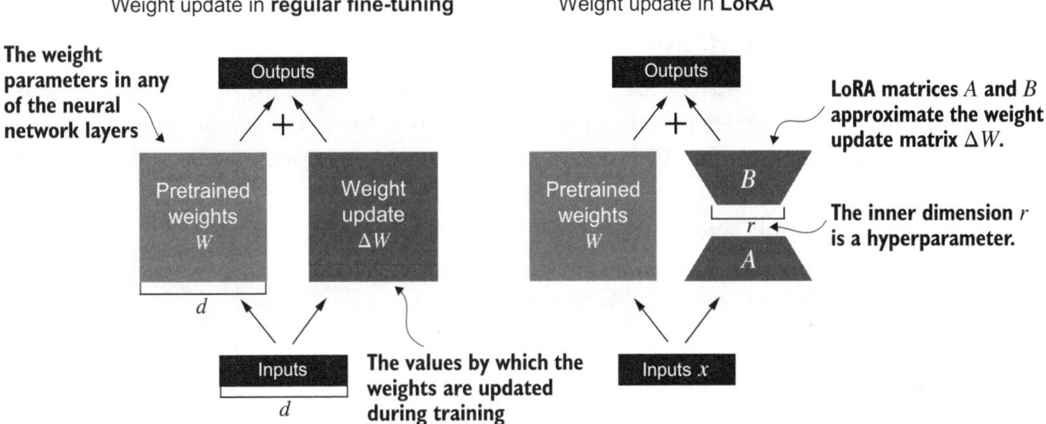

Figure E.1 A comparison between weight update methods: regular fine-tuning and LoRA. Regular fine-tuning involves updating the pretrained weight matrix *W* directly with Δ*W* (left). LoRA uses two smaller matrices, *A* and *B*, to approximate Δ*W*, where the product *AB* is added to *W*, and *r* denotes the inner dimension, a tunable hyperparameter (right).

If you paid close attention, you might have noticed that the visual representations of full fine-tuning and LoRA in figure E.1 differ slightly from the earlier presented formulas. This variation is attributed to the distributive law of matrix multiplication, which allows us to separate the original and updated weights rather than combine them. For example, in the case of regular fine-tuning with x as the input data, we can express the computation as

$$x(W + \Delta W) = xW + x\Delta W$$

Similarly, we can write the following for LoRA:

$$x(W + AB) = xW + xAB$$

Besides reducing the number of weights to update during training, the ability to keep the LoRA weight matrices separate from the original model weights makes LoRA even more useful in practice. Practically, this allows for the pretrained model weights to remain unchanged, with the LoRA matrices being applied dynamically after training when using the model.

Keeping the LoRA weights separate is very useful in practice because it enables model customization without needing to store multiple complete versions of an LLM. This reduces storage requirements and improves scalability, as only the smaller LoRA matrices need to be adjusted and saved when we customize LLMs for each specific customer or application.

Next, let's see how LoRA can be used to fine-tune an LLM for spam classification, similar to the fine-tuning example in chapter 6.

E.2 Preparing the dataset

Before applying LoRA to the spam classification example, we must load the dataset and pretrained model we will work with. The code here repeats the data preparation from chapter 6. (Instead of repeating the code, we could open and run the chapter 6 notebook and insert the LoRA code from section E.4 there.)

First, we download the dataset and save it as CSV files.

Listing E.1 Downloading and preparing the dataset

```
from pathlib import Path
import pandas as pd
from ch06 import (
    download_and_unzip_spam_data,
    create_balanced_dataset,
    random_split
)

url = \
"https://archive.ics.uci.edu/static/public/228/sms+spam+collection.zip"
zip_path = "sms_spam_collection.zip"
extracted_path = "sms_spam_collection"
data_file_path = Path(extracted_path) / "SMSSpamCollection.tsv"

download_and_unzip_spam_data(url, zip_path, extracted_path, data_file_path)

df = pd.read_csv(
    data_file_path, sep="\t", header=None, names=["Label", "Text"]
)
balanced_df = create_balanced_dataset(df)
balanced_df["Label"] = balanced_df["Label"].map({"ham": 0, "spam": 1})

train_df, validation_df, test_df = random_split(balanced_df, 0.7, 0.1)
train_df.to_csv("train.csv", index=None)
```

```
validation_df.to_csv("validation.csv", index=None)
test_df.to_csv("test.csv", index=None)
```

Next, we create the `SpamDataset` instances.

Listing E.2 Instantiating PyTorch datasets

```
import torch
from torch.utils.data import Dataset
import tiktoken
from chapter06 import SpamDataset

tokenizer = tiktoken.get_encoding("gpt2")
train_dataset = SpamDataset("train.csv", max_length=None,
    tokenizer=tokenizer
)
val_dataset = SpamDataset("validation.csv",
    max_length=train_dataset.max_length, tokenizer=tokenizer
)
test_dataset = SpamDataset(
    "test.csv", max_length=train_dataset.max_length, tokenizer=tokenizer
)
```

After creating the PyTorch dataset objects, we instantiate the data loaders.

Listing E.3 Creating PyTorch data loaders

```
from torch.utils.data import DataLoader

num_workers = 0
batch_size = 8

torch.manual_seed(123)

train_loader = DataLoader(
    dataset=train_dataset,
    batch_size=batch_size,
    shuffle=True,
    num_workers=num_workers,
    drop_last=True,
)

val_loader = DataLoader(
    dataset=val_dataset,
    batch_size=batch_size,
    num_workers=num_workers,
    drop_last=False,
)

test_loader = DataLoader(
    dataset=test_dataset,
    batch_size=batch_size,
    num_workers=num_workers,
    drop_last=False,
)
```

As a verification step, we iterate through the data loaders and check that the batches contain eight training examples each, where each training example consists of 120 tokens:

```
print("Train loader:")
for input_batch, target_batch in train_loader:
    pass

print("Input batch dimensions:", input_batch.shape)
print("Label batch dimensions", target_batch.shape)
```

The output is

```
Train loader:
Input batch dimensions: torch.Size([8, 120])
Label batch dimensions torch.Size([8])
```

Lastly, we print the total number of batches in each dataset:

```
print(f"{len(train_loader)} training batches")
print(f"{len(val_loader)} validation batches")
print(f"{len(test_loader)} test batches")
```

In this case, we have the following number of batches per dataset:

```
130 training batches
19 validation batches
38 test batches
```

E.3 Initializing the model

We repeat the code from chapter 6 to load and prepare the pretrained GPT model. We begin by downloading the model weights and loading them into the `GPTModel` class.

Listing E.4 Loading a pretrained GPT model

```
from gpt_download import download_and_load_gpt2
from chapter04 import GPTModel
from chapter05 import load_weights_into_gpt


CHOOSE_MODEL = "gpt2-small (124M)"
INPUT_PROMPT = "Every effort moves"

BASE_CONFIG = {
    "vocab_size": 50257,          # Vocabulary size
    "context_length": 1024,       # Context length
    "drop_rate": 0.0,             # Dropout rate
    "qkv_bias": True              # Query-key-value bias
}
```

```
model_configs = {
    "gpt2-small (124M)": {"emb_dim": 768, "n_layers": 12, "n_heads": 12},
    "gpt2-medium (355M)": {"emb_dim": 1024, "n_layers": 24, "n_heads": 16},
    "gpt2-large (774M)": {"emb_dim": 1280, "n_layers": 36, "n_heads": 20},
    "gpt2-xl (1558M)": {"emb_dim": 1600, "n_layers": 48, "n_heads": 25},
}

BASE_CONFIG.update(model_configs[CHOOSE_MODEL])

model_size = CHOOSE_MODEL.split(" ")[-1].lstrip("(").rstrip(")")
settings, params = download_and_load_gpt2(
    model_size=model_size, models_dir="gpt2"
)

model = GPTModel(BASE_CONFIG)
load_weights_into_gpt(model, params)
model.eval()
```

To ensure that the model was loaded corrected, let's double-check that it generates coherent text:

```
from chapter04 import generate_text_simple
from chapter05 import text_to_token_ids, token_ids_to_text

text_1 = "Every effort moves you"

token_ids = generate_text_simple(
    model=model,
    idx=text_to_token_ids(text_1, tokenizer),
    max_new_tokens=15,
    context_size=BASE_CONFIG["context_length"]
)

print(token_ids_to_text(token_ids, tokenizer))
```

The following output shows that the model generates coherent text, which is an indicator that the model weights are loaded correctly:

```
Every effort moves you forward.
The first step is to understand the importance of your work
```

Next, we prepare the model for classification fine-tuning, similar to chapter 6, where we replace the output layer:

```
torch.manual_seed(123)
num_classes = 2
model.out_head = torch.nn.Linear(in_features=768, out_features=num_classes)
device = torch.device("cuda" if torch.cuda.is_available() else "cpu")
model.to(device)
```

Lastly, we calculate the initial classification accuracy of the not-fine-tuned model (we expect this to be around 50%, which means that the model is not able to distinguish between spam and nonspam messages yet reliably):

```
from chapter06 import calc_accuracy_loader

torch.manual_seed(123)
train_accuracy = calc_accuracy_loader(
    train_loader, model, device, num_batches=10
)
val_accuracy = calc_accuracy_loader(
    val_loader, model, device, num_batches=10
)
test_accuracy = calc_accuracy_loader(
    test_loader, model, device, num_batches=10
)


print(f"Training accuracy: {train_accuracy*100:.2f}%")
print(f"Validation accuracy: {val_accuracy*100:.2f}%")
print(f"Test accuracy: {test_accuracy*100:.2f}%")
```

The initial prediction accuracies are

```
Training accuracy: 46.25%
Validation accuracy: 45.00%
Test accuracy: 48.75%
```

E.4 Parameter-efficient fine-tuning with LoRA

Next, we modify and fine-tune the LLM using LoRA. We begin by initializing a LoRALayer that creates the matrices A and B, along with the `alpha` scaling factor and the `rank` (r) setting. This layer can accept an input and compute the corresponding output, as illustrated in figure E.2.

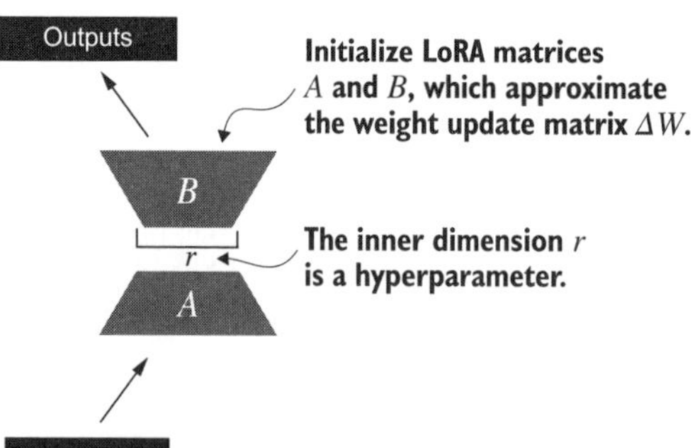

Figure E.2 The LoRA matrices *A* and *B* are applied to the layer inputs and are involved in computing the model outputs. The inner dimension *r* of these matrices serves as a setting that adjusts the number of trainable parameters by varying the sizes of *A* and *B*.

In code, this LoRA layer can be implemented as follows.

Listing E.5 Implementing a LoRA layer

```
import math

class LoRALayer(torch.nn.Module):
    def __init__(self, in_dim, out_dim, rank, alpha):
        super().__init__()
        self.A = torch.nn.Parameter(torch.empty(in_dim, rank))
        torch.nn.init.kaiming_uniform_(self.A, a=math.sqrt(5))
        self.B = torch.nn.Parameter(torch.zeros(rank, out_dim))
        self.alpha = alpha

    def forward(self, x):
        x = self.alpha * (x @ self.A @ self.B)
        return x
```

The same initialization used for Linear layers in PyTorch (annotation to the `kaiming_uniform_` line)

The `rank` governs the inner dimension of matrices A and B. Essentially, this setting determines the number of extra parameters introduced by LoRA, which creates balance between the adaptability of the model and its efficiency via the number of parameters used.

The other important setting, `alpha`, functions as a scaling factor for the output from the low-rank adaptation. It primarily dictates the degree to which the output from the adapted layer can affect the original layer's output. This can be seen as a way to regulate the effect of the low-rank adaptation on the layer's output. The `LoRALayer` class we have implemented so far enables us to transform the inputs of a layer.

In LoRA, the typical goal is to substitute existing `Linear` layers, allowing weight updates to be applied directly to the pre-existing pretrained weights, as illustrated in figure E.3.

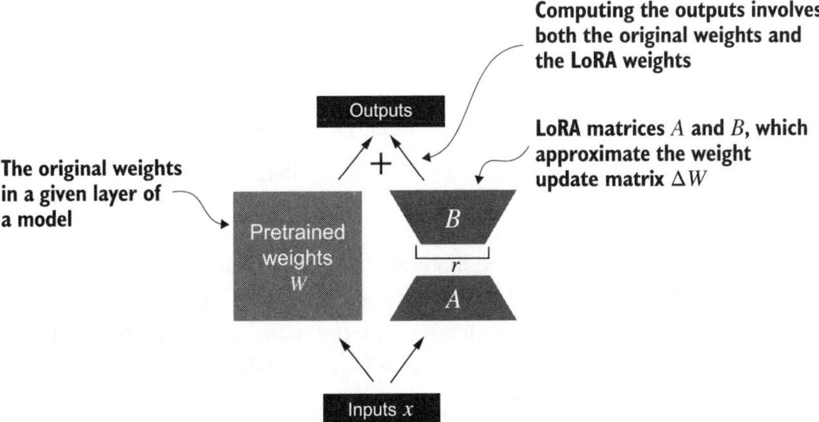

Figure E.3 The integration of LoRA into a model layer. The original pretrained weights (*W*) of a layer are combined with the outputs from LoRA matrices (*A* and *B*), which approximate the weight update matrix (Δ*W*). The final output is calculated by adding the output of the adapted layer (using LoRA weights) to the original output.

To integrate the original `Linear` layer weights, we now create a `LinearWithLoRA` layer. This layer utilizes the previously implemented `LoRALayer` and is designed to replace existing `Linear` layers within a neural network, such as the self-attention modules or feed-forward modules in the `GPTModel`.

Listing E.6 Replacing a `LinearWithLora` layer with `Linear` layers

```
class LinearWithLoRA(torch.nn.Module):
    def __init__(self, linear, rank, alpha):
        super().__init__()
        self.linear = linear
        self.lora = LoRALayer(
            linear.in_features, linear.out_features, rank, alpha
        )

    def forward(self, x):
        return self.linear(x) + self.lora(x)
```

This code combines a standard `Linear` layer with the `LoRALayer`. The `forward` method computes the output by adding the results from the original linear layer and the LoRA layer.

Since the weight matrix B (`self.B` in `LoRALayer`) is initialized with zero values, the product of matrices A and B results in a zero matrix. This ensures that the multiplication does not alter the original weights, as adding zero does not change them.

To apply LoRA to the earlier defined `GPTModel`, we introduce a `replace_linear_with_lora` function. This function will swap all existing `Linear` layers in the model with the newly created `LinearWithLoRA` layers:

```
def replace_linear_with_lora(model, rank, alpha):
    for name, module in model.named_children():
        if isinstance(module, torch.nn.Linear):        # Replaces the Linear layer with LinearWithLoRA
            setattr(model, name, LinearWithLoRA(module, rank, alpha))
        else:                                          # Recursively applies the same function to child modules
            replace_linear_with_lora(module, rank, alpha)
```

We have now implemented all the necessary code to replace the `Linear` layers in the `GPTModel` with the newly developed `LinearWithLoRA` layers for parameter-efficient fine-tuning. Next, we will apply the `LinearWithLoRA` upgrade to all `Linear` layers found in the multihead attention, feed-forward modules, and the output layer of the `GPTModel`, as shown in figure E.4.

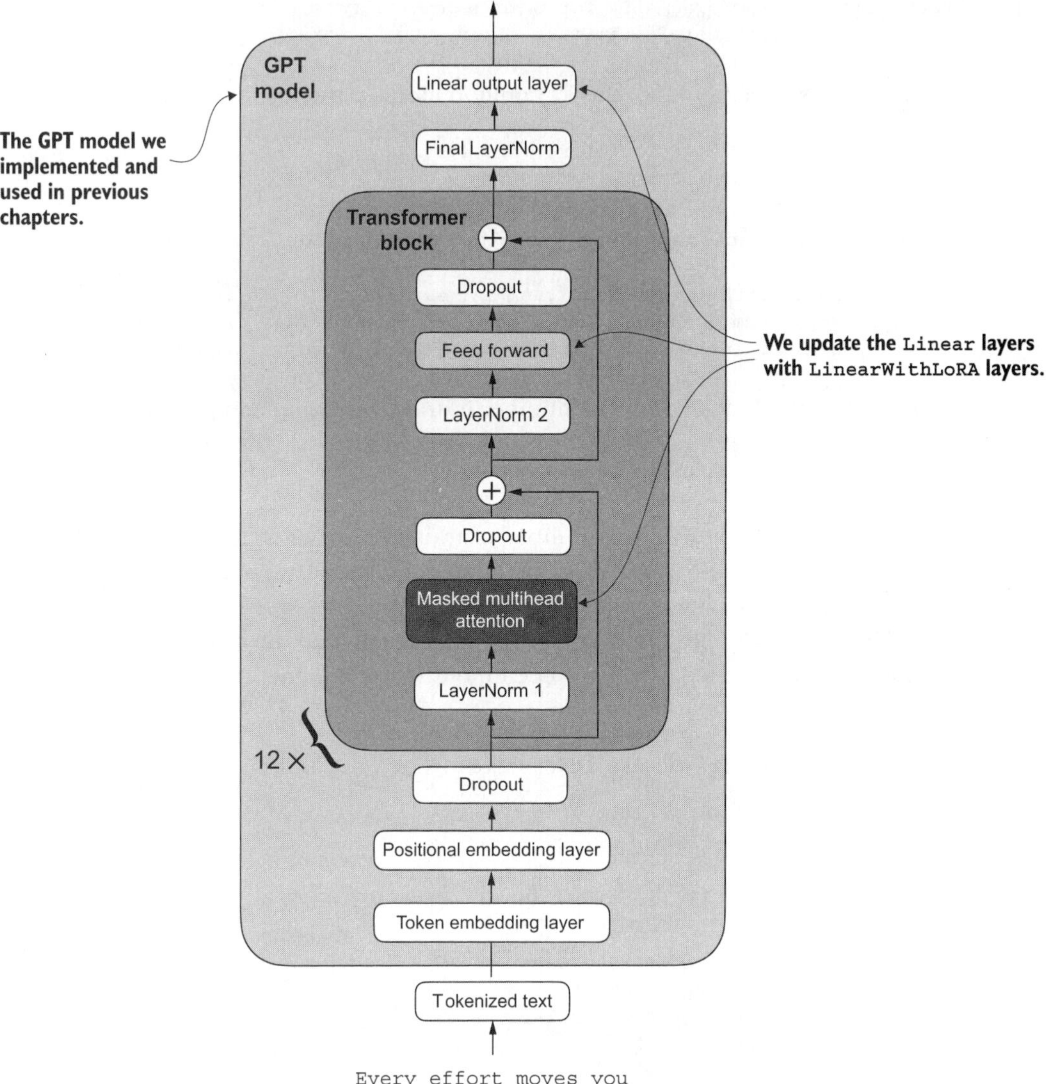

Figure E.4 The architecture of the GPT model. It highlights the parts of the model where `Linear` layers are upgraded to `LinearWithLoRA` layers for parameter-efficient fine-tuning.

Before we apply the `LinearWithLoRA` layer upgrades, we first freeze the original model parameters:

```
total_params = sum(p.numel() for p in model.parameters() if p.requires_grad)
print(f"Total trainable parameters before: {total_params:,}")

for param in model.parameters():
    param.requires_grad = False
```

```
total_params = sum(p.numel() for p in model.parameters() if p.requires_grad)
print(f"Total trainable parameters after: {total_params:,}")
```

Now, we can see that none of the 124 million model parameters are trainable:

```
Total trainable parameters before: 124,441,346
Total trainable parameters after: 0
```

Next, we use the `replace_linear_with_lora` to replace the `Linear` layers:

```
replace_linear_with_lora(model, rank=16, alpha=16)
total_params = sum(p.numel() for p in model.parameters() if p.requires_grad)
print(f"Total trainable LoRA parameters: {total_params:,}")
```

After adding the LoRA layers, the number of trainable parameters is as follows:

```
Total trainable LoRA parameters: 2,666,528
```

As we can see, we reduced the number of trainable parameters by almost 50× when using LoRA. A `rank` and `alpha` of 16 are good default choices, but it is also common to increase the rank parameter, which in turn increases the number of trainable parameters. Alpha is usually chosen to be half, double, or equal to the rank.

Let's verify that the layers have been modified as intended by printing the model architecture:

```
device = torch.device("cuda" if torch.cuda.is_available() else "cpu")
model.to(device)
print(model)
```

The output is

```
GPTModel(
  (tok_emb): Embedding(50257, 768)
  (pos_emb): Embedding(1024, 768)
  (drop_emb): Dropout(p=0.0, inplace=False)
  (trf_blocks): Sequential(
    ...
    (11): TransformerBlock(
      (att): MultiHeadAttention(
        (W_query): LinearWithLoRA(
          (linear): Linear(in_features=768, out_features=768, bias=True)
          (lora): LoRALayer()
        )
        (W_key): LinearWithLoRA(
          (linear): Linear(in_features=768, out_features=768, bias=True)
          (lora): LoRALayer()
        )
        (W_value): LinearWithLoRA(
          (linear): Linear(in_features=768, out_features=768, bias=True)
          (lora): LoRALayer()
        )
```

```
        (out_proj): LinearWithLoRA(
          (linear): Linear(in_features=768, out_features=768, bias=True)
          (lora): LoRALayer()
        )
        (dropout): Dropout(p=0.0, inplace=False)
      )
      (ff): FeedForward(
        (layers): Sequential(
          (0): LinearWithLoRA(
            (linear): Linear(in_features=768, out_features=3072, bias=True)
            (lora): LoRALayer()
          )
          (1): GELU()
          (2): LinearWithLoRA(
            (linear): Linear(in_features=3072, out_features=768, bias=True)
            (lora): LoRALayer()
          )
        )
      )
      (norm1): LayerNorm()
      (norm2): LayerNorm()
      (drop_resid): Dropout(p=0.0, inplace=False)
    )
  )
  (final_norm): LayerNorm()
  (out_head): LinearWithLoRA(
    (linear): Linear(in_features=768, out_features=2, bias=True)
    (lora): LoRALayer()
  )
)
```

The model now includes the new `LinearWithLoRA` layers, which themselves consist of the original `Linear` layers, set to nontrainable, and the new LoRA layers, which we will fine-tune.

Before we begin fine-tuning the model, let's calculate the initial classification accuracy:

```
torch.manual_seed(123)

train_accuracy = calc_accuracy_loader(
    train_loader, model, device, num_batches=10
)
val_accuracy = calc_accuracy_loader(
    val_loader, model, device, num_batches=10
)
test_accuracy = calc_accuracy_loader(
    test_loader, model, device, num_batches=10
)

print(f"Training accuracy: {train_accuracy*100:.2f}%")
print(f"Validation accuracy: {val_accuracy*100:.2f}%")
print(f"Test accuracy: {test_accuracy*100:.2f}%")
```

The resulting accuracy values are

```
Training accuracy: 46.25%
Validation accuracy: 45.00%
Test accuracy: 48.75%
```

These accuracy values are identical to the values from chapter 6. This result occurs because we initialized the LoRA matrix *B* with zeros. Consequently, the product of matrices *AB* results in a zero matrix. This ensures that the multiplication does not alter the original weights since adding zero does not change them.

Now let's move on to the exciting part—fine-tuning the model using the training function from chapter 6. The training takes about 15 minutes on an M3 MacBook Air laptop and less than half a minute on a V100 or A100 GPU.

Listing E.7 Fine-tuning a model with LoRA layers

```
import time
from chapter06 import train_classifier_simple

start_time = time.time()
torch.manual_seed(123)
optimizer = torch.optim.AdamW(model.parameters(), lr=5e-5, weight_decay=0.1)

num_epochs = 5
train_losses, val_losses, train_accs, val_accs, examples_seen = \
    train_classifier_simple(
        model, train_loader, val_loader, optimizer, device,
        num_epochs=num_epochs, eval_freq=50, eval_iter=5,
        tokenizer=tokenizer
    )

end_time = time.time()
execution_time_minutes = (end_time - start_time) / 60
print(f"Training completed in {execution_time_minutes:.2f} minutes.")
```

The output we see during the training is

```
Ep 1 (Step 000000): Train loss 3.820, Val loss 3.462
Ep 1 (Step 000050): Train loss 0.396, Val loss 0.364
Ep 1 (Step 000100): Train loss 0.111, Val loss 0.229
Training accuracy: 97.50% | Validation accuracy: 95.00%
Ep 2 (Step 000150): Train loss 0.135, Val loss 0.073
Ep 2 (Step 000200): Train loss 0.008, Val loss 0.052
Ep 2 (Step 000250): Train loss 0.021, Val loss 0.179
Training accuracy: 97.50% | Validation accuracy: 97.50%
Ep 3 (Step 000300): Train loss 0.096, Val loss 0.080
Ep 3 (Step 000350): Train loss 0.010, Val loss 0.116
Training accuracy: 97.50% | Validation accuracy: 95.00%
Ep 4 (Step 000400): Train loss 0.003, Val loss 0.151
Ep 4 (Step 000450): Train loss 0.008, Val loss 0.077
Ep 4 (Step 000500): Train loss 0.001, Val loss 0.147
Training accuracy: 100.00% | Validation accuracy: 97.50%
```

```
Ep 5 (Step 000550): Train loss 0.007, Val loss 0.094
Ep 5 (Step 000600): Train loss 0.000, Val loss 0.056
Training accuracy: 100.00% | Validation accuracy: 97.50%

Training completed in 12.10 minutes.
```

Training the model with LoRA took longer than training it without LoRA (see chapter 6) because the LoRA layers introduce an additional computation during the forward pass. However, for larger models, where backpropagation becomes more costly, models typically train faster with LoRA than without it.

As we can see, the model received perfect training and very high validation accuracy. Let's also visualize the loss curves to better see whether the training has converged:

```
from chapter06 import plot_values

epochs_tensor = torch.linspace(0, num_epochs, len(train_losses))
examples_seen_tensor = torch.linspace(0, examples_seen, len(train_losses))

plot_values(
    epochs_tensor, examples_seen_tensor,
    train_losses, val_losses, label="loss"
)
```

Figure E.5 plots the results.

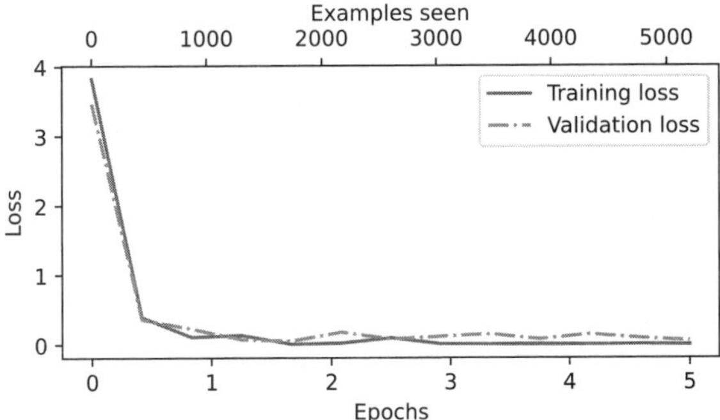

Figure E.5 The training and validation loss curves over six epochs for a machine learning model. Initially, both training and validation loss decrease sharply and then they level off, indicating the model is converging, which means that it is not expected to improve noticeably with further training.

In addition to evaluating the model based on the loss curves, let's also calculate the accuracies on the full training, validation, and test set (during the training, we approximated the training and validation set accuracies from five batches via the `eval_iter=5` setting):

```
train_accuracy = calc_accuracy_loader(train_loader, model, device)
val_accuracy = calc_accuracy_loader(val_loader, model, device)
test_accuracy = calc_accuracy_loader(test_loader, model, device)

print(f"Training accuracy: {train_accuracy*100:.2f}%")
print(f"Validation accuracy: {val_accuracy*100:.2f}%")
print(f"Test accuracy: {test_accuracy*100:.2f}%")
```

The resulting accuracy values are

```
Training accuracy: 100.00%
Validation accuracy: 96.64%
Test accuracy: 98.00%
```

These results show that the model performs well across training, validation, and test datasets. With a training accuracy of 100%, the model has perfectly learned the training data. However, the slightly lower validation and test accuracies (96.64% and 97.33%, respectively) suggest a small degree of overfitting, as the model does not generalize quite as well on unseen data compared to the training set. Overall, the results are very impressive, considering we fine-tuned only a relatively small number of model weights (2.7 million LoRA weights instead of the original 124 million model weights).

index

Symbols

Numerics

A

B

C

D

E

F

G

I

K

L

M

N

S

T

U

V

W

X

Z

RELATED MANNING TITLES

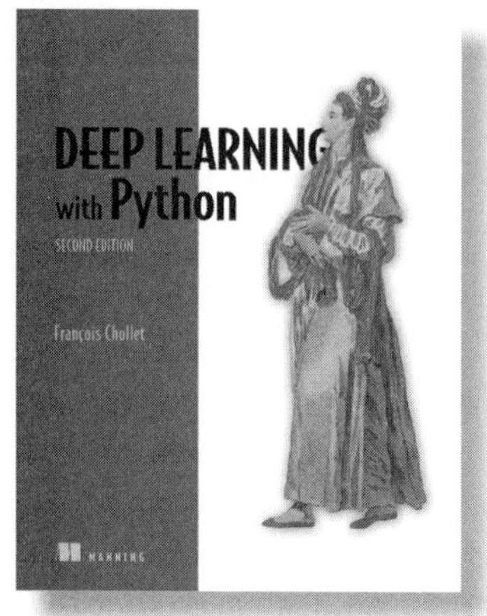

Deep Learning with Python, Second Edition
by Francois Chollet

ISBN 9781617296864
504 pages, $59.99
October 2021

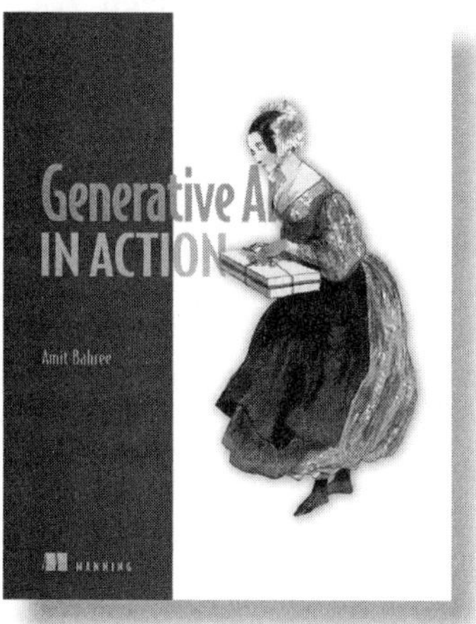

Generative AI in Action
by Amit Bahree

ISBN 9781633436947
469 pages (estimated), $59.99
October 2024 (estimated)

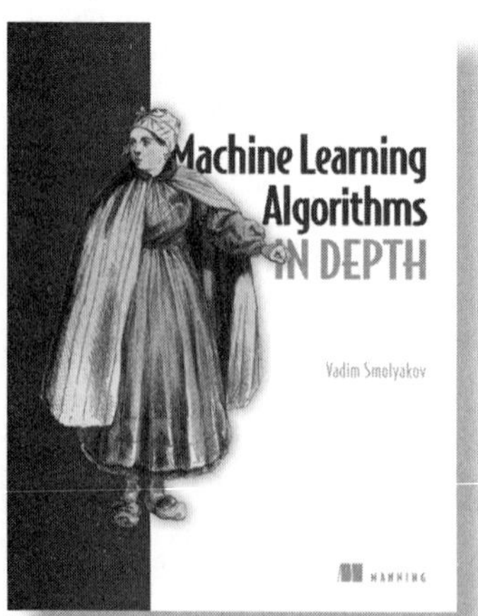

Machine Learning Algorithms in Depth
by Vadim Smolyakov

ISBN 9781633439214
328 pages, $79.99
July 2024

For ordering information, go to www.manning.com

RELATED MANNING TITLES

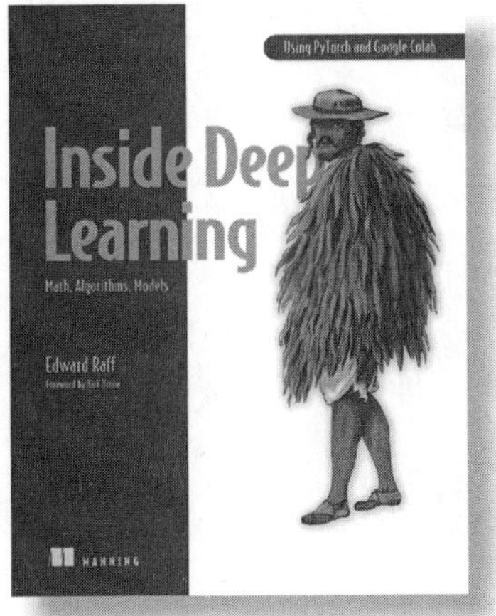

Inside Deep Learning
by Edward Raff
Foreword by Kirk Borne

ISBN 9781617298639
600 pages, $59.99
April 2022

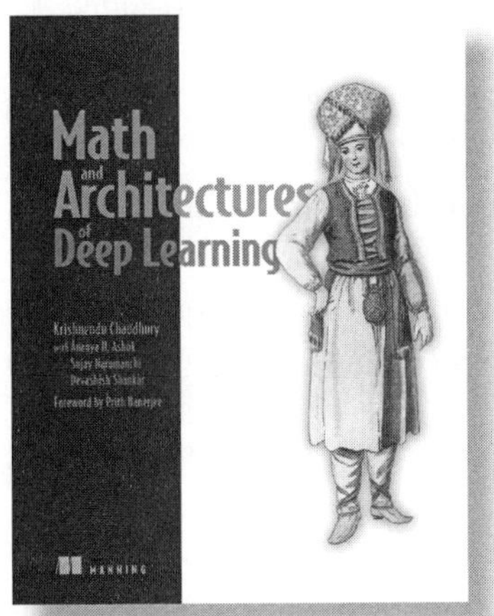

Math and Architectures of Deep Learning
by Krishnendu Chaudhury
with Ananya H. Ashok, Sujay Narumanchi,
Devashish Shankar
Foreword by Prith Banerjee

ISBN 9781617296482
552 pages, $69.99
April 2024

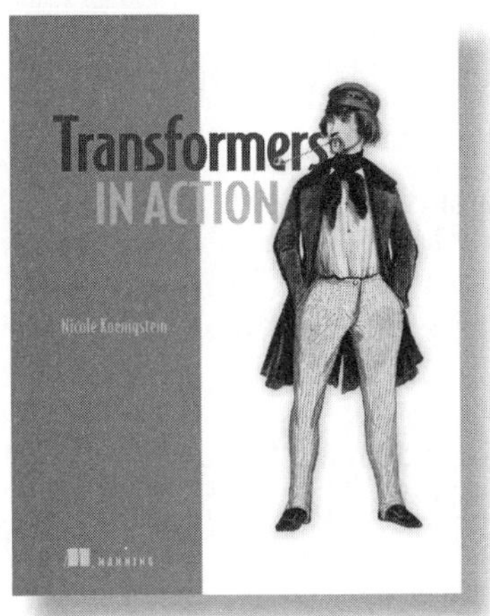

Transformers in Action
by Nicole Koenigstein

ISBN 9781633437883
393 pages (estimated), $59.99
February 2025 (estimated)

For ordering information, go to www.manning.com

LIVEPROJECT

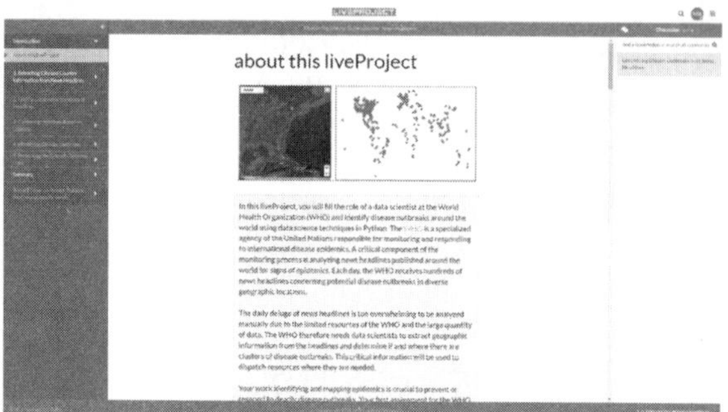

Hands-on projects for learning your way

liveProjects are an exciting way to develop your skills that's just like learning on the job.

In a Manning liveProject, you tackle a real-world IT challenge and work out your own solutions. To make sure you succeed, you'll get 90 days of full and unlimited access to a hand-picked list of Manning book and video resources.

Here's how liveProject works:

- **Achievable milestones.** Each project is broken down into steps and sections so you can keep track of your progress.
- **Collaboration and advice.** Work with other liveProject participants through chat, working groups, and peer project reviews.
- **Compare your results.** See how your work shapes up against an expert implementation by the liveProject's creator.
- **Everything you need to succeed.** Datasets and carefully selected learning resources come bundled with every liveProject.
- **Build your portfolio.** All liveProjects teach skills that are in demand from industry. When you're finished, you'll have the satisfaction that comes with success and a real project to add to your portfolio.

Explore dozens of data, development, and cloud engineering liveProjects at www.manning.com!